THE FIVE LITERACIES

OF GLOBAL LEADERSHIP

THE FIVE
LITERACIES
OF GLOBAL
LEADERSHIP

What authentic leaders know and you need to find out

Richard David Hames

JOSSEY-BASS
A Wiley Imprint
www.josseybass.com

Copyright © 2007   John Wiley & Sons Ltd, The Atrium, Southern Gate, Chichester,
West Sussex PO19 8SQ, England
Telephone (+44) 1243 779777

Under the Jossey-Bass imprint, Jossey-Bass, 989 Market Street, San Francisco CA 94103-1741, USA
www.jossey-bass.com

Email (for orders and customer service enquiries): cs-books@wiley.co.uk
Visit our Home Page on www.wiley.com

Other Wiley Editorial Offices

John Wiley & Sons Inc., 111 River Street, Hoboken, NJ 07030, USA

Jossey-Bass, 989 Market Street, San Francisco, CA 94103-1741, USA

Wiley-VCH Verlag GmbH, Boschstr. 12, D-69469 Weinheim, Germany

John Wiley & Sons Australia Ltd, 42 McDougall Street, Milton, Queensland 4064, Australia

John Wiley & Sons (Asia) Pte Ltd, 2 Clementi Loop #02-01, Jin Xing Distripark, Singapore 129809

John Wiley & Sons Canada Ltd, 6045 Freemont Blvd, Mississauga, ONT, L5R 4J3, Canada

Wiley also publishes its books in a variety of electronic formats. Some content that appears in
print may not be available in electronic books.

Anniversary Logo Design: Richard J. Pacifico

Library of Congress Cataloging-in-Publication Data

Hames, Richard David, 1945–
    The five literacies of global leadership : What authentic leaders know and you need to find
out / Richard David Hames.
        p.   cm.
    Includes bibliographical references and index.
    ISBN 978-0-470-31912-3 (cloth : alk. paper)
    1. Leadership.   I. Title.
HM1261.H35 2007
303.48′4—dc22

2007002348

British Library Cataloguing in Publication Data

A catalogue record for this book is available from the British Library

ISBN 978-0-470-31912-3 (HB)

Typeset in 10/12pt Garamond by SNP Best-set Typesetter Ltd., Hong Kong
Printed and bound in Great Britain by TJ International Ltd, Padstow, Cornwall, UK

This book is printed on acid-free paper responsibly manufactured from sustainable forestry in
which at least two trees are planted for each one used for paper production.

In loving memory of
John Allen Hames & Robert Pereira

When does one ever know a human being? Perhaps only after one
has realised the impossibility of knowledge and renounced the
desire for it and finally ceased to feel even the need for it. But then
what one achieves is no longer knowledge, it is simply a kind of
co-existence; and this too is one of the guises of love.

– Iris Murdoch, *Under the Net*

The most beautiful thing we can experience is the mysterious.
It is the source of all true art and science.

– Albert Einstein, *What I Believe*

CONTENTS

ACKNOWLEDGEMENTS   xi

FOREWORD   xvii

INTRODUCTION   xxi

PART ONE: MESSY BUSINESS   1

1   The Matrix   3

Looking Outside-In   3
Looking Inside-Out   9
Notes   12

2   Entangled Freedom   15

World on Edge   15
Imagine There's No Country   23
The Tyranny of Intimacy   27
Notes   31

3   Cathedrals and Cafes   35

Net Influence   35
Treading Water   41
Eyes on the Ball   44

Que sera, sera! Whatever will be, will be   50
From Atoms to Ecosystems   53
Bazaars, Brains, Brands and Brakes   56
Symbiotic Design   61
Who's in Charge Anyway?   69
Missed Steps in the Dance   75
Liberating Enterprise   80
Network Mastery   83
Participative Architectures   86
Closer than Close   90
Networks, Narratives and Navigation   92
Notes   97

PART TWO: CHANGING MINDS   105

4   Certainty Traps   107

All Change   107
Notes   116

5   Reinventing the Present   117

Notes   139

6   Responsiveness Rules   143

Notes   153

7   Click!   155

Notes   178

PART THREE: THE FIVE LITERACIES   181

8   Literacy I – Networked Intelligence   183

Catching the Future   183
Zero Geography   189
Infolust   192
And Citizens?   198

Designing Viability   199
Notes   208

9   Literacy II – Futuring   **211**

Thinking Matters   213
Deep Structural Patterns   216
And Yet Still Deeper . . .   217
Views from the Future   219
Notes   224

10   Literacy III – Strategic Navigation   **227**

Planning in Real Time   229
Imitating Nature   233
Strategic Activism   235
Exit the White Knight   240
(Re)defining Management   242
(RAISE)ing Consciousness   243
Navigating Emergence   246
Upgrading Thinking . . .   260
ChangeBrains and Strategic Decision Theatres   268
Notes   271

11   Literacy IV – Deep Design   **275**

Bits and Pieces We Pay For   277
The Vital Stuff (Or Method)   282
Using *Knowledge Designer*   285
The Art of Strategic Conversation   288
Seeing Through Another's Eyes   290
Growing Coherence   292
Integrating Multiple Perspectives   294
Operationalising Deep Design   301
Notes   304

12   Literacy V – Brand Resonance   **307**

Markets are Conversations   307
Brand New World   313
Wild about Work   318
Notes   324

PART FOUR: ESCAPE VELOCITY   327

13   Cracking the Code   329

    Note   340

FURTHER READING   341

INDEX   347

ACKNOWLEDGEMENTS

Ten years have elapsed since I completed my second book, *Burying the 20th Century: New Paths for New Futures*. Since then I have not published much. Some occasional thoughts have been captured in an online blog and I was persuaded to produce a couple of chapters for other people's books. My creative impulse has been channelled into the research for this book – *The Five Literacies of Global Leadership*. My colleagues and I have also used this time for extensive field testing of most of the frame-breaking ideas contained here, which has resulted in Part Four: Escape Velocity – the secret 'code' that elucidates and clarifies many of the mysteries of *five literacies* leadership, and additional materials to be found online at http://www.richardhames.com.

It is hardly surprising, after such an extended interval away, that I should find the return to writing another book both energising and challenging, especially one concerned with defining a new philosophy of leadership. The difficulty of the task may also have been compounded by circumstances in my private life, which has been something of an emotional roller-coaster over the past year or so. Readers should note that when I urge people to let go of the past in order to step into new epistemologies I do so not from some theoretical musing or moral resolve but in the harsh light of my own frailties and sets of misunderstandings – a deliberate consequence of the way I choose to live my life. I cannot pretend that I find such experiences anything other than scary and exceedingly unsettling. Yet, at the end of the day, they are also uplifting in terms of wisdom and personal growth – always assuming one is able to face them with an open heart and a receptive mind. I have no doubt that I have lived a more extraordinary life by embracing events in this way, rather than steering clear of pain. But it also means I have become intimately familiar with their humbling nature.

The past year alone presented an unusually large number of extreme highs and lows – some calculated, others not. I had to deal with the tragic and totally unexpected loss of Robert Pereira, one of my closest friends and business colleagues, as well as the death of my older brother John. As if these ordeals were not enough, they were followed in rapid succession by the collapse of what has been the most romantic relationship of my life so far, ongoing dramas within my family and, much to the consternation of many friends, an impulsive relocation from Melbourne's relatively quiet and unflustered lifestyle to the bright lights and exhilarating commotion of Bangkok. The catalyst for this most recent upheaval was a chance encounter with a young Isaan woman who has since become my partner. As we share our lives and learn about each other's cultures I am at last starting to feel an inner tranquillity I have not felt in years.

All of this, both good and bad, unforeseen and intentional, provided me with enough joy and heartache in 2005 to last a lifetime – as well as the raison d'être for not having the time or the inclination to write another book! Ultimately, though, there can be no excuse. An inventor who does not invent forfeits the right to be called an inventor. Similarly, a writer must continue to put pen to paper and publish to still be considered a writer.

In spite of that, *The Five Literacies of Global Leadership* would never have seen the light of day had it not been for the insistence of a few friends who constantly nagged me, each in their own inimitable way, urging me to stop dawdling and start writing once more. They know who they are. They will also see that in many instances their most valued advice and sensible suggestions have been taken, distorted and reinterpreted in ways with which they will possibly take issue. I accept the blame for these liberties. It is the lonely furrow all authors must hoe. I do not doubt that by accepting the advice I received at face value I could have written a better book. But it would have been a very *different* book. At the same time I trust they will not be too dismayed by the final result.

It is gratifying to acknowledge the many friends and colleagues who have significantly contributed to the evolution of my ideas and work in so many different ways over the past decade. The inspirational presence of two people and their considerable influence on my thinking has been paramount.

Marvin Oka co-created Strategic Navigation with me. Our creative partnership has been incomparable in every respect. Marvin and I worked together closely for months on end, agonising over every facet of Strategic Navigation in an endeavour to find ways of expressing the intricacies of the methodology in a form that was practical and could be clearly understood by all practitioners. In particular it needed to be simple and effective for our major client at the time – a large central government agency. Marvin's incredible memory, immense talent for design and capacity to systematically explore every crack and crevice of any hypothesis has resulted in a product that is as flawless as we can make it at this stage. It is an honour to acknowledge that many of the ideas expressed in this book are also his.

Elizabeth Winkelman has been my best friend for most of the past 10 years, bringing sunshine into my life where only dark clouds had existed. She constantly coaxed and encouraged me over this time, exhorting me to continue writing when there were so many distractions vying for my attention. Elizabeth remains my most forthright critic, selflessly analysing every idea in the most intricate detail and from every possible angle in spite of my obvious irritation with such pedantry; something nobody else was able or prepared to do. I owe her a debt I can never repay.

Numerous business associates, especially from Thoughtpost and The Hames Group, have thrown diverse, thought-provoking ideas my way while taking great delight in belittling others I would occasionally throw into the melting pot for discussion. The dialogues I have had with these most valued of friends have deeply enriched my life. For this I will be eternally grateful. They include Charles Macek, Veronica Allardice and Charles Coupland, Chris Cowan, Peter Tunjic, Fiona Matthews and Ed Kosior, Andrew Donovan, James Coulter, Michael Roux, Peter Handsaker, Jon Fink, Peter Binks, Joseph Voros, Peter Harrison, Jan Lee Martin, Paul Fox, Chris Stewart, Greg Foliente, Patrick O'Leary, John Elkington, Pamela Webb, Peter Hayward, David Tacey, Rob Pereira, Jose Ramos, Max Dumais, Richard Slaughter, Susan Oliver, Adolph Hanich, Peter Senge, Maryse Barak, Dean Joel, Tara Kimbrell Cole, Richard Neville, Oliver Freeman, Duncan Watts, Halvard Dalheim, Julie Birtles, Colin James, Gerry White, Allan Hawke, Liza Lim and Daryl Buckley, Sohail Inayatulla, Rhonda Galbally, Barry Jones, Mike Bolan, Phil and Kerryn Ruthven, Richard Jones, Mick Yates, Louise

Mahler, James Moody, Christopher Aston-James, Francois de Meneval, Gary Hamel, Tom Haynes, Bronwynne Jones, Paul Higgins, Ted Hummerston, Manfred Kets de Vries, Andy Meikle and Madeleine MacMahon, Jon Mason, Andrea Hull, Peter Schwartz, Napier Collyns, Brian Bacon, Chloe Munro, Maria Sanciolo-Bell, Tony Dormer, Rodin Genoff, Di Percy, Martin Vogel, Zia Sardar, Pat Stone, Patricia Shaw, Mike McAllum, Dave Snowden, Roy Madron, Nik Gowing, Allan Snyder, Mike Shaw, Peter Ellyard and Geoff Dale.

Naturally, ideas, however relevant for the times, demand legitimacy in practice for them to be accepted and taken seriously. *The Five Literacies of Global Leadership* would not have materialised without the enthusiastic support and trust I continue to receive from my clients – all exceptional global leaders in their own right – and other inspiring leaders. Foremost among these have been Jonathan Ling (CEO) of The Laminex Group; Nick Schofield (Chief Scientist) of Land & Water Australia; John McFarlane (CEO) and Shane Freeman (Group GM Human Capital) of the Australia and New Zealand Banking Group; Richard Branson (Founder) Virgin; Christopher Bell (CEO) of the Leadership Consortium; David Carter (Founder) and Anthony Howard (CEO Asia Pacific) of Merryck & Co; Martin Lombard (Vice President Human Resources) of World Vision; Cathy Wilkinson (Executive Director, Melbourne 2030) of the Department of Sustainability & Environment in Victoria; Michael Stanford (CEO) of St John of God Hospital Group; James Millar (CEO) of Ernst & Young Australia; Michael Carmody (Commissioner), Jim Killaly and Michael Monaghan (Deputy Commissioners) of the Australian Tax Office; John Brown (CEO) of BP; Greg Bourne and Ravi Singh, (CEO Australia and Secretary-General India respectively) of the World Wildlife Fund; Phil Clarke (CEO), Robert Marriott (HR Director), Sam Fernando (People Development Manager), David Rymer (Know-How Manager) and Peter Bartlett (Chairman) of MinterEllison Lawyers; Megan Clark (Director, Technology & Innovation) of BHP Billiton; Al Gore (former US Vice President); Scott McNealey (Founder) and Jonathan Schwartz (President) of Sun Microsystems; Goodnews Cadogan (Senior Manager Corporate Planning) of the South African Revenue Service; Lisa Gray (CEO Wealth Management) and Heather-Maree Thompson (GM People and Culture) of National Australia Bank; Jeffrey Immelt (CEO) of GE; Brian Benger (CEO) of Guild Insurance & Financial Services; Wen Jiabao (Premier of China); David Butler, (Commissioner) of Inland Revenue New Zealand and Suze Wilson (Deputy Commissioner) of the State Services Commission New Zealand.

Throughout my working life there have always been a few clients that have become lifelong friends. In this regard I acknowledge many colleagues in BP, truly one of the world's most extraordinary companies and nurturers of leadership talent. Most importantly in this regard has been my much-cherished friendship with David Nicolson (Nico), until recently General Manager of Organisational & Individual Learning in BP for the Asia Pacific region. From our very first meeting Nico was unstinting in his passionate advocacy of my ideas. Springing initially from Nico's zeal, word of this madcap yet passionate Australian corporate philosopher and strategist eventually spread to others including Vivienne Cox, Steve Davies, Patricia Lustig, Andrew Ditty, Marcus Richards, Dan Lovely, Mark Twidell, Gary Dirks, Jason Scott, Cheryl Ramirez, Ann Ewing, Brian Wishart, Vivian Li, Karen Roberts, Frila Yaman, Neil Samuels, Ann Lamont, Keith Freeland, Sabine Unruh, Tammy Lowry, Eiji Wakiwaka, Mike Bennetts, Linda Chan, Filip Huylebroeck, Larry Horton, Nicolas Le Douarec and Andreas Priestland.

The fact that The Hames Group continues to attract exceptional clients, with opportunities to co-design initiatives that are open-ended and often ground-breaking, purely through word-of-mouth marketing, can be mostly attributed to the championing of my ideas by those who represent me and promote my interests. These include the extraordinarily professional staff at Saxton Speakers Bureau, especially Helene Greenham, Sandra Rogerson, Jacqui Bridson and Winston Broadbent who have continually worked to put me in front of stimulating audiences, Charles Brass from the Futures Foundation, and Julie Ankers of Entertrainers and Speakers. More recently, the entrepreneurial flair and enthusiasm of Andrew Greatrex, who invited me to join Global Leaders Network in 2005, has given my work renewed impetus. Andrew has been avidly promoting my work to the world at large. It is through Andrew that I have come at last to believe in the true value and pioneering nature of these ideas – a revelatory gift which I appreciate enormously.

To the professionalism and enthusiasm shown by Francesca Warren, Joanna Golesworthy, Viv Wickham, Darren Reed, Sam Hartley, Tessa Hanford and all the team at John Wiley & Sons, Ltd, and to all those I have omitted to mention here but who in their own quiet way assisted the evolution of my thinking over the past few years, my sincere gratitude and thanks. I hope they enjoy reading the final product and will not pay too much attention to the inevitable gaps, flaws and other faults they are likely to find and for which I accept full responsibility.

Richard David Hames
Bangkok, Thailand
January 2007

FOREWORD

THEY ARE EVERYWHERE

The future is shaped by the quality of leadership. Sadly, several Western nations with a knack for inspiring its citizens in times of crisis, have, for the past decade, been seriously misled. So much so, that in a just world, such 'leaders' would be sitting in the dock at the Hague. Despite the protest of citizens, a few politicians and spin doctors, aided by the odd media tycoon, managed to transform the Iraqi dictatorship into a slaughterhouse. In so doing they destabilised the Middle East and squandered what's left of the West's moral authority. How could this happen? Because democracy as currently practised is a sham, writes Richard Hames in these pages, re-jigging Abraham Lincoln: "We presently have government OF the people, BY interchangeable sets of career politicians, FOR the pursuit of economic growth and development . . .". How rare for democracies to be put under the spotlight.

It is mostly the same set of leaders who turned a deaf ear to the repeated warnings on Global Warming; censoring the science, spurning Kyoto, demonising Greens, dismissing Al Gore's Inconvenient Powerpoint as 'mere entertainment'. Today's politicians are quick to extol their own gift for leadership, despite an often tragic record of needing to be dragged kicking and screaming into the 21st Century. Their true flair is follower-ship. After a key issue reaches critical mass, comes a qualified back flip. Oh shucks, I guess we should clean up our coal . . . but not at the cost of harming our economy. Except the economy has already been harmed by their lack of investment in renewable energy.

Not all politicians and tycoons live in a bubble. How could they? For 35 years at least, the world community has been undergoing a gradual mind-shift. 'I'm on full alert to avoid committing such eco atrocities as soaping myself in the creek or taking a car to the campsite', a delegate reported from a 1973 festival in rural Nimbin, Australia. 'Each of us took our rubbish to the depot, sorting it as: glass, metal, compost, or paper. After accidentally tossing an apple-core into the bin marked "metal" I spent ten minutes feeling guilty, then rummaged within. That's how Nimbin got to you.' In the ensuing decades, millions of citizens the world over shared a gradual awakening, a sense that something was amiss with the officially sanctioned shop-till-you-drop lifestyle. That which we call profit usually involves the destruction of natural capital treated as income. That kind of growth has its limits.

By no means did Westerners shift to lentils and bicycles, or foreswore truffles and luxury cars. Many mutated into millionaires, CEO'S, Buddhists, even politicians. But they often stuck a new note, projecting global idealism and slick entrepreneurship, like Richard Branson, Bob Geldof, Anita Roddick, and hundreds of others, including new generation 'shape shifters' like Bill Gates and the Grameen Bank's Mohammed Yunnis. High flyers are often flawed; presented less as role models than as heralds of a cultural shift that is finally dethroning the dominant paradigm. Scores of equally daring, if less prominent activists enliven the pages of this book. The Five Literacies are spreading.

Elephants still crowd the living room, but now we're starting to take their measure. The lumbering beasts of mass media remain cheerleaders for business-as-usual, still trumpeting the joys of consumer society. Advertising, marketing, branding, fashion, the entertainment industry, and all the associated rigmarole of promotion, spin and celebrity culture, puts hyper consumption at the core of human existence. But ever more wonder if time is running out for the Shopping Religion, which has long dwarfed traditional faiths. In 2006, the US congress of the World Council of Churches confessed to its global affiliates, 'We consume without replenishing; we grasp finite resources as if they are private possessions; our uncontrolled appetites devour more and more of earth's gift. Christ, have mercy'. The revelation is spreading that a society comprised of competitive, self interested individuals trying to get as rich as possible can hardly be regarded as sane. The Council's public plea to the Son of God was not considered newsworthy.

A handful of global corporations own and control mainstream media. Board members are mostly drawn from blue chip consumer brands and defence industries, so don't hold your breath for a rigorous commitment to peace or the promotion of a carbon neutrality. (The reaction of Rupert Murdoch's newspapers to Al Gore's movie was a spate of editorials and articles proclaiming, 'Why Al Gore is wrong about climate change'. While the motto on the masthead of his Australian flagship is 'Keeping the Nation Informed', the opposite is true.

The good news is that the digital age has marginalized the gate-keepers, allowing us to construct a richer portrait of our society, our ecosystem, our guardians. The result is often terrifying, though illuminating, as it would be for the metaphorical prisoners unshackled from Plato's cave, after a lifetime of mistaking the flickering shadows on the wall for the real world.

I've lost track of the number of revelations that first appeared on the web before seeping into the mainstream. If plane-spotter bloggers had not disclosed the flight paths of certain aircraft, the world would have remained ignorant of the CIA's criminal kidnaps and Torture Flights. On the web you can even find stills of the in-flight victims hooded and chained to the fuselage, headed for hell, guarded by shamefaced soldiers. Such images are unlikely to appear in the New York Times. But I dwell on the dark side of life and of leadership, and of what's fit to print. Plenty of uplifting initiatives are happening beyond the orbit of Governments and hit men.

As our lagging leaders lost the plot, a new story slowly unfolded in the hearts and minds of everyday citizens. The premise was clear. That the future can no longer be taken for granted – it needs to be rescued. The public's foresight started to stretch beyond limited electoral cycles and national borders. Employees took into organisations what they were discussing at home, and often found friendly ears and receptive CEOs. Sustainability task forces were set up, emissions were measured and questions arose about the 'evolving purpose' of corporations.

Even in noxious industries, such as cement and waste management, I have found a fervor bordering on the Blitz Spirit, a kind of 'can do' euphoria that took me by surprise. No more fudging, no more greenwashing. Instead of a grudging acceptance of the new realities, as exuded by most Governments, I sensed an unbridled enthusiasm. Perhaps the change of climate is changing the workplace, providing a mission beyond utility and profit. Stress and depression is giving way to resilience and daring? A gleam in the eye, a shared sense of purpose. The stakes are high and horizons are stretching. Could the real goal of business be doing good? While politicians bicker and weave, the unofficial leaders in our midst seem determined to ensure that the Earth our children inherit will still be worth inhabiting.

Richard Neville
Sydney 20th February 2007

INTRODUCTION

In the beginner's mind there are many possibilities. In the expert's mind there are few!

– Shunryu Suzuki

The Five Literacies is the manifesto of a group of remarkable people who are intent on creating better futures. These individuals do not reside only in the rich nations of the developed world but also in the very poorest parts of China, Russia, Bhutan, India, Brazil, Africa, Thailand and Indonesia. They are not always the agents of powerful governments and institutions. Nor are they necessarily elite captains of industry. On the contrary you will find them in different walks of life, doing all kinds of work. Some are household names. Others you may never know. That they have determination cannot be doubted. Their spirit, too, is as generous as their intellect is razor-sharp. They are the alchemists, seers, scientists and artists among us and they have five things in common:

1. They are passionately optimistic. They do not feel unduly burdened or constrained by problems or impediments, however grave these might appear to others. They have a burning desire to create a future that is better than the one they inherited.
2. Their curiosity about the world and their craving for wisdom compels them to explore and discover new knowledge. Their instinct is not to become expert, nor to preach, but to learn. They are reflective practitioners.

3. They recognise that individual genius is fragile in comparison with the power of collective wisdom. They spend the majority of their time liberating new ideas and mindful action through collaborating with others.
4. They are expansive thinkers. Embracing emergence and uncertainty, they understand that sustainable change comes about through intelligent shaping of the whole system of which they themselves are only a small part.
5. They are compassionate people. Profoundly disturbed by a society that perpetuates inequity, injustice, conflict, homogeneity, poverty and environmental degradation, they are determined to do their best to improve this state of affairs. Whatever business they are in, they are dedicating their lives to changing the world.

We often gasp at their audaciousness, are astonished by their all-encompassing ethos, admire their honesty and humility, marvel at their adaptiveness, misinterpret their intentions, ignore their aspirations, are blinded by the brilliance of their strategic instinct and even write them off as quirky misfits. But in stepping so boldly into new epistemologies they are giving hope to many, as well as making a great deal of competitive behaviour redundant as they rewrite the rule books. They are *five literacies* leaders and this book is a testament to their thinking, courage and vision.

In times of ambiguity and rapid technological advancement, three factors become especially critical for survival and sustainable prosperity. These are:

- Ecological viability (the capability to remain intentionally aligned with, and relevant to, changing circumstances)
- Generative learning (the capability to continuously challenge what we know and how we know it and to adapt quickly when necessary); and
- Conviviality as expressed through authentic behaviour (the capability to sustain and express a coherent internal dialogue as a guide to action).

This is as true for individuals as it is for organisations, governments, communities and indeed entire societies. Whatever eventually replaces the blemished ideology of industrial economism and its technoculture will need to synthesise these factors into a new *logic* more appropriate for the age of attention and acceleration. *Five literacies leaders* are doing just that. Their ideals, principles, thoughts, models and practices – the code that motivates them and explains their success – is captured in this book.

The extensive action research we have conducted over the past decade has unravelled a 'secret' cognitive and behavioural code that denotes an entirely new logic for leadership: a new rationale in which context, intelligence, conversation, foresight and collaborative design are all-important. Integrating insights from a diversity of alternative worldviews and belief systems, the contemporary paradigm is first exposed for what it is – a deeply flawed, self-reinforcing hotchpotch of linear frameworks and toxic practices. In its place a more resilient, moral, adaptive, intelligence-driven means of organising and managing human affairs is advocated. An ecology of *appreciative* leadership and praxis. Tracking the inherent energy, interconnectedness and nonlinear nature of global transformation, together with its profound impact on our daily lives, *The Five Literacies* establishes both the framework and justification for why such a morphogenic leadership capability is indispensable as we struggle to comprehend the new rules confronting individuals, business and governments everywhere. The book is in four parts.

Messy Business (Part One) sets the scene. I describe the changes that are happening in our world from a leader's perspective, the implications of these changes for leadership in every sphere and how the nature of leading others must change as a consequence.

Changing Minds (Part Two) describes a suite of four tenets (receptiveness, self-renewal, responsiveness and reciprocity) extraordinary leaders persistently access to learn their way into better futures. These are best thought of as an array of essential enablers: the mental models, values and behaviours required to appreciate and put into effective practice the *five literacies*. Getting to come to terms with the integral nature of these 'enablers' is crucial for any serious comprehension of the *five literacies*.

Receptiveness enables both personal and global mind changes. This is all about the ability and readiness to step into new epistemologies – however uncomfortable that might be. I examine the critical need for receptiveness – to new ideas, new ways of seeing and thinking about the world, and alternative ways of designing and managing human affairs. Many things we take for granted, from the need to inspire followers to the clever crafting of visions, are the residue of a bygone era. The jargon in which these things are enveloped and the incessant, inane attempts to measure the unmeasurable, are obsolete. At best they become part of sensible management practice. But at worst they become meaningless in the context of today's world. While they may have made sense even a few years ago, they do not add value now to our understanding of leadership. They do add costs however.

It is not easy to accept these things as mind traps; after all we have been taught they are essential elements in maintaining progress. It is even more difficult to break free from them, even when viable alternatives are staring us in the face. *Self-renewal* only becomes possible once we have dropped all pretence and become genuinely open to personal change. Self-renewal enables reinvention and the restoration of wisdom. Here I review the need for rethinking priorities and methods in a world where accepted theories about managing, organising, governing and leading have been thrown into disarray. I consider the most appropriate ways of 'thinking about thinking' in this astonishing context, focusing on the need for more open, engaging and exploratory ways to create new directions and sustainable future pathways – for ourselves and for our institutions. To help us advance these thoughts, *ecological* models, based upon the principles of living systems rather than the purely linear *economic* models of our industrial past, are proposed as the basis for more sustainable, human-centred, whole-system designs.

Responsiveness, the third tenet, facilitates intelligent reaction to events and needs. It assumes that the much-debated notions of speed, technology and globalisation, their interaction and the new social practices they have engendered, are indeed today's *killer apps*. Literally. I explain how navigational processes offer us the best opportunity to discard redundant protocols and practices that continue to weigh us down, anchoring us in the past. At the same time I point to how such mechanisms can be designed to liberate collective wisdom and spirit, nurturing resilience, impelling the capacity for innovation, and growing confidence for action.

But responsiveness without responsibility only offers improvements to the path we are already following. Something critical is still missing. *Reciprocity* enables the obligations we have as human beings – towards each other and to this planet we call home. Here we propose a compelling model of how government, learning, community and business organisations can re-engage and interact, using the principles and concept of reciprocity to design a more sustainable, prosperous and inspiring society. I examine the kinds of strategies that are needed to liberate and transform institutions in ways that are most beneficial to more people, proposing a schema that would lead to a more responsible view of corporate citizenship, sustainable prosperity and the social contract between individuals and society.

The Five Literacies (Part Three) describes the very different mindset and practices used by today's really smart leaders when dealing with the pressures arising from globalisation – in their business and in their personal lives. Central to industrial society has been a faith in the essential capacity of humanity to perfect itself through the power of rational thought and reason. Given the perilous state of our world, such human-centred rationalism must surely now be considered suspect. The dilemmas we need to confront, moreover, have arisen as a direct result of *seeing* the world this way. Not confined merely to government or to business, this view impregnates the entire fabric of Western society. Sadly, the problems caused by the shortcomings of industrial economism cannot be conveniently ignored, swept away or solved using cold, hard, reductionist logic. This has been tried and found sadly wanting. Indeed, the impeccable logic of *rational* thought and expression, together with the industrial values underpinning it, have made matters far worse, often resulting in recklessly flawed interventions that have caused irrevocable damage to the Earth's biosphere, as well as to each other.

Rational analysis, for example, fooled otherwise intelligent technocrats into assuming pollutants would have few negative social impacts or environmental costs. It persuaded us that industrial *waste* should be thrown away (as if that were even possible) rather than viewing it as potential profits going up in smoke! It allowed the first Bush administration to claim that dealing with global warming would bankrupt the US economy, although alternative views based on the end-use efficiency paradigm invariably viewed it as a profit opportunity. It legitimised the attitude that youth's addiction to drugs was just a criminal matter, rather than a symptom indicative of society's deeper ills. For a time it even convinced us that the invasion of Iraq and the *War on Terrorism* were fought in the name of human rights rather than supremacy over oil as well as a deeply ingrained, yet irrational, fear of those who hold views contrary to our own. In much the same way, it has deceived governments into believing they can control the economy, provide full employment and protect their citizens from acts of aggression. It justified our supposing the global market was *free* as we blindly continued to prop up the energy sector to the tune of hundreds of billions of taxpayers' dollars while hiding many other forms of subsidy by not accounting for them in our economic models. Sadly, it has also tricked us into expecting that international terrorism can be defeated by conventional military means and that the continued globalisation of trade will benefit developing countries more than it harms them. Rational analysis will continue to haunt us in the immediate future, of that I have no doubt.

In all of the preceding examples, at least part of the problem has been the inadequacy of current forms of human expression to represent complex ideas in ways we can all comprehend. Languages are universally used as the guide to our social reality. In other words, we construct our world, and explain its structures and vagaries to others, through the use of language. Currently, however, we lack an inclusive, knowledge-transforming language capable of upgrading our understanding of reality's evolution. The competitive, scientific, analytical, prescriptive, either-or language we routinely use to describe everything we perceive, after all, has been responsible for constructing *ways of knowing* that gave rise to our present predicament. It is utterly unsuited to the kinds of understanding we now need in order to reach beyond the industrial economism it spawned and helped sustain over a period of some 300 years.

Our inability to separate fact from fiction, the rise of the celebrity airhead and the cult of the marketable personality as the most pervasive and amenable form of human experience, along with the secularisation of a society in which money is the only universally understood data, have all but destroyed the premise of truthfulness. Otherwise we are swept along by accelerating economic growth headlong into unknown and treacherous waters. We drown in information – much of it incoherent, conflicting or frivolous. On just one single day of the many days I spent writing this book, as much world trade was carried out as in the whole of 1949. Our waking hours have become a palimpsest of signs, symbols and texts to be read, glanced at, misconstrued or ignored. An hour of judicious downloading from the Internet can put more information at our fingertips than was possible to absorb during a lifetime in Beethoven's day. Furthermore, the way we receive such information has a vital bearing on the ways we experience and interpret reality. Swamped by data and glued to the technologies that manipulate it, we have lost any sense of the sacred unity of all living things.

But what use is information we can't act upon? It smothers our ingenuity and obscures hope. Because we cannot *know* what is actually happening to a society that is global, let alone assimilate even part of it within the context of our personal lives, we are ultimately deprived of the potential to *do* anything much about changing it. Increasingly, we are aware of our own (learned) helplessness. Adrift in a hyper-real society that has become both a condition and a pleasure, we sense alienation and a lack of harmony but cannot make sense of what that might mean. Sadly, we have become blind, deaf and dumb to viable alternatives. We are trapped in the Matrix.

In this environment we urgently need the capability to design afresh the means to release us from the gravitational pull of our industrial past and to recreate optimism for the future. The means to do this are spelled out in *The Five Literacies*. Networked Intelligence, Futuring, Deep Design, Strategic Navigation and Brand Resonance are the five interrelated knowledge domains used, often instinctively, by today's truly extraordinary leaders. Collectively, these literacies offer strategies and a new behavioural code that can awaken higher levels of consciousness within us all. Freeing individuals and institutions alike, they allow us once more to create coherence and meaning from the incredible acceleration of information and complexity of interactions that threaten us with stress, exhaustion and collapse. Liberated from the trauma of not knowing *what* to do or *how* to do it, *five literacies* leadership can help restore our confidence to be mindful and act with generosity as well as providing the means to remain alert, connected, relevant and viable in a world as unpredictable as water flowing over rocks. Adopted more widely, these *five literacies* will enable us to embrace an appreciative consciousness whereby today's Matrix will be recognised for what it is – a system on the brink of collapse, comprising dangerously self-serving delusions under the guise of solutions motivated by greed and arrogance. Then, by achieving viability from one moment to the next we will be more able to compose into being the long-term framework for a sustainable and more convivial society.

Finally, *Escape Velocity* (Part Four of the book supplemented by additional materials to be found online at http://www.richardhames.com) sets out the very practical 'code' habitually applied by today's extraordinary leaders in the form of new rules, models and strategic questions. It also defines the attributes of today's extraordinary leaders in a way that can be readily understood and replicated by us all, if we have a mind to change the way things are.

PART ONE

MESSY BUSINESS

In the film trilogy, *The Matrix*, the world with which we are all familiar is a digitised fantasy – a highly sophisticated illusion fabricated by an alien life form following Earth's devastation. Those in control are superior beings, able to morph between reality and the Matrix with ease. Human minds have been sucked dry – they are mere husks, memories edited, all aspirations deleted. Inhabiting a state of naive contentment, people remain ignorant of their actual predicament. An elaborate simulacrum has become their reality. It is also their prison. Humanity's true plight remains undetected to all but a few who have cracked the code. Instead of swallowing the blue pill, which would keep them in a comatose state, they have chosen the red pill of knowledge. In so doing they are marked as heretics – troublemakers that must be eliminated. But once they have seen the Matrix there can be no going back. Their lives are changed forever.

CHAPTER 1

THE MATRIX

The tools of the mind become a burden when the environment which made them necessary no longer exists.

– Henri Bergson

LOOKING OUTSIDE-IN

The pace of life has accelerated remorselessly over the past few centuries. Our cultural evolution is an exponential trajectory in which everything is speeding up. It took from the beginning of civilisation to the year 1900 to develop a global economy producing $US600 billion in output. Today the world economy grows by that rate every couple of years! Supply chain velocity has become the most critical factor for business in maintaining a competitive advantage. Communication has become instantaneous. We are constantly on the move, yet also plugged in to the pulse of world events. Information that would have taken days or even weeks to deliver in the age of sailing ships is now transmitted within the blink of an eye. Working on the principle that 'faster is better' industrial society set out to conquer distance and duration. It has succeeded.

But speed is not free. Enormous flows of energy and materials are needed to keep pace with society's insatiable demand for food and water, goods and services, roads and runways, bridges and tunnels, electronic equipment and lifestyle gadgets. Our material evolution has been so fast and intense that the drive towards simultaneity has even thrown nature into disorder. In the process we are rapidly approaching the edge of chaos – surfing wildly on the shock waves of cultural fusion, climate change and technological wizardry as they collide and converge into an *attractor*[1] that is transforming the world in ways we may not be able to comprehend, least of all control.

Numerous other factors feed this *attractor*. On almost every economic indicator continental Europe continues to decline. The future is perceived as dark and ambiguous and the spirit of enterprise is frustrated at every turn.[2] Meanwhile China and India seem set to dominate the coming decades just as the US ruled the latter half of the twentieth century.[3] Chasms of confusion are opening up between different belief systems, provoking reckless acts of inhumanity and terrorism. Watched by millions who are starving to death, developed nations continue to plunder the environment and accumulate obscene wealth, appearing to value selfishness and greed as if these were the peak of sophistication. Consumers everywhere are demanding more and more of everything, fuelling misery in the developing world and perpetuating the gap between those who benefit from global prosperity and those who cannot.

This vast global dynamic is only just booting up. Yet it is already giving rise to a disconcertingly complex environment in which the axioms (and much of the knowledge) of the past appear increasingly inadequate. We are in the early stages of a revolutionary demographic shift that is upending political, technological and economic priorities at the same time as redefining global markets.

Plagued by indecision and ever-deepening paradox, our lives have become a tickertape parade of newness and excess. Meanwhile almost everything we supposed constant, from economic growth to rational decision making and even more fundamental concepts such as human rights and national sovereignty, have become tentative. In the face of such unrelenting novelty and tension, conventional approaches to leading, managing and organising human activities have become ineffectual. We maintain these obsolete mechanisms only because they are what we know. It is as though we cannot see any acceptable alternatives. But increasingly they do not work.

Figure 1.1 The fabricated driving forces of global transformation are smashing together at warp speed – creating a world of zero geography where change itself is accelerating exponentially.

The evidence is everywhere – if we could just *see* it. Nothing and nobody is immune. Even that most cherished of all concepts, *democracy*, has been subverted as the hegemony exerted by powerful elitist regimes engages in a purpose vastly different to that originally envisaged. Setting aside for a moment the fact that the term itself has become devoid of any meaning in a world where governments of every political persuasion routinely identify themselves as being *democratic*, all current systems of representative *democracy* are designed to pursue unsustainable economic growth and preserve high levels of inequality. *Democratic* leaders routinely apply violence in some form as a means of establishing or of preserving this so-called *democracy*. Furthermore, that is the intention! Modifying Abraham Lincoln's celebrated phrase, we presently have 'government *of* the people, *by* interchangeable sets of career politicians, *for* the pursuit of economic growth and development *through* an engulfing culture of transnational corporate capitalism'.[4] This is immoral. It is also patently unsustainable, as Michael Albert convincingly avows in his essays on an alternative post-capitalist system based on participative economics – or Parecon:

> In capitalism, owners together with about a fifth of the population who have highly empowered work decide what is produced, by what means, and with what distribution. Nearly four fifths of the population does largely rote labor, suffers inferior incomes, obeys orders, and endures boredom, all imposed from above. As John Lennon put it, "As soon as you're born they make you feel small, by giving you no time instead of it all." Capitalism destroys solidarity, homogenizes variety, obliterates equity, and imposes harsh hierarchy. It is top heavy in power and opportunity. It is bottom heavy in pain and constraint. Indeed, Capitalism imposes on workers a degree of discipline beyond what any dictator ever dreamed of imposing politically. Who ever heard of citizens asking permission to go to the bathroom, a commonplace occurrence for workers in many corporations (Michael Albert, There is an Alternative, *Frankfurter Runschau*, 27 July 2005).

The final speaker at the World Social Forum's closing ceremony in Brazil on 5 February 2002 was the Nobel Prize-winning Portuguese poet, Jose Saramago. His concluding words were these:

> Everything in this world is discussed, from literature to ecology, from expanding galaxies to the greenhouse effect, from waste treatment to traffic congestion. Yet the democratic system goes undiscussed, as if it were a given, definitively acquired and untouchable by nature until the end of time. Well, unless I am mistaken, among so many other necessary or indispensable discussions, there is an urgent need to foster worldwide debate on democracy and the causes of its decline, on the part citizens play in political and social life, on the relations between States and international economic and financial power, on what affirms and what negates democracy, on the right to happiness and a worthwhile existence, on the misery and the hopes of humanity or, to cut down the rhetoric, the hopes of the simple human beings that make up Mankind, one by one and all together. There is no worse deception than self-deceit. And that is how we are living.

A more *convivial*[5] model of society is feasible, but it will only be achieved if we can bring into being an entirely new paradigm of participative citizenship, where Lincoln's phrase would describe the democratic system as being *of* the people, *by* thinking, acting and learning together, *for* the co-creation of just and sustainable societies.[6]

Alas, our addiction to the beliefs and habits of a bygone era, matched only by our seduction for the new, is insidious. Blind faith in numbers and the opinions of experts, the appeal of arcane knowledge, the valuing of profits over people, the suffocating dogma of dependency (particularly upon the state and its elected representatives) the bizarre conviction that we can predict the future (or even other people's behaviour for that matter), and the bravado-like façade of infallibility used to rationalise our negligence in degrading the biosphere, for example, all still go largely unchallenged today. How can this be so?

The true nature and purpose of the human condition is unfathomable. Inexplicable and immensely complex, it remains beyond our current comprehension. We may occasionally experience moments of enlightenment – brief insights, a fleeting sense of déjà vu, perhaps, or memories from a deeper consciousness. Some may sense the sheer exhilaration of being constantly *out of control*.[7] Others encounter mostly despair as we drift into a scary future few would have intentionally chosen. Most of us, though, are just world-weary. Our public lives have become a sham, warped by fashion, trivia and the coruscating banality of screen celebrities, politicians, sporting heroes and omnipresent brands. Estranged from a world of our own invention, albeit one that escaped our grasp decades ago, we are now captive to its unrelenting prodigality. As hope and optimism recede, to be replaced by an overwhelming sense of helplessness and futility (especially among the young and the disadvantaged), changing things for the better is no longer an option. It has all become too difficult! Yet change we must, for the tedious conventions and artifice of this regimen ensnare us within a corruptive worldview that is utterly inadequate for resolving the tumultuous upheavals we experience in our daily lives.

The world we inhabit, the corporate world of industrial economism,[8] is at once both fact and fiction. It *is* the Matrix. In reality there is no such thing as a free market. Capitalism, too, is mostly a fiction.[9] What the Matrix *has* created is a darker side of capitalism – an elitist corporate system and bureaucracy posturing as a free market where producer power extends its influence over consumer demand and where corrupt CEOs, cheating Wall Street analysts and number-impaired accountants pursue their vested self-interests at the expense of society at large.[10]

All encompassing and horribly oppressive, the Matrix nevertheless has its narcissistic charm. It is as easy to become complicit in the deception as to remain oblivious to its existence, unaware that we are so beguiled. Held within its thrall, we continue to conjure madcap schemes; clinging to pitifully deficient ideas in the belief that conditions will remain sufficiently stable for long enough to bring success – whatever we imagine that to be. It is impossible to persist with these practices and worldview for very much longer without risking mayhem and ultimate collapse of the social order. The real world dances to a different rhythm now. An unstable, chaotic rhythm that alters in a flash. And completely without warning!

So new ways of knowing and designing society and its interactions are essential; new institutions, frameworks, tools and techniques are urgently required. Moreover, these must be allowed to evolve so that they remain pertinent to our needs. If ever there was a time to discard the models and orthodoxies prescribed by the high priests of industrial economism it is surely now. No longer sufficient in today's world, these relics (or, more accurately, the way they are practised) must be consigned to history. One such relic is the system of social discourse we call *representative government*. Another, the pseudo-scientific edifice of *management*. Yet another, the system of free enterprise labelled *capitalism*. All three are intended to help us achieve the outcomes we need as a society – but none have kept pace with our true predicament. Moreover they have produced despair and fear where hope and inspiration are essential.

Take the discipline of management for example. Hatched in the factories of the industrial revolution and incubated by the military over two world wars, it has grown fat and awkward. Jam-packed with flawed theories, irrelevant practices and other quackery, it is now little more than a worn-out charlatan promising miracles it cannot possibly deliver. Rather than remaining vital and compelling, the entire legitimacy of management and its orthodoxies are questionable in today's context. The same is true of leadership. Like the Emperor's new clothes in the well-known children's fable adapted by Hans Christian Andersen from an old Spanish tale, contemporary management and leadership practices are supposedly fashioned from the finest of industrial fabrics, shamelessly endorsed by self-interested aficionados and constantly paraded before us on the catwalks of the consultocracy. It takes childlike innocence to not be deceived by such an elaborate hoax. Why, even the perpetrators of the sting have been duped by their own ingenuity. They have melted the fine line between the feigned and the real.

Occasionally we may catch a glimpse of their impoverished nature, perhaps through the damage they wreak on ordinary people, their institutions and the planet. At other times we may ponder the absurdity of the contrived artifice, theatricality and treadmills that keep us enrolled in relentlessly meaningless activities calculated, it seems, merely to ensure a growing legion of business gurus and management consultants has an endless supply of guinea pigs on which to test their latest crackpot ideas and top executives can reap grossly inflated rewards for being mediocre. Naturally, we try to banish such heretical thoughts from our minds, while those with a vested interest in maintaining the scam are quick to extol its virtues, inculcating in our consciousness, every minute of every day, the paucity of viable alternatives. It is almost impossible not to be duped. The Matrix engulfs everything. The code required to disable it is impenetrable. But crack it we must. For while it prevails we remain permanently trapped within its deceits and empty promises.

Is it possible, then, to break free from our arrested state? It has to be. There is a multitude of people around the world who are not taken in by appearances. They recognise reality for what it is, are deeply frustrated by the current situation, and feel the need to contribute to the development of a new paradigm of democracy and citizenship – and thus to a new paradigm of leadership. This frustration is already giving rise to the emergence of more passionate, smarter global leaders. Leaders who recognise the power of collective wisdom over individual genius. Leaders who are informed by sources other than the mainstream media. Leaders who think and act systemically. Make no mistake, these people are tomorrow's heroes and they are practising an entirely different kind of leadership. *Five literacies* leadership.

LOOKING INSIDE-OUT

Instead of just adding to a field that is saturated with predictable tenets based on time-honoured assumptions, *The Five Literacies of Global Leaders* sets out to explore and challenge the meaning of leadership in a world that is increasingly uncertain, intimately connected, fiercely competitive – and harrowingly unfair! Leadership today is profoundly different from what it was yesterday. And it certainly will be different again tomorrow. Nothing can be taken for granted in today's world except that the context is changing all the time and the world of industrial economism, the wellspring from which past leadership theories and stories sprung, is crumbling fast. In the final analysis, *five literacies* leadership is the essence of a more enlightened, *convivial* form of leadership that will take us to higher levels of consciousness and capability. This book explores what *five literacies* leadership is, why it is so important, and what is so inherently different about its practise from more familiar models of leadership.

Examples of *five literacies* leadership already abound, for this is not some pie-in-the-sky theory but the initial stages of a new philosophy of leadership. Just look around you. All over the world and in all walks of life, *five literacies* leaders are inventing better ways to meet the needs of a global society. They come from all walks of life and are not necessarily well educated or in positions of authority. They habitually acquire wisdom through generative learning and, though they recognise their value, tend to be unpretentious people. They concede a greater responsibility to society than has previously been the case. Through the application of ecologically intelligent design they envisage the creation of ample crops and goods from benign production processes that access renewable energy sources and emit no waste or pollutants. They collaborate to defeat disease, poverty, injustice and the mindless destruction of the biosphere. They know that their success is utterly dependent upon the networks of relationships they can foster through their example and the inspirational resonance they can engender within the community. And they have shifted their focus from next quarter's profits, the votes they may win at the next election, or their own self-serving ends, to the rights of future generations. Why? Because they are not deluded. They see reality as it is and have come to understand that these things are the right things to be doing.

Is it feasible for others of us to perceive the entire praxis of industrial economism for the hazardous illusion it creates? Certainly. One need only choose to do so. Can we, then, break free from the stranglehold of a system that should be consigned to the industrial age? We can and we must. The technoculture we wear like a second skin was, after all, invented by us, and what we have made we can also expunge. Besides, it has already done more damage than we can humanly bear.

Possible ways forward, however, are littered with traps for the unwary. For a start, awareness brings with it other, more heroic, obligations. Deficiencies within the current paradigm will only become intolerable when we stop pretending the system works and are prepared to try something different. This will entail our embarking upon an internal journey of discovery, challenging our deepest assumptions, embracing alternative ways of knowing about the world, tackling past demons and facing fears of the future head on. We will also need to share our rites of passage with others if we are to arouse them from their comatose state, such is the alluring power of the Matrix.

Above all we have to be prepared to throw stuff away. Not the material waste that clogs up our landfills – but the cognitive waste in our heads that stifles possibility, ingenuity and progress. You know what I mean. They are familiar things like blindly competitive behaviour, results-based thinking, artificial boundaries, excessive bureaucracy, preposterous measures derived from exclusively linear or economic analysis, a belief that speed is good, contempt for nature, discriminatory hierarchies, the need to attribute blame when things go wrong, insufferable egos playing with other people's lives, tolerance of tedious and pointless work, meticulous planning that hardly ever produces significantly different results, redundant procedures and the like. Even attitudes designed to censure artistry and imagination while defending incompetence, must perish, at least in their present form. Indeed, most of what we currently believe to be typical, indispensable or inevitable (including the perks that come by virtue of class or status) should be banished. That will take both courage and resolve.

So, what is the most appropriate and viable societal episteme for our brave new global age? What will it look and feel like? Will it have an Asian face, for example? How will it be different from the model of industrial economism fabricated over the past 300 years in the West and to which we so tenaciously cling? It will certainly not be designed by elites whose sole objective is profits before people. Nor will it have much of the external gloss and trappings we have come to expect. It will inspire and liberate, more than it oppresses. Because there will be no sophisticated aura to maintain, no pretence to delude, nor technicalities to keep secret, it will not be as costly. Indeed, it will almost certainly lack the suffocating artifice to which we have become accustomed. It will perhaps feel more *instinctive* because its genesis is in natural systems. In fact, it may be so beguilingly simple that many will initially reject it purely on these grounds.[11]

Perhaps this all sounds too far-fetched – a trifle melodramatic or excessively idealistic. So, before rushing ahead to destroy the Matrix we should consider the alternatives. There is a critical decision to be made. And it is a moral one. We can cling on to the prevailing attitudes and practices of the industrial age: by swallowing the blue pill of amnesia we can continue in our deluded stupor, ignorant of any deeper sense of the human soul and of human destiny – but resigned to a future spinning increasingly out of our control. The ideology of certainty will cloud our decisions once more. The righteousness of the developed world will ensure that the rich get even richer while the globalisation of poverty continues unabated. Empirical rationalisation will validate every failure and any sense of enlightenment will be deleted from the collective unconscious as we continue to apply the flawed conventions of a bygone age . . .

Or we can choose to swallow the red pill of enlightenment. The craving to see the world for what it really is, and how it could be, will outweigh any desire to return to the egotistic irrelevance of past knowledge. We will navigate a new terrain – a terrain fraught with apparently unresolvable dilemmas, complex ambiguities and dynamic uncertainties. A terrain brought almost to ruin by our reluctance to pose existential questions coupled with an inclination to ignore the signs of collapse all around us. While it is destined that we should choose this journey, (there is really no alternative) the way itself is still unclear and unpredictable. If the destination was a mystery, any path would do. But we know where we need to go. And for extraordinary leaders there can be no thought of turning back.

NOTES

1. In physics, *attractors* are patterns representing all of the possible states of a system. Like gravity they pull us into their orbit. They are also an aligning force – helping bring coherence to chaos. Thus *family* is an attractor, as is *culture*.

2. The Organization for Economic Cooperation and Development (OECD) released its report, 'Going for Growth', in February 2006 that details economic prospects in the industrial world. The conclusion is clear: Europe is in deep trouble. In spite of all the talk about the rise of Asia and the challenge to America, it may well turn out that the most consequential trend of the next decade will be the economic decline of Europe. The European Union has a combined Gross Domestic Product (GDP) that is approximately the same as that of the United States. But the EU has 170 million more people. Its per capita GDP is 25% lower than that of the United States, and, most important, that gap has been widening for 15 years. If present trends continue, the chief economist at the OECD argues, in 20 years the average US citizen will be twice as rich as the average Frenchman or German.

3. As the world roils between terror and trade, Asia is by far its most promising and most explosive region. India's integration into the broader East Asian economy is a fundamental dynamic reshaping global trade and geopolitics. The Indian economy is growing slightly more slowly than China, but will probably continue to grow fast for longer, given that the population of more than a billion people is substantially younger than China's. Half of it is under 25. China is also faced with a challenging domestic agenda of reforms – such as the establishment of an independent legal

system, for example, which may slow the economy significantly in the medium term. At the moment, though, China is booming and has become the world's fastest-growing economy. Its growth will slow eventually, but there are still hundreds of millions of Chinese yet to integrate into modern economic life, so the potential for sustained high growth is there for at least the next decade.

4. Madron, R. and Jopling, J. *Gaian Democracies*, Green Books, London, 1998.

5. A *convivial* society would be self-organising and collaborative in ways that are 'appreciative' of all stakeholders' needs. In a convivial model of democracy, for example, economic growth and development would be based on *sufficiency* (rather than *efficiency*) and would be driven by *appreciative* principles embedded within technological innovation. These principles would exhibit a concern for the improvement of the human condition while emphasising interdependent collaboration and harmony; social justice and equity; intimacy; community; and an enhanced ecological balance.

6. Exactly as advocated by Roy Madron and John Jopling in their call for democracy as an open source and sustainable model of community learning at www.wwdemocracy.org. Michael Albert's work on participative economies (Parecon for short) also delves deeply into a possible new post-capitalist paradigm at www.zmag.org/parecon/indexnew.htm.

7. Kelly, Kevin, *Out of Control: The Biology of Machines*, Addison-Wesley, Chicago, 1994.

8. *Industrial economism* is the term first used by Hazel Henderson in her book *Paradigms in Progress* to explain flaws in the old industrial paradigm. Many different names have been given to the emerging paradigm. Recently deceased futurist Robert Theobald often referred to the twenty-first century as 'the healing century' while Hazel Henderson calls it the 'solar age' or the 'age of new enlightenment'. I prefer the 'age of appreciative ecologies' which refers to the need to move beyond simplistic economic models. Only by embracing ideas and models from living systems can we hope to appreciate the dynamic complexity of our world, while accepting its essential unmanageability.

9. Even if it were not, the great economist John Maynard Keynes noted that capitalism is not just, beautiful, virtuous or intelligent. Not only that it doesn't even deliver the goods!

10. J. K. Galbraith suggested that one of the greatest frauds in capitalism concerns ownership. Owner authority is a sham. In reality shareholders are fully subordinate to corporate management. The second fraud is that which measures progress exclusively by the volume of production of material goods and services – or Gross Domestic Product (GDP). GDP measures the production of consumer goods in the economy – not artistic endeavour or education or literature or the arts – or even happiness. In this context social

success means more automobiles, more TV sets, more computers, more microwave ovens and more weapons. Yet the best of human civilisation is the artistic, literary, religious and scientific accomplishments that emerged from societies where they were the true measures of success.

11. Wheatley, M. J., *A Simpler Way*, Berrett-Koehler, 1996.

CHAPTER 2

ENTANGLED FREEDOM

Our brain has been programmed for a world characterized by the need
to manage things. But this world has vanished. The new world is characterized by the need to manage complexity.

– Stafford Beer

WORLD ON EDGE

Driven by the creation and widespread, rapid dissemination of new
knowledge, today's global businesses are swept along in an unyielding
torrent of change. The emergence of science fact from science fiction
in fields like nanotechnology, robotics and genomics, for example, is
mind-boggling. When an edition of *Playboy* can be bought from a
news stand in Indonesia, the world's most populous Muslim nation;
when the possibility of a global bird flu pandemic becomes more
certain after deaths in Europe; when a bizarre blend of impulse and
fantasy, posing as US foreign policy, escalates geopolitical nightmares
around the world, adding fuel to the fire of fundamentalism and
terrorism; when a Chinese businessman can buy a MiG-21f plane from

a US eBay seller to decorate his offices in Beijing,[1] and when political leaders like Colonel Gaddafi of Libya can shake off their tyrannical image to become voices of freedom and democracy, then, quite literally, everything we believed to be constant is open to change. Our world is continually transforming. Sometimes it seems as though everything is spinning out of control. It is altering who we are, what is important to us, and how we live our lives. We are all feeling the shock.

Caution must be exercised here. I do not want to descend into the hyperbole that so often accompanies such claims. Human beings are rarely the victims of blind chance. Perhaps being 'out-of-control' has become more ideology and futurist cant than fact? Most of the issues facing us today are the result of poor decisions in strategic conception, design and execution, in addition to consequences that were unforeseen at the time. The really important question is whether we can now design our way out of the situation we have created. Perhaps it was always like this . . . But somehow I doubt it. While new knowledge systems and their accompanying technologies have previously ushered in societal transformations, such as the agrarian and industrial revolu-

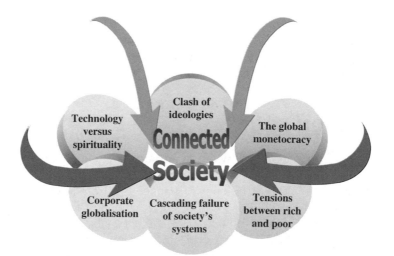

Figure 2.1 The shock waves of systemic change and their consequences have been partly triggered by our ability to connect with anyone, anywhere, almost instantly. This is a phenomenon that could only have been generated through exponential acceleration in technological breakthroughs.

tions, profound disparities between our own situation and that of previous ages are becoming clear. Globalisation hasn't occurred in simple sequential phases, where advancement was made from one distinct phase to another, but through an accumulation of inventions and practices piled on top of one another. The industrial revolution did not replace agrarian society. It added an additional layer of mobility, speed and interaction. Likewise the information age did not replace industrial society. It added yet another layer of complexity. But as more and more layers have been added, and the tentacles of the new knowledge system have spread wider, more and more people have been able to compare their own situation with that of their neighbours. As a result, differences have become more stark, geopolitical tensions have intensified, and the planet's ecological footprint has increased to the point of meltdown.

It is for these reasons that what is happening today is extraordinary. The complexity we have created is unprecedented. And, in the sense that it is impossible for the rational human mind to keep pace, today's changes are essentially unknowable. The scale, triggers, speed and trajectories of this revolution are all unfamiliar since, unlike its nomadic, rural and industrial predecessors, today's upheaval is not the consequence of some isolated discovery, historical event or new invention, but rather the collision of a myriad such factors.

Firstly, we are more intimately connected with one another than ever before – even in disease and death. There is, quite literally, no place left for us to hide from the clamour resulting from connectivity. Insinuating itself into every crack and crevice of our waking life, it personalises events and their consequences. Global television broadcasts assault us 24 hours a day with images from diverse cultures, allowing us to live through each other's achievements, miseries and aspirations, almost as if they were our own. Mobile telephony and instant messaging ensure that news is instantly available to those of us who have access to these technologies. Do-it-yourself broadcasting sites like YouTube are creating opportunities for any individual, irrespective of their location, to create, share and profit from their ideas.[2] Meanwhile the Internet, file-sharing protocols, weblogs, Podcasts and online communities such as MySpace, Bebo and Xanga have sprung up in cyberspace with such ferocity that they are recognised as powerful political, marketing and social tools.

Secondly, this connectedness is instigating an evolution of worldview, profoundly shifting our perceptions of humanity, progress, democracy and the mutual obligations we have towards each other.

For example, while the rise of China and India continue to capture the minds of many Western business leaders, we saw for the first time something resembling a global conscience react to the tsunami in Asia, Hurricane Katrina and the earthquake in Kashmir. Awareness-raising events, organised by artists like Bono and Bob Geldof and patronised by celebrities like Nelson Mandela and Oprah Winfrey, as well as new organisations like Green Cross International,[3] politicise the boundary-less nature of a host of adverse social outcomes including violent conflict, diseases like malaria and HIV Aids, displacement, deprivation, child prostitution, poverty and environmental sustainability in ways that resound within this new collective ethos.

Thirdly, as the convergence of digital and genomic codes alters long-established patterns of human production and consumption, we are fast reaching a tipping point in human development. The human race is getting smarter. Much smarter! Whether or not that translates into being wiser, of course, has yet to be determined. In the West we can reasonably pinpoint the start of this learning curve in knowledge, for the scientific revolution in Europe, followed by the Enlightenment, marked a fundamental gear change in human capability. No longer searching for ways simply to fit in to a natural or divine order, human beings sought to change it. Once people found ways to harness energy they were able to build machines that released far more power than any human or horse could ever do. The rise of new machinery like the steam engine drove the Industrial Revolution, creating in its wake a whole new way of life. Similarly, new communications technologies like the telephone, fax and Internet augmented human capability, changing the way resources are used and freeing us from physical location.

Today the search for new knowledge continues unabated, compelling an ongoing revolution in the health, well-being and prosperity of humankind. The speed at which new knowledge is diffused today is extraordinary and continues to accelerate. And while this is possibly the single most important trend of our time, convergent technologies (explicitly digital and genomic code together with nano-scale engineering) have become the inexorable drivers of that trend. If that were not enough, these new technologies are also stimulating *consilience* – literally the collision of knowledge from different disciplines – as never before.

The result is a shift in control away from the centre to the fringe, coexisting extremes and new delineations between utterly different realities – demarcations epitomising the harsh gulf between the poor and the affluent in this world. For example, in at least one of these realities, power is still wielded by authoritarian politicians, capitalists and landowners. Corruption is endemic at virtually every level within the system. Often, even the systems of justice and education are not immune. Here, people are trapped by their *material geography* and by their inability to access new technologies. They are locked-out of the wealth being created by others who inhabit a more fortunate reality. There, in a world of great fortune, a different reality struts and frolics its goods to almost obscene excess. In *zero geography*, you and I pursue creativity and innovation in ways and at a speed that is astonishing. Real power belongs to anyone who has the means to attract attention and make their ideas popular. Nowadays that means access to the World Wide Web.

The edges between these and other paradigms are constantly fraying and re-forming to the extent that, while they are hard to explain they are even harder to explain away. This process of continuous transformation is changing how all of us think, work and react to global events. It is creating apparently unresolvable absurdities and cruel inequities, generating vast material wealth on one hand and massive resentment on the other. It is even transforming what it means to be human. The fact that this is happening within a global knowledge economy means that we must not hesitate to re-evaluate the logic, criteria, intentions and principles underlying everything we have inherited and, if need be, redefine conventional wisdom in the light of these new realities.

Nothing should be exempt from such scrutiny – from the links between conflict and natural resources to urban security, social discourse, the fundamental causes of terrorism the notion of 'demography as destiny' and even concepts like ownership and governance. Take intellectually property (IP) rights, for example. To most people, piracy conjures up the music recording industry, which has been devastated by the (currently illegal) peer-to-peer file-sharing capability of MP3 and other new technologies. Counterfeiting, too, evokes images of the street vendor in the dodgy back-street markets and shopping malls of Asia where it is possible to purchase impossibly cheap Rolex watches or the latest hit movies on DVD. I recently purchased a Breitling wristwatch from a street stall in Bangkok for US$50. This 'Montbrilliant' copy is virtually indistinguishable from the real article which retails for around US$5500!

In this digital age, literally anyone who has a new invention, a creative idea or a technological breakthrough is at risk of being ripped-off. It matters not a jot whether we are talking about the automotive, pharmaceutical, entertainment, software or any other intellectual-property-dependent sector. To the executives and armies of lawyers in major corporations this is the dark side of the Internet age. It is something that needs correcting. What could be more obvious than protecting the huge investments that have been made over many years and that are now at risk. But is it quite that straightforward? Digital technologies, which are a boon to consumers and businesses alike, make all data and information easily replicable, able to be transmitted at the speed of light around the world. When theft is rendered effortless, it becomes more pervasive. This is precisely what has happened. Indeed the amount of piracy and counterfeiting could well be taking the global economy towards a different kind of tipping point. The Business Software Alliance estimated that 35% of software deployed worldwide in 2005 was pirated. In some countries the figure exceeds 90%! This is unparalleled. And we don't have the faintest idea how to deal with the problem.

Pharmaceuticals are harder to duplicate than computer files but even here industry losses are thought to be in the billions, while individuals who unwittingly ingest counterfeit drugs, do so at their own risk. The overall cost is anyone's guess. Counterfeiting and piracy is estimated to cost companies around the world more than US$600 billion a year, roughly equal to Australia's GDP. Although these are global issues, they have a disproportionate effect on countries like the US and Japan whose economies are increasingly driven by innovative, technologically sophisticated businesses, with intellectual property becoming an increasingly larger part of the total.

As important as intellectual property is to the economy today, it is going to become even more crucial in the future. Yet as IP crime escalates, solutions become harder to envisage while policing becomes futile. Unless, that is, one is prepared to rethink the issues, admit that this is a case of market failure in the global knowledge economy and recast both logic and expectations (of what constitutes criminal activity) in the context of today's realities. While corporate lawyers with vested interests and unlimited funds will undoubtedly continue to demand tighter regulations, more universal laws and tougher barriers, many creators of intellectual property and contrarian lawyers like Lawrence Lessig are starting to question the validity of these old laws and to propose alternative ways of sharing and earning money from intellectual and creative activity. Lessig asks why, just at the moment when digital technologies give to our kids the most extraordinary powers of creativity, we should try to shut that down. If Shakespeare and Disney and Miles Davis were not pirates when they used remixed materials, what principled reason is there to condemn their digital equivalents? Surprisingly the growing open source and 'Creative Commons' movements includes many large multinational corporations such as IBM and GE for example.[4] They appreciate the dynamic circumstances in which they are operating today, understand the inequities inherent in conventional approaches to copyright and patent laws and recognise, too, the threat to our cultural heritage by the abuse of copyright law, particularly with regard to the fair and reasonable use of information in the public domain.

Perhaps theft then, is not the real issue. When even works that have no economic value or commercial benefit are locked away from public consumption under absurd copyright restrictions, perhaps it is the law itself that is the real problem. New technologies and new forms of collaboration, coupled with new social practises arising from these, demand that we rethink what knowledge is for, how it can benefit society as a whole, and how practices that were once illegal for well-argued reasons can be legalised for even better reasons. It might be different if everyone in the world had equal access to the drugs, software and ideas we all take for granted in a free society. But that is not the case. Every year millions of poor people die of diseases like malaria because of appallingly inept government policies that provide the big drug companies with little or no motivation to produce affordable cures. Economist Michael Kremer, the Gates Professor of Developing Societies at Harvard University, proposes a market-orientated 'aid' system whereby rich donor governments, and even the World Bank, commit to purchasing a viable drug or vaccine that can then be developed for a specific illness.

It is not just pharmaceuticals that are needed by the poor. Learning and access to education give people the knowledge to contribute, to be self-sufficient and to feel respected and valued. Ideas are the essence of human knowledge and enterprise. But ideas are locked away in the millions of sentences crafted by countless authors throughout history, in the pages of books and stored in libraries all over the planet. Accessing these ideas is not possible for many people who might then use them to liberate themselves and their communities from poverty and oppression. Besides these books are all protected by copyright conventions that place clear restrictions on their purchase and use. Brewster Kahle, however, sees an opportunity here that is too good to miss. He wants to create a global information democracy.

Citing the ancient Library of Alexandria as his inspiration, Kahle spearheads the Open Content Alliance, a consortium backed by the likes of Yahoo and Microsoft, which has the rights to scan collections like the British Library, and to make those millions of pages available to anyone with a web browser.[5] Couple that with the production of a US$100 notebook computer (powered by clockwork) with smarter browsers[6] and one has the possibility of creating an explosion of access so profound that it is almost impossible to comprehend.

Naturally it is not just the need to deal with global inequities that is important but the whole structure of business and government and their relationship. Multinational corporations, bounded by traditional mindsets and shareholders' demands for immediate returns are beginning to see the need to reconceive everything they had previously taken for granted. A few examples point to the shift in consciousness that is occurring. Within the past decade, in an era of unconscionable greed and excess, BP broke free from the pack, admitting global warming was a reality and that it had a responsibility to mitigate the symptoms of climate change by progressively moving *beyond petroleum*. The company currently spends around 40% of its budget on renewable energy and is looking to increase that figure. Another example of this company's ethical leadership occurred more recently when, in August 2006, it shut down production in the Prudhoe Bay oil field in Alaska after discovering severe corrosion in 12 separate sections of transit pipelines. Prudhoe Bay produces 400,000 barrels of oil per day, about 8% of the US oil production. As a consequence there was massive criticism of BP's motives from within the US. In spite of that the shut down continued until the company was sure that the site could do no damage to the fragile arctic environment. Under the stewardship of CEO Ray Anderson, Interface spent millions of dollars in a commitment to reverse the environmental damage being done by its factories and highly toxic processes. The company is now a model of how to eliminate pollution and waste from the production process. IBM donates hundreds of its patents to the open-source Patent Commons Project, turning a philosophical movement into a tangible business strategy in just one play.[7] And so on . . .

There will always be prominent cases where greed or mismanagement grab the headlines. Enron and WorldCom spring immediately to mind, for example. But most corporations now understand the advisability of being ethical, honest and open in their dealings. Make no mistake, changes and re-evaluations of this nature are altering everything we have known, taking everyone back to zero. Nation states, large multinationals and even entire societies that do not comprehend the significance of these changes will be unable to avoid disaster and potential collapse. It matters not how big or rich you are today. Past reputation, too, is of little value in today's fickle world.

The past cannot be considered a preamble to the future. Nor can there be any room for complacency in an unforgiving, knowledge-driven world. For the first time in our history, the extent and sophistication of human knowledge is such that we have the means to create a civilisation that is wiser and more equitable than in the past. A planet that is ecologically sustainable and where the inhabitants cherish all life. At the same time, we have unintentionally produced an incendiary brew where terrorism, ecological devastation, poverty and conflict thrive, inexplicably causing humanity to turn on itself. Wildly disruptive perturbations and astonishingly complex dynamics resound globally from this unfathomable fusion. What is more, everything is accelerating so fast that we are all having trouble making sense of it let alone trying to keep up. It is as though change has triggered a new 'Big Bang'. Quite literally, our world is on the edge!

IMAGINE THERE'S NO COUNTRY

In the celebrated words of John Lennon, 'Imagine there's no country. It's easy if you try'. Much of what we have taken for granted is in decline. Formerly prevalent value systems founded on village and community life, religion, the family and loyalty to the firm are fast mutating as consumer envy and materialism colonise our consciousness. Once-venerable institutions (including the probity of law, academia, medical practice, the ideologies that gave birth to both communism and capitalism, and even the concept of the nation state itself) are now threatened as, through the rapid fusion of ideas, technologies, markets, institutions and cultures, entire belief systems collide and ricochet – indifferent to tradition and trampling over even well-established boundaries.

Nowhere is this fusion and uncertainty more obvious than in the geopolitical sphere and in the demographic changes that are occurring around the world. Even nation states are not immune from this volatility. Of the flags and national anthems comprising today's United Nations 75% did not exist 50 years ago. Many of them have been fashioned from the remnants of hare-brained schemes, flawed ambitions and wars. Other nations have disappeared as quickly. When the Berlin Wall collapsed, an event that heralded the break-up of the USSR, East Germany virtually disappeared from the map in two weeks!

In 1994, up to a million Rwandan Tutsis were massacred by Rwandan Hutus in just 100 grisly days. Yet Hutus and Tutsis lived together peacefully enough before German and Belgian colonisers decided that the taller, thinner Tutsis were a finer race than the stockier, darker Hutus, and endorsed them as such. Not all of Africa's troubles have their roots in colonialism, but the conflicts in central Africa provide a particularly stark reminder of what can happen when nations are drawn up with artificial boundaries out of a patchwork of smaller nations.

The idea of a racially homogeneous nation state is a relatively modern one. Most of the world's great empires have been formed by waves of conquerors of different races. The extent of migration that is taking place today, though, means that the typical nation-state is soon likely to be multi-ethnic, multi-racial and multi-cultural. Never before have humans had such ability, or derived such impetus, to seek greener pastures. Global demographics and economics will ensure that the twenty-first century is characterised by even larger movements of people around the world. An estimated 95% of the world's population growth is taking place in poor countries, which tend to be black. Meanwhile, in rich countries, which tend to be white, nearly all have birth rates below replacement levels.

Some nations, like the US and Australia, for example, became prosperous largely as a result of migrants. We began this new century with the proposition that Europe, which has hitherto been predominantly white and Christian, may not be for much longer. In some cities of England, such as Leicester and Birmingham, it is predicted that black and Asian populations will be in the majority within a decade. France is now estimated to have more Muslims than practising Catholics. Germany has some three million people of Turkish origin, some of whom have been there for three generations. In the United States there is already an Hispanic majority in southern California and in many other parts of the country blacks and Hispanics will outnumber whites within a few decades. Islam will become a bigger force in the West in coming decades simply because immigrants from Islamic countries have more children than the native populations. Within five years, it has been estimated that over 50% of the world's children who are under 12 will be Muslim. It really doesn't matter what measures are taken to keep them out, the migrants will keep arriving for two reasons: they want jobs and a better life and the developed countries need their labour. The United Nations estimates that Germany will need a million migrants a year to retain its present ratio of workers to dependants.

All of this indicates that ethnicity can no longer be considered a rational basis for nationality; and that, if the idea of the nation-state is to survive, countries will have to find ways of unifying their citizens other than through a common race or creed. Indeed, if the world is not to be even more conflict-ridden in the twenty-first century, humans will need to get over their hang-ups about race. There is some evidence that this is already happening. Notwithstanding the rise of neo-Nazis in Germany and extreme racist activities in Austria, France, Spain and Italy, the movements of millions of people from Africa and the Middle East into Europe have so far taken place without huge conflict and bloodshed. Of course, how fragile this apparent tolerance is, or whether it would hold in the event of a catastrophic economic downturn, has yet to be tested.

Whether we are talking about government or business, institutions or communities, the real point is that we have moved into a revolutionary era once more. An era where knowledge is in a state of flux and almost everything we have taken for granted is under threat. Markets have morphed into public conversations. News is often more glitz and *infotainment* rather than serious reporting of crucial issues. Politicians have entered the domain of extreme sports, flirting with fear like trapeze artists in a circus – yet oblivious to the public dangers they unleash. In some parts of the world even the judiciary are joining in the fun. Meanwhile technologies run rampant. Genomic code will soon challenge and change us in ways for which we are as yet totally unprepared. Digital code has already altered our lives irrevocably, liberating those who have access to new technologies while creating a technology-poor underclass in those who haven't. Chat rooms, blogs, CD burners, MP3 players and other technological marvels may astound, even terrify, anyone born before 1970, but for most technology-rich teenagers, the first generation truly growing up in the digital age, the technology that makes all that ready-in-an-instant, pop-it-in-the-microwave, send-an-SMS-by-mobile style of information-sharing possible is just part of daily life, along with the toaster and the TV.

These youngsters live private lives in an increasingly public arena. There have been surprising side effects too. For example, a restructured, deconstructed vocabulary of symbols and language shortcuts has emerged alongside this new pop technology. Why look up your personal horoscope, the weather or the latest movie screenings in the newspaper when you can have them pushed to your mobile phone as you pass the cinema or have them waiting in your email inbox each morning? Why waste time typing sentences when you can say 'brb' instead of 'be right back' or 'gtg' as a shortcut for 'got to go' and 'cya' when you really do have to say goodbye?

There can be no doubt that our kids have learned to speak digital while most adults still speak digital with a pronounced, often hilarious, accent. The Internet has spawned a whole generation whose social interaction is increasingly electronic. Chances are that you already know couples that forged e-relationships that have blossomed into e-marriages or that have eventually broken up by texting each other. Technology's influence on mating choice extends beyond the Internet's great cyber-singles bar. New technology is also increasingly used among young adult males as a status symbol to show off or to 'preen' much in the manner of mating birds. Researchers at the University of Liverpool reported that young men in pubs and bars use their mobile phones as 'lekking' devices, meeting in groups and displaying their technology as a symbol of status and wealth in much the same way that male grouse congregate and show off to attract mates.[8]

Whether or not culture has shaped our biology in the past, is irrelevant; we will soon consciously control our own evolution in the future. But when technologies shift to such an extent, the human knowledge monopolies built around them crumble to dust. Everyone is forced back to zero. Such has been the case with the clergy, with teachers, with medical practitioners, accountants, bank managers, sound engineers and blue-collar workers. Once the unassailable guardians of arcane knowledge, these and numerous other professions have been dispossessed of their authority, legitimacy, indeed some of their very existence, by the Internet. Their special status in society has vanished. This same shift now heralds the demise of leadership as we know it.

Adults, especially teachers and parents, have been brought up and indoctrinated to say 'I know'. Experimenting with interactive technology allows kids to learn faster than most adults who are more fearful of clicking in case they are wrong or cause the computer to suffer a nervous breakdown! The kids have become the mentors. According to a US study, *Growing up with Interactive Media*, published in 2000 in partnership with the University of Texas, today's kids in the US spend as much time living in a virtual digital world as they do in school, or with family and friends. ABS statistics from August 2000 show that digital penetration in Australia is increasing. In households with children under 18, 72% had a computer and 47% had Internet access. In August 1998 the figures had been 64% and 23%, respectively.

The biggest shift is that kids are now empowered to generate their own media. They are not passive consumers of product any longer. That is what the digital age is doing. This new culture of technology even has the potential to alter the patterns of human evolution as evidenced by the physiological changes to the fingers of young Japanese kids who spend so much time sending text messages to each other.

THE TYRANNY OF INTIMACY

The Internet brings a fresh, slightly precipitous mode and impetus to trade, education, communication and the exchange of information. At the same time its prismatic nature connects heretics, mavericks, entrepreneurs and provocateurs with no single coherent platform, spawning virtual communities ranging from militaristic and criminal networks to the anti-corporate protest movement. United not by political party but by some other loose affinity, and intent, very often, on changing the prevailing system of global capitalism, it empowers organisations lacking legal standing, corporate identity, bricks and mortar, or even leadership, to mobilise activities on a whole range of issues – from the exploitation of cheap labour in the sweatshops of South America, to human rights abuses in the oil fields of Nigeria, to environmental damage caused by mining, forestry and the nuclear cycle.

As I have already noted, distance is no longer an impediment to business. Today the tyranny of distance has been superseded by the tyranny of intimacy. Indeed a crucial aspect of the digital age is the unprecedented intrusion of the mass media into our daily lives. Though insidious at one level, this extraordinary capability allows us the freedom to interact instantly with (and be influenced by) people in markedly different environments and from utterly dissimilar cultures.[9] Powerful trends like these are gathering a seemingly unstoppable momentum as they overturn long-held 'facts'.

Naturally there are some facts we can accept as constant truths – at least for the moment. We know, for example, that the boundaries that once existed between the public and private sectors, between businesses and their customers, between one business and another and even between one nation and another, are blurring and realigning. The advent of simple business models like franchising, and the fact that airplanes constantly overfly foreign air space, has meant that local and regional thresholds have been utterly dissolved. We also know that markets are transforming into networks. But even the blurring is becoming fuzzier now! Nothing is that clear any more.

Potentially, these realignments may fundamentally alter the nature of democracy. As the role of government changes, so the influence of non-government organisations (or NGOs) increases faster than at any other time in our history. Speed coupled with our ability to connect with others – anywhere and at any time – is creating a world in which there are now no such things as local issues. An end to welfare and the welfare state becomes a real possibility, with calls for a new social contract balancing the honouring of individual rights with a more communitarian (and global) compassion. Self-help has now become essential as institutionalised help all but disappears.

Globalisation, a factor within the broader phenomenon of globalism, seems intent on subsuming national economies into a single market – with global brands and global corporations with global reach. This has come about through the incredible connectivity evidenced by new technologies. We are now witness to a bewildering fusion of social and cultural factors. Even to the development of global systems of ideas. Scientific method, for example, is now a global way of understanding the world in which we live. The English language, too, has become the universal language for air traffic and air safety.

Globalisation, of course, attracts both benefits and dangers – especially as new linkages become possible, for example with criminal and terrorist networks. Meanwhile, the complexity characterising this networked society is contagious, touching all aspects of our lives. The mind-numbing rate of change, coupled with the intrusive nature of the global media, makes it almost impossible to draw breath – or to escape! Can you even begin to imagine how this might impact you and your family in the years to come?

The restructuring of capitalism feeds this global marketplace. And, as the world moves from mass consumerism to mass personalised consumerism, so we begin to feel the results of an increasingly flat and 'weightless' world.[10] Transactions and interactions occur at blinding speeds. Increasingly complex business and regulatory environments result as the economy dematerialises into intangibles and value is created not by capital or labour but by services, brands, blueprints, intellectual property, innovation and design.[11] New ideas have become the most valuable commodity. The rules governing what we do and how we do it are also changing quite dramatically. One need go no further than the changes that have occurred in the balance between competition and collaboration, for example. While competition was absolute in the industrial economy, remaining viable in today's knowledge economy requires the collaborative leveraging of scarce resources across entire business ecosystems and network clusters. This often means cooperating with almost everyone in the supply chain, from suppliers to end-users, and even with fiercely competitive rivals. Take for example the fact that it is now possible to run Microsoft's Windows XP operating system on a Mac! In a reciprocal move, Apple has made concessions to Windows users allowing them access to its hugely popular iPod music players and iTunes music store.

Such cooperation can be on many levels, of course, ranging from the clustering of physical facilities to enable closed-system linkages of production inputs and outputs,[12] to alliances for procurement or the sharing of non-core services across a federal grouping. In many instances, cooperation may even extend to in-process ventures and relationships with those with whom we are positioned competitively in the marketplace.

Again, in the knowledge economy, and linked to the principle of collaboration, is the concept of abundance. Abundance has become as important to business today as scarcity was in the industrial world. From the advent of the fax machine (where a critical mass of customers was a necessity for the product to be useful) to the latest in file-sharing protocols and open-source software, new technologies have opened up opportunities for dramatically extending and deepening market reach. This in turn has shifted business practices as well as customer perceptions of value. It has legitimised collaborative design and development. Expeditionary marketing, where new products are released in a *beta* format to be tested in the market (thus helping to identify and eliminate bugs or to improve features) before their official launch, is now commonplace as a result.

The coupling of the principle of abundance with technologies like the Internet has also led to the advent of entirely new industries. Pioneered by upstarts like Google, Yahoo!, Amazon and eBay, it has resulted in markets where network knowledge is captured, sorted and used to enhance the value proposition for individual customers. In all of these examples, the principle of abundance assumes the capturing of market share, by getting customers to use products as quickly as possible, is critical to success. In many instances this has even meant that companies are willing to give certain of their products away in

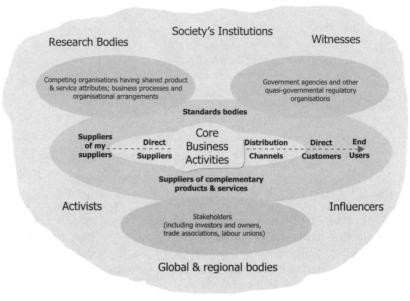

Figure 2.2   The competitive model of discrete industry groupings no longer accurately represents what really happens in global markets. Modern business ecosystems comprise myriad connections and relationships (many of them collaborative in nature) of members all interacting in ways that enable their own and each other's survival. Adapted from James F. Moore, Predators and Prey: A New Ecology of Competition, *Harvard Business Review*, May 1993.

order to build brand awareness and capture what was previously an uncontested market space. At least in these market categories, head-to-head competition has become a futile practice while collaborative strategies have become the most powerful means for rendering competitors and competition irrelevant.

Yet a third example of how many of the principles underlying business have changed is the impact of the Internet on markets. Business transactions increasingly occur in virtual space, diminishing the importance and relevance of physical spaces and geography. Success now depends on grasping this emerging *common sense* and using it to cope with the speed of global networks and the knowledge economy.

This is all very well if you happen to live in the more affluent parts of our world. Sadly, the positivist, materialist, technologically optimistic paradigm underpinning 300 or more years of *industrial economism* (a cruel hoax that continues to be peddled to poorer nations under the guise of economic development and progress) has come badly adrift. At least 100 million more people are living in poverty than just a decade ago while the gap between rich and poor is continuing to widen. According to a policy paper published by the Geneva Centre for the Democratic Control of Armed Forces in March 2004 between 113 million and 200 million women around the world are demographically 'missing'. Every year between 1.5 million and 3 million women, many of them children, lose their lives as a result of gender-based violence or neglect.[13] These killings are not silent – all the victims scream their suffering. It is not so much that the world does not hear them; it is just that we choose not to pay attention. Meanwhile, the challenges of poverty, overpopulation, famine, illiteracy, environmental degradation, financial distress and misgovernance have never been greater.[14]

NOTES

1. In May, the *Beijing News* newspaper reported that a Chinese businessman had bought a MiG-21f plane from a US eBay seller for $US24,730 ($32,600) to decorate his offices.
2. www.YouTube.com was created by members of the music industry with the aim of making music videos freely available to the public. It has since become a tool for anyone to upload and broadcast content of any kind and, in so doing, is revolutionising the way in which media works. By general consensus, websites like this are blurring the boundaries between fiction and reality. They are also responsible for the inevitable convergence of television and the Internet and the demise of standardised free-to-air content.
3. Founded in 1993 by former USSR President Mikhail Gorbachev, the mission of Green Cross International is to help ensure a just, sustainable and secure future for all by cultivating a new sense of global interdependence and shared responsibility regarding humanity's relationship with nature.
4. The Creative Commons enables copyright holders to grant some of their rights to the public while retaining others through a variety of licensing and contract schemes including dedication to the public domain or open content licensing terms. The intention is to avoid the problems current copyright laws create for the sharing of information. All these efforts, and more, are done to counter the effects of what Creative Commons considers to be, in the words of chairman Lawrence Lessig, a dominant and increasingly restrictive permission culture, 'a culture in which creators

get to create only with the permission of the powerful, or of creators from the past'. Lessig maintains that modern culture is dominated by traditional content distributors in order to maintain and strengthen their monopolies on cultural products such as popular music and popular cinema, and that Creative Commons can provide alternatives to these restrictions.

5. The ancient Greeks attempted to copy every book in existence to create the great Library of Alexandria.

6. Tim Berners-Lee, credited by many as the inventor of the World Wide Web, is currently working on an intelligent browser which he calls the Semantic Web, aimed at making it easier to find useful information on the Internet.

7. Another good example of this shift of awareness is the work being undertaken by Tomorrow's Company, a UK-based think-tank and research organisation, which is looking into the purpose and role of global business in the future. Tomorrow's global company will address four key questions with the aim of helping global business develop a clear idea of its role, the conditions for success in the future and the implications this will have for business strategy and leadership: (i) What should be the role of a company in society, globally and locally? (ii) How should the future collaboration between the wealth-creating enterprises, the financial institutions, government and civil society be developed and managed? (iii) How can companies lead, manage and benefit from a diverse workforce whilst maintaining a strong core purpose and set of values? (iv) How can companies address their critics and form productive relationships which yield positive outcomes?

8. *Human Nature*, **11**, p. 93. May 2005.

9. Numerous recent studies point to such patterns. See particularly: Levine, R., Locke, C., Searls, D. and Weinberger, D., *The Cluetrain Manifesto*, Perseus Books, Cambridge, MA, 2000; Mazarr, M., *Global Trends 2005: An Owners Manual for the Next Decade*, St. Martin's Press, New York, 1999. Henderson, H., *Paradigms in Progress: Life beyond Economics*, Berrett-Koehler, San Francisco, 1995.

10. Coyle, D., *The Weightless World: Strategies for Managing the Digital Economy*, MIT Press, 1998.

11. I am especially interested in 'strategic' innovation. This involves making new connections, re-imagining relationships, linking different economic and knowledge domains, and experimenting with new combinations of ideas, resources and capabilities. In this way we innovate by learning from the world rather than just imagining we are being creative within our own narrowly designated fields and disciplines.

12. A fine example is the industrial ecology model. Here waste from one production process is fed as raw material into another production process.

13. These figures include 'honour' killings, selective abortion and infanticide, starvation, medical neglect, results of the international sex trade, rape, genital mutilation and domestic violence.

14. *The State of the World's Cities* – a report published by the UN in 2006 that outlines urban trends in the twenty-first century, suggests that poverty and inequality will characterise many developing-world cities and that urban growth will become virtually synonymous with slum formation in some regions during the coming years. The report monitors five indicators regarding the speed of global urbanisation: (i) The lack of durable housing: it is estimated that 133 million people living in cities in the developing world lack durable housing. (ii) Lack of sufficient living area: overcrowding is a manifestation of housing inequality and is a hidden form of homelessness. (iii) Lack of access to water: although official statistics reflect better water coverage in urban than rural areas, surveys show that in many cities the quantity, quality and affordability of water in low-income urban settlements fall far short of acceptable standards. (iv) Lack of access to improved sanitation: over 25% of the developing world's urban population, or 560 million residents, lack adequate sanitation. (v) Lack of secure tenure: a global survey in 60 countries found that 6.7 million people had been evicted from their homes between 2000 and 2002 compared with 4.2 million in the previous two years.

CHAPTER 3

CATHEDRALS AND CAFES

Bringing life into organizations not only increases their flexibility, creativity, and learning potential, but also enhances our dignity and humanity as we connect with those qualities in ourselves.

– Fritjof Capra, The Hidden Connections

NET INFLUENCE

Ok. So the world is not neat and tidy. We might prefer that it was, indeed we usually behave as if it was. But it is not. It is messy and uncertain. Even more so in the wide wild world of business! Although we try to bring order to our working lives, routinely applying the latest management tools and techniques to help give the impression that we are on top of things, nothing could be further from the truth. Not only that, we appear to be making matters far worse by tenaciously applying archaic solutions to 'wicked' issues, as if we didn't have the imagination, foresight or courage to invisige new possibilities.

Because our previous strategies were unsustainable, the future can no longer be a simple continuation of our past. The future has to be transformational. While economic globalisation and political integration are essential components of societal transition, they are not the whole process. Previous transformations in society have been all-encompassing bifurcations that have touched every aspect of our lives, from politics and business to technology, environment and culture. Throughout history these bifurcations have impelled the progressive integration of different peoples, enterprises, economies, societies and cultures in systems of more and more people and larger and larger dimensions. But while these were local, national or regional in the past, today's shift is global. Humanity's sociocultural evolution now extends to the whole planet.

Many people still have difficulty comprehending this basic fact. They fail to see that old notions of reality are slipping from their grasp and new ones rapidly taking their place. We are now inhabiting a world dominated by living networks.

In spite of this we continue to design organisations and institutions of government as if we had never met other human beings with thoughts and dreams and feelings of their own. We rarely examine the unintended consequences of our actions; even though by not doing so we put at risk the very means for our continued health and well-being. We constrain spirit and imagination, preferring instead to focus on banal, quantifiable tasks that suboptimise performance and cause distress, conflict and confusion. We practise oppression rather than liberation. We compartmentalise people's lives in order to play them off against each other. We then capriciously alienate those who actually do the work by rewarding a small minority for efforts that are mediocre and uninspiring. And all the while we conveniently ignore the fact that these behaviours could well be interpreted as clinically psychopathic by any self-respecting psychiatrist!

So why do so many of us continue to act so? The answer stares us in the face. In contemporary society the disciplines of designing, organising, managing and leading have become axiomatic. Although designed for another age these orthodoxies have become sacrosanct. Yet they are also increasingly irrelevant and out of touch with the global issues facing us, as well as the science and technologies that are transforming the way we think and feel. All that needs to change. Recent discoveries in the new science of networks, including degrees of separation, synchronicity and 'small-world' phenomena, are rewriting our understanding of complex systems and the interdependence of human activities and behaviours. The implications of these breakthroughs for organisational design, for leadership and for management

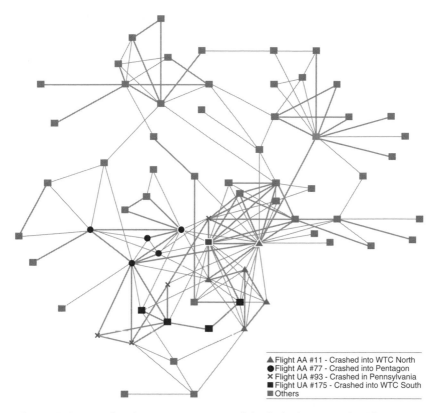

Figure 3.1 An after-the event mapping of the links between the 9/11 terrorists reveals new insights about how they were operationally organised. Copyright © 2006, Valdis Krebs, http://orgnet.com/hijackers.html.

are profound. Challenging conventional wisdom by exposing as false many of the assumptions we have previously held, they cast doubts on many 'best practice' conventions, highlighting numerous deceptive, non-productive and ultimately damaging practices that many of us still take for granted.

Thanks largely to a plethora of scientific and technological discoveries made during the past century or so, we are now in possession of some extremely perceptive theories about the nature and structure of reality. If we really want to understand the world in which we live, it must be through these new explanations, rather than through our preconceptions, received opinion or even common sense. Our best

Table 3.1 Different worldviews imply different organisational operating systems and, by implication, different sets of tools. When these tools and techniques differ markedly from the espoused worldview, confusion is created which can lead to stress and cultural breakdown.

Industrial economism	Knowledge ecologism
• Cartesian knowledge	• Quantum knowledge
• Static industries	• Dynamic ecosystems
• Competitive relationships	• Symbiotic relationships
• Outcomes predictable	• Outcomes uncertain
• Planning for results	• Navigating towards potential
• Focus on rules	• Focus on intelligence
• Culture can be managed	• Culture is emergent
• Heroic leadership	• Leaders at all levels
• Functional separation	• Functional integration
• Personal mastery	• Network mastery

hypotheses are not only 'truer' (and therefore less distorted) than what we once thought to be true, they make far more *sense* than common sense. However, accepting and applying these theories, together with the evidence and credentials that authenticate them, requires us to overtly discard many popularly held beliefs and accept, instead, explanations so counter-intuitive that they can, at first, seem utterly absurd. To great leaders, of course, they are universal truths.

Although most of these theories appear to relate primarily to the ways of science, to the structure of the universe, to human destiny – indeed to the very construction of human consciousness – the domain of social activity and discourse, too, is inextricably implicated in ways that will ultimately see the emergence of entirely different types and patterns of work, learning, leisure, government and commerce. Yet nowhere do these theories seem more incompatible with current practice, nowhere more disturbing to acknowledge, than in those very same areas of human enterprise. We have arrived at a watershed in history where the growing interest in planetary governance structures and 'glocalisation', for example, seem a logical next step for humanity.[1] Regrettably this idea presents itself at a time when mainstream media are reporting a trend to 'resource nationalism', with many indicators pointing to a potent resurgence by the nation-state.[2]

Are we really facing a choice between a planetary society and resurgence of the nation-state? And what of privatisation? Will the idea of *ownership* itself topple, giving way to new forms of administering access to the finite resources we all share? Or can we imagine a whole new way to manage the affairs of humanity? If we were to choose a better way, what could it be? Who would own the resources in such a society; the governments of nation-states, corporations, the commons? Seriously 'wicked' questions like these are not being asked, let alone pondered in any significant way, except by a few academics like Professor Irwin Laszlo.[3] And while energy, especially oil, is currently centre stage in the global theatre, growing shortages of food and water are waiting in the wings.[4] It does seem ironic that just as today's thought leaders begin to engage in serious conversations about an emergent planetary culture, signals from the margins suggest the geopolitical world may be moving in the opposite direction.

Yet the reasons for this paradox stare us emphatically in the face: by accepting the relevance of such radical ideas, we are set on challenging many of the basic assumptions we have held about life and work – its means and its ends. By accepting the sapient validity of the new we automatically invalidate many of the principles upon which our institutions of government, business and learning are predicated. Besides, why would those with power and influence change the status quo when they are doing so well by it?

The fact that the discovery of this body of new scientific theory happens to coincide with a far greater global awareness of human limitations (the fragility of our environment, the paucity of our imagination, the egocentric nature of our deeds, the finite nature of our resources) coupled with a growing sense that unrestrained economic growth and development may not necessarily equate to progress or the advancement of the human condition, doesn't make its manifestation any less scary.

No simpler, nor finer, example of the profoundly unsettling nature of the new science exists than the theory concerning the basis of human interaction. As a species, the human race has given itself an extraordinarily bad press. Anything likeable about us we tend to dismiss as the result of a fairly recent invention called civilisation. Anything remotely nasty we attribute to evolved 'human nature'. From cradle to grave we are constantly reminded that human beings are 'naturally' competitive. This belief has given rise to a system for the organising of human affairs that is essentially adversarial. The media sustains this credo and most industry policy is based upon it. Even survival itself, we have determined, is about competition, as a consequence of which much of our daily existence revolves around principles of rivalry and so-called 'healthy' competitive behaviour – examinations; grants and scholarships; selection, promotion and career development performance management; business takeovers; patents; politics; the law. The list is endless.

Yet modern biology no longer supports this jaundiced view, tentatively concluding that human beings have instincts to be both compassionate and cooperative from a very early age. The secret of this good side to human nature is that, compared with other animals, we are uniquely ill-equipped for self-sufficiency. Like ants and bees we cannot live outside of a communal society. We actually take pleasure in being socially connected. We cannot do without it. So dependent have we become on divisions of labour, for example, that few people today can feed, clothe and shelter themselves entirely through their own efforts. Many people regret this and yearn to rediscover the virtues of a simpler age of self-sufficiency.

In truth, there never was such an age for our species. From time immemorial, human beings have been obsessed with exchange, pacts, contracts, bargains, fairness and reciprocity – concepts virtually unknown to most other species. Nor does such a theory of cooperation necessarily contradict the prevailing paradigm in both economics and biology: that people act predominantly out of enlightened self-interest. It does, however, raise profound questions regarding the ways we have traditionally designed and put to use our social, economic and political institutions. And it totally screws up any selfish, conditioned responses we may have had to the ultimate purpose behind work, enterprise, wealth creation, public service and government. If we examine the relationships between this biological concept of human nature and other new theories drawn from cybernetics, neuro-linguistic programming, social ecology, systems dynamics, epistemology, and the new science of complexity, chaos and self-organised criticality, a startling, yet unusually evocative, pattern of connectedness emerges; an 'entanglement' demanding *ecological* (not just *economic*) approaches to the organisation and management of human affairs.

Initially, this *ecological* paradigm is likely to have the most influence on governance, business and trade. In the industrial age, most corporations would have conceded that a successful business model was good for up to about 40 years. Today, companies that have tied themselves to that model invariably atrophy and die. Only corporations that adopt new business models, or that create generative waves of development, will continue to grow and prosper over the longer term. The same appears to be true for governments and societies, albeit with extended timeframes – a simple proposition that has significant repercussions. It means, for example, that it would be foolish to divorce the purpose and functioning of private enterprise and public service from the dynamic necessity for global society to change. It means, too, that we should be ready to jettison social strategies that continue to divide humanity or that are unable to stabilise environmental degradation or eradicate social injustice. And it explains why 'real-time' approaches to strategy (in any sector) are not simply about a new way of doing business but about providing a model of ecological harmony capable of creating a 'culture of permanence'[5] within our society. In effect, what we are imagining here is a viable replacement for the highly toxic and unsustainable Western strategy of unfettered materialism, unchecked acceleration and rampant economic growth and development – the strategy that, even today, motivates most business activity.

TREADING WATER

In the early 1980s, a select club of companies that included Shell, Mitsui, Stora and DuPont carried out a benchmark investigation into corporate longevity. This apparently disparate group of 27 global corporations came together through curiosity. Specifically, curiosity as to which aspects of their internal capability were responsible for enabling them to adapt to changing circumstances better than most others, to the extent that some of them had remained in business for at least a century or more. Put another way, the study was an attempt to discover any shared self-replicating properties that enabled sustainability of the business in the long term – a search for unique *genetic* qualities, if you will. These were all examples of firms that had survival at the core of their aspirations. These companies were in business, any business, as long as it helped them continue as a viable working community. Over their long lifetimes, each one changed its business portfolio at least once – some of them several times. Yet each one retained its unique identity. DuPont, for example, started out as a gunpowder manufacturer, became the largest shareholder of General Motors in the 1930s, and is now mostly involved in the production of speciality chemicals and bio-fuels. Mitsui's founder opened a drapery shop in Edo (Tokyo) in 1673, went into money changing and converted into a bank after the Meiji Restoration in the nineteenth century. This company added coal mining to its operations and, towards the end of the nineteenth century, ventured into manufacturing. The first written mention of the Swedish company Stora dates from 1288. In those days it was a copper mine. During the ensuing 700 years, new activities were added that replaced the old core business. The company moved from copper to forestry to iron smelting to hydropower and, nowadays, to paper, wood pulp and chemicals. While in hindsight each one of these changes seems massive, they were for the most part gradual, almost imperceptible. Yet they demonstrate a flexible attitude to the 'core' business of the time.

Initially, outside of the participating companies, little interest was shown in this study by the management community at large – possibly owing to the bewildering profusion of fads already occupying the minds of 'progressive' corporate executives at the time, but more likely due to the implausible nature of the study's conclusions. Before this work was undertaken, we should remember, the most common metaphors for corporate life were essentially mechanistic. Only later did more social metaphors of the tribe, the clan or the team, become popular. Now, however, startling evidence was advanced linking corporate longevity to the rate and quality of learning within the whole enterprise relative to changes in the external environment. The study gave particular emphasis to data supporting the notion that the most 'successful' global corporations (in terms of sustained growth and profitability) appeared to behave as if they were living organisms, maintaining their ecological 'fit' by continuously upgrading their ability to respond rapidly to changes in their environment.

This single insight, if correct, was a time bomb ticking away in the offices, factories and boardrooms of major corporations and within the classrooms of business schools. Akin to Einstein's preposterous assertions regarding the relativity of space and time (in a world pervaded at the time by the rational theories of Newtonian physics) the Shell study, at least to those few people who were able to fathom its profound implications, had the potential to blow the world of management theory into smithereens.

The study revealed that the two key motivations shared by these firms were: (i) remaining in business (survival) and (ii) the development of their full potential (capability). But perhaps the most interesting characteristic of success exhibited by all 27 companies was openness to learning, flexibility and adaptiveness – what Shell's Arie de Geus explained as, 'an extreme tolerance to the new'. In effect, this seemed to imply that the less control a corporation had over changes in the external environment, the greater the levels of tolerance required in order to be successful. Or, to look at it another way, a management policy of low tolerance, coupled with high levels of centralised control, required two basic conditions to be fulfilled: (i) the corporation should have some control over the world in which it is operating; and (ii) this world should be relatively stable.

Of course, both these conditions are rare today. The major lesson arising from the Shell study is that any corporation desiring success and longevity, particularly in an environment that is hostile and volatile and in circumstances where the need to adapt swiftly to changing conditions is paramount, would be well-advised to initiate a policy of minimal controls and shared learning. The study provided ample evidence that successful survivors create sufficient internal freedom to cope with a world of changes that they have no hope of controlling.

Since then, a considerable number of research projects have been undertaken, exploring every conceivable link between an organisation's business performance and its social ecology. The pioneer in this field is undoubtedly Stafford Beer.[6] Through his meticulous work into viable systems, we now have a far better understanding of the characteristics required to create and sustain an organisational system. In the late 1980s, a distinguished Professor of Marketing at Harvard University, Igor Ansoff, validated the significance of a strategically aligned culture in the optimisation of business intent. A few years later another American researcher, Professor John Kotter, discovered that a strong, aligned, adaptive culture, which was also 'strategically appropriate', could be relied upon to deliver exceptional business performance over time, regardless of changing strategies. Other practical investigations carried out over the past 15 years or so have revealed how *tacit* knowledge – rather than more explicit rules, goals and directives – may be responsible for up to 80% of actual organisational performance. More recently, inquiry into organisational learning has resulted in a profusion of diverse ideas, texts, conferences and consulting assignments, not to mention an entire family of new functions and services – a profusion that still shows little sign of abating. Much of this work, though focused ostensibly on management, also has huge implications for leadership.

Which is all well and good; except that none of this new knowledge seems to have resulted in anything other than cosmetic finetuning in the field of leadership. Mostly we continue doing what we have always done. Although it often feels as though we are moving forward this is most often a delusion. We have been treading water. For whatever reasons, transformative change to our institutions, organisations and the ways these are managed and led, has not yet transpired.

Indeed, until now, relatively few attempts have been made to create a new knowledge base for managing the fast-moving, strategically aligned, knowledge-creating enterprise of the twenty-first century. *The Five Literacies of Global Leadership* does just that: initiating an authentic revolution in strategic leadership philosophy and practice that sets it apart from the practice of management once and for all. But why, given all the emphasis on change and innovation over the past 25 years, is genuine organisational transformation relatively rare? Undoubtedly much of it has to do with our ability to convince ourselves into believing almost anything at all. But perhaps it also has something to do with the difficulty each one of us has in imagining other possibilities and alternatives to that which are already in place.

EYES ON THE BALL

In 2002 an experiment was conducted at a conference entitled 'Toward a Science of Consciousness' sponsored by the Centre for Consciousness Studies at the University of Arizona in the USA.[7] Observers were asked to pay close attention to two teams of participants who were tossing a ball back and forth. Audience members were told to count the number of times the ball was being caught and thrown. While they were doing this an actor dressed in a gorilla costume walked through the space in which the two parties were throwing the ball back and forth – directly through their line of sight. Incredibly, when questioned afterwards, almost half the audience had not seen the gorilla. This anecdote illustrates the immense challenge each one of us confronts every day in shifting our mental models away from what 'we know' to be the truth, to embrace the unknown, the uncertain and the unexpected. It also depicts the problems faced by all modern enterprises in growing the passion to reinvent business models, responding appropriately to market opportunities and competitive threats, extracting maximum value from innovation and continuously upgrading the thinking of those executives whose job it is to adjust to increasingly greater complexities and paradoxes.

If we go through life paying attention only to our immediate individual needs we run the risk of becoming materially affluent to such an extent that we become unaware of other possibilities and closed off to communal growth and spiritual renewal. The chance to change remains blurred. Perhaps totally off our radar. We can only become aware of this and bring opportunities into sharper focus, by shifting our mental models – the lenses through which we see and comprehend the world and our relationship to it. This *is* the only way problems are transcended, issues are transformed and beneficial change is realised.

Seeing the gorilla, though, is only the beginning. The fact is each of us is persuaded to think and behave a certain way. Although we may deny it, what we think about, and consequently what actions we take, is heavily biased from birth. This is because the very act of thinking is shaped by our perceptions – highly selective filters that wash over or edit out anything remotely inconsistent with our most deeply held (inherited and acquired) convictions. Even when we think we're being open-minded, or original, it is our perceptions, derived from deeply held beliefs about reality (our *worldview*), that guide us into doing what we actually think.

Take, for example, Thomas Hobbes. Hobbes adopted the mechanistic worldview of Newton and Descartes and attempted to apply it to the human realms of politics and society. He argued that, by starting from first principles, he could construct a rational science of society. The problem was that Hobbes' first principles were nothing of the kind, but simply subjective assertions shaped by the tumultuous times in which he lived – seventeenth-century England, riven by civil war. To Hobbes, it was axiomatic that people seek to dominate others, only relinquishing power voluntarily if it is necessary for their self-preservation. In order that some individuals do not take advantage of other people's willingness to cooperate Hobbes reasoned people should transfer their rights to a higher power, granting it a mandate to enforce this cooperation. In this way the community is united into a single body. Hobbes called this the Leviathan. We would probably call it the state. Although Hobbes' worldview may appear somewhat brutal from a modern perspective it established the notion that reason could be accommodated in politics. Unfortunately, while the natural sciences have moved on, we're still suffering the effects of attempts to apply the mechanistic, atomistic philosophy of the seventeenth century to the management of human affairs today.

Numerous, diverse worldviews coexist in today's society, all jostling for our allegiance in one form or other. Some, such as those embracing the world's great faiths and political ideologies, become universal in their appeal, resonating naturally with their devotees' perceptions of right and wrong, true and false, good and evil, sometimes for centuries at a time. Others, like Darwin's theory of natural selection, Einstein's depiction of relativity, or Erwin Schrödinger's stranger-than-fiction model of quantum entanglement,[8] are based on direct observations and hypotheses.

As imagery of these concepts seeps into our awareness they develop a veracity, directly shaping our understanding and expectations of how things work – at least until more plausible explanations come along. Spawned from a potent mix of individual and collective beliefs, values, experience and motivations, each dominant worldview generates a discrete *knowledge system* that sets it apart.

Every knowledge system has an inherent lingua franca comprising moral imperatives, through which issues are subjected to analysis, and a self-reflective source language of shared myths, stories, metaphors and associated values, which are called upon to sort and make sense of reality. This lingua franca allows us to become conscious of what we choose to *see*. Yet what we *choose* to see is what is meaningful to us, and what is *meaningful* is determined by the worldview . . .

Although these lingua franca permeate society, facilitating sense-making and reifying coherent inventions of 'the truth', we are rarely conscious of them, or of our allegiance to a particular worldview, except perhaps on deeply emotive levels when in a state of personal moral crisis, or when we have to confront these differences head on. This became clearer to me recently when adapting to the quirks of life in rural Isaan. Almost everyone in this part of Thailand conforms to a cultural worldview that I find beguiling yet naive and somewhat problematical for someone more accustomed to Western beliefs. For example, in Isaan strong credence is given to the power of the super-natural. This, combined with the traditional devotion to Buddhism as well as recognition of the potency of Western science, creates an eclectic system of faith that is hard to get a real fix on. When someone is suffering from a migraine, for example, it means that a visit to the local shaman is as important as taking prescription medicine from the pharmacy and 'making merit' at the village Wat. All three measures are seen to be equally important, indeed necessary, elements towards restoring the health of the individual. In more serious cases of mental illness, where someone might be suffering from paranoia or psychotic delusions, for example, the patient will be accompanied by all manner of friends and acquaintances on these visits that, by their very pres-ence, help to amplify the 'good luck' required in order for the patient to be restored to full health. Although it would be easy to dismiss such worldviews as primitive, at least from a purely contemporary Western viewpoint, this would be shortsighted. And wrong! The fact that they help sustain an essential component of Thai tradition and culture is what really matters. It is this fact that should be respected by people within and external to that tradition.

The deceptive yet persuasive power of worldviews was illustrated recently by George Lakoff.[9] Referring to George W. Bush's 2004 State of the Union address, Lackoff noted the difference between what was *said* by the President and what he actually *meant.* This speech, Lackoff asserts, was based on an internal logic in which national politics was perceived through the metaphorical lens of a conservative, 'strict-father' family.

> The strict father sees the world as a dangerous and difficult place, where evil lurks, and competition will always produce winners and losers. His job is to protect and support his family, and as moral authority, teach his kids right from wrong. Through example and painful punishment, he instils in them an internal discipline to act morally and become self-reliant. Moral people are disciplined and deserve to prosper. Those who are undisciplined are not moral and should not prosper. Mothers may comfort, but must be prevented from coddling, lest the children become undisciplined, immoral, and dependent. When the children are mature, they are on their own and parents should not meddle in their lives. This family moral system, projected onto the nation, defines a radical form of conservative politics that Bush supporters implicitly understand and that provides the internal logic that lies behind the speech.

Lakoff is very perceptive; and accurate. Like Nixon before him, Bush has wrapped himself in the American flag, the need for national security, his high office and a claim to be the defender of America – the man who can show terrorists not to mess with the USA. His critics are attacked as being soft on fighting terrorism, or being knee-jerk partisans, when all they want is for their president to stay within the law. Few would question President Bush's goal: protecting Americans from further terror attacks. But every thinking American should question his means. Never in history has a US president asserted claims to such unchecked power.

Let us examine this situation more closely in the light of the past five years. The United States initially responded to the attacks of September 11, 2001 by declaring a global 'war on terror'. More recently, it has redefined the conflict as the 'long war'. Some have even gone as far as to suggest that the post-9/11 world is the beginning of a third world war.[10] Of course the audacity of the 9/11 attacks and the instantly exposed weaknesses of the most powerful economic and military nation on the planet indicated extraordinary times ahead. President George W. Bush's comeback was predictably dramatic. But few could have foreseen the global turmoil his declaration would unleash. Five years later, ties between the Muslim and Christian worlds are tense, diplomatic alliances have been redrawn and insurgencies rage in Iraq and Afghanistan with civilians the favoured target of suicide bombers. Instability reigns supreme. At its heart, the US and its allies maintain, is terrorism. On the other hand Western imperialism, religious intolerance and a desire to corner global markets in natural resources like oil, must surely rank among the root causes of such geopolitical chaos?

What is clear to me is that governments everywhere have over-reacted to the point where they have elevated the risk of terrorism to one that is essentially 'existential' – they claim it threatens our very existence and our way of life. Accordingly, political responses have ranged from the whimsical to the patently absurd. For example, in Australia, fridge magnets were mailed to every household in the country urging citizens to *Look out for Australia. Help protect our way of life from a possible terrorist threat.* More recently, while navigating the security gauntlet at Bangkok's new international airport on a flight to New York, a small tube of lip balm from my wife's carry-on bag was confiscated. This is ludicrous. How is it that we've allowed the world to change around us in this way?

Part of the problem is the confusion and fear caused by the message that terrorism poses an 'existential' threat. Much of the way that Western societies have reacted since 9/11 has been shaped by this conviction. It is a belief that remains widely accepted and seldom contested. Why? Where is the evidence? The overthrow of Western imperialism is indeed the declared aim of the terrorists themselves. But why would we suppose they have the capacity to demolish our entire way of life? Even nuclear terrorism, which would cause terrible suffering and disruption, would hardly threaten the underlying fabric of Western societies. The truth is that terrorism poses a small, but not negligible, danger to the safety of each one of us. However it does not pose a threat to our society at large. Issues like climate change and environmental pollution carry far greater risks.

Once again, the problem is overwhelmingly one of perception. In the face of a threat that so many of us are told is existential, thorough policing and security intelligence diligence seems hardly enough. Consequently we are seduced by our own misperceptions of the situation into wildly inappropriate policies and even the subsequent erosion of individual rights. When the complex pattern of reasons, motives and pretexts that propelled the US into Iraq is finally untangled, I suspect an important factor will prove to be an overpowering need to be seen to be doing something bigger than police work in the face of an existential threat. But now, having made that decision, political leaders are locked into an account of the threat that justifies their actions. And the more serious and demanding the commitment to Iraq appears, the more apocalyptic our leaders need to make the threat sound in order to justify landing us in it.

> Five years on, the way the West's leaders talk about terrorism is now much more shaped by the need to justify what they have done since September 11 than by any sober judgement about the threat of terrorism itself. That is why Tony Blair thinks he has to say that we are engaged in a global battle 'utterly decisive in whether the values we believe in triumph or fail'. It is why President George Bush thinks he has to say that if the terrorists are not defeated in Iraq they will have to be fought in America.[11]

How do we extract ourselves from this cycle of misperception and counterproductive response? We need to start examining statements like these much more carefully in order to ask: Do they ring true? Where is the evidence and what is its source? Do they provide a realistic basis for policy and action? Because before we can establish a more balanced, coherent, sustainable and successful approach to the issue of terrorism, we are going to need to start describing it much more realistically.

By referring to these examples it is not my intention to suggest that President George W. Bush is evil or the only Western leader to openly defy the law. The decline of freedom in Britain is not news, yet introducing the new Legislative and Regulatory Reform Bill has demonstrated Prime Minister Blair's taste for absolute power and a disdain for democracy that is unprecedented. This new bill marks the beginning of the end of true parliamentary democracy in Britain. In its effect, it is as significant as the US Congress abandoning the Bill of Rights in 2005. Like Bush, the Blair clique does not enter into debate. For the radical in Downing Street, 'sincere belief' in one's own veracity is quite enough.[12] Such is the power of worldviews.

These examples illustrate an important point: worldviews do not change the way things are. Rather, they project particular versions of reality onto the minds of those predisposed to accept them. These interpretations are then used to help justify or disguise what might otherwise be seen as irrational, immoral, criminal, or perhaps merely 'odd' behaviour.

QUE SERA, SERA! WHATEVER WILL BE, WILL BE

As a coherent and orderly picture of the world developed within society over centuries, it made sense for its members to believe that the numinous power behind this reality was itself coherent and orderly. By and large, we are assured by physicists, religious leaders and mystics alike, the world evolved according to a set of universal laws. These laws invariably depict a rational and unified worldview within their particular tradition. It is hardly surprising that we have collective faith in this notion, especially given that we force it to accommodate the otherwise underlying tensions between science and spirituality. Whatever one's bias, so much attention is now accorded the tangible world of things and events we even tend to measure human progress almost totally in terms of economic development. In the developed world, growth is the mantra, while success is gauged by the amount of material wealth that can be accumulated and spent in any given year.

Much of contemporary society is driven by an ethos of materialism. The cult of avarice colours the palette of information and ideas that shape our society: its purpose, aspirations and values. It punctuates differences, reducing civilisation to a productivity index and anaesthetising us to alternative, equally valid, voices and expressions of progress. Incessantly observed, reported on and vicariously experienced, this shared fiction has become our *common* sense. Alternative or dissenting voices are progressively marginalised. Deeply immersed in a constant theatre of activities, events, rituals and social interactions, society's insatiable appetite for material wealth has become the rationale of daily life for many. Over time, this narrative has become the overarching pattern of our culture, shaping our entire social order. Initially through family life, and then via education, television and the popular press, it influences the processes by which we are socialised. It forges our sense of identity, what we should aspire to, and what life is for. And, because it influences what we believe we *need* and what we believe to be *important*, it sways our sense of where our true interests lie. We do not challenge this story, because we believe it to be 'the truth'. Quite simply, it is taken to be the way things are. And because we *know* it to be so, the story is sustained through our collective communicative behaviour.

As this story arises from perceived common interests and is embedded in the pattern of social arrangements and relationships defined within society, it has immense potency. And yet its power is vested not in any particular individual, place or institution, but in a single narrative emanating from everywhere. Naturally, the meaning we make of all this is contingent upon the personal information coming at us from our inner world of values, beliefs and assumptions. Because each one of us instinctively interprets our perceptions of the external world through the lens of our inner world, we see the world as *we are* – not as *it is*. If, at times, our subjective projections of our objective reality seem crass or ambiguous, this inner world of beliefs and perceptions is, by comparison, infinitely more mysterious. Through MRI[13] and similar digital imaging technologies, the human mind is beginning to divulge its secrets. Cognitive science[14] opens up an entirely new inner world that we're only just beginning to understand.

Take human perceptions for example. Shaped within worldviews by various *ways of knowing* we've devised for exploring what it means to be human (things like religion, politics, science, philosophy and art), perceptions habitually seduce us into believing that it is in the nature of things for all kinds of phenomena to be the way we 'see' them, or 'expect' them, to be. In essence, our perceptions allow us to create illusions of reality. Yet, by reinforcing a particular version of the truth, perceptions also make us blind, deaf and dumb to the legitimacy of alternative worldviews. This explains the tension and fear we experi ence wherever worldviews collide, as illustrated by opposing fundamentalist groups in the Middle East, for example, where peace fails even to get a foothold; in the stance of China to Taiwan or India to Pakistan over their disputed territories; and in the West's posturing with regard to Iraq, Iran and to North Korea.

Becoming alert to particular *ways of knowing* and the unseen perceptions informing a certain worldview opens cracks through which we can peek, grasping the inner workings of the knowledge system in play. Here we can sense how perceptions are being organised and manipulated. Looking beyond the illusion's compelling external veneer we are then able also to challenge our inner assumptions with far greater ease than would otherwise be the case. Though science and spirituality are only two ways of knowing about the world, they have come to embody how we routinely come to terms with ourselves and the human condition. One or the other infuses most contemporary worldviews. Together they create a sense of *wholeness* experienced as enlightenment or wisdom.

In pre-literate communities, as in those quarantined from the excesses of consumerism by time, geography or privation, it is totems, the seasons, natural events and superstition that guide understanding. Affiliated knowledge systems focus on wisdom, emotions, reverence, meditation and the soul. For the rest, science holds sway. In literate societies it is the lens most commonly used to explain the way things are. Its apparent certitude and empirically based logic possibly account for the esteem in which science is generally held. In fact scientific knowledge has become so highly regarded that it determines not only how we *see* the world but also *what* we do (or do not) and *how* we do it. Science accounts for the way we govern, organise and manage our affairs. It has become our indestructible article of faith – the exuberant protagonist in society's subliminal epistemology. But herein resides a paradox, for science, like any other knowledge domain, is essentially evolutionary. The agrarian revolution might have been delayed for centuries had it not been for breakthroughs in astronomy, which then allowed for the possibility of agriculture.

Likewise, the advent of modern management theory in the later years of the nineteenth century was predicated on a physics that offered a more comprehensive explanation of tangible things. Thus, from this standpoint, the industrial revolution was never about new machines, factories or production methods, but the shifting *context* for how business might now be done. The same can be said of today's global business environment. Over the past few decades, physics has advanced from a discipline concerned principally with physical matter to one focused on connections, relationships and behaviour. At the same time, extraordinary advances in biology and the life sciences have evolved our understanding of who we are and have even given us the gift to create life itself.

We have now reached a moment in history where we can go far beyond what was previously thought possible. The *context* has shifted once more. In moving forward, we recognise the role modern scientific management played in getting us to this point. But it is equally vital that we appreciate the philosophy underpinning the new science, and its deeper interconnectedness with spirituality, so that we can continue our journey of discovery and apply this to the design and management of human affairs.

FROM ATOMS TO ECOSYSTEMS

The primary worldview (and related knowledge system) that grew to maturity between the industrial revolution and the invention of the H-bomb, one with which we in the West are most familiar as it allowed contemporary capitalism to emerge, is essentially Cartesian.[15] Newtonian science, together with linear, reductionist thought, resulted in new means for production. These systematised production methods were then made even more efficient by engineers like Frederick Taylor who advocated the division of labour into functionally related units and the reduction of routine tasks into their simplest possible components.[16]

Newtonian logic is best characterised as the ability to manage and measure tangible things. Analysis, results-based thinking, and organising mechanisms based upon machine-like hierarchies, are parts of a distinctive behavioural *code* used to justify the linear nature of cause and effect. Spirituality is inconsequential here. Material progress holds sway. Shrewdly labelled *industrial economism* by the US economist Hazel Henderson,[17] Newtonian worldviews generate distinctive architectures, propelled by reductionist principles,[18] where *productive* economic activities prevail, and are therefore highly prized, while other, more creative activities are perceived to be *less productive*, and therefore of less value to society. The pressure to be, or remain, productive leads to a desolate, somewhat demeaning situation where everyone, from poets to politicians, are forced into a relentless contest to prove their (utilitarian) worth.

This dispiriting situation even extends to our fascination with leadership. Pandering to a regulatory environment fixated on measurement, compliance, control and constraint, MBA courses are pumping out a generation of 'leaders' who are temperamentally, emotionally and intellectually incapable of managing any change in themselves, let alone in the dynamic organisational and business realities we are bound to face in the future.[19]

All is not lost, however. While industrial economism still motivates and sustains much of what we do in the developed world, its supremacy has started to falter. Reason and logic, seminal factors in its development, are now pointing to alternative, more appropriate knowledge systems and, thence, to new worldviews. Why should this be so?

Throughout history, the more fundamental shifts in societies have arisen not from government edicts and the results of battles fought but through vast numbers of people changing their minds – sometimes just a fraction. Some of these shifts have given rise to profound transformations – for instance the transition from the agrarian to the industrial age in Europe. Others have been more specific, such as the termination of slavery as an acceptable institution, the rejection of British colonial power in India, the failure of communism in the Soviet Union and the opening up of China to global markets. In such instances, it is largely a matter of people remembering that no matter how powerful the economic, political or military institution, it is able to persist only because it has legitimacy and that legitimacy arises from the perceptions of people.

Where people give legitimacy they can also withhold it. A challenge to legitimacy is the most potent force for change in history – inspiring revolutions, bringing down despots and ushering in democracy. To that force must now be added another, equally empowering principle. By consciously shifting the fundamental views we have of reality (the manner in which we perceive, think, value and behave), we can change the world. There are distinct signs that such a paradigm shift is underway, particularly aided by reality-shifting technologies that are now emerging. Everywhere one detects murmurings of the need for a new social order. Meanwhile, the old order decays, as evidenced by the militarisation of societies; unbridled materialism; the drift towards anarchy, long-term unemployment and homelessness; the continued plundering of resources from the developing world; disconnection of youth and growing urban violence; violation of the social contract between society and the individual; an inability to arrest the environmental destruction that rampages on a broad front; the inherent futility of the 'war against terrorism'; and a growing schism between the rich, consuming Northern hemisphere and the populous, poverty-stricken South.

The shape of the new is not yet clearly discernible, although we seem to glimpse elements of it from time to time in a hotchpotch of new kinds of entrepreneurial enterprises, new forms of community, alternative economies and other social innovations that embody values and principles congenial to a new paradigm. Maybe we're beginning to see there is more to life than money and possessions. More likely is the realisation that industrial economism's attendant institutions and applications appear incapable of remedying the most intractable of society's problems. Indeed there is a growing suspicion they might actually prolong them! Advances in science and technology, too, present us with opportunities to approach these issues differently. Possibly it is also because the unintended consequences of industrial economism, evident in the intolerable threat posed to the human species by poverty, militaristic geopolitical interventions, social injustice, drought and biospheric degradation, has resulted in society's moral centre shifting once again to embrace the sanctity of all life.

The chaos of all this is palpable enough. Innovative technologies and cultural fusion are converging to pitch the more developed nations headlong into an unbounded world where connectivity proliferates and economic value resides in myriad fleeting intangibles. Many of the rules underpinning industrial economism, once uncontested, now serve only to hinder and frustrate. Confusion and uncertainty reign supreme in a global soap opera where trusting relationships are critical and business is transacted opportunistically and at phenomenal speeds. Imbued with massively disruptive forces and dynamics way beyond our comprehension, this quantum world(view) is characterised by the need to embrace ambiguity, uncertainty and paradox. Integral thinking, connecting, relating and narrating are now seen to be part of an intrinsic 'code' used to illuminate and deal with complex, asymmetric phenomena.

The science offering the most coherent explanation of this messy, ambiguous world is not Newtonian physics but the rapidly unfolding science of adaptive systems, nonlinearity, emergence, free-scale networks and small-world phenomena. This is not the stuffy science learned from school textbooks but the world of spontaneous behaviours, stories, diseases, friendships, ecosystems, fashion, fads, crises, rumours and markets.

Cartesian approaches to organisational development and the leadership of change were predicated on the assumption that it was possible to predict, design and control reality. Network science unlocks us from such deceits, letting us see the world as a living system of dynamic flows and interconnections rather than a banal clockwork mechanism. Living systems like ecosystems, animals, organisations, economies and societies are not 'made' in the conventional sense. There is no simple hierarchy. No 'one' single person or team is in charge and there is certainly no central hub demanding compliance of any kind. The incessant, chaotic, essentially unknowable, interaction of all individual components ensures that living systems are in a constant process of renewal – and *emergence*.

Emergence has changed our understanding of the relationship between the physical, material world and the invisible, non-material world. We still live with the legacy of Newtonian science and the belief that the *real* world is that which we can touch and feel and directly experience. But emergence reveals the significance of the invisible world and the defining role relationships play. So the science of networks offers an alternative way of perceiving the world that is immediately relevant to contemporary leadership, governance and management. It reveals a world of unexpected linkages and interrelationships, a connected society within which entirely new possibilities are taking shape regarding the organisation of human affairs.

If the turmoil and complexity we encounter every day is better explained by this new science, how should we perceive today's practices? What assumptions need to change? What might we need to *see* differently? More precisely, how should our approach to designing, organising, managing and leading human activities shift, given this utterly dissimilar view of how things actually work? To begin to appreciate these issues we must first identify the axioms underpinning this 'connected' reality. Only then can we begin to recognise the factors that matter as we begin to make sense of the changes that might be possible.

BAZAARS, BRAINS, BRANDS AND BRAKES

Beginning in the early fifteenth century, a few audacious explorers from a handful of nations, England, Portugal, Spain, Holland and China among them, took to the high seas at the behest of their rulers to discover the world beyond their known borders. In their quest for foreign lands these voyagers opened up new trade routes, creating vast empires in their wake and subduing any resistance from indigenous inhabitants. Thus, the process of colonisation became the first phase towards globalism. Colonisation persists to this day, though it is more evident in the colonising of minds by global brands, rather than nations colonising lands. The empires of the future will indeed be empires of the mind.

The second phase of globalism was triggered by the Industrial Revolution, sometime towards the latter part of the eighteenth century, and is now commonplace. Spearheaded by prosperous conglomerates (mostly in the US and Europe), motivated by the need for cheaper labour and new customers, this period of globalism saw companies enter a seemingly unending dance of financial restructuring, process re-engineering, outsourcing, expansion and relocation of production facilities overseas in pursuit of lower costs and access to additional markets for their goods. When most of us talk about *globalisation* we are usually referring to this phase, as well as the disruption it continues to bring to workers, as much as the ubiquitous presence of particular brands in shopping malls from Bangkok to Dubai and Sydney to Los Angeles.

But during the latter years of the twentieth century the world shrunk yet again. Suddenly and with very little warning, access to fibre-optic telecommunications propelled connectivity to a whole new level, ushering in a plug-and-play era in which almost any intelligent individual with a notebook computer and a web browser could connect and collaborate with anyone, anywhere. This third phase of globalism was driven by innovation, living networks and the efficiency of global supply chains. Volatile, yet empowering, rules that previously made sense were now reinvented. Beijing, Bangalore and Boston became instant neighbours as workflows were disaggregated and reaggregated in myriad ways that wiped out any advantage (in terms of power, resources and infrastructure) developed nations once had.

The impacts of these three overlapping waves of internationalisation offer extraordinary opportunities for any business prepared to invest in new ideas, experiment and reinvent the way value is created. But the burden of bureaucracy, the gravitational pull of the past and a lack of creative stimuli weigh heavily on some organisations, especially in an era where speed is of the essence. Although interconnectivity, technological convergence, liberating relationships, speed of interaction, and the laws of increasing returns, economies of flow, and abundance, for example, are all characteristics of today's networked economy, perhaps the most critical factor for any leader is how they 'frame' this reality while 'waking up' to everything that is going on around them. We call this *learning metabolism*: the time it takes for an individual or an enterprise to identify, process and react (appropriately) to a particular chain of events in the external environment.

Contemporary markets have become pure network. They are surprising and inherently chaotic. Because they are dynamic flows rather than discrete events it is impossible to out-think them. They are capricious, scrambling all conventional sense of time and constantly mutating before our eyes. The speed of these market networks is astounding, occurring instantly. Business leaders work at the interface between external realities (markets) and internal leverage (their organisation's capacity to perform in those markets).[20] This is their playground and they are mesmerised by it. Being business people with business interests, skills, language and expertise, they are drawn to the market's vibrancy as well as its exhilarating uncertainties. Theirs is a world of change – of spot deals, customer value, hedging, risk and endless entrepreneurial opportunities.

They learn to respond to events in the marketplace as rapidly as they can. But there is an inevitable time lag between these responses and market dynamics. This may be seconds (as in the case of foreign exchange markets, for example) to weeks or even years (as is the case with aeroplane manufacturers or major infrastructure developers). In any case, the learning metabolism of business is much slower than markets – even when a company's business intelligence capability is finely honed and alert to changing conditions. By its very nature, the learning metabolism of government regulators is invariably slower than business. This will continue to be the case until governments develop the ability to focus on anticipating the systemic consequences of their policies, rather than over-reacting to discrete problems in the market as they occur, with greater numbers of imposed controls, which are merely symptomatic of an over-regulated system. This inevitably leads to a situation in which corporations are encouraged to short-circuit, and even cheat, the system.

The real laggard, however, is the tool universally used by organisations to equip them with the capability to respond appropriately to market opportunities! Management. Held in thrall to conservatism, backed by ignorance, cumbersome routines, bureaucratic paraphernalia, costly legacy mechanisms and futile attempts to control every possible risk, management moves sluggishly in comparison to business – and glacially in comparison with the dynamism of markets!

Occasionally, traditional support functions like information technology, human resources and finance can be so out of touch, that an organisation's learning metabolism can actually flat line.[21] In these situations managers remain blissfully unaware of the strategic business imperatives and opportunities around them – although they will deny this. Naturally this is deeply frustrating for customer-facing business leaders who eventually see management as hindering rather than helping their own efforts. Unfortunately, this is closer to the truth than many realise. And it isn't because managers are lazy, incompetent, negligent, or simply doing their best to stall progress. Far from it! They are, however, recklessly indifferent to the assumptions upon which their earnest toil is based. They often ignore facts, pretending that oscillations in the system are due to some kind of malevolence that can be systematically stamped out. And they are also certainly sceptical of evidence indicating the need for a more encompassing worldview.[22]

Markets, business organisations and even regulatory agencies, aren't discrete entities. Nor are they static. On the contrary, they are symbiotically related. Dependent on each other for their very existence, they are intrinsically connected, via literally millions of links, inter-actions and transactions, into an ecosystem which is never at rest. Momentum, energy and opportunities are created by the market. Business responds, as rapidly as possible and in ways intended to maintain the market in a more-or-less permanent state of positive arousal, a phenomenon the new science refers to as 'living on the edge of chaos'.

Meanwhile, deep in the bowels of the organisation, the *management factory* moves at a snail's pace by comparison.[23] The management factory specialises in trapping people in energy-sapping, demoralising, demotivating and disempowering work systems. The effort workers are compelled to waste in creating a simulacrum of efficiency for audit purposes – as if it were possible to fatten a pig by measuring it – is quite extraordinary.

The really absurd thing about this is that targets and audits tend to burden the best people in the system, who conscientiously try to make it work, while the unscrupulous continue to manipulate it anyway – and are then immunised by officially getting away with it. But assum-ing managers are not focused on such wasteful activities as perfor-mance appraisals and meeting mindless targets plucked out of thin air, their job is to grow organisational capability to realise potentiality in ways that deliver stakeholders' needs – as rapidly and as efficiently as possible.

There are always plenty of additional diversions, many of which conspire to slow down an organisation's learning metabolism. Attention must be given to emergent risks, for example. Competitors need to be kept at bay. New alliances must be sought and valued relationships sustained. The 'license to operate' granted to the company by society must be constantly safeguarded and pressures from various govern-ment agencies dealt with. Staff need to be won over, market analysts convinced, new talent needs to be engaged – and kept. Above all, conflicting demands from customers, suppliers, staff, shareholders and regulators, all of whom are capable of applying the brakes in an effort to shift the system in ways that will benefit them, need to be constantly resolved. In this situation it is hardly surprising that inertia, delays, redundancy and waste are created, firstly in any exchanges between the business and the market, secondly by the support functions' valiant attempts to help sustain core business activities. This inertia increases the further away from the market an activity occurs. This resembles the deterioration of blood in the body's circulatory system where the heart, as the metabolic pump, propels oxygenated blood around the body. The further away from the heart the blood travels, the weaker this flow becomes. The blood loses oxygen and colour along the way, changing in consistency from a free-flowing scarlet to a sticky, reddish purple.

Similarly, the market is the locus of business energy, except that information, not blood, is now the material. Almost like osmosis, front-line business people and entrepreneurs pick up on this energy because they are close to the market. But as information and activities flow away from the market's heart, so the signals weaken and distort. Lethargy grows, each successive delay warping knowledge regarding the actual state of the market. By the time this information gets into the management factory it has deteriorated to the extent that it is all but meaningless. This drag gives rise to a 'ratchet' effect. The market evolves in real time, driven by any number of emergent factors. Nothing can halt its pent-up energy. Indeed these days it often appears to be spiralling faster and faster out of control. Business reacts to the market as best it can and as close to real time as possible. After further delays, management attempts to respond to business calls for help. But because the management factory is dependent on second-hand knowledge of the market, its responses are invariably hit or miss. Besides, the responses themselves are often something of a curiosity; too slow to be of much use to the business, divorced from reality and frequently totally out of phase with the original need. So disconnected are they from the original market dynamic (which has since changed yet again) that they manifest as a series of irrational knee jerks, rather than as coherent strategic enablers. From a business leader's perspective it is as though a commotion born of a thousand egos has flipped intention on its head to reflect collective misinterpretations around achieving some abstract goal. What emerges is often just a mess!

As markets become more competitive, pressures on revenue, profitability and shareholder value increase, and the obligation to meet stakeholders' derived demands[24] gathers pace, the 'ratchet' becomes weighed down by more and more dubious activities designed by the management factory to maintain its image of productiveness. Meanwhile the 'drag' increases. Burdened by the need to meet increasingly impossible goals with fewer and possibly scarcer resources, functional managers become more and more focused on the 'here and now', inadvertently jeopardising business aspirations while allowing strategic

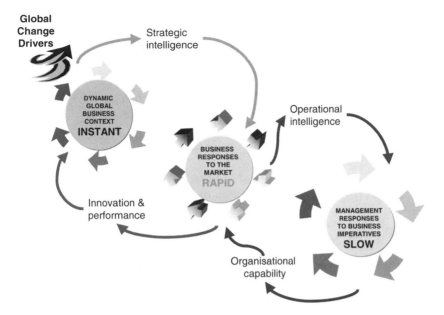

Figure 3.2 The 'ratchet' effect is a phenomenon in which differing metabolic learning speeds (inherent in markets, business and management) interact to create a frictional 'drag' on organisational responsiveness, thereby encumbering business effectiveness.

opportunities to lapse. This is regrettable because the market–enterprise interface should also be the field of play for demonstrating the true value of support functions. Functional experts should not cower from it, nor be distracted by developing esoteric practices divorced from the realities of the market. True synergy is only created when functional experts work hand-in-glove with business leaders on their organisation's capability to interact within that space. Exhortations from business leaders to their support functions to become 'more strategic' means just that: ultimately it is the only way the dynamic space between the external market and the internal organisation can be contained.

SYMBIOTIC DESIGN[25]

There are few ways of remedying this. It has become almost a pathological condition. In spite of good intentions, most attempts to devise viable alternatives to the customary 'chain of command' configuration still found in the majority of organisations do not contribute any long-lasting value to the business. Some simply misunderstand the impact imposed frameworks have on people and their performance, while others do enormous damage by disrupting, and even destroying, critical knowledge and intelligence flows across the enterprise. As enabling tools, organisational structures should promote effectiveness and add value – not make it more difficult for people to go about their business. To approach organisational design without this in mind is foolish. Yet it is all too common.

This cavalier attitude towards organisational design can at least be partially explained by the fact that most of us, unlike *five literacies* leaders:

- Rarely take into account the more critical of today's business drivers (such as the need for deep collaboration, intimate stakeholder relationships, broad global networking and immediate access to real-time intelligence and learning).
- Ignore the context (i.e. conditions in the business ecosystem that would indicate whether or not certain types of organisation will perform better than others).
- Begin by using a set of flawed assumptions concerning the governance and collective behaviour of people and their mutual interaction.
- Design organisational architectures that are too inflexible to adapt to changes in the business environment and in society.
- Prefer to use technocrats to design *for* – rather than *with* – people – resulting in a plethora of look-alike work spaces.

Such formulaic thinking is apparent in the vogue for various forms of compartmentalised, matrix and portfolio configurations, in the majority of standardised outsourcing arrangements,[26] in joint ventures, in the absurd vacillation between centralisation and decentralisation, and in the fashionable, yet ultimately futile talk of 'flatter' management structures – all without any real consideration of uniquely dynamic context. Although these designs appear to create the illusion of progress (because they can and do improve *efficiency*, which has become our single, most obsessive measure), they trap us in our own history.

Like the future, history is a compilation of selective memories that are constantly subjected to various filtered interpretations. We gain meaning from these interpretations and this meaning becomes 'what

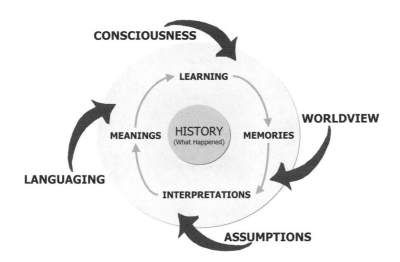

Figure 3.3 We unconsciously reinforce our beliefs about reality to create a history that is highly personal and extremely difficult to unlearn. Real transformation begins when we become conscious of our inner prejudices and beliefs formed from past experiences and learning. We cannot simply ignore the past and focus on the future because we are conditioned by our chosen history.

we have learnt' from these experiences. They are individual and unique – highly refined personal expressions of particular moments in the past. Nevertheless we are wedded to them, believing them to be the totality of what actually happened. Transformation (as in a change to a different state of being) occurs when we are able to subject these memories to closer scrutiny, perhaps comparing our own versions of reality with others who were present or who heard differing reports. Changing our assumptions, our language, our worldview or our consciousness, all enable transformation to occur.

So compelling is the force of the past, so resilient in validating (and thereby maintaining) the status quo, it is gravitational in its impact; a force so strong that we are incapable of escaping our predicament unless an external agent is able to shake us out of our inability to see a different reality. Consequently, all of these so-called design 'solutions' miss a fundamental point: none of them replaces (or even seeks to replace) the bureaucratic 'logic' within the enterprise with anything significantly different – or more viable. In other words, these solutions do not:

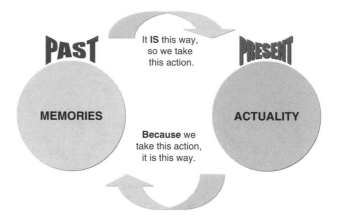

Figure 3.4 Structure-function traps suppress future possibilities by rationalising how we have become to be the way we are today. It seems preordained that it should be this way – and no other way! We sometimes refer to this as the gravitational pull of the past.

- Speed up the capability of the business to respond adequately to dynamic change.
- Guarantee greater returns to shareholders over the long term.
- Make the business any more cost-effective over the long term.
- Automatically shift the model of leadership from punctuating external events to creating a healthier context for change.
- Encourage strategic foresight or the development of different ways of knowing about the corporation and its evolving purpose in society.
- Focus the entire organisation on innovation and performance.
- Assure the gathering of appropriate strategic intelligence nor its use in making wiser, more viable decisions.
- Advance opportunities for organisational learning and development.
- Embed deeper, more fulfilling relationships across the enterprise and beyond into the broader business ecosystem.
- Diminish the amount of pressure and stress on people.
- Tolerate diversity or novelty of any kind (if it can be at all avoided).

In fact, in spite of much rhetoric to the contrary, most of the available evidence suggests they have the opposite effect to what is intended:

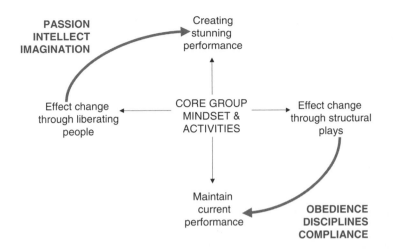

Figure 3.5 Attempting to transform an organisation can so easily fail through insufficient focus. Half-hearted attempts to liberate passion and imagination tend to neutralise energy and create a mess! When managers also insist upon detailed attention to compliance, balancing loops are created that simply reinforce the status quo.

increasing bureaucracy, confounding people's understanding of how they can best add value while emphasising their individual short-comings, suppressing their inclination to be creative and establishing meaningless targets that encourage mediocre performance. Essentially, bureaucracy encourages the organisation to act as if it were blind, deaf and dumb to everything going on around it. One might even argue that the cost of inaction would be far less than the constant merry-go-round of restructuring and other so-called 'change' activities that have become routine for lazy managers attempting to hide their distinct lack of imagination and ability.

So what is it about the bureaucratic model that is so attractive, other than the power of the individual over the many? After all, it's only one model of organisation. Are there any alternatives to its more flawed short-comings? Of course there are. They exist everywhere we look in nature and are based on the use of systemic intelligence to adapt to changing conditions. We have come to refer to this capability as 'consciousness' and it is sought after persistently by *five literacies* leaders.

From the perspective of *five literacies* leaders, the key to more effective organisational design is in the streamlining or even elimination of the 'ratchet' effect – the inevitable, yet unintended byproduct, of bureaucracy. This entails getting rid of linear, hierarchical operating systems and instituting instead, a cybernetic, intelligence-driven, relationship-based approach to governance and 'control'. This, in turn, increases learning metabolism, thereby helping raise the consciousness of the whole enterprise to new collective levels of awareness.

One way *five literacies* leaders have of encouraging this shift, for example, is to change the reporting relationships between customer-facing businesses and support functions. In order to add value, and avoid irrelevance, support functions would not respond to business needs but, in partnership with the business, to market dynamics and global change drivers. But in order for this strategy to succeed, business leaders and functional experts alike must let go of the 'supply-and-demand' notion whereby the business makes specific requests, often translated into service-level agreements, to which functional experts respond the best they can. This is rather like a sick person using the Internet to self-diagnose their condition and instructing their GP as to the prescription they need. They ignore conflicting symptoms and a host of other possible causes simply because they are unconsciously incompetent to know about those things. As the old saying goes, 'a little knowledge is a dangerous thing'.

There are three other obvious weaknesses in the traditional service agreement model:

- Focusing the spotlight solely on today's urgent requirements invariably encourages short-term thinking, thereby increasing strategic risk. Requests from the business should encompass meeting current needs while anticipating future demands in the ever-morphing, market–enterprise interface.
- Without actual knowledge of the assumptions underpinning business requests, and the language being used to express these needs, support functions can only respond from their own current, highly filtered, sets of misunderstandings. These can be way off target.
- Attending solely to today's business issues and requirements may distract from adequate focus on the market–enterprise intersection. This is a hugely complex space, demanding ongoing intelligence and dialogue to be effectively leveraged for competitive advantage.

An additional, though unintended, consequence of the bureaucratic service model is reinforcement of the 'ratchet' effect: delays accumulate in ways that amplify 'drag' as well as open up the possibility for further misinterpretations and distractions. This can also lead to a lack of confidence and low self-esteem on the part of functional practitioners who always find themselves several steps removed from where the action really is. By the time they can respond in a manner that pleases everyone, the situation, and therefore the demand, has changed. To make matters worse, they probably instinctively realise this and yet, fearful of appearing incompetent, continue doing what they have always done. Thus the ratchet effect is reinforced yet again.

Instead of allowing this situation to prevail, business leaders and functional experts alike must create an operational symbiosis, taking joint responsibility for a learning space wherein opportunities can be explored and strategic responses coordinated. In this space the role of the business leader is to look *inside-out* while that of the functional expert is to look *outside-in*. Constantly conversing with each other to create a shared understanding of the whole system and its dynamics, their dialogue becomes the means for eliminating operational drag. Just as a doughnut cannot exist without its hollow centre, so business leaders and functional experts cannot exist in isolation from each other. By working together they create a commonwealth of knowledge that is infinitely more compelling than the empire of knowledge existing within each of their discrete 'silos'.

Enormous benefits are generated by using their (separate) knowledge to inform, mature and invigorate this relationship, a relationship that is necessary to accomplish the kind of strategic alignment so critical in today's competitive business environment. The only way support functions can become (and remain) immediately relevant to the business is if they, too, focus on the dynamics of the market–enterprise interface in partnership with business leaders. They have to be there, seeing the same things, interpreting them according to their expertise, debating what it is they 'see' and co-designing appropriate responses. This is the reason support functions are so relevant today. They can help optimise capability in ways that would simply be overlooked by the business. Ironically, it also explains why many support functions are perched on the edge of inconsequence: they do not realise that facilitating this partnership *is* their value! Theoretically, dismantling the internal supply-and-demand arrangements in the context of this partnership is eminently feasible. After all, these internal customer–supplier contracts are merely relics of a bygone era. In practice, though, it requires open-minded business executives capable of setting aside

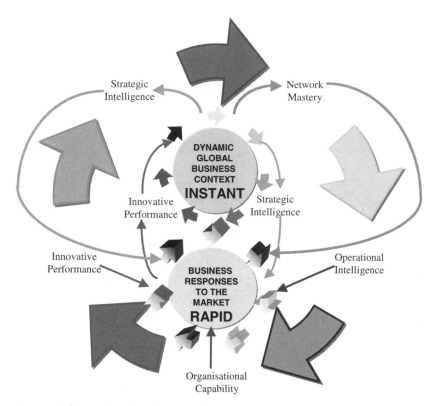

Figure 3.6 In distributed networks structures the 'ratchet' effect is all but eliminated. Drag is minimised by positioning the organisation's functional expertise in a shared 'learning space' with business leaders, and enterprise knowledge and learning metabolism increases.

preconceptions to become adept at network mastery; an organisation able to explore alternative ways of relating, communicating and learning within the enterprise; and a management mindset prepared to trust the self-organising qualities of robust social systems. To find all of these qualities present in a single organisation at the same time is relatively rare.

The same is true of governments and the thinking behind government policy. Solving the 'drugs problem' by cutting off the supply on the streets would be an example of linear thinking. In that case, dealers will react by cutting the doses with other chemicals and raising prices – causing addicts to steal more to feed the habit and run even

worse health hazards. The problem has been 'solved' in the reductionist sense, but in any systems view matters have actually been made
worse.

There are two other important properties of complex human-
activity systems. Firstly they can't be managed by the use of crude
performance targets, which bend them out of shape and make imple-
menters 'look the wrong way' – at the targets rather than the needs of
their clientele. Nor, secondly, can they be managed by reductionist
command-and-control methods, because of the many unintended consequences these bring. Instead, such systems have to be carefully
managed for long-term, incremental improvements by introducing
learning processes rather than specifying outcomes or targets, and their
success judged by users, not governments. Where in our organisations
can the possibility for this kind of conversation and learning space be
found? How should we design mechanisms that will work best to create
the conditions in which such conversations flourish? The formal hierarchies in most organisations do not easily allow such relationships to
develop. So where is the strategic opportunity? Surprisingly, it may well
be found in the cultural cracks and crevices of the corporation – in
those shadowy spaces where corporate life is relatively unordered,
energy is free-flowing, and few managers ever actually venture.

WHO'S IN CHARGE ANYWAY?

At first glance, the modern corporation appears monolithic. Impregnable. A bastion of power, masculinity and dehumanised jargon. And
yet it is among the most effective of instruments devised for aggregat-
ing and managing human activities. From the Santa Clara Supreme
Court case in 1886, that gave corporations the legal status of a *person*,
to the acceleration of corporate power through globalisation and into
government, corporate culture has been so institutionalised as to
become virtually unchallenged and beyond critique.

However, corporations are not the success we imagine them to be.
Paraphrasing John Maynard Keynes' critique of capitalism, most
contemporary corporations are not intelligent, beautiful, just or virtuous. Nor are they secure from a range of contemporary pressures,
which is clear from the ways in which their supposed invulnerability
has been tested in recent years. Reckless strategies (e.g. Monsanto's
proposed GM innovation, cleverly if cruelly dubbed 'the terminator'
seed by canny green activists), skyrocketing executive salaries,

mismanagement, and an outbreak of scandals associated with unethical governance and misconduct (e.g. the collapse of Andersen Consulting, Enron and WorldCom and incidents such as the gross overstating of oil and gas reserves by Royal Dutch-Shell) have tarnished the public image of corporations in much the same way as alleged claims of sexual misconduct among the priesthood persist in undermining the, once unimpeachable, authority of the church today. As one of society's most powerful contemporary institutions, big business bears more than a passing resemblance to the medieval Church. In this respect corporations (or at least their more prescribed attributes) are today's great 'cathedrals' of global commerce.

Like their namesakes, today's corporate cathedrals have ordained leaders (presidents, directors, managers and supervisors) whose task is to maintain the faith (capitalism) by upholding the approved system of human rules and morals (company law, rules and regulations) while preserving the cult of worship (performance excellence). A semblance of authority is preserved by means of a negotiated system of delegations and controls (the chain of command) issued by the organisation's leaders. This group spend their time ensuring sanctioned dogma (corporate vision) is translated into communal rituals (the work) as they preach their message of hope (brand) to an assembly of worshippers (diverse stakeholders). Culturally desirable conduct is inculcated by means of an appropriate recognition and reward system (pay and promotion). Meanwhile, the incentive to collective action is promoted by tales from the gospels (plans and other corporate messages).

But ordained leaders, too, are subservient to a higher power. Though often unnoticed, and certainly missing from any organisation chart, an elite cadre of high priests (inner cabinet or 'core group'[27]) exercise overall supremacy. Bound by a common philosophy, this elite group wields enormous power in the conventional sense. This is derived solely from their intimate loyalty to, and feelings for, each other. Although they never admit it, they are often there to serve their own purpose, which may or may not align with the best interests of others, including shareholders.

From within the hallowed precincts of the corporate cathedral it is easy for ordained leaders to imagine they control the whole organisation. Most behave as though they do. This is a cruel illusion. The charts and hierarchies that claim to map the organisation's social systems are largely fictional, political constructs. Despite our best efforts at management and control, no 'one' is in charge. What is more, the formal nature of the cathedral (albeit necessary in some form or other if viability is to be sustained) is responsible for barely 20% of business results . . . At best! Why? Because, although the cathedral is the primary source of order and control for the business, it is not a closed system. On the contrary, it is just one part of an inherently complex, and increasingly global, business ecosystem[28] in which collaborative relationships and shared knowledge provide the impetus for creating value and wealth. The cathedral can't even claim to *represent* the whole enterprise although it is the skeleton on which everything else depends. There are so many facets to business that are outside the scope of the cathedral to control. Ultimately, no amount of edicts or institutionalised procedural formalities can compensate for the diversity and richness that exists within, and beyond, the organisation. Because of this, ordained leaders spend a great deal of time and energy dealing with a communicative reality riddled with novelty and unintended consequences.

Today's complex market dynamics are well beyond the capacity of any single business to contain. Besides, the fact that people are essentially unpredictable, communicating and interacting impulsively makes it impossible to regulate for every eventuality. To attempt to do so is simply not possible; curbing creativity, dulling initiative and reducing the natural tendency of the organisational community to remain vibrant and progressive. As we engage with each other, the nature and quality of our relationships compose us into being, as they do the quality of the world we create and experience. Like all living systems, human systems self-organise in response to meaningful information. Just as we explore and try to shift the behavioural patterns of our organisations and communities, so must we pay attention to the quality of the information society uses to bring itself to life.

So let us assume the coexistence of a contrasting, subliminal, distributed, and therefore more informal, *shadow* side to the rather forbidding and obdurate nature of the corporate cathedral. We will call this *shadow* side the cafe. Everyone in the extended enterprise is a member of the cafe including, of course, ordained leaders. But the cafe is the epitome of everything that the cathedral is not. Purposeful action here is entirely voluntary, growing out of the actions of its members. Imposed directives are absent. Bound together by common interests, life in the cafe is altogether different from the orderly, somewhat artificial existence mandated by the cathedral. Indeed, it is far more evident from activity in the cafe that the organisation is not a machine but a self-regulating *living* system. Although the cafe is the primary source of disorder (the black energy of the organisation if you will) it has no central design. Its very nature impels self-organisation, out of which inspiration and innovation appear as and when required. In the chaotic intimacy of this networked community there are no official leaders, each individual adding value to the network and stepping into leadership roles as required. And because it is a distributed system it is extremely resilient compared with centralised or decentralised structures.

In the cafe, most official dogma and decrees from the cathedral are greeted with a healthy scepticism, frequently becoming the basis for self-deprecation and wry humour. Work still takes precedence, but results are achieved in ways that may sidestep or evade the cathedral's more prescribed directives. Gossip, personal experiences, new and heretical ideas, corridor conversations, spur-of-the-moment reactions to unfolding events and unintended consequences all interact in different ways, contributing to the cafe's messiness yet uncanny ability to cut through bureaucracy to get things done. In fact the cafe, not the cathedral, appears to be the main reason organisations rarely descend into anarchy and chaos.

Five literacies leaders realise the potent disorder of the cafe as much as they appreciate the logic of the cathedral. Because of this they invariably balance the need to liberate the cafe's energy with maintaining just the right amount of order (via the cathedral) in order to keep the whole system working effectively. In so doing, leadership effort is focused primarily on networks and narratives, particularly as engendered within the cafe's 'commune*cology*'. This 'sense-making' system is the most vital, yet undervalued, aspect of any enterprise, comprising:

- The web of interconnected relationships existing between all its members. This vast network extracts and synthesises relevant information from the environment for use (as intelligence) by the organisation. Without intelligence the business cannot self-organise. Without *new* intelligence nothing *new* will ever happen.
- The innate narrative which provides a sense of what the organisation represents (and is supposed to be) to individual members. As it recreates itself moment by moment, the organisational community constantly refers to this story, filtering the profusion of information available to it in order to identify only that which is meaningful.

The cafe is at once many things: a cellular network, a vast feedback mechanism that can be used to amplify change within the organisation, a skin of sensors stretching across the enterprise, an emergent community of mind . . . Because of this richness, the cafe plays a particularly important role in the translation and diffusion of messages across the organisation. Ideas and innovations can reach anyone almost instantly via the cafe. What is more, the cafe's scale-free topology amplifies any inherently memetic qualities such messages might contain.[29]

Although the cafe is far too complex (i.e. has too much variety) for any single individual or group to control, its potency is realised in a resilience and resourcefulness that the cathedral cannot hope to match. The disorderly informality of the cafe is responsible for 80% of the organisation's results . . . At least! Which is why, for example, smart leaders encourage their people to use the Internet for unrestricted play, investigative browsing and personal emailing. Far from being a waste of the company's time and resources, it is learning that can be shared and then applied to enhance capability.

At a self-regulating level, no member of the cafe exists as a self-sufficient entity but only in relation to others. In fact this 'entanglement' may be the only rationale for talking about *organisational* capability.[30] Ultimately, if we are able to use the cafe to create sufficient intelligence gathering, file sharing, information swapping and issues resolution on an as-needed basis, the organisation's learning must become independent of individual human supervision and intervention, since the network itself will have the means (information and resources) to solve specific problems.

The cafe also happens to be the means by which cultural coherence is maintained and messages about shared identity and purpose shaped and conveyed – much of it by word of mouth and subliminal messages – or what has recently become known as viral communication. Viral communications can be extremely powerful – yet also perilous. People are subject to enormous stresses in today's fast-paced workplaces. The pressure to perform, to think creatively, to adhere to a set of corporate values, to make sense of a bewildering patchwork of issues, and to comply with an ever-growing number of rules and procedures, are all present in the modern enterprise. These demands, usually arising from attempts by the cathedral to remain competitive while maintaining order, rapidly become an intrinsic element in the cafe's social fabric – sometimes to such an extent that an entrenched cultural belief may actually replace specific directives. This is yet another example of how perceptions can mislead.

Take for example, the fact that people make meaning even when nothing has been said. Silence speaks volumes if the context (for what is not being said) is apparent. I have stumbled across many instances where people simply imagined they heard a particular directive because they had been part of the corporate cafe long enough to anticipate such points of view from their ordained leaders. Typically they then comply with these 'ghost statements' as if they were real. Yet it is all fiction!

This is often how organisational systems become dysfunctional and unhealthy cultures are formed. It is where those seemingly in power attract co-dependent behaviour as 'the children' scurry around trying to please the 'the parents'. This deluded state, where the co-dependent's boundaries are confused with the person for whom they are performing,[31] has become a common way of avoiding responsibility for one's own behaviour in many contemporary organisations. People tell themselves that they are merely doing what is expected of them. Never mind that much of it is imagined.

This behaviour is seen in alcoholic households, dysfunctional business organisations, religious sects, government agencies and the hallowed halls of academia. People read intent and meaning into casual (or even imagined) statements. Then they assign legitimacy to their fiction. And if you question those who are doing the 'scurrying' they will swear they were told to behave this way. They remain convinced they were directed to do so, forgetting entirely that they had anticipated what the cathedral would want from them, then merely complied with their own imagined directive. In their minds, fiction is turned into fact and they remain loyal to it.

This is what many people do in the cultures they work in, the industries or companies or trades or churches or families to which they belong. They become obscenely obedient to the system, to the extent that they imagine what the system wants and conform to these rules in order to be perceived as loyal members. They will then swear they were instructed to obey the rules or were intimidated when confronted with the facts of the situation. The notorious physical and psychological torture of Muslim prisoners by American soldiers in Abu Ghraib serves as one extreme example. But there are literally thousands of situations in the workplace where imagined directives dictate how people behave and to which they remain loyal.

The remedy to behavioural fusion of this kind is for leaders to encourage openness, honesty and individuality across the enterprise. Where people are encouraged to share their own stories and aspirations, where they are open to all kinds of feedback and learning, where they are not oppressed by irrelevant rules and restrictions, and when individual authenticity and responsibility become commonplace, dysfunction diminishes and profound conversations in the cafe become potent vehicles for assuring organisational viability.

Those of us who are familiar with life in a large organisation will have spotted a bittersweet paradox in this metaphor: stimulating the effectiveness of the cafe invariably impacts operational effectiveness in positive ways. Yet the more ordained leaders attempt to control (aspects of) the cafe, presumably to improve performance, the more likely it is that the organisation's overall performance will deteriorate. Attempts by the cathedral to corral the cafe with red tape greatly diminish its potency. Simply leaving it to its own devices, however, also poses a risk. As the cafe contains the greatest variety, positive and negative feedback mechanisms,[32] and the most feral and resistant cultural elements in the organisation, it cannot be ignored. To do so would be to court disaster. Equally, the cathedral cannot expect the cafe to just obey orders. Life in complex systems is never that simple!

Unlike the highly selective *on-off* systems crafted by ordained leaders in the cathedral, communication is not discretionary in the cafe. While we can choose some dimensions of what, how and when to communicate, we cannot choose *not* to do so. The cafe's radar is always *on*, and our communicative behaviour, whether as individuals or as an organisation, is always broadcasting from deep inside our inner world, speaking of who we are and what we stand for, in a continuous stream of word-of-mouth marketing and self-reflection. Given this complexity, how can ordained leaders relinquish their need to control everything in ways that preserve order, disentangle unintended effects, and breathe new life into the business? How can alternative sets of ideas emerging from the cafe establish their own inherent legitimacy? How might the 'core group' be expanded to engage a critical mass within the organisation? How could the intentions of the cathedral be brought into a more fruitful alignment with the rejuvenating energy of the cafe? More explicitly, how might we re-imagine the nexus between cathedral and cafe in order to take advantage of the emergent dance between order and chaos?

MISSED STEPS IN THE DANCE

Unlike *five literacies* leaders, the majority of ordained leaders in government agencies and corporations have no basis for realistic normative planning. While they might cling to a favoured organisational theory, they habitually misunderstand the very system they are influencing. As Stafford Beer famously quipped,

> Those leaders who become famous for being 'realistic' and 'responsible' turn out to be outrageously irresponsible just because they are so unrealistic.

The unrealism to which Beer refers boils down to an inability to appreciate what is actually occurring in the broader business ecosystem coupled with a refusal to think deeply through the inevitable systemic consequences of their strategic intentions.

Part of the resolution to this paradox lies in enabling ordained leaders to carry out their most dignified role: that of ensuring the ongoing viability of the whole enterprise. The real choice they have in this regard is not to use new tools, cut costs to the bone, improve quality or work harder (although one or more of these might be in order) but to change their worldviews, frameworks and strategies so that the future they create is different from the future they would have encountered had they *not* made those changes.

In today's environment, where issues emerge from nowhere and things can shift so rapidly, ordained leaders need courage as well as near-instantaneous information to be confident that they can achieve this.

> Frankly, there is not much point in knowing what happened yesterday – because even yesterday is the purest history. Nothing can be done about it any longer. But if we can get hold of a close idea of what is going to happen next week, then we have at least a chance of doing something about that. And certainly knowing what has been happening over the last few days is the best basis for estimating what is likely to happen over the next few days.[33]

If their information is out of date, of dubious accuracy, or they fail to receive algedonic signals of systemic distress, their decisions are likely to be worse than useless.[34] At times they can be extremely damaging. This is particularly the case with high-risk financial resource and investment decisions,[35] although the capability for developing new strategic trajectories, too, depends upon sound strategic intelligence and extreme sensitivity and responsiveness to the business ecosystem. Bureaucratic models do not usually allow for such high levels of responsiveness. Fortunately there is an alternative to the mind-numbing acceptance of even greater levels of bureaucracy. This is where understanding dynamic systems rather than machines, and heuristics rather than forecasting, becomes an imperative. For although the problem of speed cannot be solved, it can be *dis*solved. How? By getting rid of all the time-lags where these are an impediment to performance; by deploying a real-time nervous system so that the enterprise is more 'conscious' of the emergent dynamics of which it is a part; and by encouraging a diverse range of temporal responses to problem solving and issues resolution. In this way, the time it takes for an organisation to identify, process and act upon new intelligence (its learning metabolism) can be increased many times while people do not feel they are losing the plot or become neurotic about things getting out of control.

Within any complex system, such as a corporate entity or a government department, for example, there are fundamental rules which,

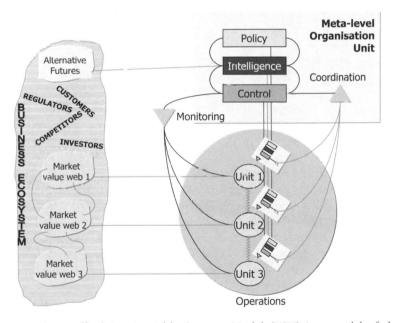

Figure 3.7 Stafford Beer's Viable Systems Model (VSM) is a model of the recursive organisational structure of any viable system. A viable system is any system organised in such a way as to meet the demands of surviving in changing conditions. One of the prime features of systems that survive is that they are adaptive. The VSM expresses a model for a viable system, which is an abstracted cybernetic description that is applicable to any organisation that is a viable system. Reproduced from Beer, A.S., Platform for Change, Chichester, John Wiley & Sons, Ltd, 1995.

when disobeyed, lead to instability or a failure to learn to adapt and evolve. When CEOs, senior bureaucrats and government ministers wonder whether to centralise or to decentralise organisational structures they are typically answered by dogmas. When they ponder whether planning is oppressive and therefore inimical to freedom they are answered with doctrines. When people seek an end to officialdom they are answered with a managerial expertise which, judging from its record, has absolutely no effect. Managerial cybernetics, the science of organising in real time, allows us to quarantine the problems of organisational structure from the ruck of prejudice. If dogma, doctrine and expertise fail to provide effective answers, then what criterion of effectiveness should cybernetics use? The answer is the criterion of *viability.*

The use of viability as a model for cybernetic governance is not a new idea. Stafford Beer's Viable Systems Model, created over 30 years ago, has been used extensively as a conceptual tool for understanding organisations, redesigning them and supporting the leadership of change. Despite its successful application by numerous private and public sector organisations, as well as within an entire nation-state, however, the notion of viability has not been widely accepted.[36] There are two main reasons for this. Firstly, the ideas behind Beer's model (including recursion and variety, for example) are not intuitively easy to grasp; secondly, they run counter to the great legacy of thinking about the design of organisations dating from the Industrial Revolution – a legacy that is only now starting to be challenged.

Organisations have customarily been viewed as hierarchical institutions; closed systems that operate best according to a 'top-down' command structure: strategic plans are formulated at the top and implemented via a cascade of instructions through the tiered ranks. Control is exercised through some form of 'performance management' system that rewards or sanctions staff according to perceived accomplishments. Apart from constraining rather than liberating human potential, it is now widely accepted that this *modus operandi* is far too slow and inflexible to cope with the increasing rate of change and complexity enveloping most organisations. Recent developments in technology have helped usher in a new concept of network organisations with real-time information widely distributed to reach and be used by all those who actually perform the work. The ground is now fertile for viewing the organisation itself in a new light: as an open system; a community of interlinking learning networks where strategic conversation is the main enabler of decision making and performance.

However, there is also much confusion about the nature of this new-style organisation. Ask the members of any large enterprise to explain their organisation's structure to an outsider and a series of vague, confusing and often conflicting interpretations are likely to ensue. It is becoming increasingly apparent that it matters much less who reports to whom, as who needs to *talk* with whom and how all the pieces of a complex interrelated jigsaw fit together to form a synergistic whole. Yet it is precisely this sense of 'the whole' that is so often missing. A clear danger with looser, decentralised structures is that overall cohesion and synergy may be lost in the attempt to spawn a multitude of business units and profit centres capable of responding to different market pressures and organisational support requirements. Knowledge and information then often become trapped in local silos, reducing the chances of people working in cooperation with others across organisational boundaries. People working in different parts of the enterprise are simply unaware of related issues and activities that ought to concern them because the organisation has lost its connecting tissue.

The reverse is true of centralised structures where 'fringe' knowledge is all but ignored. For example, in their rush to 'de-layer' and rid themselves of costly bureaucratic controls, many organisations are charting their course to oblivion through other means: instead of creating recursive structures that provide long-term viability, they are blindly axing units and people, or setting up shared services models, without due consideration of their actual and potential contribution to the viability of the whole enterprise. Without a framework to examine the functioning of the organisation as a complete, living system, many cost cutting exercises achieve one-off savings at the expense of longer term organisational effectiveness.

Models of viability offer a way of gaining both functional decentralisation and cohesion of the whole. They are underpinned by fundamental cybernetic principles of communication and control in complex organisations. These principles offer a way of providing true autonomy and empowerment within an integrated framework, together with the necessary supporting links between the individual parts. In short, they provide a framework for designing highly responsive and adaptive organisations that balance external and internal perspectives and long- and short-term thinking. Viability-centred models provide the capacity to respect the relational and recursive nature of an enterprise, to nurture it into a healthy balance, thereby making it intrinsically adaptable to change. The process of reinvention then becomes a continuous, spontaneous dynamic within the organisation, rather than something imposed in fits and starts by the cathedral, or worse, from a hostile external source.

Cybernetic systems of governance also avoid polarisation, offering the possibility of finding a balanced set of organisational arrangements that align the rights and expressions of every individual (the cafe) to the aspirations of the business (the cathedral) as well as the pragmatic imperatives of discrete business units with the shared expertise of the whole enterprise. Furthermore, feedback mechanisms ensure that people across the organisation are intimately linked into operational governance in ways that are enlivening and motivating. Being at once themselves independent viable systems with a right of individual choice, and also members of a community, which in turn has a right of collective choice, viable systems create both coherence and efficiency. By integrating cybernetic controls within navigational practices, we avoid the dogma, doctrine and expertise associated with bureaucracy, the lack of flexibility apparent in autocracies, and the deprivation of direction and guidance that is so frequently absent from permissive systems.

Of course, merely reconnecting the cathedral and the cafe by instituting a method of cybernetic governance is insufficient to fill the void brought about by stripping bare the management factory. It will certainly help eliminate waste, focus attention on what is important, improve overall effectiveness, and enhance coordination between operating units and channel intelligence where it's most needed. The business will become more resilient because of it. But even viable 'control' systems will not necessarily liberate entrepreneurial energy, punch holes in traditional operational 'silos' or result in the kinds of performance that allow some businesses to dominate their niche. Something way beyond a rationally engineered design is needed for this to occur. A fusion of innovation, vision, serendipity, passion, intuition and appreciation – it is the alchemical quality that separates the great from the merely good. It happens when uncommon people interact in uncommon ways, creating fresh dialogue to focus on possibilities and the realisation of their potential. I call it *Deep Design*. Deep design is the fourth of the *five literacies* and it is brought about by a special kind of collaborative dialogue called strategic conversation.

LIBERATING ENTERPRISE

Strategic conversation is not simply better talk but the means for generating wiser, more appropriate decisions that transform current conditions. Typically it employs a narrative process intended to enable reflective practice regarding: (a) how we perceive and interpret the world; (b) how we can be at one with those processes; and (c) how we are able to fathom the consequences (both positive and negative) of those choices. Strategic conversation is vital if *Deep Design* is to occur. More often than not, this entails the cathedral's leaders finding appropriate ways of high-jacking the cafe's conversational space, to ensure that it becomes strategic, thereby making the whole enterprise far more aware of changing business conditions. This is the territory of real-time systemic facilitation and integral praxis, where methods like Transformational Narrative[37] and Strategic Navigation,[38] new breeds of operating system in which specially designed, sophisticated applications focusing on strategic learning and intelligence, are given licence to self-organise within agreed boundaries, are becoming indispensable. Navigational systems treat strategy as a process – a continuous braiding of intelligence creation with insightful action. They are purposefully designed to embrace complexity and emergence, to recognise patterns and their trajectories, and to respond mindfully to changing external conditions in real time. Attempts to press gang old or inappropriately designed applications into these dynamic operating systems do not work. They either cause the application itself to crash, or the system to respond in much the same way as the human immune system reacts to the introduction of a virus or foreign body. Rejection.

When too many people ask too much from too little, systems go into a state of overload. This is often preceded by a trigger event of some kind that heralds a cascade of failures and the ultimate collapse of the system. This is precisely why the current situation concerning global warming is so worrying. All the measurements and reports of dire consequences still do not accurately forecast with any precision the rate of deterioration. We do know that no reliable upper limit can be put on how quickly the planet is warming up. We know that the Earth's temperature could rise far higher from greenhouse gases than previously expected. We know that Greenland's water loss has doubled in a decade. And we suspect that the huge Western Antarctic ice sheet may be starting to disintegrate. However, it is still impossible to predict what all of this really means or how close we are to a catastrophic phase transition. When we do understand it will probably be too late to do anything about it.[39]

Similarly, human systems can shift into altered states, particularly distressed states – and seem to do so with alarming frequency. What is it about corporate management systems that cause failures to occur in a manner reminiscent of phase transitions? We now suspect it may have something to do with the artificially contrived customs habitually employed, particularly in our rather bizarre conduct towards each other, within most corporate environments, that fail to monitor the vital signs of the organisation. But it probably has much more to do with flaws in the design of the original system: design is an elegant term for what, in most cases, would have been an inelegant piecing together of a structure from many small components whose individual behaviour could be predicted but whose collective behaviour was not really understood at all. Such is the level of organisational design even today.

For example, the demands on any contemporary business are extraordinarily complex and fiercely competitive. The burden on value-adding support functions, too, is fast reaching a state of overload. Stress is becoming palpable as individuals try to achieve impossible targets with fewer resources. At the same time they are being urged to think longer term, put themselves in their customers' shoes and come up with innovative solutions to problems, all the while promising alignment with any number of fashionable, quick-fix, initiatives posturing as responsible strategy.

In this climate transformation, in the form of phase transitions, is not negotiable. It is inevitable. But it is unlikely that it will ever turn out as intended. Emergence wins out. To counter this, functional professionals have rapidly to acquire the strategic expertise and confidence to step into a shared space with their business partners. Like these colleagues they must comprehend what goes on in the market, but from their own distinct perspective. Simply by standing in this shared space, the learning metabolism of the whole enterprise accelerates while drag from the management factory is reduced. When this is achieved, support functions are able to guarantee the exceptional levels of service and operational excellence demanded by business leaders with very little of the angst previously borne with such stoicism. They move into an altogether different zone, similar to the euphoria experienced by high-performing athletes and artists.

To make this shift will be tough, perhaps impossible and even counter-productive, if attempted solely from within the cathedral's known ways and preferred bureaucratic protocols. While the cathedral must always maintain the viability of the whole enterprise, it is the ad hoc, spur-of-the-moment, non-directed nature of the cafe that is the best departure point for this kind of intervention.[40] Ultimately, though, the integration of both cathedral and cafe is essential and this can be achieved through the use of intelligence-driven, recursive, viable systems.

Arguably the wisest way forward is to reframe this problem by identifying, challenging and then overturning those orthodoxies that no longer adequately serve the business; that is by changing the operating system and its associated frameworks. In this regard, one compelling strategy might be to find ways of unshackling the organisation's capability to respond in real time to complex business issues by aligning cathedral-like *orderliness* with cafe-like *connectedness*.

Business today must respond to unprecedented volatility. Rapid responses and initiatives are often demanded from systems that were designed in a more leisurely age. Much depends on learning. But learning, like electrical energy, can't easily be stored. It has to be generated and used when and where it's needed in order to retain its value. If that isn't possible, the custodians of knowledge become expensive and expendable. This is the pressure all technical experts face today. In this environment, how long will it be before impatient business leaders simply give (what they perceive to be) non-value-adding support functions the flick?

Or is there a way leaders can reinvent the rationale of management and the management factory to ensure both functional decentralisation and cohesive viability of the whole enterprise? What if the new science of networks could be used to transform support functions in ways that enabled real, sustainable breakthroughs in business performance? That articulated compelling and innovative ideas in a language which business immediately understood? That increased the speed at which learning could be applied across the enterprise? That anticipated future trends, deduced needs and found solutions to the most difficult of business issues? How much would such *network mastery* be worth to a large multinational corporation these days?

NETWORK MASTERY

Since Peter Senge's influential book, *The Fifth Discipline*, was published in 1990, much has been made of the role personal mastery plays in organisational performance – and rightly too. Personal mastery refers to the development of one's own proficiency and is often likened to a life-long journey with no ultimate destination. Along with teamwork, personal mastery was the saviour of training professionals in the 1990s, leading to the popular practice of mentoring and business coaching with which we're so familiar today.

> People with a high level of personal mastery are able to consistently realise the results that matter most deeply to them – in effect, they approach their life as an artist would approach a work of art. They do that by becoming committed to their own lifelong learning.[41]

In the new global economy, however, the practice of personal mastery must be a given. This does not negate its importance. But personal mastery alone is insufficient to compete successfully in today's global markets. Just as development must now shift from the individual to the collective, it is network mastery that forges global leadership; that enables strategic collaboration; that liberates performance beyond the merely competent. Network mastery is the ability of a distributed group or community to consistently accomplish those things that could not be achieved by any of them individually.

In 1974 Mark Granovetter, a Harvard sociologist, made an apparently unexceptional discovery. It is *who* you know that matters! His study involved asking several hundred white-collar workers how they'd landed their jobs. More than half credited a personal connection. Duh! I hear you sputter . . . But then it got interesting. As Granovetter probed more deeply he found that four-fifths of these indirect hires barely knew their benefactors.

> As it turns out, close friends are great for road trips, intimate dinners, and the occasional interest-free loan, but they're not much use for job leads and blind dates. Why? Because close friends move in the same circles and know the same people.[42]

In other words, it's not so much who you know, but who you *vaguely* know. Granovetter called the phenomenon 'the strength of weak ties'. He had discovered the secret of social networks: the node with an unusually large number of links, the hub, or the connector.[43] I will refer to these people as *attractors*.[44]

Attractors have an extraordinary knack of making friends, which is why they play such a vital part in social networking. Organising soirees with people they barely know, attending conferences in quest of new alliances, and owning address books brim full with contacts from all walks of life, attractors are the societal thread linking diverse people and ideas into a vast web of relationships. The architecture of extensive networks is dominated by a few, highly connected hubs. Part of society's uniqueness is that it is composed of literally millions of these social clusters. Whether it's a village, organisation, club or profession, we're all part of these small worlds, where everyone knows everyone else. The more visible these clusters are, the more influential they become. In fact the rest of the network is barely visible by comparison.

Attractors play a special role in these small worlds, linking us into other people's worlds through their web of weak ties while providing a tipping point for change within the network itself. In order to acquire new or different information, networks need to activate weak ties and attractors do this particularly well. Far from content to inhabit their own small world, the most powerful attractors link into other clusters that then become bridges into the outside world. In this way their influence increases while impressive artworks, books, novel ideas, unique products, unlikely partnerships and technological innovations develop in their chaotic wake.

While attractors have a significant role in spreading news and stories within a network, they also show us that network mastery doesn't require us to pay too much attention to content[45] but to the nurturing of weak ties, the acceptance of emergence, and the enabling of generative learning, in real time, across the network, and according to the dynamics of the moment. The latter is dependent upon two mutually dependent factors: *code* (those local 'rules' determining how the community self-organises) and *topology* (what actually manifests from the code in terms of collective behaviours, culture, structure etc.). This is not to imply that technical knowledge is unimportant. It simply means that content, by its very nature, will change depending upon the business context. What's far more important is the speed at which access to new assets (including knowledge) can be created and distributed across the organisation (community or industry cluster) to meet clients' derived demands and to create new markets.

Take for example, the city of Wenzhou in Zhejiang province, south of Shanghai. Here the manufacture of cigarette lighters began in the mid-1980s when locals brought them back from Japan as gifts. The enterprising citizens of Wenzhou broke the gadgets down into their component parts and quickly learned to reproduce replicas. By 1990 more than 3000 small entrepreneurial families in Wenzhou were making lighters. Intense competition between these families soon forced a shakeout. The smaller family businesses switched to making components for the lighters while the larger companies focused on assembly and distribution and the Wenzhou network, a network of some 700 companies operating as a single cohesive, interdependent entity, was born. Over the next few months specialisation, low overheads and the absence of bureaucratic trivia drove down manufacturing costs sufficiently to allow the network entry into the international market. Although lighters were initially sold on price, higher margins were earned as the network learned to produce new designs faster. By 2003 the Wenzhou network manufactured 750 million lighters and enjoyed a 70% share of the world market, wiping out most of the Japanese and South Korean companies that once dominated the lighter business and thriving in markets that require rapid responses to changes in demand.

This is only one example of China's highly flexible, low-cost producers. There are many others using their innate appreciation of relationships and 'guanxi' to operate in industries where changes in style affect demand.[46] Foreign executives usually ignore these networks because they don't conform to the standard notion of a globally competitive organisation. But there is much we can learn from them in terms of network mastery. Their flexibility and ability to anticipate trends cannot be underestimated, especially as the 'Made in China' tag has already created powerful allies among global distributors and retailers. When these diverse networks gain access to the investments necessary to build brands they are sure to become an unstoppable force.

The intriguing thing about this particular example is how fierce competition became the trigger for autonomy and cooperation between the various members of the network. In similar examples from all around the world, collaborative behaviour is producing a tipping point in the shift from cathedral-type organisations to cafe-type communities. But what does collaboration really mean? Surely controls assure better performance, not the freedom to do as one likes? On the other hand, if collaboration is such a powerful force, how could it be leveraged even more effectively towards innovation and change? Where does collaboration fit in such a globally competitive environment? And what does an organisation need to do to benefit from the tension between competition and cooperation?

Ultimately, any form of collaborative practice depends on the evolution of an *architecture of participation* within the enterprise. And that is inextricably bound up with the potency of free energy bouncing around the cafe.

PARTICIPATIVE ARCHITECTURES

On one level, our cultural evolution can be seen as a trajectory of increasingly sophisticated (unconscious and conscious) cooperation enabled by technology. Indeed it seems that certain cultural innovations, or *metatechnologies*, trigger human societies to reorganise at higher levels of social cooperation. This can be seen in the hunting and gathering habits of indigenous communities, for example, where customary levels of foraging by the family unit occasionally expand to wield a tool (the social network) far more sophisticated than usual. In the Middle Ages the metatechnology of capitalism pushed the hierarchical class structure of feudal society to transform into a new way of organising social activity: the market. Today, smart technologies like the Internet are doing the same, creating new opportunities for distributing power to the commons. Author Robert Wright concludes:[47]

> Natural selection, via the evolution of 'reciprocal altruism' has built into us various impulses (such as generosity, gratitude, obligation and trust) which, however warm and mushy they may feel, are designed for the cool, practical purpose of bringing beneficial exchange.

Management consultants have been 'spruiking' the importance of an *empowered* workforce for decades. Yet, for all the hype, the formal bureaucracy of the corporate cathedral still exerts an almost gravitational force to constrain and keep others firmly in their place. Information is often the first in line to be contained. Knowledge frameworks and work systems designs, ranging everywhere from problem solving to project management, typically adopt linear, sequential processes, where important decisions are escalated progressively upwards in a hierarchy of professional decision makers. All of which creates *empires*, rather than a *commonwealth*, of knowledge.

This fixation on control through regulation, dating back to the end of the Middle Ages in Europe, is flawed, rigid and ponderously slow, especially in comparison with the speed of markets. Too much control ties up the capacity to create and share knowledge, severely curtailing learning and development – which is contrary to any organisation's best interests. But there is also ample evidence to suggest that excessive controls, especially in the form of mindless obedience to 'the rules' and a concentration on diligence, actually increases costs, dampens motivation, diminishes innovation, encourages time wasting and game playing, stifles learning and has a long-term debilitating effect on morale.[49]

Meanwhile the trend towards greater accountability gathers pace. Across all sectors of the economy attention is increasingly focused on corporate governance, rules and regulations, compliance and risk management, while organisations continue to centralise and repress operations in the vain hope that this will actually *improve* performance. Perhaps it can in the short term. But in the long term such thinking is disastrous.

Empowerment and altruism seem totally at odds with such trends, particularly as these qualities demand a climate of mutual trust, focused commitment, cooperation, mutually beneficial relationships, and the opportunity to try new things from everyone involved, in order for them to be successful. Clearly, a new architecture of participation is warranted: one where capability is unshackled at the same time as risk is contained. Today that has become possible. Other, more collaborative competencies, are being applied to human production in ways that are more effective, innovative and robust than the assembly line was a century ago. In this context, much of the cathedral's formal dictates (whether in functions, units or channels) can be replaced by small, interconnected, networks of practice. Working in parallel, like the cells in a brain, affiliated networks of collective intelligence can get results faster than any single contributor or group. Furthermore, minimal controls are required in order to keep the entire enterprise focused on performance. The result is predictable: as unnecessary bureaucratic practices and controls are discarded, costs go down and creativity is unleashed. Lower costs enable greater opportunities for investments in learning, growing organisational capability and experimentation. Positive energy increases. Performance improves. It really is as simple as that.

Participation serves as both a business and civic model principle today. From the citizen engagement site Love Lewisham,[50] online talent contests and the online picture sharing of branded websites like Flickr, to Internet activism,[51] customer-designed and curated products, micro-lending cooperatives and even the exclusive eBay-style bargain hunting of a business like iBood,[52] engaged customers, members and citizens have become the new Chief Creative Officers in entrepreneurial-minded organisations across the planet, all thanks to the immediacy of new technologies like the Internet.

The most remarkable of the new collaborative approaches, however, is modelled on a method that for more than a decade has been closely associated with the development of computer software: *open source*. It is called *open source* because the collaboration is open to all and the source code is freely shared. Open source processes harness the distributive powers of new technologies, like the Internet, allocate the work out to many, and use their piecework to build a better whole. The open source method involves a broad body of collaborators, typically volunteers, whose every contribution builds on those before. Just

Share the objectives	A broad group of contributors agrees on a focal point and intended consequences for a specific collective effort.
Share the work	Projects are distributed among a mass of volunteers which creates 'architectures of participation'. No other model can possibly match the sheer brainpower it harnesses.
Share the results	Open source etiquette mandates that the creation be available for everyone to modify and develop and that any improvements are shared by all. This is the triumph of participation by the many over ownership of the few.

Figure 3.8 The principles of *open source* as a collaborative network method.

as important, the product of this collaboration is freely available to all comers.

Open source is now spreading to other disciplines, from the hard sciences to the liberal arts. Biologists have embraced open source methods in genomics and informatics. NASA has adopted open source principles as part of its Mars mission, using 'clickworkers' to identify millions of craters and help draw a map of the Red Planet. In online publishing, wiki.com has created an evolving English dictionary with entries and improvements from thousands of volunteers. There are open source projects in law and religion. There's even an open source cookbook! For all its novelty in organisations, open source processes are nothing new. Similar ideals can be traced all the way back to Ptolemy, circa AD 150. The same ethic is to be seen in Amish barn raising, in the creation of the Oxford English Dictionary and, more recently, the Wikipedia, and in the mapping of the human genome. What *is* new is the use of open source development in organisations to share work in ways that create conditions more favourable to innovation, adaptiveness and rapid response.

So, if open source offers so much, how should we now approach organisational design, given that the knowledge requirements of business leaders and functional professionals appear to be so different? How can we ensure that the dynamic periphery between market and organisation becomes the focus for collaborative inquiry and decisive action? What means should be used to switch the 'operating system' from one that is closed and controlled to one that is open and dynamic? These questions bring us back full circle to the principles of scale-free preferential networks and the potential for reconceptualising the nature of leadership (and therefore management) within large corporations through expeditious and shrewd use of the cafe and its culture.

CLOSER THAN CLOSE

Reductionism was the powerful driving force behind much of the twentieth-century's scientific research, the assumption being that if we could only understand the parts we would be sure to comprehend the whole. Unfortunately we didn't allow for the dynamic nature of complex systems: knowing the details, even intimately, doesn't guarantee the whole system will function as you would like or expect. Complex systems, like those found in organisations or in nature, follow a common design. A few natural laws govern their structure and evolution.[53] Among these laws, one of the most important is the law of interconnectedness. Complexity teaches us that nothing happens in isolation and that most phenomena and events are interconnected in some form or other. Recently, network scientists have gone even further: they argue that we all live in *small worlds* where everyone is linked to everyone else. In these small worlds, networks are pervasive.

Hidden deep within their fractal structure, networks have properties that reduce or expand our ability to do things with them. The smallest changes in a network's topology,[54] like the addition of a single individual to a team, for example, can leverage open previously hidden windows onto new worlds, allowing numerous diverse possibilities to emerge. The addition of just one person drastically changes the network itself. When a sufficient number of people are added, such that each individual is connected to at least one other person, a unique giant cluster (which we commonly refer to as *community*) emerges. Each community is a small world in its own right. Numerous small worlds, all interconnected, form a single community we call *society*.

In 1929 Hungarian author Frigyes Karinthy first proposed the outrageous notion that each individual in this global society is linked to any other individual through at most five acquaintances. In 1967 Stanley Milgram, a Harvard professor, turned this idea into a much-celebrated, ground-breaking study, on interconnectivity. The term 'six degrees' was coined by playwright John Guare. We now know that small separations are common in just about all networks: species in food webs appear to be two links away from each other, molecules in the cell are separated on average by just three chemical reactions, while we are all just one link away from our closest friends.

The six degrees theory suggests that despite the enormous size of society, it can be easily navigated by following social links from one person to another. We can even afford to be very provincial in choosing our friends as long as one or two of those friends have some weak ties. Weak ties offer us shorter paths to particular individuals and even a few such links will significantly grow the resilience of a social network. This is very different from the Euclidian world to which we are accustomed and in which distances are calculated in miles or kilometres. Our ability to reach people has much less to do with the physical distance between us than our ability to find the *pattern that connects* each other.

Naturally, not all social links are equally useful; it depends on what we are trying to do. Some links may lead us down blind alleys while others may take us further and further away from our intended destination. Recognising this, we continually re-interpret the value of social links, going with synchronicity,[55] choosing the most suitable 'attractors' with whom to interact by engaging an almost instinctive kind of social search engine, and finding the shortest path through a labyrinth of possibilities.[56] Organisational cafes are free-flowing communities as well as complex, evolving, scale-free networks.[57] Their web of social clusters grows, link by link, as new people enter the organisation, move around, and self-organise in ways that are novel and unpredictable. They adapt, too, as people leave, friendships mutate and relationships are rewired. In spite of this, the organisational cafe is far from being democratic. Growth, preferential attachment and *fitness*[58] all conspire to ensure that a few highly connected groups or individuals emerge to become all the rage. This introduces a *rich-get-richer* phenomenon where attractiveness and visibility help more connected hubs become even more popular and influential.

Unlike the discriminatory methods and barriers of entry used for the selection of ordained leaders, the only provisos in the cafe have to do with human preferences. In other words we are free to choose our friends. Often, new acquaintances link us into new social clusters. And yet, although individual choices remain highly unpredictable, the cafe community follows strict evolutionary patterns. Indeed, the very act of linking can tip our own small world into a different state. Acting in unison, yet without prior warning, the addition of only a single link to a community is all that's required for a spontaneous phase transition such as this to occur.[59]

Social ties are crucial in activating the small-world energy of the cafe – just as the flow of intelligence through the establishment of real-time feedback loops is the most critical function in preserving the 'cathedral's' integrity. Attempt to reduce or remove these links, or to substitute imposed couplings in their place, and the intricate web of social interaction that is the hallmark of the cafe will dry up and vanish. This is conspicuous where well-meaning architects have used mechanistic design criteria, based upon economic efficiency rather than on social contact, to build office spaces that isolate individuals from each other. It is also evident in situations where leaders, coming from a strict *command and control* mindset, try to seize control of communications for their own narrow purpose. In both cases, preferential attachment is destroyed and the power of the enterprise to innovate and remain adaptive is considerably weakened.

Create new ties, provide more spaces and opportunities for social interaction, however, and richer, more diverse conversations are sure to ensue. Furthermore, the uneven topology of scale-free networks ensures there is no critical threshold likely to slow down the dissemination of *attractive* messages. Even if a message has few memetic qualities, it will usually spread and persist in the cafe like a virus. The high speed of communications devices today enhances this capacity for *instant messaging* by collapsing space-time in ways that 'shrink' organisational networks. This accelerates learning, extending the reach of the organisation globally and affording the luxury of maintaining and reactivating social contacts that, just half a century ago, would almost certainly have died out.

NETWORKS, NARRATIVES AND NAVIGATION

Compared with nature, where redundancy is an integral feature, design flaws and failures, as well as intended and unintentional consequences, corrupt many human systems. Even the most supremely engineered systems are not immune from such vulnerability. In circumstances where these systems are expansive or interconnect individual nodes within sprawling networks, the risk of collapse becomes exceedingly high.[60]

The speed at which errors proliferate in large social systems like corporations triggers classic examples of cascading failures, which are then attributed to deficient processes, human culpability, technological failures or communication gaffes. This is why the overly engineered, elaborately structured, bureaucratic procedures built into the management factories of our major corporations and government departments have themselves become the real problem. Production-line mindsets, standards, sequential value-chains and control methods, so innovative in manufacturing environments during the industrial era, have become the vogue in organisations just about everywhere.

There is even an expectation these days that a well-managed business needs these things in abundance so as to present a serious façade to the market and to remain competitive. The implication is that we're somehow negligent if our organisational systems lack the steroid-sculpted, globally branded managerial toolkits such as Six Sigma, Balanced Scorecard, ISO 9000 series, 360 Degree Feedback, Customer Relationship Management, Lean Manufacturing . . . The list of 'must-haves' on any self-respecting executive's shopping list is a bottomless pit of tools in which anecdotal hype and competitive chic alone drive sales.

But here's the problem: there is very little evidence to suggest that any of these fads are valid in every type of situation, and a lot of research suggesting they are not. Some of them have been effective, in a limited sense and in very specific circumstances, while others of them have done a great deal of damage. Most, however, while intuitively appealing, are empirically contradictory. It is hardly surprising, of course, that initial reactions to any risk posed through uncertainty or unpredictability should be to tighten regulatory controls, demand impeccable behaviour and institute strict assurance measures. Sometimes the reactions from the custodians of the management factory can appear positively Stalinesque – take the erosion of human rights perpetrated by the Bush administration in the US after 9/11, for example. It doesn't take long to experience the futility of such responses.

In organisations, morale, trust and loyalty are almost impossible to recover once they have been eroded by a dysfunctional work environment, where individuals feel devalued or discounted altogether in comparison with profits. More problematic still is the anxiety and stress accumulating from the unthinking, mostly generic, application of these tools and protocols, even in the most thriving and successful companies.[61] Today's employees are expected to be flexible, open to change, take risks, do more with less, tolerate ambiguity, view instability as normal, and accept that a long-term relationship with an employer can no longer be expected.

Table 3.2 Some inconsistencies between operating systems and applications. The use of inappropriate applications causes stress, ultimately leading to collapse of the operating system in use.

	Old operating system	New operating system
Assumptions about reality	The world is stable and certain. With skill and effort we can control our destiny, decide on our future vision and get the results we promise	The world is complex and uncertain. We cannot always predict what will happen, but can respond instantly and innovatively to events as they occur.
Dominant language in use	Develop formal relationships Engage experts Seek senior managers' approval Put numbers above all else Stick to the game plan Engineer for efficiency Respect boundaries Take your work seriously Plan in advance in detail	Develop preferential relationships Engage attractors Permission to lead Put values above all else Use intelligence to adapt Design for adaptiveness Transcend boundaries Have fun Learn your way forward
Typical applications	Six Sigma Balanced Scorecard Total Quality Management Benchmarking Strategic Process Control Performance Appraisal	Generative Learning Networks Systemic Mapping Strategic Navigation Collaborative Inquiry Strategic Foresight Open Source

It is difficult to believe that this is the lingua franca of today's corporate operating system. Stress arises from the tension between the use of all-encompassing, prescriptive-based tools (*applications*) in conjunction with this managerial vocabulary (*operating system*) urging authenticity, leadership, creativity and excellence. Applications and operating systems are out of kilter, perhaps even utterly incompatible. In many organisations it has now reached a point that is unmistakably counterproductive: where each additional regulation or control tool acts rather like a Trojan virus in a computer, causing the whole operating system to malfunction and crash. Meanwhile managers push for more of the same, largely unconscious of the damage they are instigating. The ruthless aspect of conflicting applications and operating systems is abundantly clear. The re-engineering of corporations may sound progressive and sensible, especially to shareholders, but the price workers pay is an undercurrent of bewilderment, anxiety and diminished loyalty and commitment, their morale eroded by a chaotic and often dysfunctional work environment in which individuals are devalued or discounted altogether.

From government agencies to multinational corporations, small enterprises, even sports clubs, universities and charities, the principles on which we've become reliant for design are no longer effectively meeting our needs in a world characterised by dynamic change and volatility. Instead, they choke responsiveness, suffocate creativity and cause needless stress. Furthermore, they frequently instigate responses and initiatives from management that are downright foolish. This is immediately apparent in the bizarre formality of large organisations. Through the management factory, the organisation's executives always seek to design mechanisms that limit the amount of variety in evidence – even to the point of mandating what is deemed to be 'suitable' apparel, for example, and what can or cannot be used to embellish a work station. Such efforts invariably fail simply because such a goal is impossible to achieve. It runs counter to nature. However well intentioned, the strictly limited variety inherent in the cathedral[62] is quashed by the irrepressible diversity of the cafe. Containing far too much complexity to keep in check, the cafe inevitably self-organises in ways that approximates the healthy diversity of a living ecosystem where the highly interconnected nature of the network guarantees a topological integrity and an unusually high tolerance to errors and failures. In fact the only way to break apart a scale-free network is to simultaneously wipe out a hierarchy of highly connected hubs. In normal circumstances, any such strategy carries an unacceptably high risk in terms of ongoing viability.

As Malcolm Gladwell points out, tipping points cause cascading failures within systems. However, most systems failures are not instantaneous. Discrete flaws and symptoms of impending catastrophe can go unnoticed for a long time before triggering a sequence of malfunctions that then becomes unstoppable. Attempting to decrease the frequency of such cascades merely makes those that do tip even more disruptive. Conventional wisdom and, I readily acknowledge most mainstream thinking on the practice of management, both support the myth that change is generated and sustained by a core group of ordained leaders within the cathedral. This would still be a rational position to hold if it were not for the knowledge emerging from the study of scale-free networks, which exposes the imperfections embedded within most conventional approaches to management and organisation. In fact, the most effective tipping point for organisational transformation, though still the least understood, is the potent social metabolism of the cafe. This is now the optimum leverage point for strategic innovation and sustained performance – but only when it is thoroughly understood. Establish the conditions whereby people are able to connect preferentially and communicate with ease, encourage partnerships between business leaders and support functions, direct development and innovation towards open source tools and activities, demolish the management factory's red tape, defy convention by designing the organisation for speed rather than efficiency, liberate people in preference to controlling them . . . These are the raw genetic materials that enable generative learning networks. Amounting to a set of rules for designing, organising and managing in today's connected economy, this organisational DNA comprises an integrated praxis balancing the logic of cybernetics with the spirit of humanity. There are four critical enablers in this philosophy:

- *Open receptiveness* – the ability to be open to change of all sorts.
- *Self-renewal* – the capacity to let go of the past and discover the new.
- *Vigilance for responsiveness* – the ability to navigate prevailing conditions in real time.
- *Appreciative reciprocity* – the ethos of working collaboratively.

Using these enablers, the praxis of **The Five Literacies** allows globally coherent activities to emerge in the absence of centralised authority and control. This praxis is a new social innovation, a language capable of liberating performance reaching far beyond yesterday's dreams. It is the means for providing the propulsion needed to break free from past paradigms in creating and leading the globally distributed learning communities of the future.

> The last function of Reason is to recognise that there are an infinity of things which surpass it . . .
>
> – Blaise Pascal, *Pensées*

NOTES

1. Glocalisation is a trend to bypassing the nation-state with direct connection of local business nodes to a global economic grid. Glocalisation allows both greater integration with the world economy and the shifting of power from central government to local communities. This new direction has encouraged 'clustering', the collaboration of related businesses in geographic regions for the purpose of competing in the global market. Harvard Professor Michael Porter suggests that 'clusters represent a new way of thinking about national, state, and local economies, and they necessitate new roles for companies, government, and other institutions in enhancing competitiveness'.

2. Bolivia has nationalised its natural gas industry; Venezuela is raising taxes and royalties on foreign companies. Ecuador is nationalising oil; Russia is limiting foreign ownership of energy ventures and talking about taking control of projects from Shell, and others. China is 'prowling the globe in search of energy resources', especially Africa, Saudi Arabia and Kazakhstan (not to mention Australia). Source: Business intelligence agency Williams Inference, May 2006.

3. In a long article for *Kosmos Journal* (www.kosmosjournal.org), Irwin Laszlo describes some popular understandings of what the future might be like, then demonstrates why such conventional thinking is unlikely to be helpful, by describing the known processes of complex change revealed by the study of chaos theory.

4. The world is now eating more food than farmers grow, pushing grain stocks to their lowest level in 30 years. Rising population, water shortages, climate change and the growing costs of fossil fuel-based fertilisers point to a calamitous shortfall in the world's grain supplies in the near future. Source: National Farm Union of Canada, June 2006. Nor can we rely on technology to fix this, says Lester Brown, president of the Earth Policy Institute. 'There isn't much land left on the planet that can be converted into new food-producing areas. . . . Unlike the Green Revolution in the 1960s, when improved strains of wheat, rice, maize and other cereals dramatically boosted global food production, there are no technological magic bullets waiting in the wings.' In the case of water, the double impact of shortages and privatisation has led to riots in communities whose water rights have been sold, with disastrous consequences for the locals. All of this adds up to an alarming set of challenges. Will these shortages and the rise of resource nationalism encourage the renaissance of the nation-state after all? That would confound 20 years of speculation that the nation-state will give way to more local and global systems, largely because of the difficulty of managing the movement of things like information, money, work and pollution across national borders. And if the nation-state strengthens, how might this affect the long-standing

practice of national governments divesting their responsibilities to private enterprise?

5. Real time refers to a fluid atemporal domain – an expanded 'now' in which past and future meld into the present. Working in real time does not mean that everything occurs at the speed of light. On the contrary it is assumed that some things are better done more slowly, like nature's processes. This accounts for the 'slow' movement in areas like organic produce, restaurants and transport, for example, that are occurring all over the world. Explicitly, the capacity to perceive critical events should occur instantaneously. Synthesising intelligence and reflecting on this as the basis on which to act, however, should take longer. To act precipitously, especially if that means curtailing time for proper reflection, is a contemporary phenomenon that has been proven not to work. Real-time strategy implies the separation of perception from action; thus any number of reaction and transaction speeds are possible, depending upon the context.

6. Stafford Beer was a British cyberneticist and management thinker. His biggest independent project was never completed: In 1970 Beer was approached by Salvador Allende's elected socialist government of Chile to develop a national real-time computerised system Cybersyn to run the entire Chilean economy. When General Augusto Pinochet seized power in a violent military coup in 1973, the Cybersyn project was abandoned. Beer continued to work in the Americas, consulting for the governments of Mexico, Uruguay and Venezuela. He also wrote a series of four books, based on his own Viable Systems Model for organisation modeling: *Platform for Change, Designing Freedom, Heart of Enterprise* and *The Brain of the Firm.*

7. 'Towards a Science of Consciousness, Tucson 2002', Tucson Convention Center Music Hall, Tucson Arizona, 8–12 April 2002. Sponsored by the Center for Consciousness Studies at the University of Tucson.

8. Quantum entanglement describes the properties of two quantum particles that bump into one another. After the interaction, it is impossible to tease apart the two particles' characteristics. Once they become entangled, all the information about the particles lies only in their joint properties. If something affects the quantum state of one particle, it will inevitably affect the quantum state of the other, no matter how far apart they are. Einstein famously dubbed this *spukhafte Fernwirkungen:* 'spooky action at a distance'.

9. George Lakoff is Richard and Rhoda Goldman Distinguished Professor of Cognitive Science and Linguistics at the University of California, Berkeley, and a Senior Fellow at The Rockridge Institute.

10. Former US House speaker Newt Gingrich defining the current global environment on Fox News, 19 July 2006. Meanwhile President George W. Bush likens Osama bin Laden to Hitler. Such exaggerations have become increasingly prevalent in the post-9/11 world.

11. This entire argument is taken from Hugh White, Visiting Fellow at the Lowy Institute and Professor of Strategic Studies at ANU, in an article published in *The Age* newspaper on 11 September 2006 entitled 'Terrorism a threat – but not to our way of life'.

12. John Pilger's book, *Freedom Next Time*, published June 2006 by Bantam Press.

13. Magnetic Resonance Imaging uses electromagnetic radiation to obtain images of the body's soft tissues.

14. Cognitive science is the study of those brain mechanisms responsible for our thoughts, moods, decisions, feelings and actions. In other words cognition refers to everything taking place in our brains that helps us to know the world. Included here are such mental activities as alertness, concentration, memory, reasoning, creativity and emotional experience.

15. After the philosopher Descartes and his mechanistic view of reality.

16. An engineer and one of the fathers of scientific management, Frederick Taylor pioneered systematised work design at the Midvale Steel Plant in Pennsylvania beginning in 1881.

17. Hazel Henderson is best known for her work in evolutionary economics, particularly the measuring of human progress using whole-of-system indicators. She is author of *Paradigms in Progress: Life Beyond Economics*, Berrett-Koehler, San Francisco, 1991.

18. Reductionism was the driving force behind the trillions of dollars spent on disassembling nature during the last century. It maintained that to comprehend a system such as nature we must first decipher its component parts, the assumption being that once each part is understood, the whole will make sense. Now we are close to knowing almost everything there is to know about the smallest pieces but no closer to understanding nature as a whole.

19. In Search of the Collaborative Individual – Enabling Leadership Emergence in Complex Adaptive Systems, Neil McAdam, Winter/Spring 2004 Edition, *Mt Eliza Business Review*, Melbourne, Australia.

20. The term capacity as defined here is a systems concept: what outputs is the total system capable of generating in each part, given the limitations imposed on any part of the system by other parts? Potentiality is the performance of which the system would be capable, 'if only . . .'.

21. A term used to denote death.

22. Approximately $US50 billion is spent by corporations each year on 'change management' initiatives which, by their own measures, largely fail to live up to expectations.

23. To my knowledge this term was initially coined by management thinker John Seddon from the Vanguard Group.

24. Derived demands are needs arising from dynamic situations that require immediate action or attention. An example would be the flick of a switch to turn on the lights in a darkened room. The demand for light is met

almost instantly. Derived demand service design is about arranging things so that people who need things done are connected to other people and equipment that get things done – on an as-needed real-time basis.

25. Symbiosis is a mutually beneficial relationship between two people or groups.

26. As advocated, for example, by Charles Handy in his theory of 'shamrock' organisations.

27. Kleiner, A., *Who Really Matters: The Core Group Theory of Power, Privilege and Success*, Allen & Unwin, New York, 2003.

28. The notion of a business ecosystem upgrades the industrial era's perception of discrete 'industries' in which the relationship between a company's core business activities and its customers, competitors and suppliers are the only significant relationships. The idea of a business ecosystem extends and surpasses this notion. It depicts the entire network of (present and future) relationships, information flows and value points linking all stakeholders – including government bodies, the community, activists and regulators, for example.

29. First proposed by evolutionary biologist Richard Dawkins in his 1976 book, *The Selfish Gene*, a *meme* is a self-propagating or contagious idea that infects a social population by virtue of its uncanny 'stickiness'.

30. It is something of a fallacy to talk about organisational capability in the context of individual development. The capability of the organisation is at once *greater than* and *different from* the capability expressed by its individual members.

31. Psychologists call this 'fusion'.

32. Positive feedback reinforces and amplifies information, while negative feedback dampens it down in an effort to maintain the status quo.

33. Fanfare for Effective Freedom, Cybernetic Praxis in Government. Delivered by Stafford Beer to The Third Richard Goodwin Lecture at Brighton Polytechnic, Moulescoomb, on 14 February 1973.

34. We rely on a viable system to function continuously. Algedonic signals are precautionary signs that the system is stressed and about to fail. Different from routine information, algedonic signals in an enterprise are transmitted via special neural pathways (information channels) set up by ordained leaders as part of the 'change brain' system within Strategic Navigation.

35. It is well known that economic movements operate in irregular cycles. In this context, out-of-date information is not merely late; it is *precisely incorrect*. It represents a pattern that has past, but because the information is late this is not recognised. By the time executives discover a crisis, it is actually over. But they take action without understanding that, and therefore choose exactly the wrong action each time which causes further instability.

36. Stafford Beer implemented his Viable Systems Model in Chile from 1970 at the behest of the Marxist President, Dr Salvador Allende who had asked Beer, 'How should cybernetics be used in the exercise of national government?' The political environment was extremely unstable at the time. The real question was whether the government could get a sufficient grip on the economy before an inflationary time bomb blew up in its face. In the event it did not.

37. Transformational narrative is an intelligence-based form of critical dialogue, intended to engage all members of an enterprise, which then forms the basis for strategic change through collaboration.

38. Originally designed by Richard Hames and Marvin Oka for the Australian Tax Office, Strategic Navigation is a real-time strategic management methodology based on the principles of complexity and living systems.

39. In physics a phase transition is the sudden transformation of a system from one state to another. The distinguishing characteristic of a phase transition is an abrupt sudden change in one or more physical properties as in the formation of ice when water is cooled.

40. Viability here is understood as the effective exercise of cybernetic control through the synthesis and distribution of real-time intelligence throughout the system.

41. Senge, P., *The Fifth Discipline: The Art and Practice of the Learning Organization*, Doubleday Currency, New York, 1990.

42. Watts, D.J., *Six Degrees: The Science of a Connected Age*, Heinemann, London, 2003.

43. In his book *The Tipping Point*, Malcolm Gladwell argues a case for including connectors, mavens (collectors of knowledge) and marketers in any social network.

44. I am not using the term 'attractor' in the strict scientific sense. For me, attractors create social coherence, pulling others into their orbit and liberating collective energy and intent.

45. A reference to the technical knowledge functional professionals bring to their work. For example, in HR this knowledge may relate directly to recruitment, curriculum design, coaching, facilitation, etc.

46. *Guanxi* is the innate Chinese approach to personal connections – an individual's social capital within a particular group.

47. Wright, R., *Nonzero: The Logic of Human Destiny*, Vintage Books, New York, 2000.

48. Dating from the end of the Middle Ages, the invention of the clock allowed time to be precisely controlled. Prior to the clock, longer cycles (night, day and the seasons) coordinated human activities. The institution of clock time, invented by monks to coordinate prayer times, was rapidly adopted by tradespeople and mechanics. Clock time was later commandeered by the factories of the industrial revolution to control production cycles more

efficiently. Clock time, however, is just as arbitrary as any other measurement. Essential in terms of coordinating complicated schedules, clock time has nevertheless become a tyranny in its own right. Real-time potentially enables an escape from that tyranny.

49. Research undertaken and validated by Professor Gary Hamel, Chairman of Strategies and Visiting Professor, London Business School.

50. Initiated in February 2005, Love Lewisham involves residents in keeping the southeast borough of London clean. After installing special software on their cameraphone, observant townspeople can snap a picture of 'offending graffiti' or overflowing litterbins, enter location details and send it to the local council. The picture is then posted on the council's website, and cleaning crews are sent to resolve the issue.

51. Internet activism is increasingly used as an effective tool to lobby government and change unfair or ineffective policies. Organisations like Alternet (www.alternet.org) promote refreshingly challenging views from the mainstream propaganda and news agencies. Open Democracy (www.opendemocracy.net) goes further by organising online protests and petitions; while organisations like Getup! (www.getup.org.au) uses the latest online tools to address significant issues in ways that facilitate participative democracy.

52. iBood – 'Internet's best online offer daily', a Dutch company launched in October 2005, ships goods to most European countries. Modelled after the US-based Woot, in the first two months after it started iBood's turnover was 1.1 million euro, and expected turnover for 2006 is between 6.5 and 8 million euro (source: Emerce).

53. Sometimes referred to as 'local rules'.

54. A network's topology is the total array of relationships between all linked elements in the network.

55. Synchronicity is an example of self-organisation, pervasive in nature, where individual pulses are brought into the same phase of oscillation over time.

56. Through the use of relationship maps, or causal loop diagrams, for example.

57. The topology of complex social networks bears little relationship to the more randomly uniform networks of, for example, the highway systems connecting cities. Visually and structurally, social networks look more like airline maps, where a few major airport 'hubs' dominate activity and define the network's topology. The vast majority of other airports are tiny in comparison. These complex networks are organised according to power laws rather than the natural bell-curve distribution seen in the highways model. Because no node can claim to be characteristic of all other nodes it is called scale-free.

58. In this context, fitness can be defined as the ability to make friends and attract others more easily than other, competitor networks.

59. When order suddenly and spontaneously emerges out of chaos, (from water to ice, for example) it is termed a phase transition.

60. The introduction of any new mass technology (telegraph, railway, radio, telephone, air travel, etc.) has always been accompanied by a naive package of marketing hype and spectacular promises. Today we know that new technologies have unexpected consequences.

61. Researchers at the National Institute for Psychosocial Medicine in Stockholm studied 24,000 employees who worked for a variety of organisations in the public and private sectors in Sweden between 1991 and 1996. They found that those organisations that were the most successful and that grew most rapidly (an average of 18% annually) had the highest levels of long-term sickness absence (more than 90 days) and hospital admission, especially among women. Failing organisations which cut staff to save costs in times of recession – the practice known as downsizing – are known to increase stress for workers and have been linked with a rise in heart disease deaths among employees. But this is the first study to suggest that working for a successful enterprise may also be bad for your health.

62. Variety is understood in the cybernetic sense of the total number of possible states of a system. The greater the number of individuals, the greater the possible variety. For example, a small executive unit cannot hope to match the variety present in the whole enterprise. In spite of this, many executive teams focus on effecting greater control over the organisation by attempting to reduce variety.

PART TWO

CHANGING MINDS

Magic is power. So, too, is faith. Both are invisible yet they trap us in certainties we hold to be 'the truth'. The law, capital, ownership, scarcity, information and ideas are all forms of power, as are affiliation, passion, intention, imagination and collaboration. Power paints a patina of legitimacy on individuals that can be misleading. Ultimately power is simply a dynamic within relationships. As such it is a constraint – an emergent property[1] arising from the need to respond to the actions of others in particular ways. In society, power embodies monopolies of self-interest and influence whose *raison-d'être* is self-evident to the majority. If we are to combat the prisons of invention that trap us so easily in obsolete forms of leadership we need to be able to break free from old thinking.

NOTE

1. Emergence is a key concept in the science of complexity. Emergent properties arise from the complex interaction of the various parts of any system. When these parts interact, something different and entirely surprising, results.

CHAPTER 4

CERTAINTY TRAPS

A great many people will think they're thinking when they are merely rearranging their prejudices.

– William James

ALL CHANGE

In pre-literate societies, and even in some relatively sophisticated communities to this day, fear and superstition ensured the village shaman was held in awe. Throughout history, arcane knowledge gave clerics, teachers, physicians and scientists immense authority. Sovereigns held sway through the wealth they accumulated from combat, matrimony and taxes taken from those who toiled the land. Later, politicians exercised authority over the state through rule of law. During the past quarter of a century, hegemony has been gradually wrested from nation-states by entrepreneurs who controlled the movement and utilisation of capital and labour. Today, global business empires have become supreme, their structures symbolically dominating the urban skyline just as temples, palaces and government buildings have done in past ages – a reminder of the ephemeral nature of power.

With the possible exception of collective memory, nothing endures forever.[1] All living matter exists within a continuous cycle of regeneration, growth and decay. Within a couple of generations we even forget almost everything about our predecessors, including their appearance and lifestyle. Even power monopolies crumble, especially when the group's beliefs, concerns or technologies change. In Western society, during the course of the twentieth century, all three of these components shifted significantly. Belief systems have been shaken to the core by extraordinary scientific discoveries and by events ranging from the Holocaust to the collapse of communism. Our primary concerns have become almost uncontainable. We struggle to come to terms with diverse issues ranging from an increased tendency of the state to intervene in the lives of its citizens to escalating family violence, civil disobedience, international terrorism, the alienation of youth, euthanasia, genetic engineering, global pandemics and climate change.

More palpably, innovation of all kinds is occurring at blinding speeds, enabling the rapid fusion of cultures, the emergence of a single market economy and radically altered patterns of human productivity and consumption. Even the ability to create a hybrid human–machine biology is now within our grasp. Little wonder, then, that this volatile mix creates an uncertain and apprehensive social milieu. That the power monopolies previously enjoyed by monarchs, governments and corporations are unravelling, and new ones being formed, faster than ever before, should come as no surprise. But, while we have become unshackled from a range of arbitrary boundaries settled on, and imposed upon us by others (moral, biological, political, social, economic and geographical) power itself is *dematerialising* just as knowledge increases. What is more our learning curve is accelerating exponentially. This fact has not yet sunk in. Of course, the implications are far from clear.

Take corporate entities, for example. We've always assumed that business institutions, those monuments of twentieth-century capitalism, would endure. They are singularly focused on economic value, are perceived to be a pinnacle of human progress, and are built to last. Buildings, management systems, hierarchies, processes and protocols are all designed to endure. Or are they? Surely there comes a time when the most incomparable and elegant of designs no longer fulfils its original intention? What if our assumptions regarding the supposed longevity of business corporations are simply wrong? What if the very focus, structures and mechanisms designed to ensure corporate sustainability actually achieve the opposite of that intent? What if the patriarchal, corporate model of power is becoming obsolete as we watch? What would be the symptoms of that extinction? If we look closely, we might be seeing just that today.

As old-style corporations grow more corpulent, typically through mergers or acquisitions intended to improve shareholder value, many suffer from diseases we recognise in human beings including dementia, myopia, cancers and sclerosis. Out of touch with social and market needs that are transforming faster than at any other time in our history, many old-style corporations have become disposable – unfit and unworthy to survive for much longer. The stench of corporate collapse is in the air. Too complacent by far, too competitive, narcissistic and inwardly focused, too rigid and sluggish to adapt to changing conditions, these dinosaurs of a bygone age are being replaced by a new species of networked enterprise – collaborative, intelligent, self-organising, ethically responsible and, above all, built for speed.

But why should such a collapse of power be happening now, at the zenith of our development as a predominantly capitalist society? Communism is tainted. Markets hold sway. The owners of global corporations are supremely influential and even have their own club.[2] So what is going on? Should we attribute the demise of corporate power to misplaced greed generated by a form of capitalism shaped by individualistic values? Or is it simply negligence? A dearth of leadership? Or mismanagement perhaps? Are there other, more inherent defects that cause our enterprises and institutions to implode after just a few years? If so, what steps might an enterprise take to prevent premature decline? Or does it have more to do with today's bewildering global business environment? Can we blame the context for these uncertainties?

Not only are we at the turn of another century and a new millennium, we are snarled in the transition between one epoch and another. The sun is setting on the fossil-fuelled age of industrial economism. Meanwhile, another revolution dawns, heralding the first global knowledge age. An age likely to be characterised by tumultuous changes to who we are, what is important to us, and how we live our lives. On this helter-skelter journey, nothing is the same today as it was yesterday. All we can know for sure is that it will be different again tomorrow. No wonder we're all feeling confused and powerless!

It is crucial that we understand the quandary we are in. Only through a comprehensive understanding will we be able to make wise choices and bring all our resources to bear on facilitating a paradigm shift. But in order to make better sense of our predicament we must first learn to distinguish between reality and illusion; fact and fiction. To begin, we must hold ourselves accountable for having fashioned the world as it is today. The built environment, with all its amazing diversity and affluence as well as its disturbing shortcomings, is a direct consequence of the ways human beings have thought, felt and acted through the centuries. Today's world is how it is because we made it that way. If we had intended something else then presumably we would have designed it differently.

Well, perhaps not! Notwithstanding technological perfection (which is probably unattainable anyway) and a jumble of human traits such as ego, vanity, rivalry and self-interest, at least four other interdependent factors stand in the way of our ever constructing a perfect world:

1. Surprise – When complex systems of any kind interact, they produce surprises that simply can't be accurately predicted. Other than to react instantly, especially when what is actually occurring doesn't accord with what we had intended, there is little we can do to prepare for such novelty. Take the *Challenger* space shuttle disaster, for example, an event that is lasered onto the world's collective retina. This catastrophe occurred when one complex system (weather conditions) reacted with another complex system (physical materials) with unpredictable results. In effect, ambient temperatures froze the O rings in the space shuttle's massive booster engines, causing them to become brittle and rupture. This malfunction could only have been prevented had serious concerns regarding the performance specifications of the O rings been conveyed to NASA early enough for them to calibrate the operational risk of launching in such icy conditions. They weren't.

2. Linear thinking – The conceptual models we use to structure the way we think are often extremely narrow and rigid. While this is critical for analysing, categorising and labelling, such demarcation doesn't necessarily translate into the enlightened comprehension of a whole system. Consequently, because these models do not easily facilitate a thorough grasp of relationships, transformations over time and other dynamic variables, we often remain blissfully unaware of the true complexity of any situation. In fact, our habitual use of linear models and results-based thinking perpetuates the illusion that we are solving complex structural issues when, in reality, all we are doing is resolving a few, discrete, easily detected, symptoms. NASA engineers had not adequately tested any space shuttle Go/No

Go launch scenarios arising from poor weather conditions because such matters were considered to be well outside the scope of the engineering brief. Such decisions were traditionally a matter for launch personnel.

3. False assumptions – It matters not whether one is highly intelligent or totally psychotic, all humans hold relatively fixed views about their own reality. Even the most consummate thinking founded on impeccable logic is invariably embedded in deeply held convictions about how things work, what is right and wrong, what is real and what is not real. These convictions lead us, all of us without exception, into making erroneous assumptions and taking things for granted. But beliefs change, sometimes radically, as fresh insights are gained that improve our understanding. Turning to our NASA example again, the manufacturers were apparently aware of the design fault in the O rings but did nothing to draw it to the attention of NASA because they had incorrectly assumed the shuttle would never be launched in such inclement weather conditions.

4. Impulsive behaviour – Human behaviour is inherently unpredictable because so much of what we do is spontaneous. However well intentioned, our actions will always have unintended consequences because of this trait. We are not good at monitoring the systemic impacts of our actions to ensure that what we get is indeed what we want. In the NASA example, the impact of temperature on the properties of the materials used in the space shuttle's O rings, although known to a few engineers, was never translated into meaningful information for launch control. If NASA had known that the performance properties of the O rings were compromised under such freezing conditions, the countdown would have been postponed and the disaster averted.

Apart from the first of these, about which we can do little except to embrace uncertainty as a fact of life, the three remaining factors are fundamentally concerned with how we frame and structure our thinking to create what is usually referred to as a *commonsense*[3] of everyday assumptions. *Commonsense* results from the generally accepted models we use to acquire and organise knowledge, but also from embedded patterns of behaviour. If we could only find ways to change these patterns, by escaping the oppressive legacy of past hubris and prejudices for example, we could create a startlingly different world. Without a more universal appreciation of the behavioural limits imposed by our habitual tendency to think in linear, dualistic, reductionist and primarily economic terms, however (our current *commonsense*), we will not halt the damage we are wreaking on each other and on the biosphere; nor will we execute viable alternatives to the future we are drifting towards. In fact, we will not even begin to comprehend such things let alone talk about them.

Blind pursuit of economic growth and development (or any other one-dimensional strategy for that matter) must not be an option any more. A desire for further economic growth should specify growth of *what* and to *what end*.[4] Intelligent economic growth, for example, can provide the resources for creating a world in which crushing poverty, social exclusion, famine, ill health and injustice are things of the past. Or it can create more of the same. It can produce more pollution on a planet already choking with toxic waste, or be directed towards industries that reduce, eliminate and even reverse the effects of pollution altogether. Both types of growth create work. We need to agree what sort of work we want.

For far too long, industrial economism has trampled over the indigenous wisdom, sense of community and benevolent spirit of the human soul, inflicting upon us a world that is simply too contaminated, competitive and disturbed to be sustainable. Integral models and inspired insights are desperately needed to help restore hope, dignity and prosperity and to shape society in ways that are most beneficial to the majority of people. This will also entail deconstructing many of the more rigid myths that mould our thinking about the future and reconstructing these to reflect today's realities. One such is the myth of technological determinism – the mistaken conviction that the invention and adoption of particular technologies is somehow unavoidable.[5] Yet another, the myth of ideological superiority – that particular philosophical principles will endure simply because they appear to be sacrosanct at a particular period of time.

There are many other myths that perpetuate inequality, poverty, pollution, injustice and waste. Institutionalised learning, for example, has led to the fragmentation and perhaps irretrievable loss of human knowledge. Another is the belief that modern agricultural methods have reached some kind of perfection. This is one of the most ridiculous myths of our time if one considers the damage done to the Earth through Western agrarian models and practices. A couple of simple examples will suffice to illustrate this lunacy. It takes 20,000 litres of water to grow one kilogram of coffee, 11,000 litres to make a McDonald's Quarter Pounder, and 5000 litres to make a kilogram of cheese. Meanwhile, back on the farm, these practices translate into impending disaster. Millions of farmers in China, India and Pakistan now use pumps to suck up water beneath their fields, removing about twice as much as is replaced by rain. Where 10-metre wells once yielded water, now tube wells as deep as 400 metres are running dry.

The main reason we fall into these traps is that we find it almost impossible to imagine with any great clarity what alternatives could fill the void. Of course examples abound of people who are defying conventional wisdom and proving the foolishness of such myths. Take Jose Felipe Rebeiro in Brazil, for example, the pioneer of a new kind of agrarianism, combining small mixed farms with local knowledge and high-tech as is needed. Rebeiro is showing local people how they can make a far better living by exploiting native trees for their abundant and numerous fruits, drugs and pigments than they ever can from soy farms, which in any case are owned by foreign companies that employ as few people as possible in the name of efficiency. Examining the ancient art of agro forestry in India, Rebeiro has also pointed out that cattle are essentially woodland animals: dairy cows given shade yield up to 30% more milk than cattle injected with hormones which eventually find their way into the human food chain with as yet unknown consequences.

Innovations of this nature are a constant and usually make a great deal of sense with hindsight. But hindsight is just that! Although powerful elites, such as the military, politicians, judges, corporations and the bureaucracy may influence change more than the achievement of any single innovator, the future can never be predictable, as any thorough study of history will show. So many factors, including cultural context, socioeconomic conditions, group mores, government policy and pure serendipity invariably help shape the outcome.

Another deeply ingrained myth, one that is barely challenged today, concerns the phenomenon of progress. In the West, for example, it is commonly assumed that life is improving and that we are on a (mostly scientific) trajectory towards a state of considerable material prosperity. Adherents of this view (including, as one might expect, many of the world's most affluent nations and their institutions such as the World Bank, IMF and WTO) cynically ignore the fact that progress in one area is often bought at the expense of impoverishment elsewhere. Globalisation has not brought prosperity to all, but it has brought poverty to many. An alternative, though related, view is driven by the somewhat medieval notion of continuous disintegration and decay following humanity's fall from grace in the Garden of Eden. Many in the environmental sustainability movement, for example, continue to call for a dramatic downscaling in human production and consumption to avoid further environmental catastrophe and ultimate species extinction.

Yet another myth concerns that of a single predetermined future. Unhappily there is no such thing as 'the future'. Oh, if life were that simple! The future is not singular, but multifaceted and multidimensional. Through each personal decision, as well as through our daily actions, we are helping to fashion multiple 'micro futures' that coexist within a breathtaking variety of shifting dynamics and contexts. These tumble chaotically into being – concurrently desirable and undesirable, viable and impractical, predictable and surprising – depending upon the context and one's perspective. If that were not sufficiently complex, they then proceed to coalesce and interact unpredictably, creating an emergent global dynamic that is forever shifting. To that extent 'the future' is utterly inexplicable, strange and speculative. Yet we cannot avoid the responsibility for creating the world the way it is. The future will always remain a social construction evolving from human desires and interactions. Future generations are bound to judge us for the decisions we make today.

Of course, comprehending the present is no pushover either, in spite of the fact that we are conditioned to focus on the temptations of the current moment. For it requires us to *sense* and *discern* the salient patterns connecting everything happening around us, to instantly *make sense* of the underlying dynamics and interdependent nature of these patterns, to *appreciate* the diverse ways in which they could (and are) playing out, and to *respond* by designing actions that are appropriate and that align with our intentions and values.

So what will it take to create a more viable world for future generations? We must certainly learn to let go of the past – though prudently. Personal experience should not be discounted. In fact it is invaluable. As philosopher Georges Santayana reminds us, those that do not remember the past are condemned to repeat it. Our minds constantly synthesise generalised patterns (archetypes or mental models) derived from our concrete experiences. These mental models influence how we understand the world and also shape future behaviours. We often forget, however, that all experience is contextual. What worked in a particular situation, in a particular culture and at a certain time, may be totally inappropriate for today. Furthermore, memories warp and twist over time to such an extent that each successive memory becomes almost a discrete reinterpretation of the original experience.

We must also find other ways of escaping today's mind traps that persistently threaten to delude us – usually without our even realising it. For example, most organisations are still configured in ways that focus on efficiency – particularly the efficient production of tangible goods. The compartmentalised functions and other elaborate means used to achieve efficiency is a model inherited from our industrial past. Enticed by its financial benefits in an industrial context, (speedier processes, using fewer people, resulting in fewer errors and lower costs) we have incorrectly assumed that this model can and should be applied as a universal method for organising any business today. But, even ignoring the social consequences, which are many and profound, efficient processes are next to useless for leveraging tacit knowledge, generating innovation, processing intelligence and ensuring service quality, for example. These require redundancy, human contact, time for reflection and the nurturing of creativity.

Finally we will need to evolve a new episteme in which to *see* the world differently. If we were to become really conscious of the ways in which the filters[6] we habitually use to organise and sort information prejudice our ability to comprehensively discern reality, we would be staggered by our intolerant, bigoted, short-sighted attitudes. Only then might we become more inclined towards developing a *transformational* competence – using multiple viewpoints for informed decision making rather than relying on our own needs and narrowly biased views. At the same time, if we were able to create palpable *memories of the future*, integrating alternative intelligence, collective aspirations and new wisdom into stories that profoundly resonate within the human heart, it is just possible we could review the most critical of global issues and dilemmas, reperceiving them in all their astonishing variety and richness and complexity.

It is possible we might then also conceive the world (and our relationship to it) afresh. We might see the commonality between the peoples of the world rather than focus on those differences that set them apart. We might acknowledge the irreparable social and environmental damage we are wreaking in the name of economic development, merely to prop up for the time being a lifestyle we wish to maintain or are still striving to achieve. We might even find a way of transcending our tenacious celebration of industrialism, with its inflexible definitions of human welfare, efficiency, energy and undifferentiated per capita-averaged growth, in order to design whole-of-system interventions better able to secure a peaceful, more ecologically conscious, sane, gender-balanced and equitable world.

NOTES

1. Memory is an essential component of biologically adaptive systems. It emerged only when life and evolution gave rise to systems of *recognition*. The term collective memory is used to describe aspects of heredity, immune responses, reflex learning and various forms of consciousness that are inexplicable. Take, for example, the extraordinary journey begun every northern autumn by millions of monarch butterflies. Gathering in the United States and Canada, they fly 4000 km south to their winter retreats in the fir forests of Mexico travelling up to 200 km a day. Between November and March, the butterflies blanket the trees in Mexico's Michoacan state with a sharp orange hue while millions of wings spread a soft murmur through the leaves. No other insect makes such a journey en masse. Scientists continue to puzzle over how and why the monarchs return to the same patches of trees high in the mountain peaks. The mystery deepens when you realise the monarchs don't even have the benefit of memory (as we understand it) to guide them; those leaving Mexico will never get home – they die en route after reproducing. It takes four or five generations of monarchs, each living for approximately one month, to reach Canada and the US. The ones born in the autumn will delay sexual maturity and live for up to eight months – long enough for them to complete the journey to Mexico, survive winter and in the spring begin the journey again.
2. The World Economic Forum held at Davos each year is attended by many of the most powerful people on the planet.
3. Antonio Gramsci referred to commonsense as an encrusted form of thinking that carries within it a residue of popular ideas.
4. I refer here to a report entitled, *The Wellbeing of Nations*, published by the OECD, Paris, 2001.
5. Technological determinism is the idea that a particular technology, such as the alphabet, electricity or the Internet, is so powerful that it is beyond our control. I reject such a notion. The adoption of new technologies is never inevitable but rather the result of an emergent dynamic and interactions between the cultural context, social mores and government policy.
6. These filters commonly include any assumptions, beliefs and values we might hold that ultimately determine our attitudes, opinions and behaviours regarding any given issue.

CHAPTER 5

REINVENTING THE PRESENT

The distinction between past, present and future is an illusion – although
a persistent one.

– Albert Einstein

It is our custom to react to volatile and unstable conditions, and the
problems arising from these, in one of two ways. Often we will continue to apply remedies that are failing, redoubling our efforts and
enthusiastically allocating extra resources to the issue while blindly
ignoring any data that might conflict with our obdurate preconceptions
and views of a rational reality. Why? It's actually quite simple. Firstly,
human beings generally dislike being proven wrong. In some cultures,
this can bring about an embarrassing loss of face and even dishonour.
Secondly, we tend to rely more and more on measurement rather than
use observation and wise judgement. While analysis and calculations
are useful in many situations, the measures we adopt are often open
to misinterpretation: they can be used in ways that convince us we
are on the right track, even when we are not. The unrealistic calls for
further economic growth and development as a response to the detrimental social impacts and environmental costs caused by that very

strategy, is an example of how impoverished our judgement has become in that respect.

Occasionally, however, we might attempt to reconsider the entire situation, viewing changing circumstances through fresh lenses in the hope of noticing something different or seeing a factor we had previously overlooked or understated. But rethinking entire systems and their conditions is never an easy thing to do. It takes time, imagination, humility and deep reflection to understand what caused the current state and, above all else, a willingness to let go of past preconceptions.

Any expression of a different reality entails the development of new mental models as well as the application of appropriately designed tools and techniques. Many of the existing ones are stale, having created the simplistic economic remedies and myopic political agendas that gave rise to the unsustainable situations in which we now find ourselves. For example, continued use of industrialism's reductionist ethos, dogma and models will only cause us to become mired in more of the same. Such expressions of alternative futures also require dedicated methodologies that allow us to overcome the quicksands of the past while inventing practical, coherent and meaningful futures out of the dynamic cosmic dance of a complex, continuously evolving present.

The ability to reflect sensibly and inventively on alternative futures is extremely challenging for most people simply because our fascination with the present is so all encompassing. It overwhelms us by its immediacy – as the sphere in which our most routine thoughts, feelings and actions connect and play out. Because of this, our rational spirit acts rather like an immune system, assuring us that tomorrow will simply be a continuation of today, even when our most deeply embedded instincts caution us that this cannot possibly be so. Take the relationship between business and society, for example. For generations the sole purpose of business was to create wealth. It has always been left to other institutions, such as the Church, the state and patronage from wealthy citizens, to provide for people's spiritual, educational and social needs. Today, however, there can be little doubt that business has a vital role to play in shaping a coherent, appreciative society. Although still unacceptable to some, because of their submission to the overwhelming nature of the present, in itself formed by past experiences, smart global leaders acknowledge that it is no longer possible for them simply to continue to mind their own business. In the process of becoming the most prominent and powerful of global institutions, business has acquired far broader obligations to society.

Leaders that miss or ignore this imperative may thrive for a while. In fact their booming business may well give them the illusion of continuing success. Ultimately though this path is unsustainable. Consumers are demanding much more from business these days. They want new products for a sustainable world and they are insisting that corporations fearlessly align the interests of people, business and the planet. Why? Because they want to stop cheating their children by continuing to fund their lavish lifestyles from the future. That is why customers everywhere are seeking out ethically responsible alternatives to current offers. Business leaders that are not prepared for this and who uphold greed as their prime strategy, will perish. Customers will take their custom elsewhere. When this happens it is already too late. Profits will be harder to come by, the business will be marginalised and insolvency will rapidly ensue. It is important to remember that society permits businesses to operate in the first place. The survival of any business is dependent upon people purchasing the goods and services on offer. If people stop buying, the business ceases to exist. Given the basic values and behavioural shifts occurring today at a grassroots level, it should come as no revelation that such licence can be withdrawn – perhaps quite suddenly and without warning – if the company is perceived to be acting inappropriately, unethically or against the wishes of the majority.

In April 2000 Monsanto CEO Robert Shapiro proclaimed that genetically modified (GM) foods would solve the world's food problems. Responding to the urgent needs of millions of starving people, Shapiro's company had allocated considerable resources to the design and manufacture of GM foods in the hope that Monsanto would carve out a special niche for itself as a company with a soul and that profits would automatically follow. By any conventional standards the business principles were correct. However, the conditions under which Monsanto intended to sell these new GM products were entirely out of sync with society's rudimentary understanding of GM science and its lack of tolerance for multinational corporations 'holding the developing world to ransom'. Within a few weeks GM food protests erupted in Europe as questions of adverse side effects entered the public debate. Consumers voted with their buying power, rejecting not just Monsanto's products but also their shares. The company's stock plummeted and, irrespective of the science involved, the dangers of proceeding were seen as too great. Massive public opposition had stopped the company in its tracks.

These changes in society's conscience are not just a passing fad. Nor will these problems simply go away. On the contrary, they seem likely to escalate. Incited by well-informed activists such as Naomi Klein,[1] Monsanto and agribusiness companies like them are now facing a groundswell of public opinion as new allegations fly thick and fast. One claim given popular credence suggests that a complicit industry is intent on contaminating the whole food chain to such an extent that it will become impossible to regulate the GM industry. For many years similar claims have been made against the tobacco industry where class actions are now leading to litigation on a scale that could eventually bankrupt the industry. More recently, the practices of some of the world's largest pharmaceutical companies, particularly the relationships they foster with the doctors who dispense their drugs and the alleged manufacturing of social anxiety in creating new markets for their products, have come under increasing scrutiny. As reported by Ray Moynihan and Alan Cassels in their recent book *Selling Sickness*, many of these companies are intent on 'disease-mongering':

> Thirty years ago Henry Gadsden, the head of Merck, one of the world's largest drug companies, told *Fortune Magazine* that he wanted Merck to be more like chewing gum maker Wrigley's. It had long been his dream, he said, to make drugs for healthy people – so that Merck could 'sell to everyone'. Gadsden's dream is now reality, driving the marketing machinery of the most profitable industry on earth.[2]

In 2002 Merck was faced with clinical trial results showing that patients taking Vioxx, a painkiller, had five times the number of heart attacks as those taking an older drug. But the company refused to accept the most obvious explanation – that Vioxx might be dangerous to the heart. Merck continued to sell Vioxx for four more years, until another trial confirmed Vioxx's dangers, before withdrawing the drug. Now Merck faces 14,000 lawsuits, covering almost 30,000 plaintiffs, contending the drug caused heart attacks and strokes. The company says it did nothing wrong and plans to defend every lawsuit.

Examples like this, and there is no shortage of examples from the corporate world, clearly illustrate the need for organisations and their leaders to come to terms with the politics of change in all its unpredictable richness and variety. It is vital for companies to develop intimate knowledge of their customers' desires and aspirations and act in accordance with the real needs of society. Such profound knowledge, however, can only ever transpire if we are able to:

- Develop ways to appreciate the autopoietic[3] nature of our social and business ecosystems, however we may define these.[4]

- Establish what links, relationships and information flows really matter to different people, in different geographies, over time.
- Agree what is significant, and less so, as we cooperate with each other to create pathways into sustainable, 'preferred' futures.[5]

Inevitably, it also compels the application to our own circumstances of more organic, nonlinear models for dealing with the multidimensional nature of change today – ecological models that integrate, but also enable us to think far beyond the simple-minded, mechanistic structures of *industrial economism*. Without such a refined appreciation, business institutions will continue to view the world through the window of an obsolete paradigm, misdiagnosing their 'success' and forfeiting any leading role they might have assumed in enabling a more coherent and prosperous society.

The task of reinvention and renewal is never an easy one. We are mostly oblivious to the countless assumptions we employ to interpret our corporeal experiences. Indeed, many of our most deeply imprinted values and emotions actually thwart any innate ability we might have to recognise the legitimacy of those whose beliefs differ from our own. Nor, as already implied above, are we particularly conscious of the ingrained models and cultural archetypes we habitually use to reflect upon the ways we think. Toss in the fact that we invariably resort to using only the thinking tools with which we have become familiar and we stand a very good chance of repeating past mistakes, even when we believe we are being truly original and inventive.

Many of the so-called advances in managing and organising during the past half century, for example, are little more than age-old ideas convincingly rebranded and packaged to appeal to our insatiable craving for anything new. Eagerly touted by superannuated old-paradigm experts seeking to recycle themselves, the thinking itself invariably remains frozen within the prevailing Cartesian worldview. To believe otherwise might be considered delusional. But believe it we do, so clever is the marketing of ideas today! Even genuinely unique developments are often, and at times quite cynically, co-opted for industrial age pursuits rather than as the means for optimising human potential, reconceptualising the concepts of growth and progress, and creating a more sustainable, ecologically viable world.[6] Meanwhile it becomes more and more difficult to discern between genuine innovation, the repackaging of old ideas and sheer garbage.

Comparable fallacies have taken root within the business community as a consequence of the tedious media hype surrounding the so-called *new economy*. While the products of digital technology appear to be nullifying many tenets of *industrial economism*, previously assumed to be immutable, such as the relational shift between traditional competition and networked cooperation,[7] for example, it is far from clear how some other business fundamentals might evolve. We are unable just yet to distinguish fact from fiction. And yet this very fact separates truly great leaders from the pack of also-rans who are content merely to manage their business as it is today – pruning costs where possible but otherwise keeping their heads firmly in the sand. *Five literacies* leaders, on the other hand, have the courage and intelligence to look far into the future and to embark upon risky ventures, demanding change during times of the greatest success and prosperity.

Naturally, others eventually try to copy this lead in an effort to piggyback on success. Fearful of being left out in the cold and eager to be a part of the new gold rush, increasing numbers of corporations are being taken in by the relentless propaganda surrounding social ethics, environmental responsibility and, of course, new technology. The fervour for new technology in particular has led some firms into launching websites in the naive hope that this alone will transform them into *new economy* firms. Oblivious to the fact that they are often only pursuing one of the oldest and most common of business strategies (that of minimising production costs) they fail to grasp that what is actually required in today's volatile market conditions is authentic distinctiveness. Innovative products, for example, and unique business models that seamlessly integrate design, production, distribution and service. Some firms do get it. Others probably never will. But in tomorrow's environment only authenticity is viable in the long term.[8]

But what is fact and what is fiction in the so-called *attention* economy?[9] How can we tell the difference when everything we encounter is designed to capture, track, quantify, manipulate, seize, buy, sell and control our attention; where 'real' advertising is incorporated into 'unreal' digital games; and where the boundaries between reality and hyper-reality are increasingly blurred? Over the past few centuries, human brains have been conditioned to deal with a rational world characterised by the need to manage tangible *things*. We have become expert at fabricating a world of unbridled consumerism where economic value resides in tangible goods; reductionist logic and reason are used to explain most things; and predictive strategies are consistently used in an attempt to find permanent answers to narrowly defined problems. In this world we rely on science and technology to solve our ills. And we buy, buy, buy as if there is no tomorrow – even when we throw much of it away! Energy from non-renewable resources is assumed to be there for the taking. Competition is regarded not as a cultural construct springing up out of specific circumstances that continues to be condoned, but as an inherent part of human nature. Progress equates to economic growth and expansion. Any perceived 'lack of progress' is treated with further doses of economic development even though this often contributes to the social and economic deterioration of unsuspecting communities. In this urbanised authoritarian world, order is obstinately sought through hierarchical institutions. Patriarchal corporations contentedly function behind laws that hold them accountable as individuals – whatever the costs of their activities to society or damage done to the environment, which is often considerable.

Like it or not, this is the essence of the industrial episteme. It is our *indust*-reality and it feels as natural as the air we breathe. Exceptionally, human beings are the only species to have invented their own ecology. Ironically, conditions within that ecology now threaten our own self-destruction, along with the extinction of thousands of other species. Blessed with a track record virtually unblemished by success, other than our domination over nature, we have been trapped within this noxious invention for over 300 years. And after 300 years it is slowly choking us. Although industrialism has brought vast material wealth to around 10% of the world's population, devastating poverty and environmental damage has also followed in its wake. It may even have ruined the biosphere of the planet beyond redemption. We do not really know. Yet developing nations hunger for its alchemy, viewing its alluring materialistic façade with envy and aspiring to create their own versions as swiftly as they can.

Perhaps we should not be too concerned, however, since the industrial world is in decay, imploding under the weight of its overindulgence. And, with it, the logic that has given rise to its excesses as well as the values it espouses. In spite of denials to the contrary from those who cannot comprehend the unprecedented nature of the changes we are living through, human society may be shifting to a fundamentally different kind of morality and infrastructure. We have seen similar upheavals at various times in our history. The agrarian and industrial revolutions, for example, both dramatically changed the basic patterns of human production and consumption. But we've experienced nothing on the scale of today's massive disruption, which has the potential to touch every living soul on the planet in one way or another!

The world we are now frenetically creating is a digitally connected world. A breathtaking world in which information, together with the phenomenal speed at which it can be transmitted, is conjuring entirely new possibilities. A disconcerting world in which many of the conventions we have used for managing, making meaning, organising, trading, learning, communicating, playing, designing and governing are being recast. A bewildering world in which long-prevailing myths are being exposed,[10] value systems suddenly threatened and where once venerable institutions, such as the law, politics, business corporations and the nation state, are no longer considered trustworthy.[11] A volatile world of extremes, where the impoverished are forced to abandon any hope of a normal life or allow their resentment to erupt in ferocious acts of malice and international terrorism.

A few fundamental processes have ignited this contemporary hurly-burly. By themselves, these processes are unexceptional. It is the extraordinary dynamism created by their accelerating convergence, however, and the detritus they leave in their wake, that cannot be ignored. This dynamism has allowed global capitalism to run riot. Electoral choices are drying up as citizen's concerns are subverted to the needs of big business. In the meantime, corporations play one nation off against another in efforts designed to minimise regulation and lower wages while reducing human rights and disregarding environmental constraints.

Elected representatives everywhere have undermined their own usefulness, to the extent that democracy itself is now threatened as boundaries become even more blurred. This is evident on several fronts, from the geopolitical to the purely commercial. For example, in July 2006 the shocking might of the Israeli military machine inadvertently accorded legitimacy to its enemies by engaging Hezbollah in the field of battle. Illegitimate political coalitions like the G8 regularly meet to protect their own economic self-interests but act as though they were the legally elected representatives of a united world economy. Bodies such as the World Trade Organisation (WTO), that affect the lives of millions, remain unelected and unaccountable. Their decisions, however, are binding. Thus far the WTO has ruled in the corporate interest in all of its deliberations concerning the environment. Indeed, it has so lacked accountability that even its own Third-World delegates have been excluded from meetings affecting their future.[12]

In spite of these trends, and even though global capitalism appears to be gathering an almost unstoppable momentum, it may also be sowing the seeds of its own destruction. A global capitalist future is by no means preordained.[13] Globalisation is not just crashing on our heads from another planet. The rules of globalism are not unambiguous, inevitable, or necessarily irreversible. Corporations are clearly taking advantage of existing ambiguities and uncertainties. Such is their inherent nature. And in adopting the role of spruikers for corporations, governments have certainly been remiss.

If business interests have prevailed as an end in themselves, however, without regard to more widespread benefits that corporate activity is supposed to deliver, then the system we have designed is defective. It is never too late to change a flawed system. Increasing global inequality is in no one's interests; not even those who have done well out of globalisation. Many economists will argue that capitalism is the most effective means yet created for producing wealth and assuring material progress. Even if this is the case, capitalism urgently needs to be reinvented, so iniquitous has it become. The game is still there for the playing. We have a moral and collective responsibility to ensure that the benefits arising from capitalism are shared more equitably than in the past.

There are signs that this, too, may already be happening. For example, there is a devolution towards smaller, decentralised and networked communities underway in many parts of the world. Extremely large units it seems (both corporations and states)[14] in addition to their addiction to centralised planning, homogeneous values and bureaucratic control have become increasingly unmanageable. On the other hand, the growth of some multinational corporations, amounting almost to a merger madness, appears to be almost unstoppable – their brands and influence insinuating themselves into our everyday lives.[15]

Since the early 1970s, citizens movements have sprung up everywhere, most expressing a desire for greater autonomy, proposing alternative policy agendas[16] and all the while crying out for greater accountability from governments and corporations. Enabled by the Internet, these rag-tag social movements are now able to communicate with ease across national boundaries and time zones. Service industries have increased significantly in number over the past 50 years to the extent that they now employ far more people than manufacturing industries. This shift from the tangible (possessions) to the intangible (experiences) may also signal a long-term change in society's values that could eventually undermine the more rampant aspects of materialism. Likewise, the energy-consumption shifts that have been transforming industrial cultures since the 1960s continue to result in many more organisations taking the social impact and environmental costs of their production strategies into account. And as political democracy and economic democracy become disentangled, we discern the willingness of repressive regimes to tolerate the global 'free' market.

At one level, all the above observations appear to be factual; part of a grand pattern of transition between one age and another. This in itself, of course, may be an illusion. Facts can quite easily become fictions, and vice versa. This is why it is far more problematical to predict with any accuracy, for example, what specific conditions might signal the fracturing of China into autonomous regions or a reunification with Taiwan; how different aspects of globalism might unfold; how current government policies can rapidly unravel creating unintended complications in their wake; or how swiftly notions of security might shift from purely nationalistic, military self-interest to embrace multinational environmental and social concerns.

Ultimately, however much we try to convince ourselves to the contrary, human pursuits (both overt and covert) continue to shape the future, unleashing surprising developments and creating further unpredictable complexities. In this uncertain world, sorting fact from fiction is sometimes absurdly difficult, especially at levels of detail. Much depends on the veracity and integrity of the stories we choose to communicate – or not. For example, if global communications really are creating 'one world' why are news media increasingly provincial and inward looking? And if the corporate media is worried about falling audiences among people of non-Western backgrounds, to what extent is the media itself to blame? Has it anything to do with an underlying belief within corporate media that they have a monopoly on 'the truth' and that other media transmitted merely conspiracy theories?

> For all the increasing tensions between Arabs, Jews, Christians, Muslims and neo-conservatives, many are united on one thing: increasing, and increasingly visceral distaste for the output from large English-language broadcast media organisations such as BBC television and radio (though not its World Service radio network) and CNN. There are many reasons for this, but three stand out very clearly:
>
> • The question as to why so many of those who broadcast for large media organisations find it difficult to portray neutrally the lives of those who live in poverty and for whom faith is integral to life – whether in the West or in the East.

- The tendency to reduce events that are achingly complex into simplistic debates, and ones that are mostly devoid of history, context or insight.
- The entirely justified belief that, all too often, large media organisations lead their news bulletins with stories whose origins lie in a press release, press conference or unattributable briefing by the government – even if this is not always acknowledged in news reports.[17]

One thing is sure: if more people from Jewish and Muslim communities are refusing to watch or interact with journalists from the establishment media, it means that these groups are slowly being starved of essential sources of knowledge, information, and commentary on current events. They will instead have to increasingly rely on speculation from reporters, on hidden cameras and microphones, and on briefings from government departments or intelligence agencies in western countries. There will, as a consequence, be very little scope to confirm or to check the accuracy of the information they are being provided. News will increasingly be news when a government minister says it is and we will all be the poorer for it.

Another feature shaping our perception of reality is the effect today's pervasive 'culture of complaint' is having on everything from journalism to scientific research. For example, an increasing willingness to litigate at the drop of a hat has produced media networks that shy away from any material deemed to be 'offensive' (an imprecise term linked to an equally vague understanding of 'community standards') or that could cost them money in fines and troublesome publicity. In spite of denials to the contrary, such behaviour invariably trickles down to the creators of programmes who then self-censor in order to make their material more marketable. The compulsion to avoid being offensive has led to a false narrative in which the term *offence* is spoken of as though empirically understood and accepted by all.

In his most recent book, *Censoring Culture: Contemporary Threats to Free Expression*, art historian Robert Atkins notes how conflict (particularly in terms of television and moving images) often drives the media to play equally negative and positive roles in society. He explains this by citing the controversy surrounding a show about the Holocaust at the Jewish Museum in New York a couple of years ago. This admirable and highly intelligent exhibition, comprising contemporary art related to the Holocaust, attempted to broaden public conversation about the Holocaust.

The museum was very aware that this show might be controversial but went to great lengths to ensure that the material could not be considered objectionable. They studied it with community groups and curators brought their board into the discussion. Eventually the museum mounted a very commendable exhibition that raised important issues. But they made the mistake of publishing the catalogue two months before the exhibition opened. One of the tabloid presses owned by Rupert Murdoch read the catalogue and looked at the pictures. Of course, none of these editors could possibly imagine that a work of art might be different in person than it is on a printed page. The press savaged the museum two months before the show opened, suggesting that the show was a blatant celebration of Hitler and his regime. This undoubtedly increased the circulation for the newspapers but also put pressure on politicians who came down firmly on the side of the 'censors'. The exhibition was closed without further debate.

Much corporate funding, too, is tantamount to censorship although it happens behind closed doors. Phillipe de Montebello, the director of the Metropolitan Museum of Art in New York, pointed out to *Newsweek* in 1982 that, like every other museum, the Metropolitan Museum of Art relies on corporate funding to keep it going. He cited the 2005 exhibition *Chanel*, which was almost totally funded by the House of Chanel. This show was a completely one-sided and uncritical view of Coco Chanel, who appears to have had quite a dubious past as someone who made her money during Vichy France buying properties that previously belonged to Jews. It isn't really the function of a museum to mount such shows. As tax-exempt institutions, museums have a mandate to pursue a purpose that is essentially educational. Although in this case the museum did not act out of any inherently evil motive, the need to survive financially, especially in times such as these when government subsidies for the arts remain so incredibly low, inevitably creates conflicts of interest that remain hidden from public gaze. Whether it's in the art world, publishing, science or politics, today's practitioners are inhibited by so many social conditions (ranging from copyright laws to stringent policing of the Internet) impeding freedom of expression, that it is difficult for anyone to see through the layers of deceit, exaggeration and hyperbole. The subtle, insidious nature of modern censorship has defined the parameters of what we are and are not willing to say. In that sense it has become a camouflaged shaper of reality.

Another, more obvious, human activity shaping our reading of the future is the rate of technological innovation, especially the flood of new computerised gadgets inundating world markets that is now the most tangible face of the digital age. Consumers everywhere take this endless stream of novelty for granted. We wear technology like a second skin, imbuing it almost with a sense of piety. Indeed, it has become so indispensable that the world's entire telecommunications grid depends upon it operating without any glitches – a part of the global 'e-topia'[18] increasingly enveloping us. But is new technology really that significant? Or is that, too, merely another passing fad?

Virtual Society, a multinational project sponsored by the Economic and Social Research Council in Britain, found many of the social claims associated with the Internet, for example, to be hyperbole at best; myths perpetuated by the industry to promote its products. Although we are repeatedly presented with a picture of escalating Internet use, there is also evidence of saturation and a subsequent drop-off in use among many millions of young people. A recent global survey indicated that growth in the use of the Internet has come off its sizzling pace, even as people become more dependent on cyberspace for work and leisure. In 2005 the global online population grew at just 5%, well behind the 20% seen in 2004. Growth will slow again in 2006 in spite of the use of newer devices, like iPods, wireless notebooks and mobile phones for accessing the Internet.[19]

On the other hand, perhaps measuring growth of the Internet in the coming years will be less about user volume and more about consumers' reliance on this medium as a way of life. Whether it is checking news feeds, using VoIP telephony (where the strongest early adopter markets appear to be in 'old' Europe), blogging, or picking up a podcast, people continue to expand and apply new depth of Internet use that has not been seen before. Meanwhile in East Asia, the urban Chinese market is evolving rapidly into one of the most dynamic Internet-based economies in the world, with among the heaviest Internet usage of any of the countries measured at 17.9 hours per week online!

As fears of a global economic downturn hover like a ghost in the ether, a sudden and unexpected dip in Internet advertising revenue has forced many media groups to reorganise their online strategies and reaffirm their faith in newspapers and television stations. Then again, what if the unthinkable should happen and the Internet stalls. David D. Clark of MIT warns that, for the average user today, the Internet resembles Times Square in the 1980s: exciting and vibrant but with drugs, robberies and insane people. Times Square has been cleaned up, but the Internet keeps getting worse. Security patches aren't keeping pace.

Some 43% of US users have reported spyware or adware on their computers; IBM says viruses and criminal attacks jumped by 50% in the first half of 2005; Symantec reports that spam surged 77% at companies it monitored in the last half of 2004 and that 60% of all email was spam. At a time when more Internet connections are being made than ever before, is it possible that this particular piece of technology will not change things as dramatically and rapidly as we have been led to expect or will simply disappear? What is fact and what is fiction?

Or take as another example the situations arising from our arbitrary division of the planet into a number of artificial compartments known as 'countries' that take it upon themselves to enact and enforce laws, with or without the consent of their citizens. Many alternative thinkers have argued the nation-state is being so weakened by the political and socioeconomic factors underpinning globalism that it may be doomed as a useful institution. They point to the fact that on almost every significant issue in so-called Western democracies, the public sector is being marginalised. National sovereignty is being ceded to big business (perhaps unintentionally) as statism becomes more irrelevant at every turn. Rabid xenophobia and issues of national identity take centre stage in many countries. Meanwhile the incredible growth of the knowledge economy and its associated industries is occurring in spite of government regulation, not because of it. On the one hand the nation-state seems doomed. On the other, patriotic fervour breathes fresh life into the corpse. It is true that there are moves in certain parts of the world to lessen the effects of national borders. This is particularly noticeable in Europe, the continent that has suffered most in the last two centuries from the ravages of nationalism. It is now possible to travel from one end of Europe to the other with a single passport. Is this progress, or could it simply be seen as a return to the situation that existed before the nineteenth century gave rise to the nation-state?

While temporary travel is one thing, permanent immigration is quite another. Most European countries are locked in debate over who should be allowed to live where, and violence and intimidation against immigrants is widespread. Even countries that were largely built through immigration, such as the US and Australia, are becoming more and more wary as to whom they will admit. The 'poor and huddled masses' in North Africa are yearning to enter Europe, the southern border of the US is one long immigration queue, and Asia is awash with political and economic refugees. This is unlikely to end. Where does that leave the nation-state in terms of relevance? What is the fact and what is the fiction?

Obviously, these are exceedingly complex issues. So let us, for a moment, ponder a few relatively simple ideas that also pose some thought-provoking contradictions. In 1938, the *New York Times* confidently predicted the demise of the common pencil. In 1975, *Business Week* predicted paper was running out. In 1980, IBM calculated that the world market for personal computers over the next decade would be 275,000 machines. The actual number proved to be 60 million! Over the same time period the volume of office paper used in the US doubled from 42 kilograms to 84 kilograms per head. More famously, oil has been forecast to peak anywhere between 1970 and 2010.[20] This kind of predictive thinking is perpetuated in many of our most eagerly accepted management myths. *Endism*, for example, foresees the end of the corporation and bureaucracy, the end of books, television and mass media, the end of the personal computer, the end of the nation-state, monarchies and politics – even the end of history! I do not imagine for one moment that all these things will necessarily survive. But it's quite another thing to predict no need for such institutions and organisations. Paradoxically, one way to sort fact from fiction is to develop peripheral vision – to look *around* not just blindly *ahead* in order to perceive patterns of connection that signify something more tangible than fleeting chimera.

The gap between prediction and reality shows how far off track some forecasts can get. What seemed inevitable just a few years ago, such as flatter organisations, self-managing teams and smaller companies, now just seem quaint. And what was improbable then, now seems blindingly obvious. Rather than flatter organisations, for example, the numbers of non-production staff in manufacturing has risen steadily as a proportion of the total workforce.[21] Highly centralised data systems have entrenched top-down management, putting decision making in fewer rather than more hands. And despite claims of the new economy spawning ever smaller and agile companies, large companies are actually consolidating. The big are getting bigger. The rich are getting richer. Wordwide mergers soared 30% to a record $US1.2 trillion in the first quarter of 2000, with AOL's $US164 billion purchase of Time Warner among the 10 largest.

Again, perhaps hot-desking and telecommuting were more wishful thinking rather than fact. When British Telecom embraced telecommuting it discovered some of its employees were going stir crazy from the isolation. Their solution was to pipe background chatter into home offices. Likewise, when Chiat-Day moved to hot-desking as a means of keeping their workforce on the creative edge, they were confronted by a civil disobedience campaign. So, even in issues as apparently clear-cut as these, it is not always possible to avoid delusion. How then can we even begin to discover the truth?

Well, for one thing, it would certainly help to reverse the trend of the past 500 years and start reintegrating human knowledge. For another, we must start posing sharper, more perceptive questions. Unstable ambient conditions could be monitored more attentively: that would be more likely to generate a deeper understanding of the fundamental forces impelling 'surface' activity – the order within chaos. Multiple viewpoints could be sought more frequently, instead of immediately discarding interpretations that jar with personal experience. It would help profits if businesses were to listen to their customers more attentively and it would benefit society if elected governments took better note of their citizens' longer term desires. Perhaps the real key, though, is to appreciate the interdependent, ever-shifting, dynamic between themes and issues (*content*) and the framework in which those things interact (*context*).

It is now simply impossible, indeed pointless, for us to live our lives in segregated compartments. Our organisations and communities teem with human transactions and relationships, creating a complex emergent social ecology that can both encumber and enhance. Ultimately, though, it is this exchange of ideas, the social networks and physical proximity that facilitate innovation – the lifeblood for any enterprise today. This is why Silicon Valley and similar industry clusters around the world, as well as global supply chains, for example, make a mockery of another *endism* – the death of distance. Furthermore, it is the social nature of work and learning that highlight some of the limitations of traditional management theory, particularly in such areas as business process reengineering and statistical process control, for example. Both of these methods invariably take a monolithic view of organisations and focus on economic efficiency, productivity and effectiveness. Ill-equipped to deal with the complexity of human interaction, they ignore all the fuzzy, imperceptible, apparently non-value-adding stuff occurring in the background – including the unconscious knowledge, undisclosed talent, informal networks and lateral ties that are totally hidden from the expert brought in to focus on processes.

The point is that, although the rate of technological innovation is a significant driver of change, making predictions about innovation *per se* is incredibly foolish. Innovation is primarily about human beings – with all their diversity, imprecision and unpredictability. You will find the results of all this chaos everywhere; in our schools, corporations, cities and parliaments. Capricious, intuitive, ambivalent, spontaneous and working to a different kind of logic, humans are ultimately the ones who determine what information means and why it matters.

And so, for all the talk about global villages and electronic frontiers a stroll down the village footpath for a chat to neighbours is still one of the most satisfying of human experiences. And a pencil and paper still come in handy. Which only illustrates the perils of separating raw data from its situation and text from context: it creates one-dimensional *tunnel* thinking. Tunnel thinking is the most noticeable failing under-pinning the digerati hype and fervent prophecies of the end of the world as we know it. It is the kind of thinking, too, that fails to acknowledge the complexities of the soft systems that smudge the edges, particularly the ways that help people learn, reflect and converse together. Library catalogues, filofax organisers and black-edged letters may be on the way out, but when the world is drowning in so much information, paper is proving to be more resistant than expected. The fax with the annotated scribbles down the side, tablet notebooks and self-adhesive notes direct-ing us where to look further have entrenched it.

So how do we tease out ambiguous fictions from irrefutable factual evidence? Where do we draw the line between tolerance of certain views and instant rejection of others? Is it purely a matter of intuition? Research? Validation perhaps? And if the latter, what constitutes accept-able proof? Or are we simply creatures of habit after all, accepting information on the basis of numerical or anecdotal evidence even when our every instinct contradicts such passive and unquestioning agree-ment? It is not as though these are unimportant questions. What we see through our eyes, (literally our window onto the world) along with the preconceptions and filters we have in place to interpret what we see, determines what actions we are likely to be able to take to change or improve things. If *what* we see or *how* we see it is flawed or too narrow (and, as illustrated in the above examples, it often is) then our vision will be defective and our aspirations will fall far short of our potential. We will see only what we expect to see (or want to see) and any responses to which we commit ourselves will most likely be off target – lacking the coherence, unity and effectiveness we seek. No individual, organisation or society can expect to survive today's volatile environment with defective vision, especially if outmoded models, inaccurate maps and incomplete data are still being used to interpret and make sense of what is being seen.

This is particularly the case for business. As markets become smarter faster than most companies, so the need for continuous reinvention and development of new business models, guided by new maps of the strategic landscape, become a necessity. Inclusive mental constructs of reality are needed since the old ones are not sufficiently eloquent to explain the emergent complexity of our world. In fact a more integral understanding of how our world actually works, including what is essential and what is not, is also urgently required.

Then there are also the tools we need to enhance communication with each other, to explore our most unresolvable dilemmas and accommodate the kinds of paradox that increasingly beset contemporary institutions. Over 200 years of corporatism, sexism, colonialism, racism and elitism are entrenched within our management practices. So much so, that most organisations can still only communicate in the most contrived, humourless bourdon of mission statements, marketing brochures and 'your-call-is-important-to-us' engaged signals. Simplistic either–or solutions are of no help whatsoever when conditions change so dramatically within hours or even minutes of our having arrived at a 'correct' decision. More sophisticated methods are needed to explore collaborative approaches to problem resolution. They need to be designed to reflect the complex richness of the human condition, viewing issues holistically rather than as simple linear problems for which there can be only one correct answer.

Regrettably, unorthodox notions such as these are only just beginning to hold credence with those entrusted to manage our business corporations and government institutions. We mostly cling like limpets to the past, rejecting out of hand any suggestion that the management *science* we have so painstakingly perfected over two centuries should now need replacing. Perhaps we are becoming more sceptical or are simply disinclined to believe that today's problems are so incredibly complex in comparison with those of our predecessors. For whatever specious arguments are advanced to preserve and protect the status quo, there really can be no disputing that the field of management to which we have become so devoted had its genesis within industrial culture. In the end, therefore, it is just another dispensable product of *industrial economism.* And if the mechanistic tools and techniques of this product are no longer sufficient for our needs, then these too are dispensable.

Contemporary strategic management practices comprise highly evolved systems for planning, control and coordination, resource deployment, accounting, monitoring and reporting. Increasingly, the best of these use technology in ways that provide a comprehensive current depiction of the business. Or that is the intention, at least!

During the past decade, massive shifts have occurred in the production functions of firms, which, to date, have been the major assets driving value and creating growth. Meanwhile, the trusted mechanisms upon which we constantly depend for accurate monitoring, measuring and reporting have, to all intents and purposes, stagnated. They remain bogged down in old paradigm thinking.

Accounting, for example, arguably the most pervasive and impregnable measurement and reporting component of Western management orthodoxy, is becoming increasingly irrelevant in the evolution to an *appreciative* age.[22] In our industrial past, numbers gave us permission to believe. Because changes in the strategic landscape were gradual, even foreseeable, numbers reinforced the impression of stability. This, in turn, provided confidence for taking action, a vital strategic element in determining how and when to make competitive forays into the industry-dominated marketplace. Today's strategic landscape, though, is in a constant state of disruption. Boosted by the knowledge economy and the information-based business ecosystems it spawns, stasis is now death. Accounting is hopelessly ineffective at capturing the dynamics and drivers of the knowledge economy, where value is created not through *tangible* goods or observable transactions but through *intangibles* such as brands, designs, patents, intellectual property, unique ways of working and franchises. Furthermore, as noted by US economist John Kendrick, there has been a general increase in the contribution of intangible assets to world economic growth since the early 1900s. In 1929, for example, the ratio of intangible to tangible business capital in the US was 30% to 70%. By 1989 that ratio had flipped to become 63% to 37%.

Conventional accounting practices, too, cannot accurately capture the value of contributions made by people – their ideas, energy and endeavours. Neither can they be used to assess with any degree of accuracy the strategic viability of an opportunity, or even the ongoing performance of a project in these new dynamics. They can't answer explicit questions like: *Is our company paying too much to acquire the knowledge-based assets of their company?* Even more generic questions such as: *Are knowledge-based companies overvalued on the stock market?* seem to be beyond their means to resolve. It is not as though such questions can't be answered. They are really not that complex. Just complicated.[23] Such questions go far beyond the capabilities of traditional methods of accounting. As a consequence they no longer deliver adequate accountability. And yet we continue to use a 500-year-old system (including published balance sheets that may represent perhaps only 10–20% of the true value of a company) to make daunting decisions in a volatile business environment in which the essential assets that create value have fundamentally changed. Accounting is not the only culprit of course. Because of changes in society, there will always be a need to upgrade and reinvent management practices. At the same time, we must create altogether more elegant, strategically appropriate systems for managing the value arising from intangibles.

There can be no doubt that current accounting methods can be improved. On the other hand, perhaps an entirely new system of knowledge, comprising authoritative ways of calculating knowledge assets, knowledge earnings (actual and potential) and for valuing the kind of structural capital that gives a company the potential to innovate, could be designed.[24] Although challenging, such a system would have obvious advantages. It would allow the valuing of employees' contributions more accurately. Fewer mistakes would be made in terms of valuing a company's true worth. Investors would be able to make better decisions with less distortion than at present. Even more important, the market would have real-time information of a firm's value.[25]

There are probably numerous investment executives and financial analysts who would vigorously oppose such changes, claiming them as unnecessary or misleading. They believe their privileged personal networks give them access to confidential information they would lose once that information became publicly available. I suspect most senior managers, too, would flinch and resist any reform of this nature. They are, after all, perfectly happy with a system that reduces their legal liability – and that of their accountants. Some are probably convinced that time-honoured accounting methods still provide sufficient means for them to manage comprehensively and effectively. Many others, however, are unlikely to have given these issues much more than a passing thought, so programmed into the collective unconscious is our almost reflex acceptance of the suitability and sacrosanct nature of current management methods.

It should come as no big surprise, therefore, to learn that the majority of us still trust in a management orthodoxy that is wholly unsustainable in today's global knowledge economy. As a consequence we persist in educating aspiring young executives as though the prevailing system is exemplary, requiring only slight modifications for it to endure indefinitely. It is true that some management education programmes masquerade under fairly obvious and unremarkable veneers by using trendy jargon or paying lip service to the latest fads. But scratch below the market hype of most courses, including growing numbers of MBAs, and all you will unearth are the recycled, tired and festering worldviews of *industrial economism.*

This is precisely where *five literacies* leadership is lacking, yet is most needed. We are now running on blind faith, our gaze permanently fixed on the rearview mirror of past experience that reflects only by chance our present direction and impending state. Existing methods for managing and organising funnel us into being past orientated. Homogeneous. Expert. Corporate. Paternalistic. Risk-averse. And Eurocentric! Burdened, too, by a legacy of inherited assumptions and administrative paraphernalia, they have become far too sluggish to generate confidence in any but the most dim-witted or traumatised of politicians, bureaucrats, executives and company directors. Above all they prohibit imagination, serendipity, passion, reflection, humanity, spontaneity, intuition, novelty and lucidity – vital qualities for remaining viable in the uncertain and complex global business environment likely to characterise the coming age of *appreciative ecologies.*

All in all, we are likely to find the renewal of business processes and protocols, so that they remain prosperous while becoming culturally, socially and environmentally viable, the most challenging and profound of obligations. Especially if we continue to be stifled by a reluctance to reinvent methodologies for organising and managing human activities. As we learn to better comprehend the multifaceted, nonlinear characteristics of the world we are creating, two important insights emerge. First, we are realising that our world is actually unfathomable (and therefore largely unmanageable in the traditional sense) due to the chaotic connectedness and astonishing rate of disruptive change inherent within global interdependencies. Second, it has become obvious that only multidimensional change models, like those employed in nature's living systems, for example, are able to capture anything approaching the true dynamic nature of this complexity.

The reasons for this are staring us in the face. Living systems are morphogenic: positive feedback loops impel different parts of the system over critical thresholds simultaneously. This capability allows living systems to change *how* they change, constantly generating novelty and evolving surprising new structure. If communities, governments and business organisations are to have any hope of remaining viable during the turbulent transition from the age of *industrial economism* to the increasingly digital age of *appreciative ecologies* they, too, will need to apply morphogenic models of change. By designing organisations and their practices around ecological principles, however, it is inevitable that an alternative philosophy of business and its management will ultimately evolve.

Aligned with society's appreciative ethos, management praxis will integrate *appreciative* concepts into a more sustainable social and environmental framework rather than focus on the purely business related, ego-driven models of our immediate past. *Appreciative* ecologies will give rise not merely to improvements on past practices but entirely new methods founded on integrative models and techniques that are more in harmony with today's uncertain and dynamic global conditions. And, of course, entirely new capabilities will be required in order that we can adequately fulfil our redefined roles within society. This is what the capacity for renewal means and it is already integral to the space in which truly smart leaders play.

Although it remoulds almost every known organisational convention, for example, one of the more significant innovations within the *five literacies* knowledge base is the manner in which Strategic Navigation uses intelligence. It is commonly recognised that, as greater numbers of critical factors change within an organisation's *external* environment, so complexity increases and additional changes are required *internally* to maintain strategic 'fit'. Real strategic responsiveness (crowds and communities acting coherently in the moment, like the Mexican wave phenomenon) only becomes possible and subsequently sustainable where strategy is a continuous, collaborative cycle of collecting information, synthesising significant patterns, and responding to these as rapidly as possible by making subtle yet appropriate changes in previously identified capability leverage points. Typically these are to be found in the organisation's infrastructure, knowledge and skills base, technologies, plans, cultures, social networks and frameworks.

This approach is essentially heuristical (exploratory) and continuous in nature, reliant as it is upon the organisation acting to the best of its ability on available intelligence, keeping a close eye on the results, and making appropriate corrections as rapidly as possible if intentions are not being realised. In Strategic Navigation this exploratory approach to negotiating systemic conditions in real time is allocated to a designated group of highly skilled people who work from distributed nerve centres (decision theatres or operations rooms) to shape and evolve the organisational system. The kind of strategic learning illustrated by these 'decision theatre' practices enables consciousness of the moment within the context of an expanded 'now'. It facilitates *responsiveness* and *adaptiveness* – the ability to remain focused while changing instantly. It creates energy and it enhances confidence for taking informed action. Effective strategic learning of this kind is necessary in order for organisations to remain viable. Experienced as a continuous braid of thinking and acting, and navigating the waters between the past and the future, it is this propensity towards shared learning that creates the momentum for change without which any preferred future is sure to fade.[26]

NOTES

1. Author of *No Logo*, Flamingo, London, 2001.
2. Moynihan, R. and Cassels, A., *Selling Sickness: How the World's Biggest Pharmaceutical Companies are Turning us all into Patients*, Nation Books, New York, 2005.
3. Autopoiesis refers to the capacity of an organism or living system to exhibit a self-organising (or adaptive) nature.
4. We all inhabit social and business ecosystems. Personal ecosystems, for example, comprise our relationships with people and institutions that are important or necessary for our personal health and well being. Likewise, business ecosystems comprise the various stakeholder webs, together with their relationships and influence over each other from one moment to the next, that are vital to maintain if the business is to fulfil its niche within that ecosystem and therefore remain viable. As discrete industries, forged at the time of the Industrial Revolution, continuously change in a bewildering game of shifting alliances and strategic partnerships, so the boundaries around traditional industry groupings begin to merge and blur – to such an extent that the term 'industry' becomes almost unusable in the context of the knowledge economy. More expansive still than the customer–supplier networks of the so-called extended enterprise, business ecosystems are the socioeconomic communities comprising a number of interacting 'agents' (customers, suppliers, regulators, intermediaries, lead producers, competitors and other stakeholders) that co-evolve over time in alignment with the directions set by one or more principal members.
5. Although the future is essentially unknowable, human beings have always endeavoured to create a different world from the one they currently inhabit. Where structures and outcomes form a unified vision within a community, depicted in expressions of a 'preferred' future, they become both aspirational and inspirational in a strategic sense.
6. One possible reason for this state of affairs is that the funding for the development of new management technologies frequently derives from

conservative business sources intent on becoming more efficient global profit maximisers within the current business paradigm (e.g. Citibank's funding of research into chaos theory undertaken by the Santa Fe Institute).

7. It has long been recognised by biologists that all living systems require a balance between competition and cooperation in order to survive.

8. According to Brian Prentice a research director of Gartner (*Gartner Group Report – July 2006*) it is better not to believe the hype when it comes to new technologies. In quantifying the true potential of emerging products, a technology can still be relatively immature but carry very high visibility. In tracking the successes and failures of particular technologies, Gartner has come up with an 'evolutionary hype' cycle. This cycle begins with the technology 'trigger' and moves through a number of stages, the first of which is described as a 'peak of inflated expectations'. While technologies with inflated expectations will not necessarily fail, they are prone to un-realistic optimism. For instance, the commercialisation of digital paper, which contains tiny beads that can change color to form text and images, is likely to be driven mainly by mobile display manufacturers for the next two years rather than finding immediate mainstream application. Mashups, which integrate multi-sourced applications or content into a single offering, will also experience delays on the path to mainstream acceptance owing to vulnerabilities in combining data and logic from multiple sources. Next in the cycle comes the 'trough of disillusionment' which hits after a tech-nology has failed to meet its hyped expectations and media interest begins to fade. Despite originally very high hopes for the tablet PC, for example, it has not become mainstream. While some innovations do not survive the trough of disillusionment, others move beyond it to reach what Gartner refers to as 'the slope of enlightenment'. This is where the true benefits of a particular technology begin to be appreciated by the mainstream. This can lead to a 'plateau of productivity' where a product is widely adopted and reaches a certain level of stability. A good example of a product that has entered these latter stages is VoIP, which is now consid-ered a proven technology by most consumers and enterprises with domes-tic and global carriers staking future service portfolios on VoIP-based technologies. Despite the changes in specific technologies over the years, the hype cycle's underlying message remains the same: Don't invest in a technology just because it is being hyped, and don't ignore a technology just because it is not living up to early expectations.

9. Variously referred to by different commentators as the 'knowledge' economy or the 'experience' economy.

10. For example, the gender myth of the male breadwinner, inextricably linked to a deliberately narrow definition of 'full' employment, assumed a male head of household and was therefore predicated on the exclusion of women (or over half the population) from the workforce.

11. Politics is one such example. Recent elections in many Western democracies have been too close to call, with low voter turnouts indicating a growing impatience with mainstream politics, perceived political corruption, spin doctoring and sound-bite campaigning. This became most evident in the 2000 election for the US presidency between George W. Bush and incumbent Vice President Al Gore. Although Gore won the popular vote, a single state, together with five Justices of the Supreme Court, were key in making Bush the eventual winner. The closeness of the race erupted in a public furore when the integrity of the voting system in Florida, as well as the role of the Electoral College, were openly challenged.

12. Hertz, Noreena, *The Silent Takeover: Global Capitalism and the Death of Democracy*, Heinemann, New York, 2001.

13. Given scraps of intelligence regarding, for example, global demographics such as birth rates and migration of Muslims to Asia (rather than Europe), the unstoppable nature of the Asian economy led by China and India, the failure of the Western alliance to deal effectively with the root causes of terrorism, coupled with growing anti-US sentiment as a result of ill-advised foreign policies and naive worldviews, it is possible to craft a plausible long-term scenario in which Western civilisation and its instruments have collapsed and where personal safety, a high quality of lifestyle and security is best enjoyed in an Asian bloc where the dominant political system is one of benign authoritarianism rather than 'classical' democracy. This is unthinkable to many in the West but is not impossible to envisage in the longer term and is, I believe, a distinct possibility given current socioeconomic and geopolitical trends.

14. An obvious example is the break up of the old Soviet Union symbolised by the dismantling of the Berlin Wall in August 1991.

15. This in spite of the fact that possibly 70% of mergers and acquisitions fail to live up to the initial flush of excitement as well as the promise of greater returns for shareholders through rationalisation and other economies of scale.

16. Typically centred on self-reliance, human rights and meeting the basic needs of grassroots populations.

17. Ehsan Masood, Project Director for the Gateway Trust, writing in Open Democracy on 22 August 2006 in an essay entitled *Big Media, Small World*.

18. 'e-topias' refers to a new form of urban infrastructure – one that will create sustainable cities as well as making social, economic and cultural sense in an electronically interconnected world. The term is increasingly used by those technocrats and politicians who are dedicated to transforming our fractured society into a wired global village where 'working smarter' is used to overcome all of the problems caused by *industrial economism*.

19. 'The Face of the Web' study conducted by Ipsos Insight surveys 6500 people in 12 countries annually.

20. The late Dr M. King Hubbert, geophysicist, is well known as a world authority on the estimation of energy resources and on the prediction of their patterns of discovery and depletion. He was probably the best known geophysicist in the world to the general public because of his startling prediction, first made public in 1949, that the fossil fuel era would be of very short duration, 'Energy from fossil fuels', *Science*, 4 February, 1949. His prediction in 1956 that US oil production would peak in about 1970 and decline thereafter was scoffed at then but his analysis has since proved to be remarkably accurate.

21. Data taken from the US Bureau of Labor statistics.

22. *Appreciative age* – the hypothesis of a self-organising society able to learn its way into preferred futures, in ethical reciprocity with its environment and in ways that are 'appreciative' of all its members needs, expectations and desires.

23. Complicated (from the root *plica* meaning fold upon fold) differs from complex (from the root *plexus* indicating a woven pattern).

24. Structural capital is another form of knowledge asset that has to do with the unique way companies like Dell and eBay, for example, do business. Structural capital is considered to be a part of knowledge earnings.

25. Proposed by Baruch Lev, Professor of Accounting and Finance at New York University and author of *Intangibles: Management, Measurement and Reporting*.

26. There are two questions critical to improving any situation: Where do we want to be? How do we get there? If we have no destination in mind any path will do. If we know where we want to be, however, (in other words we have a preferred future) we can take courses of action that enable a relatively smooth journey.

CHAPTER 6

RESPONSIVENESS RULES

Modern organizations need to learn quickly about changes in their core technologies and also about shifts in their environments. Fast perception is vital. But when it comes to action, different tempos can apply.

– John Thakara, *In the Bubble*

Traditional notions of leadership seem to be a bundle of problematic concepts – like vision and the idea that leadership is somehow measurable. Typically, most leadership theories all too often ignore the context within which the thing called *leadership* is exercised. Many people almost exclusively assume that the roll of a leader is to punctuate a set of external circumstances, assuming that context is beyond the scope of leadership. But if a *leader* exercises *leadership* in a context wherein all decisions he or she makes is limited, and there is an 'other' responsible for that context, then who is actually 'leading'?

Context in most companies (including their networks) seems to be a conspiracy born of a thousand egos which flip intention, and thereby causation, based on the intellectualised pursuit of a few conflicting goals. What emerges is a mess. In this mess, leaders who attract attention rely on a sharp mind and clear convictions to navigate their way through numerous obstacles. But there are people in this same mess who manage to create a pattern or environment that provides a healthier set of circumstances wherein which others are able to make better decisions. These are *five literacies* leaders and they behave in uncommon ways:[1]

- They are thoughtfully opinionated.
- They practise a fidelity of intention.
- They are incredibly well connected and take great delight in linking people and ideas.
- They are curious and passionate about learning.
- They don't suffer from an overwhelming ego – often they go almost unnoticed for this reason.
- They practise a generosity of spirit.

This type of behaviour ripples through orders of consequence beyond measurement to emerge into what we call context. In other words, they help to create that which is unintended but on which every company relies for their success. Viability. Regrettably, for these poor souls, seldom does anyone point the finger and call them a leader, unless this is obvious by virtue of their public standing. They may have no visions or grand plans, no employees or management teams to supervise, no KPIs by which they can be measured and rewarded. But none of this means they are not leaders.

Perhaps this deeper form of *five literacies* leadership is an aesthetic. Something that is felt deeply rather than seen. Art rather than pornography?[2] The same might be said of organisations. We have always imagined our organisations to be nothing other than stable, predictable, mechanisms operating in an environment that is equally fixed and predetermined. Of course, nothing could be further from the truth. But the illusion of stability is seductive. Held within its thrall, we conjure madcap schemes in the belief that conditions will remain sufficiently stable for long enough to allow success, thus reinforcing our conviction that we are masters of the future. Oblivious to systemic consequences, we then proceed to hand down our plans from *above* for compliant execution *below* without ever establishing the real-time feedback mechanisms that will allow us to see whether our original intentions are being realised. Or even if these are still strategically appropriate. In this 'command and control' environment choice, creativity and order exist only by prior design. Emergence and evolution are totally ignored.

More pernicious still is our psychological dependence upon these practices. Unseen and unchallenged they ensnare us within a prevailing worldview that is utterly inadequate for managing the cataclysmic upheaval we are experiencing in society. Companies persisting with this worldview do so at their own peril, for global markets are dancing to a different tune. Three interdependent themes are creating the need for an entirely new leadership praxis. One that is mindful of the principles underpinning complex adaptive systems[3] and that will enable organisations to learn, operate and change in the here and now:

- *There is no need to wait.* Global connectivity enables corporations to make important decisions (and serious money) around the clock. Furthermore the phenomenon of regular business hours has all but vanished. Call centres, for example, routinely handle enquiries from halfway around the world in order to benefit from different time zones. In effect, time has collapsed into a continuous 'now'. It is no longer a constraint.
- *Experiences are richer.* New information and communications technologies like the Internet enrich and transform every transactional experience – affording access to the enterprise in deeply personalised ways that allow us to compare products, ponder investment decisions, interact with staff – even help design new goods and services.
- *Everything is speeding up.* Successive generations of computers are reducing cycle times while simultaneously collapsing transaction costs – speeding up everything from work flows and business processes to the acquisition of strategic intelligence.

No enterprise has the luxury of choosing whether or not to engage in the experience-enriched, time-compressed turmoil of this new global economy. Technology is forcing small businesses, large multinational corporations and government bureaucracies alike to be responsive to market dynamics that can shift in a flash. And without prior warning! Meanwhile customers with access to global markets make highly personalised demands in real time, taking their custom elsewhere if their needs are not precisely met.

The implications for managing and leading contemporary organisations in real time are profound and, once again, challenge much of the logic we have previously valued and learned to take for granted. The holy grail of performance excellence, for example, something all great companies constantly strive for, is not necessarily all it is cracked up to be in today's environment. In fact continuous performance excellence can actually shipwreck the healthiest business. You might not realise that by looking at the number of publications available on every aspect of performance planning, management and improvement all urging us to achieve excellence in order to assure longevity. Over the past five years almost 40% of all management books published have been about ways to improve business performance and large numbers of schemes, processes and tools are devised to help managers achieve this goal. It stands to reason that excellent performance is what customers want and consequently is what any business must achieve in order to remain viable. But remember, we are not dealing with rationality any more. Because of the complexity of business today we are dealing with a paradox even here.

And the paradox is this: a business must provide excellence in order to compete effectively in today's global markets. But excellence is not sufficient by itself. There are two traps awaiting the unwary. Firstly, in striving to achieve excellence, performance standards are frequently set so high that customer expectations become difficult to achieve and even more impossible to sustain – in other words *over*-promising and *under*delivering. In this situation the smallest mistake or lapse can trigger an immediate fall from grace. Secondly, assuming excellence *can* be achieved, sustained levels of exceptional performance can actually be detrimental if customers are not constantly aware and do not appreciate the value they are getting. Outstanding performance by itself, especially recorded over years at a time, can only guarantee complacency in today's 'experience' economy.

In fact the better and more consistently services are provided, the greater is the danger that such performance becomes commoditised. Companies that routinely provide excellent service to their clients run the risk of appearing invisible as they become an integral part of the client's organisation. They only become noticed when something goes wrong. This can lead to a single negative situation defining an entire relationship between themselves and their customers, which can result in a loss of credibility, trust, rapport, reputation and, ultimately, market share. The trick is to provide sustainable service excellence and also to ensure that clients know just that. Finding new ways to remind customers about the value they are getting and the impact this is having on their business is paramount. To remain invisible in *zero geography* is negligent. *Five literacies* leaders and their businesses create attention through the consistent morality, ethos and transparency of their actions. They recognise the value of being seen and heard, constantly finding ways to attract the attention of customers and potential customers.

Four qualities are important in this regard:

1. *Meeting derived demands*[4]

   Operating in real time demands constant, mindful interaction with all stakeholders so that responses to their derived demands can be as near instantaneous as possible when that is required. If more than a few hours are needed to 'link and think' you are not functioning in real time. Crucial opportunities will be missed, competitors may gain an unassailable advantage and your customers will go where their demands are better met. In effect you become invisible to the market. Not everything needs to be done instantly of course – some experiences (like eating food, taking an evening stroll or riding a city tram) are meant to be savoured – although we seem to be losing the ability to relax and reflect at a slow pace so hectic has life become. Remember, too, that it is in *meeting* (not *exceeding*) derived demands that actual performance is judged. Improving on one's previous performance, by offering more features at less cost, for example, will not necessarily translate into higher perceived value in the market and in any case will probably be matched rapidly by competitors, thereby eradicating any potential advantage. In fact strategies like this are more likely to shift the customers' view of commodity performance upward and the customer to take that new, improved performance for granted. It is only within the context of creating resonant value (value innovation at lower cost) that such offers become feasible due to the quantum leap that is apparent to the market generally.

2. *Removing barriers to responsiveness*

   Producing to derived demand requires jettisoning many traditional organisational functions and processes that shackle or slow down the ability to remain responsive. These include, for example, inventory buffers, bureaucratic distractions, overly detailed plans, annual forecasting and inflexible approaches to budgeting or resource deployment. Running lean management practices helps, but identifying and eradicating all the factors that impede responsiveness is just as critical. This requires managers to view product offerings through the eyes of the customer and be willing and able to match service quality with their perception of value.

3. *Installing a strategic intelligence[5] capability*

   Rapid response to derived demands requires absolute reliability and integrity. But qualities like these are dependent upon adequate business and strategic intelligence. Knowing what is happening in the total business ecosystem[6] of which we are an integral part, making sense of it, then turning this information into intelligence to change *what* we do (and often *how* we do it) is critical in today's business world. This is the first literacy of global leaders. Just as crucial is anticipating what might happen in the future and how we can best respond should circumstances take us by surprise. Establishing a robust strategic intelligence capability requires investment in new organisational infrastructure comprising, for example, real-time audit processes, strategic performance feedback mechanisms, systems for distributing and sharing new knowledge and integrated methods for sensing and making sense of information, developing foresight and managing systemic risk.

4. *Reinventing niche*[7]
   Traditionally, most business models were thought to have a shelf life of around 40 years. Nowadays they can change almost every few months. Businesses constantly reinvent themselves in order to remain aligned with their niche. But future success is not guaranteed simply by competing in the same markets. Continuous strategic innovation is now critical. The ability to enhance the value of the business while lowering costs by moving beyond current competitive space into uncontested markets has become indispensable. W. Chan Kim and Renee Mauborgne of INSEAD,[8] refer to this as 'value innovation'. What they describe is a part of what I refer to as *brand resonance* – the fifth literacy of global leaders. Thus, the ability to remain fluid, to keep changing, embracing uncertainty, complexity and ambiguity as autonomic routines of organisational life, together with the creative harnessing of imagination and intellect now become vital. Reinventing niche is one way to ensure that the business becomes as nimble and adaptive as change itself.

These four qualities are all characteristics of systemic *viability*. Viability means being self-sustaining over time. But it is only possible to remain viable if we intimately connect our inside and outside worlds in ways that integrate knowledge and promote learning to ensure responsiveness and adaptiveness. The extraordinarily swift arrival and immediate impact made by companies like Google, Alibaba.com, Amazon, eBay, Flight Centre, OneWorld Health, Cirque du Soleil, Dell, Ryanair, AirAsia, The Body Shop, Swatch, Nokia, CNN and Bumrungrad Hospital[9] for example, all of whom have come up with innovative business models, overturning long-held assumptions, rewriting the rules for their industry, and transforming relationships in the process, have demonstrated that in the shrinking world of the knowledge economy, insistence upon relevance to an historically established core purpose is not a criterion for viability. Nor are cutting-edge technologies, low-cost marketing or being a high value-added producer or service supplier. Even exercising a monopoly, as many government agencies have traditionally done, is no guarantee of continued success. Openness and responsiveness to strategic intelligence, however, are prerequisites, as is imagination and the development of an organic ability to rapidly apply learning deduced from that intelligence. Arguably, these are the *only* prerequisites, particularly if we want to explore outside the confines of that which we already know and are intimately familiar.

Once again it all comes back to being as open and as adaptive to change as is feasibly possible. In the turbulent transition from our industrial past to a networked future, organisations will only survive if they are capable of continuously reinventing themselves. They must learn to adjust instantly, like living organisms, changing as and when required to maintain alignment with the broader ecosystem of which they are a part. We know that viable organisations appear to behave like living organisms. In fact, the most naturally occurring viable systems are living systems. Unfortunately, living systems are extremely complex organisms, almost impenetrable in their ability to defy logic and reason. In certain environmental conditions, however, living systems have enormous benefits over other, more conventionally structured forms of organising as they tend to *distribute* intelligence outwards. As a consequence, living systems are more:

- Accommodating – adjusting to new or changed circumstances more easily.
- Resourceful – shifting their locus of adaptation over time from one part of the system to another in order to evolve and remain robust.
- Resilient – small failures and individual mistakes are relatively inconsequential and big failures are held in check by becoming smaller failures at a higher level within the system's hierarchy.
- Boundless – by organically extending networks beyond the bounds of their initial states, living systems build their own scaffolding to initiate further structure.
- Novel – through the exponential combinations of many individuals as well as the tolerance of individual imperfection and variation, distributed systems generate perpetual novelty and disturbance.

Apart from their distributed nature, there appear to be at least seven more critical organising principles underpinning viability within living systems.

Table 6.1 The organising principles of natural living systems

Organising principle	Implications for viability
1. Emphasising the nature of *systemic relationships* between an organism and its environment, **ECOLOGY** posits that all things, however apparently separate, are ultimately connected and must therefore affect each other.	We should always take into account how our decisions and interventions may affect the business ecosystem(s) because the whole system will react in some way to our actions – whether intended or not. A reaction may not be instant, nor at the most obvious location. But we can be sure that there will be a reaction at some point in time.
2. Intimately linked to ecology, the notion of **NICHE** is an organism's unique status, role and value it fulfils within a broader ecosystem. Its ability to fulfil this niche directly affects its prospects for survival.	In order to fulfil its niche, our organisation will need to constantly modify and maintain its 'fit' with the business ecosystem, as the ecosystem itself changes over time.
3. **COEVOLUTION** refers to the reciprocity that occurs in interacting species in order for them to evolve. Biological organisms adapt to, and create each other, from one moment to the next, simultaneously weaving themselves into one whole system. The fundamental idea here is that of *adaptation*. Specifically, the capability of the organism to adapt its niche in response to the needs of the total ecosystem.	Applying both to every individual (learning to adapt to the changing needs of the organisation) as well as to the organisation (as it redefines or, at times, even completely transforms itself in response to the changing needs and demands of society) coevolution will often manifest as distinguishable phases in the lifecycle of the organisation as it's identity and role mutate over time.
4. Living systems have a way of evolving into entirely new forms which, at times, are unpredictable and therefore surprising. This is known as **EMERGENCE**. Some viruses, for example, appear to change how they change, making it extremely difficult for research scientists to understand their true nature. When we understand more about the dynamics of	Because emergence is essentially spontaneous, and can neither be predicted nor effectively planned for, it requires special attention. We will need to establish procedures to (a) identify significant emergence as it occurs and (b) treat it, should it pose a strategic risk to the enterprise, or a systemic risk to the business ecosystem.

Table 6.1 *Continued*

Organising principle	Implications for viability
coevolution, however, such novelty is to be expected. In other words, the fact that we encounter surprises is really no surprise.	
5. As far as we can tell, **INTENTIONALITY** is unique to human beings in that we are able to engage ourselves in a process called *consciousness*. We are able to choose a path, and by choosing the direction in which we want our lives to go, are able to bring meaning and purpose to our daily activities.	Based on the clarity of our intentions, how well we are able to share and communicate them, and the degree of coherence underlying our strategic choices, we are capable of making our organisation more purposeful, more meaningful, and more future-full for all stakeholders.
6. **AUTOPOIESIS** is an important characteristic of all viable systems. It means the system is able to self-regulate in order to continuously recreate its unique role within the ecosystem of which it is a part. An integral part of autopoiesis is the system's natural ability to deal with all manner of stresses and inconsistencies. It is galling to realise that management as it has been contrived, is not nearly as effective as self-regulation – although it is neater and tidier in comparison.	Unlike most orthodox management systems, which impose levels of control to minimise the degree of turbulence within the system, self-organising systems are also self-managing to the extent that they do not require (or may simply absorb) imposed authority or control so as to ensure continuing growth and adaptiveness. The World-Wide Web is a fine example of this faculty to continually self-create.
7. **INTELLIGENCE** is the capability developed by sentient organisms allowing them to adapt and to purposefully coevolve in response to perpetual novelty in their environment. Any viable system is reliant upon intelligence, as well as its rapid processing and enacted responses, for its very survival and adaptation.	Timely, relevant, distinctive and continuous streams of information are needed from all parts of the business ecosystem (and beyond) in order for us to synthesise appropriate strategic intelligence for change and for innovation. The most critical factor in this respect is the speed at which issues can be identified, processed and acted upon.

These principles may also point to the possibility of viability within human organisations and communities. But only if we can transcend some entrenched beliefs concerning orthodox management practices. Today there is an urgent need for organisations to be viable – implying a mix of ethical responsibility, engaging sincerity and extraordinary performance. Indeed systemic viability, along with strategic relevance, innovation and speed of learning, will soon be recognised as the crucial factors determining survival and well-being within an increasingly complex, global, highly uncertain and forever changing social and business environment.

In order to achieve higher levels of viability (and be able to sustain this over time) organisations need to steer their way through unknowable chaos. Sometimes, the larger business ecosystem in which an enterprise is niched may change so completely that the niche becomes redundant in a matter of days, or even hours. When this happens, the current form of the organisation may need to be instantly replaced by a more optimum configuration. It is the sheer speed of change in today's business environment that presents the most crucial challenge for designing and implementing coherent organisational strategy. In order to be able to respond instantly (but intelligently) to changing circumstances, we need to conceive of strategy not as some static, arcane, secret and unyielding plan, but as a pliable, collaborative, learning process impelling the organisation from its present state to a mutually preferred future. A fluid, real-time approach to strategic leadership, such as this, requires new mental models regarding the role and praxis of the enterprise; new infrastructure to liberate such thinking; and the development of a new praxis to ensure that intelligence and foresight are used to drive and enable generative learning.

Strategic Navigation, the third literacy of *five literacy* leaders, is one such approach that facilitates rapid change across an organisation.[10] Overturning much of the conventional management wisdom of our industrial past, Strategic Navigation uses ecological metaphors (concerned primarily with learning and transformation) to balance the more familiar economic metaphors (concerned primarily with controlling and producing) habitually used by managers to this day.

By weaving together strands of intelligence about an organisation's past, present and future in the context of the business ecosystem, and by becoming more deeply conscious of how mind traps (such as the 'gravitational pull' of the past) filter our perceptions of reality, Strategic Navigation focuses our attention on the optimisation and integrity of the whole system. Essentially, based upon the principles of viable living systems outlined above, this literacy enables learning, growth and viability for any enterprise operating in the most hostile and unpredictable of global business environments. Strategic Navigation also resolves many of the time-related prejudices, anomalies and fallacies we fabricate, and then spend our time apportioning blame, in the process of rationalising the challenges we encounter in dealing with an increasingly complex and volatile global business environment. Take the problem of short-termism for example. One of the most common of today's misconceptions, it is frequently expressed as a disturbing incongruity between society's need for long-term vision and the 'indecent short-termism' demanded by market analysts, CEOs who are rewarded on quarterly results, and unwarranted shareholder dividends. In many respects this framing of reality is both foolish and misleading. It arises from our tendency to think in dualistic terms: in this case opting to place certain aspects of the issue (like executive salaries, or returns to shareholders, for example) within one or other of these two domains. In fact tensions between these two extremes only exist if we choose to frame it this way.

Short term and long term are not mutually exclusive, but part of a continuous dynamic. Both are critical to business survival. In any case crucial differences between short term and long term are fuzzier and have lost much of their meaning today. It is possible for both to be considerably compressed while being far more elastic, depending upon the context. Realistically, the short term can range anywhere between the immediate moment of the 'here and now' (on a trading floor) to days and even weeks (in policy development). Likewise, the long term is extended in both directions by today's uncertainties. Viability comes down to expansive long-term thinking as well as focused short-term execution. Reframing short-term imperatives and performance within the context of achieving longer term success and acting in accordance with a coherent ethos of guiding principles, immediately dissipates such previously feared anomalies.

NOTES

1. This insight and analysis are provided by Peter Tunjic, Director of Thoughtpost Legal (http://www.thoughtpost.com.au).
2. This and similar questions are routinely posed by Thoughtpost Pty Ltd, an Australian company specialising in the creation of uncommon approaches to strategy and board consciousness.

3. A complex adaptive system is able to learn to adapt to changed environmental conditions by virtue of its capability to detect, process and act upon intelligence.

4. Derived demand refers to goods or services (like electricity supply or paramedic services, for example) that are instantaneously produced and consumed. Dell's business model, for example, is based upon derived demand: your new Dell computer comes into being just two hours after it is ordered. Car manufacturers are moving this way as are commercial fisheries and tax agencies.

5. Intelligence is a higher order learning capability developed by human beings encompassing (a) the continuous acquisition of information that enables us to discern *critical* changes in systemic conditions, coupled with (b) the processing of such information in ways that give new insights into *when* and *how* we might respond to such changes, given our particular preferences and intentions.

6. As discrete industries, forged at the time of the industrial revolution of the nineteenth century, continuously change in a bewildering game of shifting alliances and strategic partnerships, so the boundaries around traditional industry groupings begin to merge and blur – to such an extent that the term 'industry' becomes almost unusable in the context of the knowledge economy. More expansive still than the customer–supplier networks of the so-called *extended* enterprise, business ecosystems are socioeconomic communities comprising a number of interacting 'agents' (customers, suppliers, regulators, intermediaries, lead producers, competitors and other stakeholders) that co-evolve over time in alignment with the directions set by one or more principal members.

7. The niche is a coherent alignment of the following factors: (a) what the enterprise was set up to do; (b) the unique value it brings to this purpose; (c) the competencies it needs in order to fulfil this value-add; and (d) the value provided by the enterprise to its people.

8. Kim, W. Chan and Mauborgne, R., *Blue Ocean Strategy: How to Create Uncontested Market Space and Make the Competition Irrelevant*, Harvard Business School Press, 2005.

9. Located in Bangkok, Bumrungrad International Hospital has become the global leader in medical tourism within the short space of five years. In 2005 Bumrungrad treated 70,000 Arabic patients alone. The new world-class outpatient clinic has a capacity of 5500 patients a day – the largest of any hospital in the world.

10. A frame-breaking management methodology devised by Richard Hames and Marvin Oka in 1996 to assist the Australian Taxation Office in dealing with real-time strategic issues and planning.

CHAPTER 7

CLICK!

Now, the Web is enabling the market to converse again as people tell one another the truth about products and companies and their own desires.

– David Weinberg, *The Cluetrain Manifesto*

In these early years of the twenty-first century we are witnessing unprecedented growth and prosperity – albeit shared between a relatively small number of the world's most highly developed nations. Our deep and lasting love affair with new technology, together with booming industrial economies, have provided the citizens of these countries with healthier lives, greater material wealth and less laborious work. We live longer than ever before. Many of us have greater personal freedoms. Our elderly, sick, disabled, unemployed and poor are mostly catered for (albeit within the bounds of a fairly unyielding system), and many discriminations, particularly those based on religion, sex and race, have declined markedly. The Human Genome Project, by wide consent one of the most important scientific undertakings of our time, and similar research into proteins and stem cells, hold out the promise of virtually unlimited alleviation of human pain and suffering.[1]

Yet, paradoxically, there are deep levels of malaise within our society – a disenchantment with what the future may hold. We seem to have misplaced those very qualities that make us human. Nowhere is this more apparent than in our business corporations. Uninterrupted prosperity seems to have become the norm after the war years. Wealth was something taken for granted in Western society. Furthermore, it ingrained itself deeply into the psyche of all eurocentric nations. Relieved from economic uncertainty, people were free to pursue happiness. Even the spectre of a nuclear holocaust did little to diminish our enthusiasm for modernism. Seduced by visions of a utopian society, we imagined an era where all social problems would be swept away on a flood of rising prosperity and growth. We anticipated a society in which workers and families would benefit from rising incomes and stable jobs; where poverty, racism and crime would abate and personal self-fulfilment would be almost limitless. We not only expected these things – after a while, we thought we were *entitled* to them.

This heady trust in a continuous boom did more than just distort our view of reality. Governments began to operate on the assumption that resources, if not infinite, were almost so. Far too much was expected of prosperity and technology as a cure for social ills. And the idea of *entitlement* subtly nullified personal and institutional responsibilities, fostering a tendency for everyone to search elsewhere for solutions to the most perplexing problems. Governments looked to a surging post-war economy to pay for ambitious infrastructure programmes; companies looked to governments to prevent recessions; and workers and families looked to corporate and government welfare benefits to guarantee their security and living standards. Meanwhile we continued to allow the fragmentation of human knowledge, condoned corruption in high places, and tolerated violent conflicts, war and poverty – as long as these did not encroach into our own lives.

The most destructive flaw in this post-war vision was that it rested on a vague concept of *progress* – an assumption that all aspects of life would constantly improve for everyone. Yet, with hindsight at least, it is easy to see that some of these expectations of entitlement were inconsistent. It was always too perfect to happen, and the belief in its practicality created the social equivalent of a mythological chimera: it arrogantly presumed that we could engineer a constant economic boom, which we cannot, and that such vigorous wealth would automatically erase all social and personal problems, which it could not. Ultimately, it confused survival with advancement.[2]

The fundamental wellspring of popular disillusion today is the fact that this society, with its comforting certainty and order, has failed to materialise. The vision of *progress*, which once provided social cohesion, has been undermined by the cumulative weight of so many dashed expectations. We are caught between the false promises and hedonistic desires of the past and the insistent, hostile, uncertain social and economic conditions of the present. Society knows this in its bones. Yet to this day, politicians approaching an election consistently promise things that can never be delivered with any degree of certainty, peddling hopes for votes. Meanwhile, an ingenuous public, embittered by the superficial posturing and ritualistic ideological exchanges, increasingly sceptical of traditional institutions, and fearful of a future from which the reassuring assumptions and securities of the past have been stripped, resorts to maligning those in authority and despairs at its own destiny.

While much human behaviour remains a mystery, occasionally appearing to defy all rational logic, an awful lot can be explained by comprehending the worldviews in play; the deeply ingrained (albeit mostly hidden) systems that shape personal values and ultimately account for the behaviours we see played out in the full glare of public life. Because we live in such an abundant and complex world there is a rich diversity of worldviews out there. One has only to look at the contrasting rhetoric between extreme views in politics, for example, to appreciate how powerful worldviews can be. Adherents to each worldview not only see critical issues differently, they then make extravagant claims in terms of preferred ways of dealing with those issues. Adherents to alternative worldviews are frequently ridiculed or feared, so strong is the ingrained nature of a dominant worldview.

Today in developed regions of the world the *technological* paradigm completely dominates most others. It pervades mainstream political and business thinking. Its impact can clearly be seen in relation to proposed action on almost any serious issue. Take climate change, for example. The difference in approach between nations that have adopted the Kyoto Principles on Climate Change, and others including the US and Australia that are signatories to the Asia-Pacific Partnership on Clean Development and Climate, are the direct results of altogether different worldviews. Both outcomes were easy enough to predict. Advocates of the *technological* worldview, exemplified by the Asia-Pacific Partnership, trust absolutely in the ingenuity of humankind to find rational, scientific solutions to climate-related problems. To these insiders, their 'answer' to the problem of global warming is a real-world, mature-person's solution. No economic pain, no mandatory targets, no international commitments and no need for open, accountable negotiations. Neither is there any place for the great unwashed of the environmental movement or the community at large. Far better to keep it in the family of power-suited industrial and political brokers, the few who can really get things done. Electronic power will keep flowing, the giant developing economies of Asia will keep growing, and no government will have to do anything it doesn't want to do. In contrast to this optimistic scenario, the *sociological* worldview which has given rise, among other things, to the humanisation of work, advocates considered incremental change. This is the worldview that inspired the Kyoto Protocols. Its advocates will persist in decrying the efforts of the Asia-Pacific Partnership, as will others with yet different worldviews.

For example, the protestors who vented their frustration and anger at the meeting of political and business leaders that formulated the Asia-Pacific Partnership in Sydney in 2006, were predominantly adherents of a *biospheric* worldview – an apocalyptic paradigm championed by deep ecologists, which advocates immediate, substantial, action on a variety of fronts, coupled with the setting of ambitious targets, to reduce the damage already done to the Earth's biosphere. To these observers, the Asia-Pacific solution is an empty vessel; a fig leaf to cover the embarrassment of George Bush and John Howard, the only Western leaders to have reneged on commitments their predecessors made at the UN Kyoto conference in 1997. In their opinion the Partnership will deliver nothing of benefit to the climate, because technology alone cannot bring the huge reductions in greenhouse gas emissions which, according to consensus climate science, are needed. But neither do the Kyoto Protocols go far enough for the proponents of this worldview. They would prefer to wind back time and take us all back to a pre-industrial world.

Within the framework of the *technological* paradigm, those linear, reductionist, political and business processes we habitually deploy respond best to clearly bounded problems and conflicts. The clues to understanding this behaviour is to be found in the history of the *technological* worldview. Because any problem during the Second World War could be defeated with ample resources, appropriate technology and a suitable strategy (or, more strictly, that was the perception), the dominant post-war ideology became that of problem solving. This engendered a confidence that any problem could be solved with adequate resources, the right tools and sufficient intellectual grunt. But even if that was the case, today's issues are different. Compounded by numerous factors they are systemic in nature – unbounded, global, messy and ambiguous. We have yet to learn how best to address such complicated dilemmas. The hugely complex and uncertain challenges facing our society today ultimately demand entirely fresh design criteria, principles and approaches to organising and managing human affairs – not just more indiscriminate patching up of the current system.

The diversity of issues we are currently required to address, together with their complex nature, interconnectedness and explosive nature, lead me to the conclusion that nothing short of a total reappraisal of the human condition – exploring who we are, why we are here, what is meaningful to us and what goals, therefore, we need to pursue – is likely to suffice if we are to withstand the enormous pressures on our species to endure. What is needed is a new belief system that integrates, at the very least, elements of all three frameworks examined above. A more universally applicable paradigm: one that unites humanity rather than continuing to divide it and that elevates a new understanding of the whole biospherical system for which humans must take responsibility. An *appreciative* worldview. Clare Graves research is interesting in this regard (see Figure 7.1 overleaf).

In fact we have an obligation to adopt *appreciative* principles and actions if we intend the future of our planet to be in the least habitable for our grandchildren and their children. An *appreciative* worldview would aspire to create a global community of praxis. It would assimilate selected features from all three of the former worldviews in play (together perhaps with other less dominant worldviews such as those that prevail in socialist Brazil and 'democratic' China) to create a fundamentally new and viable society.

An *appreciative* worldview (principles, values, behaviours and systems) is the basis for the organising philosophy used instinctively by *five literacies* leaders. In that sense it is already understood and is being practised by the smartest among us. *Appreciative* systems comprise self-organising elements that collaborate in forging and sustaining human ecologies that advance by learning their way into mutually agreeable (or desired) futures. Applying *appreciative* principles ensures this can be accomplished in ethical reciprocity with the environment and in ways that are receptive to all stakeholders' needs, expectations and desires. Ultimately, the higher moral purpose of such *appreciative* systems is virtuous alignment: the survival of the whole of humankind and advancement to higher levels of consciousness. *Appreciative*

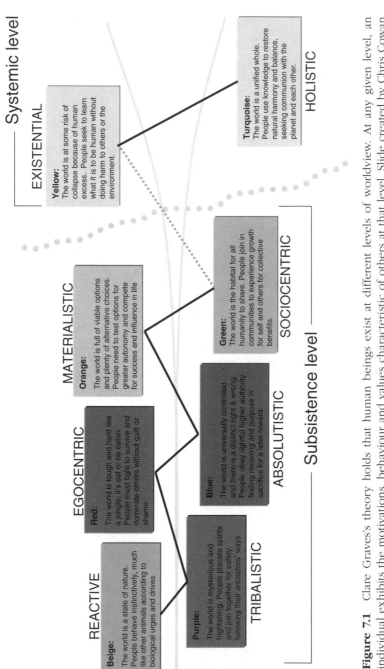

Figure 7.1 Clare Graves's theory holds that human beings exist at different levels of worldview. At any given level, an individual exhibits the motivations, behaviour and values characteristic of others at that level. Slide created by Chris Cowan as part of Spiral Dynamics. Spiral Dynamics is a registered trademark of the National Values Center and is used here with permission.

principles are compatible with the fundamentals of natural (or organic) systems. They are grounded in systems theory, use multidisciplinary approaches to decision making – and they work in practice. In fact, it is because of their affinity with natural systems that they work so exceptionally well – far more effectively than many of the quasi-scientific management fabrications which became all too familiar during the latter half of the twentieth century.

Although *appreciative* ideals are already being practised by *five literacies* leaders, and being pondered by intellectuals everywhere, it is surely only a matter of time before the whole of society begins to take notice of the escalating number of warnings from political activists, thought-leaders, new economists and even mainstream scientists, and grasps the need for such an *appreciative* (or ecological) worldview to prevail over modernism, particularly if we are to avoid some kind of global nervous breakdown or environmental catastrophe. In making such a sweeping and outrageous statement, it is not my intention to disregard or deride the potential impact of the many technological miracles and consequent increased affluence we have been promised by optimistic technocrats. But they can never provide the complete answer to humanity's current predicament.

	Unity	Alignment	Reciprocity
Self	Self-concept organised by personal values	Self-awareness and permission to fulfil one's needs	Reciprocity with others to produce mutual benefits
Group	Commitment to group purpose supported by shared values	Group members are sensitive to each other's needs	Collaborative interaction with other groups
Organisation	Organising according to agreed purpose	Collaborative interaction between groups	Cooperative interaction within local community
Community	Unity of ethical responsibility within the community	Cooperative alliances between organisations	Moral leadership within society

Figure 7.2 Appreciative relationships and values can be used to grow cohesion within and across communities of praxis.

If such a fundamental reappraisal is not forthcoming at some stage during these early years of the twenty-first century, we may precipitate a mass extinction or, possibly worse, preside over the mutation of the human species into some form of spiritually vacuous 'digital flesh'. As it is, the eroding boundaries between human beings and our prostheses – contact lenses, hearing aids, implants, genetically engineered artificial organs and communication networks – have already changed our consciousness. We are already *transhuman*. Transgenic forms, created through the interfacing of biology and cybernetics, may ultimately emerge, heralding the end of the human species as we know it. Perhaps that may not altogether be such a bad thing given the damage we continue to do to the natural systems that support human life!

On the other hand, viable alternatives to systemic structural change of this kind are too harrowing to contemplate for many people. Reasonable extrapolations of current trends indicate potentially catastrophic scenarios of global proportions. Such doom-laden scenarios appear even more feasible within the context of a contemporary culture that values technospheric solutions over humanitarian values. The possibility that we still possess insufficient knowledge to prevent the destruction that has overtaken all previous civilisations should not be overlooked. In the West we have been deliberately fragmenting human knowledge for at least the past 500 years. Maybe we should simply accept that such collapse is an inescapable part of the lifecycle and that what we are witnessing is the natural disintegration of Western civilisation. Yet, just as we are disinclined to think about the possibility of our own extinction, so cognitive preservation may be primarily responsible for our reluctance to abandon modernism in the search for more relevant, sustainable, worldviews. Human beings, it seems, will do almost anything in their power to preserve their particular worldview, even in the face of serious doubts being cast on the validity of its most fundamental axioms. We are rarely induced to relinquish even an obviously maladaptive worldview simply by logic or rational argument.

However, the need for a spiritual base – of a deeper sense of relatedness to the world around us, and towards each other – becomes more apparent each day. Many people around the world have concluded that the assumptions and beliefs on which current frameworks were built, especially those of production and consumption in the West, have become totally incompatible with the objectives we now need to pursue as a global community. Australian journalist Richard

Eckersley argues that modern Eurocentric cultures have patently neglected to fulfil that for which cultures are primarily designed: namely to give our lives meaning and to provide a clear framework of values to guide what we do.

The role and pervasive influence of culture in this regard is critical to appreciate. Cultural attributes, particularly our correlations of assumptions, convictions, values, myths and, of course, language and the arts, have always helped create and shape society's vision of itself. It is becoming increasingly apparent that Western culture is no longer contributing, as it once did, to a healthier, more robust and cohesive sense of global community. On the contrary, today's cultural endowment is moral confusion, the relentless deterioration of our institutions and personal well-being, and a rupturing of social frameworks.

Contributing to the lack of social unity, alienation, resentment and dwindling personal resilience in a society as beleaguered as ours, we can identify the following mutually dependent factors as requiring immediate attention from a whole-of-system perspective:

- Rampant materialism coupled with an insatiable desire for more – and yet more.
- Insecurities engendered by rapid change to the established order.
- An inability to absorb the various shocks associated with *newness* (especially in view of the exponentially increasing pace of change in so many dimensions simultaneously).
- The elevation of antisocial values, promoted uncritically by the media, together with a focus on bad news and the attendant mitigation of spiritual, aesthetic and communitarian codes of behaviour, which all engender despair and a lack of hope.
- The naive trust accorded most new technologies (whether benign or manipulative).
- The lack of credible and diverse role models for young people – apart from one-dimensional sports people, fashion icons, pop stars and media celebrities with their seemingly endless supply of newsworthy misdemeanours.
- Insufficient trust in the political process and our elected representatives.
- A vicarious approach to life based on the bizarre fusion of routine boredom on the one hand and instant gratification on the other.
- The lack of coherent, convincing, optimistic views of the future.

These psychosocial factors are helping to create a cultural pathology in society that is shameful and that appears to be the very antithesis of our evolutionary makeup and potential. Promoting discontent, bewilderment, permissiveness and brutality, this pathology progressively undermines our capacity and will to cope, gnawing away at the collective resolve required to tackle long-term social transformation in any effective manner. How else can we explain, for example, that 3% of all US males are in prison, on bail, or awaiting trial? Or that the world's farmers produce the equivalent of 2 kilograms of food per person per day, yet there remain 850 million people on the planet who are severely undernourished – and even more than this suffering from obesity?

People from all walks of life, young people in particular, are yearning for a future that directs more attention to the humane, spiritual dimensions of existence and less to short-term materialism and utilitarian attitudes. They seek to restore a deeper sense of community and demonstrable solidarity with some 6.5 billion other human beings who share the same fate, and are using this as a means to help overcome the West's otherwise long and relentless journey towards individualism. They are asking for a purpose that has the power to restore their faith in themselves and humankind while expanding global prosperity. A moral purpose.

Much of mainstream intellectual debate remains far too narrowly focused and theoretical to persuade people of the need for deep structural transformation. At a national level the policies that currently serve our attempts to preserve stability largely coincide with those of the most powerful economic interest groups within our society – namely governments, trading blocs such as the European Union (EU), transnational and multinational corporations, high-tech firms and major global banks. It is extremely unlikely that institutions with such explicit interest in preserving the status quo would welcome, let alone initiate, such profound changes. Conventional wisdom and prevailing practice both affirm the inevitability of the *technological* paradigm – if we confidently adhere to our progressive path of resourceful socio-technological development, we can master nature and overcome any problems we may encounter along the way. A politician would no doubt add, *'And that's a promise!'*

Today, purpose and status in our society are still vested in each individual's qualities, possessions and attainments. The search for meaning is situated almost exclusively in the material sphere of human existence, undermining those spiritual, aesthetic and ethical dimensions upon which social harmony must ultimately depend. At the same time, increasing material standards of living have not only become irrelevant to most of us in the Western world, but hostile to our very well-being. Economic expansionism – the hubris of the technological paradigm – has become a one-way street. Sadly, few people have noticed it is also a cul-de-sac.

In spite of the appalling failure of economic development in the Third World, the desirability of this worldview still remains fundamentally unquestioned. Subtle modifications in the way development policies are implemented are proposed to eliminate its worst abuses – hence rural development, eco-development and, more recently, sustainable development, which are merely cynical euphemisms adopted by the development industry to appease its critics. What our scientists, politicians and economists have taken to be economic development (that is, progress) is merely regression to a lower state of social development. Progress, in this context, is a cruel illusion. In fact, the depth of disillusionment with and within our society – particularly with mainstream political systems, which have become a cauldron for self-aggrandisement and envy; the interminable stream of corruption, selfishness and greed shown by those who have sufficient talent, wealth or influence to be setting an altogether different example to the rest of us; excessive bureaucratic bungling in everything from healthcare and family services to education and justice; and the inability of the media to engage with any of this seriously – should not be underestimated. One need only take note of the increasing incidence of depression and other psychotic illnesses, particularly in young people, which is now about 10 times greater in Western countries than it was before the Second World War. The rate of suicide, particularly in boys and young men, has been increasing in most industrial nations, particularly in younger countries like Australia, where it has trebled since the 1950s. In a recent study of 1700 Australian university graduates, whose average age was just under 22, almost two-thirds had thought about killing themselves in the past year. About 7% claimed they had tried to take their lives.

This issue is not confined to a tiny minority of young people. Nor is the apprehension and anxiety experienced by our young people confined to marginalised or disadvantaged youth, the homeless, the unemployed or the sexually abused. Data consistently indicates that such problems are endemic. It is evidence of a traumatised and sick society, a ticking time bomb set to detonate, which we continue to ignore at our peril. Increasing violent crime, delinquency, child abuse, mental illness, alcoholism and drug addiction are all symptoms of a growing dysfunctionality within society, just as pandemics and natural disasters are symptomatic of a growing dysfunctionality within the global ecosystem, and the failure of scientists, economists and politicians to understand the world in which they live is symptomatic of cognitive dysfunctionality.

Where once people had much greater certainty about their worth, position and role in society, and were also definite about the personal contribution they could confidently expect to make, for many people there is now a sense of detachment and isolation from the mainstream. We no longer have a shared sense of purpose or direction – other than acquiring the next technology fad or the latest in consumer gadgets. The technospheric world we have masterminded, through an imprudent and voracious appetite for material possessions, has lost all meaning for us. It has created a vacuum which is abrading the human soul. And, as economic development proceeds unabated, more and more people are condemned to inhabit a world to which they are ever less adapted biologically, socially, ecologically, aesthetically, cognitively and spiritually. It is as though we have created an empty self – devoid of any deeper transcendent meaning – that needs to be constantly stockpiled with consumer goods and services, celebrity gossip and other rich distractions, for life to have any value whatsoever.

Need this be so? Surely humanity should be full of optimism, the sense that the future is ours to shape, and the conviction that we have the capability to do just that? Have we really become so numb, our imagination so shackled by institutionalised solutions, so pessimistic that we cannot envisage any possible alternatives?

Before societal pessimism can be effectively combated, there is a far more immediate dilemma to resolve – a conflict between our nostalgia for the period in our history when life was carefree, less complicated and more certain – when there were no email inboxes pressing for an instant decision – and the sobering realisation that there can be no return to a past age. It is as impossible to reinstate the (relative) security of our past as it is inconceivable that we could return to traditional forms of identity and belief. The more we pursue the past, the more it recedes from our grasp and the more likely it is we compound current problems. To live in the past, or to dwell on this particular impulse, is a distraction we can ill afford. It deflects our attention from the actuality of our current predicament. And yet, with such confusion and uncertainty pervading our concrete, materialistic world, it appears increasingly probable that the ideological battles of the future will be fought out between those who believe that if we have problems it is because progress has not yet progressed far enough, and those who believe that the problems confronting us are an inevitable consequence of economic development.

Binary logic such as this is insufficient for our needs; it merely fuels our inability to address the complexities we face. It tends to reinforce current preconceptions, allowing us to make a choice perhaps between two separate, mutually inconsistent or contradictory factors but effectively preventing the synthesis of fresh possibilities. We are already well past the point where this might have been successful. Now we need entirely different thinking architectures, underpinned by more holistic, transformative logics, in order to be able to *see* alternative paths – thinking architectures and logics that embody a broad diversity and multiplicity of perspectives and that enable the synthesis of entirely new social realities and solutions. If such architectures were available, we could then begin to explore the transcendence of these extremes, redefining our notions regarding progress in the process, and attempting to reconcile materialism with environmental sustainability, and individualism with communitarianism.

There is no doubt the twenty-first century will provide the backdrop for challenges to be confronted that are intimidating in their sheer number, scale and impact – environmental degradation and pollution, climatic change, decaying infrastructures and institutions (including the family unit and the system of law and justice), new plagues of viruses, the effects of mass migration and automation, the growing gulf between the rich and the poor,[3] the provision and distribution of sufficient food for a ballooning population, international terrorism, declining opportunities for employment, redefinition of employability within the context of the digital age, regional and ethnic conflict, the complicated legislation required to ensure total genetic privacy . . . the list seems never-ending.

So far, the only solutions that have been offered for these new and daunting issues are old, disconnected, tired, unworkable. Has the impoverishment of our emotional and sensory lives depleted the courage we need for developing fresh strategies? Has our predicament anaesthetised any enduring tenacity to change? Are we transfixed by the sheer enormity of the challenge, like a rabbit caught in a car's headlights? In the end, perhaps it is simply immoral to pursue modernity further – escalating problems rather than unravelling their mysteries and then interpreting the new dilemmas that arise in such a way as to rationalise expedients requiring further economic growth, and therefore the use of further, mostly finite, resources.

The *appreciative* worldview is intrinsically opposed to the continuing rampage of modernism and the global social, economic and ecological instability that it perpetuates. Based upon ecological necessity and humanitarian principles, yet able to sustain a diverse range of self-organised, interdependent, cooperative enterprises, *appreciative* renewal offers the possibility of creating a society that is structurally and cognitively geared to the achievement of very different goals from those of the society in which we live today. It offers a society with soul – one with the will and the reason to survive. That is what *five literacies* leaders understand, articulate and attend to.

However, in spite of such inspired leadership, broader acceptance of the need for an all-encompassing shift of this kind will not be easy to achieve. For one thing, our system of education has degenerated into institutional, as opposed to vernacular, learning. Once concerned with the ethical process of socialising each newborn individual into becoming a full member of a community, education today has become little more than the transfer of detailed but socially indiscriminate information, partitioned into discrete disciplines that distort or disguise the systemic nature of significant social issues and hamper our ability to conceive and formulate appropriate solutions. By intensifying the prevailing rationalist worldview and, with it, uncompromising strategies of social domination, this unethical system sustains individuals within that worldview in such a way that alternative models become almost impossible to contemplate.

A further difficulty in promoting the need for system-based change is that, at least since the industrial revolution, influential protagonists within the mainstream of our society – those who have fully committed themselves politically, economically, psychologically and quasi-religiously to progress through economic development – play a decisive role in rationalising this worldview as well as the conditions it helps create. Those who are capable of stepping into new epistemologies mostly work at the fringe and are, as yet, mostly silent and invisible. We have yet to see them and hear them. Many of the metaphors we use, for example, to shape and communicate (through language and behaviour) our understanding of the world, are imposed upon us by people in power – politicians, religious leaders, wealthy industrialists, the media. As George Lackoff, Professor of Linguistics at the University of California, affirms:

> In a culture where objectivism is very much alive and truth is always absolute, the people who get to impose their metaphors on the culture get to define what we consider to be true.

In modern society, reductionist objectivism has dominated the priesthoods of science, law, government, journalism, morality, business, economics and scholarship to the extent that this worldview, asserting its own possession of absolute and unconditional truths about the world, has become the cornerstone of Western philosophical tradition. By far the most significant factor in this regard has been the rise of the nation-state. This utopian stratagem has become so far removed from vernacular society that it now operates under no effective social or ecological control. It is injurious to the sustainability of our planet – irrespective of the capitalist or socialist ideology on which individual states are founded, or the political authority by which they are perpetuated. In effect, the modern state has become just another interest group, concerned with little more than its own trifling interests, which almost invariably conflict with those of the society it is supposed to serve. Unfortunately, this particular interest group controls the police, the army and, to a large extent, the systems of education, law and the media.

These difficulties must not imply that we should remain paralysed by the enormity of the task ahead or by the ever-widening gap between our ideals and harsh reality. As the system of *industrial economism* reaches the end of its sustainable trajectory, there can be little doubt that the inexorable pressures towards whole system change are fast reaching a tipping point. The critical issue is the extent to which such a cultural shift towards an ecologically sustainable society can avoid the upheaval and collapse of present social structures. Everything becomes possible – except the status quo. One thing is certain, the ecological paradigm and the notion of an *appreciative* society are revolutionary concepts in that they differ markedly from the constructs we have used during the past few hundred years. Consequently the ensuing turmoil will be both profound and deeply unsettling.

Whatever the ultimate nature of the change, there are actions we should be taking now, wherever we can, to counter the oppressive impact of modernism on our lives. We must, for example, engage people whenever and wherever we can in a comprehensive, rigorous conversation on the fundamental questions of systemic change and of meaning within contemporary society. We must design technologies that facilitate collaborative, rather than competitive, processes – tools for *appreciation* that are accessible to everybody, that democratise corporate structures, and that enable radical transformation of the way we share our thoughts and shape our environments. We must learn to dream entirely different dreams – to fashion clear and compelling visions of where we want to go as a society and how we would like to live our individual lives. We must allow ourselves the indulgence of imagining altogether different possibilities for what might constitute *progress*. At the same time, any critical issues that emerge must be translated into concrete practical measures for improving the quality, efficacy, alignment and spirituality of individual, corporate and community life. We will need to discover how to redesign key aspects of our culture in ways that restore the primacy of emotion, cooperation and intuitive knowledge to our relationships with each other. And we shall need to determine how best to pursue the kinds of reciprocity that will test and authenticate the effectiveness and resilience of the new paradigm. Above all else, we will need to believe once more in the power and integrity of the individual and of our institutions to effect change through the acceptance of responsibility – a responsibility that is as much about the future and future generations as it is about our more immediate obligations.

The beliefs of some ancient cultures already embody such an outlook. The Hopi of North America, for example, believe that the interests of the seventh generation should feature as largely in any decision as those of the people actually making the decision. Being constantly enriched by what has gone before, yet constantly alert to what is to come after, seems to me to be the very hallmark of a vital, healthy culture – not some left-over, unworldly, romantic idealism as some might claim. All that stands between us and the slide into a brutal, survival-of-the-fittest, decline is the umbilical link between us, our children and their children. It is their rights, their presence, their expectations and their dreams that must now be allowed to intrude on humankind's mesmeric dance of destruction. Responsibility for creating a new ecosociety needs to reside at every level within the system – from the individual through to international institutions. We can accept personal responsibility by standing up for future generations – by treading a little more lightly on the earth and trying to do less damage. This has to be the cornerstone upon which any societal transformation will be built.

In spite of recent technological advances that threaten to supersede traditional meeting places, the same quality of life continues to be experienced within local communities of one kind or another. Local regulations, planning and politics can powerfully reinforce collaborative community and individual effort, while community accountability will enable appreciative individuals to accelerate the process of societal change. Unless or until national boundaries disintegrate totally, the alignment of appreciative communities requires national resolve and ambition in order to protect the environment and set achievable standards for individuals and businesses. In this interrelated world of ours, national efforts will require reciprocal understanding and actions from all other nations. International cooperation will also be needed to untangle the more complex issues that know no bounds – not just in terms of better management of common resources such as the oceans and the biosphere, but in recognising the commonality of all parts of the human family and in shifting the priorities and day-to-day practice of business itself.

Like any philosophy, the inherently reciprocal nature of the *appreciative* society has to be evaluated not only by what it achieves, but by its ideals. Ideals represent the highest aspirations of humankind, acting as intellectual, moral and aesthetic guideposts and also as spiritual aides. They are the 'children of their times' and, as such, contain both the inherent strengths and weaknesses of their parents – characteristics that cannot be rectified through surface changes alone. Industrial economism focused on four ideals. These can be summarised as the:

- *Scientific* ideal of perfect knowledge, the attainment of perfect truth as posited through objective analysis, validation and agreement.
- *Economic* ideal of plenty, of material wealth for all, of abundance through progress, in the sense of economic growth and development.
- *Aesthetic* ideal of beauty.
- *Moral-ethical* ideal of goodness – particularly equated during the latter half of the twentieth century with the provision of greater levels of social care.

Contemporary disasters inflicted upon local communities by global corporations or governments in Bhopal and Chernobyl; social crises arising from the military conflicts in Bosnia and the Arabian Gulf; the 2005 riots of Muslim workers in Paris and endemic corruption in state police agencies; environmental crises such as the depletion of the ozone layer, the oil spill from the *Exxon Valdez*, and the destruction of the Brazilian rainforests; corporate dysfunctionalities engendered by hostile takeovers, volatile business conditions, new technologies and rapid downsizing; personal trauma depicted by the escalating rates of youth suicide, depressive illness, and marginalisation of certain sectors within the community – such evidence challenges earlier formulations of these ideals and points to a need for a significant reconceptualisation of society's ideals.

In this regard, the scientific ideal pertaining to the attainment of perfect knowledge needs to be recast in terms of wisdom – and as 'whole-person' wisdom, rather than that 'biblical' wisdom dominated by patriarchal and gender-specific worldviews. Any newly acquired wisdom may then be put to the service of all humankind, and particularly towards the replenishment and restoration of our fragile environment. This means the reformulation of the ideal of plenty (which has led to an excess of production and consumption, and of growth *per se*) into an ideal of conviviality. The aesthetic ideal of beauty will need to be transcended into an ideal of harmony – especially in terms of the harmony that is possible between starkly different people and between nations. Finally, the moral ideal of goodness will need to be transcended into an ideal of *equality* – one that recognises the extreme threats to the individual and to the biosphere that have arisen as a result of modern technology and its application.

The embracing of *appreciative* ideals like these, and a conscience based upon reciprocity and altruism, is just one example of an attempt to pass on a more positive gift of thinking to future generations – the inestimable gift of hope, the reorientation of our society to a culture of respect for the environment – rather than one of unmindful desecration. This reformulation of ideals is anything but a trivial change in words; it signals a profound change in spirit. It has the potential to restore soul and humanity into our dealings with each other. It is the philosophy practised by *five literacies* leaders through shared intelligence and collaborative dialogue.

Faced with a crisis of consciousness, of imagination and desire, we are psychologically, cognitively, spiritually, emotionally and politically inadequate to the intemperate state of affairs we've created. The pursuit of progress seems almost to have drained us of the will and creativity to deal adequately with these problems. The key question, then, is not what we can do, but how we can become the kind of people who can, together, begin an *appreciative* conversation that might lead to potentially effective global action. That conversation must address at least four grave threats.

Firstly, we must reflect upon the threat to our entire ecological system posed by modern technology. For the first time in human history, human-induced crises have reached the potential to rival natural disasters in their destructive scope and magnitude. Furthermore, this potential is now built into the very fabric and interstices of modern civilisation. It is a direct consequence of the crisis-prone world we have created.

Secondly, we must take into account the threat to the very constitution and existence of the individual in democratic societies arising from:

- The potential risk to genetic privacy represented by (freely available) knowledge following the mapping of human DNA.
- The *dependencies* resulting from a welfare mentality in key aspects of life – including government, work, health, education and housing.
- The reduction of people to mere consumption commodities where highly paid celebrities live out the fantasies of consumers and where excessive noise and the subsequent anxiety induced can only be relieved through the constant purchase of, or stimulation by, an endless variety of unnecessary services and goods.
- The existence of a class of 'crisis-prone' organisations where the physical and mental well-being of workers is threatened by destructive political games and where skating as close to disaster as possible is sanctioned in the name of efficiency and profits.

Thirdly, the threat to the whole of human habitat, or the living landscape, must be considered. Perhaps the most insidious of all threats, this is patently manifested through the construction of dehumanised urban metropolises and of massive highway infrastructures, accompanied, more often than not, by the destruction of villages and smaller communities. There can be little doubt that the frenzy of overbuilding – the sprawling, homogeneous development of the latter part of the 20th century – is destroying the symbolic 'collective memory' of essential urban character. The endless creation, around our cities, of suburban netherworlds from which we commute to work and then to which we return to sleep is the antithesis of urban life. In our cities today, the streets are merely veins for vehicle flow, not the theatre of daily life; the parks merely lungs to clear the air, not realms enriching fantasy. For urban citizens there is no centre, only a void between fast-flowing traffic and buildings. Design on a human scale is rarely pursued today. We must also be alert and not be misled by products, projects, technologies and institutions that proclaim themselves to be 'ethical', but then use such claims to exploit both nature and people. The rhetoric of ecology is easily used by corporate power structures to confuse and mislead. Policies that are designed by corporate interests, or on their behalf, are being drawn up using *green* terms that camouflage their true identity.

Finally, we must take seriously the threat to the constitution of knowledge itself. This currently comes from at least four major sources:[4]

- *Hi-tech hoopla* – information corrupted by the media and its incorporation into a larger, more insidious *unreality.* The distinctions between information and entertainment, for example, are now so blurred that few can distinguish between them any longer. In many instances, the news has become just another fabrication in a continuous stream of infotainment. The line between reality, artificial reality and unreality, is now so thin as to have vanished altogether.

- *Data overload* – the bombardment of our senses by new knowledge. Where previous dark ages were caused by the suppression of knowledge, we may be entering a new dark age caused by the prodigious production, indiscriminate and unrelenting 24-hours-a-day assault on our senses of a disconnected mix of the banal, entertaining and earth-shattering in no particular order. Optimal flexibility for change does not come through simply increasing communication – the amount of connectivity has to be just right. Too little data can mean stagnancy; too much simply decreases adaptability through a frozen gridlock of conflicting influences. Stuart Kauffman calls this *complexity catastrophe.* In an age of accelerating connectivity, it may be that disconnection can act as a brake to keep our cultural system poised on the edge of maximal evolvability.

- *Liquid identity* – the androcentric orientation of human endeavour has emphasised abstract properties or states of mind out of which 'the truth' supposedly arises. This is far removed from, and is a distortion of, how human beings actually learn from the world and how they ought, therefore, to relate to it. Our fundamental contact with the world is not initially with impersonal objects but with that of loving parents and, ideally, a caring family and community. An *appreciative* society will require the reconstruction of our entire ontology and epistemology in order to create 'ways of knowing' that are based on (and language) ethical and compassionate relations between people and not on dispassionate, impersonal knowledge of objects.

- *Dead media* – modern society is dominated by a structure of communication reinforced by the media, whose multi-billion dollar existence is devoted to the maintenance of the context of modernism at all costs. It is precisely because of this situation that we do not have continuous and pervasive access to alternative discourse. It is not what the media *says* that's so wrong – it's what cannot be said within this context.

The consequences of all this are profound and far-reaching. There is an immediate need to begin the process of resocialisation. To be socialised is to acquire a world and a self that is inseparable from that world. Resocialisation requires the reinvention of context; the weaving together of a reality to create shared meaning in a domain of cultural consensus around *appreciation* rather than around the extremes of *modernism* as found in our immediate past. The control of context is the control of meaning. And the control of meaning is the control of reality. It is the key political issue of our time. Without the control of meaning there can be no creativity; there can be no spiritual freedom.

But it is astonishingly difficult to step out of our current context, one that has been defined through communication, simply by communicating. The same thought patterns lead only to permutations, repeatedly validating the same reality. In order to resocialise ourselves, we must find ways of stepping out of the cultural context that defines the modern realities we wish to transcend and create a new context that specifies different realities, different meanings, and different ways of talking about these meanings. We need to change the nature of communication itself in order to do this.

Most communication is determined by pre-existing context. We talk and sing things into existence – science, art and religion exist because we have spoken about these things. But today it is possible that the countercultural act of non-communication may now be required instead. This process needs to touch a new kind of interconnected reality – a deeper level of our *being* where we are capable of a consonance of shared thoughts and actions and of profound insights – a space where apparent contradictions between science, metaphysics and spirituality can at last be resolved. It can be likened to the process of creativity employed by artists, which might explain why we frequently find contemporary art annoying and uncomfortable – it does not communicate anything other than itself.

Conversation means 'to turn around together'. So we need to turn around together in the *appreciative* process of building a new cultural space for sharing ideas, motives, feelings, aspirations and intentions. This is not a process of communication – it is about saying things we don't understand or cannot explain rationally, and exploring their meaning recursively, reciprocally. The worst thing that can be said about the mass media is that at a time when we need creative conversations – both *appreciative* and critical – on a massive scale, the media can only communicate about and report on things they already know. They can only discuss problems already understood to be problems and they can only discuss them in a manner that has no possibility of participation in any direct way by anybody.

The *appreciative* revolution must focus on the inversion and undermining of the familiar structures of modernism. A system, after all, can only do what its structure and conceptual framework allows it to do. In an *appreciative* society, government, where it is deemed necessary to exist, will be about the diligent representation and empowerment of all people rather than the ideologically dependent management of mere economic factors to predetermined formulae. Educational institutions will abandon any pretext to search for a single 'truth' and will, instead, focus their efforts on improving our appreciation of diverse systems of knowledge and knowing. And the mass media will become mass personalised conversation – personalised in the sense of personal participation in a community of intention, of desire.

Perhaps the most extreme change of all must be that exhibited by business enterprise in the world of work. Here, in the space where learning, creating and consuming intersect, the transformation in *thinking, doing* and *being* must be total, ultimately transforming the very essence of what we understand by terms like *capitalism* and *progress*. Until now, the prevailing attitude of developed nations and corporations who have colonised and exploited more underdeveloped societies and their physical environments has been one of *laissez faire*. That some should suffer the consequences was considered *natural* – the survival of the fittest after struggle and where conflict was considered to be 'right'.

Milton Friedman's interpretation of capitalism, that business has only one social responsibility – that of the maximisation of profits through the engagement of free, open (and honest) competition – has led to corporate behaviour that is both detrimental to our environment and to our humanity. Milton Friedman has a lot to answer for. This belief cannot continue to be justified in today's environment – it is both morally and socially unacceptable. It would be so even if we could accept a valid definition of *profits* (which we cannot) and if it were beyond manipulation (which it is not). The value of profit, it must be recognised, exists in what it can be used for. Like oxygen to the human organism, it is certainly necessary for corporate survival. But it is not the reason for a corporation's existence. There must also be a moral imperative.

Progress has been the product of this struggle to compete, adapt and survive. But its cost has been paid for by the weak. *Appreciative* societies will bring about a more equitable distribution of wealth, thereby restoring social justice to all. The welfare-dependent, capital-istic society is convinced that every society should assume a larger responsibility for the welfare of its parts. Communitarian society, on the other hand, harbours the complementary conviction that the parts should assume a larger responsibility for the welfare of the whole. *Appreciative* society will restore the balance between these two polar-ities by focusing on net *social consumption*. The amount of consump-tion a corporation makes possible, less its own consumption, is its *net social consumption*. Appreciative organisations will consume as little as possible, operating to the benefit of society at large by contributing more than they extract. The principal objective of the appreciative enterprise, therefore, will be to maximise the rate of growth of cor-porately produced *net social consumption*. Furthermore, the strategic intention of the appreciative enterprise will be to integrate the solution of commercial problems in ways that benefit all stakeholders and their environments with the solution of social problems in ways that benefit themselves as well as society. We can barely begin to understand how to do this with models which are different from the commodity models of today's modernistic culture.

Humberto Maturana has shown us that reality (knowing and knowledge) is a construction of the observer.[?] There is a truth for every speaker. Even the new science now maintains there is no such thing as absolute knowledge. The philosophical consequences of Maturana's work principally concern the problem of ethical unity. We all desire social and ethical unity. Within the paradigm of modernism this has been achieved through coercion and manipulation: 'I have the truth. You obey it'. But we all construct the reality we know, and no con-struction is inherently superior to any other. Within *appreciative* social structures the question becomes how best to achieve ethical unity without manipulation or coercion, now that we no longer have an excuse to be coercive. Additionally, we need to discover how we can structure society to reflect this ethical unity. Ethical unity requires a structure in which there is not one voice talking the language of mod-ernism, but a plurality of autonomous communities, realised through networks of appreciative conversation, each able to control the context in which it constructs its own independent reality. It demands an appreciative society in which everyone is able to participate, in which institutions adapt and change following the changing needs and desires of the constituent population that creates them, and in which the economy continually adds value through information, ideas and intelligence.

I am optimistic in society's ability to achieve all of this because of one very simple fact. Human brains are not just discrete entities but individual cells in a globally distributed brain linked through language. Language, used *appreciatively*, is the most crucial tool available to us for shifting society into a new consciousness of alternative possibilities. Appreciative individuals, corporations and communities know this. They understand we have to take from the present to ensure our future, instead of borrowing from the future to ensure our present – they need no urging to be doing just this. Others may well be thinking and feeling their way along such a path at this very moment. And, as one appreciative organism cooperates with others in autopoiesis, creating zones of evolutionary stability in an otherwise disconcerting and disintegrating social environment, so we will advance and progress to different, more sustainable and decidedly higher level orders of worldview. An appreciative society, underpinned by reciprocity, offers a way forward, out of the clash of values between material growth and environmental erosion towards a symbolic and epistemological recovery of our humanity. It will take, at the very least, an evolution of consciousness – a shift from short-term, anthropomorphic, narrowly economic and control-orientated thinking to a long-term, systems-based, evolutionary perspective where humankind is but a part of the whole.

NOTES

1. Science is taking great strides forward in helping extend and improve the quality of human life. A vaccine to eliminate cervical cancer already exists, as do long-lasting prosthetics for the hip and knee. Within five years improved implants including bionic eyes will be available, enhanced imaging techniques will catch breast cancer earlier and new drugs will destroy dementia-inducing brain plaques. Within 10 years we will be able to regrow damaged optic and auditory nerves. Looking further out polymer bridges will repair gaps and help new cord growth in damaged spines. By the year 2050 we will have access to personalised medicines and be using stem cells to grow into any cell in the body, including the heart. We will also be seeing breakthroughs in cancer therapies, organ regeneration and brain augmentation.

2. Noted scholars like Professor Richard Dawkins passionately argue the case for evolutionary progress while others, like Steven J. Gould, are equally passionate that this is an illusion. I fall into the latter category, believing that such linear thinking is one of the causes of our inability to be truly innovative in creating genuinely alternative socioeconomic and political systems such as Parecon, for example (see www.zmag.org/parecon/indexnew.html).

3. Euphemistically referred to as 'the haves' and 'the have nots' by politically correct commentators who feel distinctly uncomfortable with reality and our culpability in sustaining this reality.

4. These examples taken from the author's chapter 'Strategic Navigation: Learning viability in a world wired for speed', in S. Herman (ed.), *Rewiring Organizations for the Networked Economy*, Jossey-Bass/Pfeiffer, San Francisco, 2002.

5. Maturana, H. and Varela, F., *The Tree of Knowledge: the Biological Roots of Understanding*, Shambhala, Boston, 1987.

PART THREE

THE FIVE LITERACIES

It must now seem obvious from everything we have explored so far that the context, and therefore the inherent nature of leadership has changed and that consequently we need altogether different expressions of leadership from those with which we have become familiar. Novel ways of breaking out of our current mental models and making our interpretations of the past more explicit must be found if we are to create viable futures and then use our imaginative capability to rethink, renew and inspire entirely new possibilities. This is why leadership in a globally networked world must focus less on the commoditised orthodoxies of twentieth-century leadership conventions and far more on the Five Literacies and their implications. Smart leaders know this. The future is catching all of us. At least we can make sure that it catches us with our eyes and our minds wide open.

CHAPTER 8

LITERACY I – NETWORKED INTELLIGENCE

We are all puppets, and our best hope for even partial liberation is to try and decipher the logic of the puppeteer.

– Robert Wright, *The Moral Animal*

CATCHING THE FUTURE

The principles underpinning *five literacies leadership* point to the poss-ibility of enhanced capability and greater responsibility within human institutions and communities. But only if we can transcend some entrenched orthodox management practices. In today's world there is an urgent need for organisations to be viable. Indeed systemic viability, along with strategic relevance, innovation and speed of learning, will soon be recognised as the crucial factors determining survival and well-being within an increasingly complex, global, highly uncertain and forever-changing social and business environment. In the exhaust-ing race for ideas it is vital that leaders grow enterprises that are nimble, adaptive, intelligent and appreciative. This necessitates finding new ways of connecting, inspiring and liberating people, their passions, imagination and intellect from the shackles that previously constrained them.

This is easy enough to say! Unfortunately the *structure-function* traps of convention (expectations, practices and habits) keep us firmly rooted in past–present loops and therefore in a set of erroneous assumptions and beliefs. Furthermore, most attempts to break out of these mind traps invite scorn and derision or, perhaps worse, all manner of rational explanations for maintaining the status quo, from those whose motives may be good but who simply do not comprehend the significance of the changes that are taking place in the world today.

The most difficult challenge confronting us in this regard is that of escaping the legacy of prejudice, arrogance and intolerance so as to make fresh sense of our reality. Without the ability to constantly raise consciousness, and hence wisdom, concerning the fundamental shifts that are transforming everything around us, we risk becoming too set in our ways. Cocooned from actuality, yet unwilling or unable to learn and adapt, the risk is that we turn our back on future poss-ibilities, seeking solace in the seductive lie of nostalgia for a past that is no longer relevant to our real needs.

To many people who are comfortable with their lives, who have found routines that bring a sense of well-being and contentment, who are not caught up in discussions about poverty, politics, trade or ter-rorism and who believe that society must be making progress because of the increasing materiality they enjoy, warnings such as this will fall on deaf ears. To many others they may simply sound over the top. But being able to see our reality clearly, and taking action to improve or change it, is far more of an issue than most of us imagine.

Making sense of the past has never been exactly straightforward.[1] As a rule we believe history to be fixed and immutable. It isn't. Even the chronicles of great leaders and earth-shattering events contain mythical elements. In fact history and time don't have much to do with each other. What we refer to as the *past* in some ways resembles the *future*. Both concepts are value-laden creations projected and inter-preted from a point in time. Most facets of the *past* are not absolute but innumerable personal adaptations of stories that are already wide open to (mis)interpretation. Undergoing constant review and modifica-tion these versions of 'what really happened' are often deleted from our consciousness if they are too awkward to accept or become too peripheral to our current concerns. One only has to compare the nineteenth-century view of European explorers as 'heroic' conquerors

with contemporary interpretations of such exploits as brazen colonisation, for example, to realise that not even meticulously documented
events from the past are as unassailable as they might at first appear
to be. Nothing is constant. In some situations the re-imagining of
history has become a deliberate, and it must be said, highly successful
ploy. Since the 1920s, China's communist elite has attempted to destroy
every artefact from the old society it associated with a degenerate past,
implanting an imagined history in its place. Erasing the nation's memory
in this way has been a conscious act which continues to this day. Even
the Party's own history is cluttered with fantasy.[2] In the great rush to
modernise Beijing for the 2008 Olympics, for example, the state is
razing the entire ancient capital, whose streets and buildings were
eyewitness to so much historical memory. Plenty of museums are being
built but these simply reinforce the Party's misinterpretation of Chinese
history.[3]

Recent events in the West, too, mutate through slight shifts of
emphasis: the 9/11 attacks on New York's World Trade Center creates
starkly dissimilar bundles of emotionally charged memories and truths
for the widows and children of the terrorists than it is does for the
widows and children of those victims trapped, crushed and vaporised
as the twin towers smashed into rubble before our eyes. There were
so many people all caught up in this terrible tragedy and yet their
histories of this one event are all utterly different. Context invariably
changes perceptions. Time too dulls the memory, such that entire
civilisations, their atrocities and their achievements, can erode, corrode
and disappear forever, leaving us with only faded impressions of what
has been.

If making sense of the past is problematic, making sense of the
future is fraught with further complications. As we journey through
life, we compose our world (and, hence, much of our identity) into
being from one moment to the next through the window of past experiences. Quite literally, the brain deciphers all perceived phenomena
in terms of such 'memory-like' filters. Indeed it is a consequence of
these perceptual filters that we tend to be most sure of our convictions
when we are able to make explicit connections between the present
moment and the past. This is why the past is so obvious in hindsight:
we make it so because of the links we make to the 'here and now'.
These projections of the past represent 'the truth' and it usually takes
considerable persuasion or inducements for us to change our minds.
The future, on the other hand, has yet to transpire. It is therefore
inexplicable, strange and more speculative.

Comprehending the present is arguably more difficult still. It requires us to sense the salient patterns connecting everything happening in the world today, to make sense of the interdependent nature of these patterns, together with their underlying structure, and to appreciate the diverse ways in which they could, can, and are, playing out.

To achieve all of this we must learn to let go of (some aspects of) the past even as we consciously break out of the mind traps that persistently threaten to misinform and deceive us – often without our even realising it. For example, if we were conscious of the ways in which the filters[4] we habitually use to organise and sort information actually prejudice our ability to comprehensively discern reality, we would be far more inclined towards using multiple viewpoints for informed decision making, rather than relying on our own narrowly biased views. At the same time, if we were able to create lucid 'memories of the future' it is possible we could use them to review the most critical of global issues and dilemmas in order to perceive them in all their astonishing variety and richness and complexity.

It is possible we might then see the world (and our relationship to it) with fresh eyes. We might acknowledge the potentially irreparable social and environmental damage we are wreaking in the name of economic growth and development. We might even find a way of transcending our tenacious celebration of industrialism, with its narrow definitions of efficiency, energy, undifferentiated per capita-averaged growth and human welfare as well as the mindless pursuit of mass production, in order to design whole-of-system interventions better able to secure a peaceful, more ecologically conscious, sane, gender-balanced and equitable world for future generations.

The *Five Literacies* can be thought of as an integral suite of meta-competencies: the expertise required across five linked domains of knowledge in order to make better sense of tomorrow's world and wiser, more mindful business decisions in that environment. They are therefore pivotal in the realisation of a new global leadership praxis that articulates a new common sense of strategic leadership in *zero geography*. They also happen to be the foundation on which any large organisation, institution, community or nation-state must depend for managing its future viability. Four conditions must prevail, however, if the *Five Literacies* are to be effectively applied.

1. **Recursive**
First, and most importantly, although the *five literacies* are not an ordered sequence or a discrete set of competencies, they are both

layered and *recursive* in nature. In other words, each literacy provides a context for the others, which then exists at every level within the larger system. Imagining the *five literacies* as skills or tools and implementing just one or two because they happen to appeal is self-defeating – a waste of time and effort. Value will be short-lived and life will rapidly return to normal if this path is taken.

2. **Congruent**

Second, the *five literacies* are incapable of yielding extraordinary results if the habits of a lifetime do not change. Tools, methods, techniques and processes all need to align with each other in terms of their underlying design criteria. The tensions caused by conflicting design criteria (for example, between systemic principles and linear measures) have the potential to do significant damage to an enterprise and instigate unwarranted stress to its people. So, in any environment where *five literacies* leadership is intended, real-time collaborative inquiry is applied in preference to top-down bureaucratic instruction. Likewise, the linking of people via preferential networks ensures the viral transmission of messages better than more conventional approaches to corporate communications.

3. **Intelligent**

Third, strategic intelligence must be valued and consistently applied when making and communicating strategic decisions. Astute readers will already have noted that this also happens to be the lifeblood of Strategic Navigation and its associated methodologies. Intelligence is not just distinctive information, nor the flow of information throughout an organisation's central nervous system, but rather a higher order learning capability all human beings use to make sense of information for knowing *when* to adapt, *what* to change, and *how* best to do it.

4. **Focused**

The blend of focused energy, unconditional concentration and passionate engagement utilised by *five literacies* leaders is something routinely sought after and experienced by high-level athletes and performing artists – but rarely in business. However, producing and sustaining elite levels of performance with the intensity and focus demanded in today's globalised environment is critical. Shifting into this atemporal high-performance 'zone' requires an ability to constantly upgrade one's cognitive, psychological, emotional and physiological capacity, as well as a willingness to help shape the conditions in which this performance becomes more polished and refined.[5] Above all else it entails the talent to constantly learn in the unending quest for excellence.

These four conditions can all be found in natural systems. Likewise, the aptitudes implied by the employment of real-time strategic intelligence to generate and extend the capacity for elite performance should occur autonomically – as they do in human beings.[6] Whenever these aptitudes remain undeveloped, as they frequently are in organisations employing traditional strategic management methods or where massive egos get in the way of real learning and change, the facility to respond instantly to changing systemic conditions will deteriorate. However, embedded within the *five literacies* the continuous making and dissemination of real-time intelligence brings about performance that is matchless.

The structural adaptiveness, flexibility and resilience arising from the application of real-time intelligence were accepted as key elements in creating sustainable organisations as long ago as a Shell longevity study of the 1980s.[7] Qualities like these are even more critical today as we navigate our way through a world of unprecedented volatility. But they can only reach their full potential in helping us navigate uncertainty if we are able to speed up the learning metabolism in ourselves as well as within our many institutions and organisations.[8] This depends on thinking differently and reflecting more deeply about business fundamentals as well as harnessing new technologies and nurturing innovation, the prime source of advantage in the knowledge economy. This is precisely why the *five literacies* are so important.

Pervasive use of the *five literacies* will add distinct kinds of value, depending on the circumstances. Undoubtedly, they best suit courageous learning leaders working in multifaceted organisations where unstable or uncertain business conditions prevail: government and state bureaucracies, local government, multinational corporations, global NGOs, community administrations (such as education, health or transportation), industry groups and large diversified businesses, for example. For these types of enterprise, the benefits will be almost immediately apparent.

As markets have transformed into self-organising living networks, many of the competencies, skills and expertise we have traditionally associated and valued with effective business practice have become obsolete. Where product value, production costs, and competitor or market intelligence were once the most critical factors in achieving adequate returns, they are not so today. In fact even long-term planning, once the hallmark of a robust strategic management practice, has all but disappeared as the instability and unpredictable nature of global markets make it almost impossible to know what will happen tomorrow, let alone next year.

This volatility has caused the sudden disappearance of skills sets and organisational functions previously thought to be permanent. Entire professions have disappeared as new ones take their place. Technology is changing work design and practice so rapidly that it is possible most of what we will be doing in 20 years' time has not even been imagined yet. It has also radically shifted the conditions, expression and practise of leadership.

In most contemporary corporations the speed of such change has caused real problems in retaining both high-level talent and specialist expertise. Information Technology (IT) departments, for example, inherit Cobol-based legacy systems that have become unworkable because of a depreciated skills base. Along with a host of other specialists (such as personnel, archives, recruitment, training, accounting, complaints, programming and planning professionals) entire layers of technical expertise, usually bracketed under the collective euphemism 'non-value-adding' functions, have been zealously ripped out of our organisations – even when they are essential to the effective maintenance of the business. Meanwhile those who previously held these positions, who just a few years ago relished the relative security and immunity provided through their knowledge, all try desperately to hold on to the specialist know-how that brought them credence and utility in the first place. But to no avail. Their world has turned upside down as other suppliers, in many cases located off-shore and seemingly able to respond instantly to the ever-changing demands of big business in a connected world, provide superior service at lower cost. Change is cruel and the shift away from old industrial business models is unrelenting.

The trend away from huge markets, capable labour and cost advantages is not just some passing fad but an overwhelming fact. In all but a few smoke-stack industries, talent and imagination, not technical skills, are now the fundamental factors of production, while attracting such talent has become the central struggle in global competition. Creative sector occupations, in science and technology, art and design, culture and entertainment, have grown since 1980 from approximately 12% of the workforce to between 30 and 40% in most advanced countries today.

ZERO GEOGRAPHY

Even the concept of vertically integrated *industries*, at least in terms of an input-based, bounded grouping of enterprises, is dubious and can be dangerously misleading in a world of *zero geography* where business models are recreated daily from new knowledge, innovation and creativity and where daily transactions number in the trillions. The most important distinction today is not the classic industry boundary but the pattern of links as well as the degree of interaction (such as technology sharing, licensing agreements, market relationships and shared procurements, for example) between these communities of companies and their extended enterprises.

Industries have been globally distributed for well over a decade now. However, since the advent of computing and advanced information and communications technologies, global business *ecosystems* – much larger, networked, more multifaceted and vibrant than any single enterprise, distributed industry or regional trade bloc – prevail. Consequently the degree of connection and networked interdependence common in global business ecosystems today is a relatively recent phenomenon. Within these sprawling networks of suppliers, distributors, outsourcing firms, makers of related products and services, technology providers and a host of service organisations and customers,

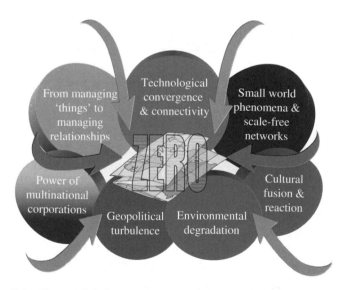

Figure 8.1   Fierce 'global' competition and intense 'local' collaboration have created a world of zero geography – a world where geography has been rendered irrelevant by changing consumer needs, sophisticated communications technologies, emotive global causes and emerging systemic conscience.

companies tend to be highly specialised and compete fiercely within narrow domains of expertise. They focus on doing a relatively small number of things well, yet depend upon each other for their mutual effectiveness and survival. In this environment most companies, including both SMEs and larger corporations, tailor their offerings to such an extent that a single product is typically the result of the collective efforts of many companies, with a significant proportion of their contributions taking the form of offerings that have no intrinsic value on their own, outside the context of the collective effort demanded by the business ecosystem.

In these loosely connected global webs and industry clusters, boundaries of all kinds are constantly transcended and restrictions we have been conditioned to accept are obliterated. Performance of any single enterprise or cluster is driven in large part by the nature and emerging characteristics of the network as a whole, which then influence the *collective* behaviour of the ecosystem's numerous members. This makes an enormous difference to both strategy and operations. And it repositions capability building as a whole-of-system requirement rather than just an internal initiative undertaken by human resources staff. In this reality economies of scale have been outmoded by the economic flows of networks. The impossible has become routine. Time has collapsed and destiny is shared here. Physical boundaries (like airspace, for example) become fluid, impractical almost to define or to standardise. Every day uncontested new markets appear out of the blue, unhampered by previous assumptions about what can and cannot work. Meanwhile, business is conducted non-stop!

Competitors are everywhere in these global ecosystems, including where you least expect to find them. As it happens, so are potential customers. And suppliers: global value webs harness seamlessly the skills and products of small operators everywhere from Seoul to Curitiba who quietly supply materials and parts for the world's computers, DVD players, white goods, solar panels, automobiles, aeroplanes, clothes, watches, digital cameras and other household gadgets. Unique products emerge suddenly without warning and are copied, somewhere in Asia, almost as fast. There are few barriers to entry in the new knowledge industries. It is even possible to rapidly establish a new business anywhere in the world, or in *zero geography*, without the trappings we have normally associated with such a venture, such as capital, premises and employees.

Meanwhile the rapid dissemination and sharing of new knowledge, coupled with the availability of goods and services around the clock, causes business ecosystems to change constantly and capriciously, morphing into new and surprising forms, and changing their topologies almost instantly as markets react to mass purchasing behaviour and peculiar anomalies in the system. This state of flux is the most important discernible difference between global business ecosystems and their antiquated industry predecessors. It means that nothing can be taken for granted here as it will have changed, possibly many times, and all within the blink of an eye.

INFOLUST

Superseding in many respects the notion of discrete, circumscribed industries, business ecosystems represent the ever-shifting intensity arising from the need to do business fast in a global environment that is changing even faster. In fact business success today is largely reliant on the:

• Size, breadth, variety, vigour and health of the business ecosystem to which the individual enterprise belongs.
• Extent to which the networks and clusters inherent within the ecosystem work collaboratively to learn from each other and consciously share information.
• Ability of each enterprise to extract additional value from critical relationships within the business ecosystem.

Over time, ecosystem members co-evolve capabilities and roles, eventually tending to align themselves with the directions set by one or more companies, this gives rise to the phenomenon of *hub* or *keystone* enterprises – nodes in the network that are more richly connected than the vast majority of other members.[9] *Keystone* enterprises play a crucial role in the health and viability of the entire ecosystem. For a start, they add robustness and resilience to the network. They also tend to be powerful influencers in their sectors in some way, becoming knowledge *hubs* and providing uncontested leadership in that space. While they might pursue their own discrete strategies just as aggressively as in the past, *keystone* companies also understand the wisdom of nurturing the health of the ecosystem of which they are a part. Like an individual species in the biospheric context, each member of a business ecosystem ultimately shares the fate of the whole network, regardless of their individual strength or wealth. Their destiny is inextricably linked. And though the roles of *keystone* enterprises may change over time, sometimes quite appreciably, the function of eco-system leadership is invariably valued (and possibly resented) by the broader community as it enables members to move toward shared visions while seeking distinction, align their investments, and find mutually supportive roles.

This phenomenon of 'linking' is one of the many new laws of scale-free networks which, if properly understood and consistently applied, can lead to exponential value creation. *Keystone* companies understand that their business and the ecosystem are inextricably linked.[10] Professor Marco Iansiti of Harvard Business School, who first referred to these companies as *keystone* companies, points out that from their earliest days these firms are unlike most others, which focus primarily on internal capability, instead taking it upon themselves to act on behalf of the overall health of their business ecosystems. They do this through various forms of *virtuous* investment: finding ways to create and exploit new value from the ecosystem and then sharing that value to achieve enormous returns both for the individual company and for the ecosystem as a whole. In taking this responsibility upon

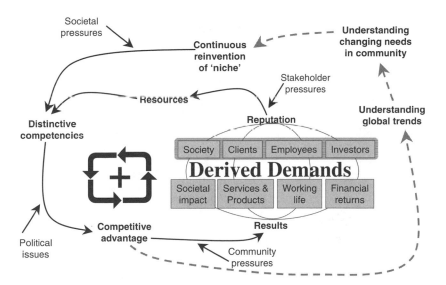

Figure 8.2 Smart companies provide exemplary leadership within their business ecosystem by first ensuring that they understand the dynamics of global markets and are able to meet the derived demands of all stakeholders in real time.

themselves they also develop the critical capability to meet stakeholders' derived demands.[11] In the midst of wild volatility and economic uncertainty, *keystone* companies provide their business ecosystems with stable and predictable sets of common assets that other organisations, including competitors, can then emulate or use to build their own offerings. These can be tangible and non-tangible assets, like knowledge or ethics. For example, Wal-Mart's celebrated procurement system, The Body Shop's use of an anthropologist to devise strategies that compensate indigenous wisdom, Toyota's search for hybrid energy sources to replace the internal combustion engine, Linux's approach to software development, and Microsoft's Windows operating system.

Notwithstanding the invisible hand of Adam Smith, whose writings still keep many executives convinced that humans essentially act out of self-interest and are not inclined to share, collaboration is also a critical factor in leveraging these resources. By pooling assets in the area of grid computing and peer-to-peer technology, for example, IBM and Avaki Corporation used a *keynote* strategy to secure corporate

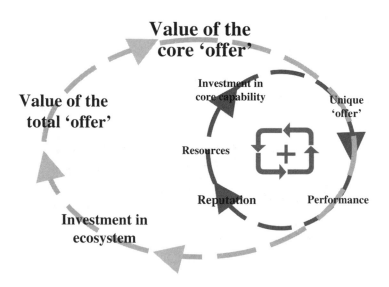

Figure 8.3 Keystone companies provide exemplary leadership of the business ecosystem through virtuous investment in the health of the whole system. They do not seek to dominate the ecosystem but their influence is massive in comparison with other players and their ROI equally impressive.

customers in the life-sciences industry, including Aventis, Johnson & Johnson and Pfizer. IBM provides the computing platform, and Avaki provides the grid-computing software. By leveraging its assets and capabilities in this way, and establishing the partnership, IBM improved the health of its ecosystem and tapped into a new global market. It has also unwittingly hammered yet another nail in the coffin of independent corporate research labs.

The online revolution has taken this desire for more information – *infolust* – and leveraging of knowledge assets to new extremes, enabling companies to collaborate in real time with large numbers of their customers, suppliers and partners – or any other stakeholders for that matter. Boeing, a *keystone* enterprise in the global aviation ecosystem, used electronic collaboration to develop its newest fleets of aeroplanes. Springwise and its global network of 8000 spotters scan the globe for smart new business ideas, delivering instant insights to entrepreneurial minds from San Francisco to Singapore. The pharmaceutical company Eli Lilly solicits requests on its InnoCentives website for solutions to product-development problems it faces. Forty companies from Dow to DuPont to Procter & Gamble now use the site where 80,000 'solvers' from 175 countries regularly come together to work. As solvers from China, the US, Russia and India began connecting online, InnoCentives launched a new conference business to bring them together to discuss novel business ideas in person.

In addition to online collaboration, the evolution of software supports online innovation. Consumers are also getting in on the act. Customer research extends beyond traditional focus groups testing physical products to web-based research, beta tests and so-called *expeditionary* marketing. Companies like Toyota, LEGO, Coach and Procter & Gamble are encouraging the democratisation of innovation by allowing consumers to tinker with products before they are released and offer up suggestions for improvement. Customers can express their design preferences using web-based technology; with a click of the mouse they can select dozens of product features from dozens of alternatives to test hundreds of designs. Prototyping is moving from physical models to fast prototyping and web-based simulations. Boeing, for example, is prototyping the new 787 without building a physical model.

Another fine example of a *keystone* company that effectively creates and leverages new value on behalf of its ecosystem is eBay. eBay creates value in a number of ways. It has developed state-of-the-art tools that increase the productivity of network members and encourage potential members to join the ecosystem. These tools include eBay's Seller's Assistant, which helps new vendors prepare professional-looking online listings, and its Turbo Lister service, which tracks and manages thousands of bulk listings on home computers. The company has also established and preserved performance standards that enhance the stability of the system. Buyers and sellers rate one another, providing rankings that bolster users' confidence in the system. Vendors with consistently good evaluations attain PowerSeller status; those with bad evaluations are excluded from future transactions. Additionally, eBay shares the value that it creates with members of its ecosystem. For example, it charges users only a moderate fee to coordinate their trading activities. Incentives such as the PowerSeller label reinforce standards for sellers that benefit the entire ecosystem. These performance standards also delegate much of the control of the network to users, diminishing the need for eBay to maintain expensive centralised monitoring and feedback systems. The company can charge commissions that are no higher than 7% of a given transaction (well below the typical 30–70% margins most retailers would charge). Naturally eBay, like Microsoft and Wal-Mart, does this because it is good business. By sharing the value, it continues to expand its own healthy ecosystem, buyers and sellers now total more than 70 million, and thrive in a sustainable way.

Collaborative practices such as those practised by *keystone* enterprises can be grouped under the category of business ecosystem (network or *swarm*) intelligence applications. They generate new value from within the ecosystem and share this; help increase productivity by simplifying the otherwise complicated task of connecting network participants to one another; make the creation and distribution of new products from third parties more efficient; enable open-source and other forms of shared research and development; and stabilise ecosystem resilience and responsiveness by continuously incorporating technological innovations into network activities.

In many respects, *keystone* companies use these practices to work themselves into an enviable position. Yet, in spite of their advantages and their overwhelming influence on the business ecosystem, they themselves invariably remain a very small part of their ecosystem's bulk. Microsoft, for example, has incredible impact on its own as well as other related ecosystems. Despite this, the company, both by revenue and staff numbers, remains only a tiny fraction of the global computing ecosystem. Even Microsoft's market capitalisation represents only around 0.4 % of the total business ecosystem of which Microsoft is a part. *Keystone* enterprises are also crucial to the overall health of the economy. Indeed their removal, in many cases, may lead to the catastrophic collapse of the entire ecosystem. Again, Marco Iansiti cites WorldCom's failures, which triggered negative repercussions over the entire web of telecommunications equipment suppliers across the US. And we are still witnessing the continued fallout from the demise of Enron which shattered confidence right across that business ecosystem in ways from which it has been almost impossible to mend.

Consequently, although the strategies of *keystone* enterprises differ considerably from most successful industrial-age cases of global success, seemingly altruistic by comparison, balancing internal strategic focus (especially innovative product development and service underpinned by capability and process fitness methods) with continuous improvement to the broader ecosystem (value creation, value sharing and the launch of collaborative communities of practice) has ensured the ongoing survival and prosperity of these corporations. In today's environment a network-centric strategy, leveraging virtuous investment as a means of improving the overall health of the business ecosystem, is simply good strategy.

Critical to this strategic understanding of business ecosystems and their dynamic morphology is networked intelligence: the systemic appreciation of emergence (in the form of possibilities and potential ventures as well as invisible downsides, asymmetric risks and other traps) coupled with the wisdom to know *what* decisions to make, *when* to make them, *who* to involve, and *how* in a context of dynamically complex change. Ecosystem networks certainly provide the means for avoiding traps and meeting the future faster – but only if networked intelligence is created by an engaged community of stakeholders and applied consistently to create new value. This usually means designing a pertinent, democratised, engaging strategic management system (the original intent behind the Strategic Navigation methodology, for example) that generates and uses real-time networked intelligence as its raison d'être, while installing new tools and techniques for enabling people to visualise the dynamic complexity with which they have to deal.[12]

Through information sharing, real-time intelligence creation, and the outsourcing of research and development to a global web of freelancers who scour the world like bounty hunters for the biggest rewards, companies are better able to respond to the markets' vagaries and derived demands, grow revenues, eliminate value-chain misalignments, decrease costs, build resilience, and improve operational efficiencies. But that is just the, albeit impressive, surface sign indicating a broader macrocosm that will most likely eventuate in higher rates of growth, more and better jobs, challenging work design and greater social inclusion within society.

Naturally, even when employing the most reliable and advanced enabling technologies and leveraging any obvious interdependencies, the task of incorporating real-time intelligence activities across a diffuse global business ecosystem (or even affiliated project clusters) is no mean feat. It requires cooperation and the integration of information and processes from thousands and potentially millions of global business partners, SMEs and customers. If that wasn't complicated enough, loyalty is fast disappearing while companies become more porous from the large numbers of outsiders working on tasks once performed within the walls of the corporation. The risks appear vast! Yet companies that have developed such strategies are realising this is much more than just a passing fad or an effective partner collaboration tool. It is a precious strategic asset. One recent study in the US concluded that information sharing with its business ecosystem partners has become the single largest contributor to Wal-Mart's margin advantage over their competitors. Very soon, grids using peer-to-peer technology to pool computing power will connect most companies and consumers.

AND CITIZENS?

What applies commercially is also happening in the public and community sectors. For example, governments everywhere, from China to India, Brazil and South Korea, are beginning the journey that will take them away from the use of proprietary, closed software, toward an open-source model where programming technology is freely available and freely shared. It has long been recognised that some of the world's most competitive (and confident) nations are those that use open-source principles in government. Finland and Denmark, for example, save millions of euros each year by employing open-source systems for bidding on government contracts. In Thailand the government is moving to an open-source system after it found coordination between government agencies and NGOs responded inadequately to the tsunami relief effort. After these initiatives, the move to participative democracy is but a small step which, in turn, is likely to produce a safer, more secure, global environment.[13]

Conventional economics, which has little truck or patience with altruism, wouldn't have predicted any of this networked information economy with its globally collaborative, open-ended modes of production, the way it has liberated talent from the developing world into the global loop, or its massive boom for entrepreneurial venture capital. But then economics itself has changed. Bioeconomics, the special form of economics seen in global business ecosystems, is rapidly rewriting the rules regarding the balance between competition and cooperation.

Somehow it is up to leaders to make sense of all of this and to reconceptualise their business arrangements to take advantage of these exciting opportunities. There is so much that governments and business need to pay attention to today – so much going on that we need to sense, make sense of and respond to wisely in order to remain viable. Networked intelligence and the principles on which it is founded – like the idea that there is strategic advantage in sharing – provides *five literacies* leaders with the means to do just that. It is the all-encompassing knowledge they create from perceiving what is going on around them that they can then use to change how things are. It is best viewed as a mixture of hypersensitive awareness to circumstances, dynamics, morphology and relationships (within and between business ecosystems) coupled to a deep understanding of the consequences, both intended and unintended, of what is happening.

DESIGNING VIABILITY

From all of this it should be clear that the creation of networked intelligence is much more than just monitoring discrete information about particular classes of stakeholder – like competitors or customers for example. On the contrary, it is dynamic, inclusive – ranging broadly (across internal and external environments), deeply (into belief systems and events) and atemporally (in terms of past, present and possible developments) – and transformative. Nowadays networked intelligence has become the basis for collaborative decision making in an environment that is global, boundless, ephemeral and, as a result, inherently complex. But it also enables flexibility, speed of response and adaptiveness in an age when those very qualities have become indispensable for any company, industry or government wishing to become and remain *viable*.

How does a company, or even a country for that matter, become and remain viable? Contrary to today's conventional wisdom, let's not necessarily assume that contemporary corporations, even those that purport to have achieved 'world's best practice' are necessarily the best place to look for role models and benchmarks for viability. Conventional corporations are fundamentally different from businesses designed as living networks.

To be really useful, many of those models must first be understood at the level of their organising principles, and not just at the level of their methods and techniques. And, sadly, when viewed at that level, we discover many of even the most highly regarded management models of the late twentieth century to be little more than unimaginative tweaking at the margins of mediocrity. Instead, let us look at the basic principles that must be in play for any corporation to be viable over time. As evidenced by the Shell study mentioned previously, such viable organisations appear to behave like self-regulating living organisms. It should therefore come as no surprise to discover that the most naturally occurring viable systems are in fact living systems.

Living systems, like human beings, are extremely complex organisms. They are almost impenetrable in their ability to defy logic and

Table 8.1 Some critical differences in design assumptions between bureaucratic corporations and living networks (the most responsive and adaptive of organisational structures).

Corporations	Networks
Management through centralised controls	Self-regulation through distributed intelligence
Adaptation through crisis	Adaptation through learning
Knowledge and authority reside within hierarchies	Knowledge and authority distributed outwardly
Knowing through analysis	*Knowing* through systemicity
Evolve through stability and uniformity	Coevolve through instability and diversity
Top-down communication emphasises authority	Wired into a 'community of mind'
Predictable and controllable	Unpredictable and uncontrollable
Intuitively resist transformational change	Continuously change *how* they change
Mostly insensitive to the environment	Highly sensitive to the environment

reason! However, we can identify seven critical organising principles underpinning the whole notion of viability within living systems, which are the key to viability within human organisations, communities and business ecosystems. They are ecology, niche, coevolution, emergence, intentionality, autopoiesis and distributed intelligence.

1. Ecology

Ecology is a natural phenomenon having to do with the innate balance of *systemic relationships* – that everything, however apparently separate, is ultimately connected and must therefore affect each other. In other words, with every decision or intervention *five literacies* leaders make, they must always take into account how it will affect the business ecosystem as the whole system will react in some way to their actions. Often it will not react instantly. It might not respond as we expect, nor at the precise location of our intervention. But business ecosystems are dynamic and constantly changing; we can be sure of a reaction in some way at some point in time. Then that will give rise to the need for further responses. For instance, in relatively recent changes to the gun laws in Australia, what at first seemed like a straightforward policy to ban semi-automatic weapons resulted in issues concerning civil rights, doubts concerning the credibility of the decision-making capacity of the government, the influence of minority lobby groups, the role and responsibility of the media, the interpretation of data . . . Even the relationships between the Commonwealth and the individual states came into question. *Five literacies* principles had not been applied.

In spite of our reductionist tendencies, a simple and straightforward government policy isn't simple and straightforward when we come to understand that all decisions, together with any actions resulting from such decisions, occur within the context of an ecosystem where all parts are continuously affected by every other part. Likewise, business corporations are not able to quarantine their strategic intentions from the vibrant web of customers, suppliers, employees, shareholders and other community stakeholders impacted by particular decisions and strategies. It simply isn't possible.

Networked intelligence creates the means whereby *five literacies* leaders can consider their responsibility to the business ecosystem of which they are a part. It demands that we make decisions not from an isolated perspective that may adversely affect the balance of the whole system but to understand the value that accrues through virtuous, cooperative investment in the whole ecosystem. This is why collaboration has become so important in business. But cooperative behaviour flies in the face of convention and is consequently difficult for managers to grasp when they have been brainwashed to see the world only in competitive terms.

2. Niche

In the context of business ecosystems and intelligence, niche is the proposition that every element within a particular ecosystem is not just related but has its unique place and role within that ecology – a relevance, purpose and effectiveness (or *fit*) it needs to constantly modify as the system itself mutates and evolves over time. In the case of individuals and human enterprise, this notion of niche can be applied to four interdependent frameworks.

The first framework chronicles the story of what we perceive to be our mission or, in the case of the enterprise, what it was set up to do and how it manages to fit[14] into a dynamically complex external environment. In other words, what is our role relative to the context in which we live and with which we interact? This framework is about *ecological* fit. The second framework has to do with the distinctive, possibly unique, qualities generated in the process of achieving this mission. This framework is about *strategic* fit. The third framework is the story of our values, beliefs, appearance, style and aspirations. This framework is about *human* fit and tells the tale of our culture, our identity and moral purpose. Finally, the fourth framework is the congruence between these respective human, strategic and ecological fits. This is *systemic alignment.* Without systemic alignment, strategic friction will increase trauma and our pathology sickens and goes into distress. Individuals will suffer from conative and other forms of neuro-physiological stress if this lack of alignment continues for any length of time. Organisations, too, will suffer similar consequences.

This principle of an ecological niche, in contrast to a marketing view of niche, is critically important for *five literacies* leaders as it demands that they are always thinking in terms of the whole business ecosystem and of the sets of dynamic interrelationships that exist between its various members.

3. Coevolution

Arising from Darwin's theory of *coadaptions* of organisms to each other, coevolution is the reciprocal evolutionary change that occurs in interacting species. Essentially, it is the notion that all things – biological, societal, and technological – adapt to and create each other from one moment to the next, simultaneously weaving themselves into one whole, interconnected system. In other words, the evolution of an organism (a human being or a social organisation like a company for that matter) is inseparable from the evolution of its environment. *Five literacies* leaders understand that, while evolution is adapting to meet one's own needs, coevolution is adapting to meet each others' needs.[15]

The fundamental idea behind coevolution, then, is that of mutual *adaptation*. Specifically, adaptation of one's distinctiveness (or personal *niche*) in reaction to the actual and anticipated needs, desires, compulsions and opportunities offered by the emerging dynamic of the global business ecosystem (small world) in which one lives and works. As far as *five literacies* leaders are concerned, this equates to strategic learning for change and adaptation. Strategic learning can be applied to the individual (relative to the changing nature of work, life, family, business, career, etc.) as well as to any enterprise or community as it redefines or even, at times, completely transforms itself in response to the changing needs and demands of society.

4. Emergence

A related hypothesis to the principle of coevolution is that of emergence, or the novel state arising from unpredictability and uncertainty. Living systems have a way of evolving into entirely new forms of life which, at times, are unpredictable and therefore surprising. The new form, or transformation, seems to have just emerged from left field. When we understand more about the dynamics of coevolution, however, such surprising occurrences are to be expected. In other words, the fact that we get surprises is no surprise at all. We expect dynamic systems to not only coevolve, but at times to also completely transform. The significance of this principle of systemic emergence should not be underestimated, especially when a corporation needs to undergo a process of organisational and cultural transformation due to its need to coevolve with the changing society it serves. Emergence can never be foreseen as it doesn't just 'emerge'. It takes us by surprise and is always entirely unexpected. Planning for surprising events and circumstances is therefore critical in contemporary life. *Five literacies* leaders understand this and are always on the alert and prepared for emergence. In this way, they avoid massive disruption and even use emergent properties to their advantage.

5. Intentionality

The fifth (quintessentially human) principle of viability is intentionality. As far as we know, this ability seems to be unique to human beings in that humans are able to engage themselves consciously in transcending the conditioning of their past by exercising choice. We are able to choose and by choosing the direction in which we want our life to go, as well as communicating this through language, are able to bring meaning and purpose to our own, and others, daily activities. Based on the intentionality behind their choices, *five literacies* leaders make their own lives and their corporations full of purpose rather than purposeless, full of meaning rather than meaningless, full of possibilities rather than forlorn and despairing. In other words, where human beings are concerned at least, viability is not only based on conditions of viability, but also choices for viability.

6. Autopoiesis

Viable systems are able to self-organise in order to create and maintain themselves in relation to the health of the ecosystem of which they are a part. This ability to self-regulate is known as autopoiesis. Unlike most orthodox management systems, mostly developed during the industrial revolution, which impose levels of control to minimise the degree of turbulence within the system, autopoietic systems are self-managing to the extent that they do not require (or may simply absorb) imposed authority or control so as to ensure continuing growth and adaptiveness.

Within these pages, you will frequently find references to *appreciative* conditions. By that I am referring to the specific category of self-organisation required in order to create a new and vibrant ecosociety from the detritus and mistakes of the past. An autopoietic system that purposefully sustains a social ecology able to learn its way into pre-ferred futures, in ethical reciprocity with its environment, and in ways that are *appreciative* of everyone's needs, expectations and desires, not only becomes viable but also convivial. From the perspective of creating a new society, this may be the ideal form of autopoiesis. *Five literacies* leaders are also *appreciative* leaders – intent on creating an appreciative society in which fairness and equality triumph.

7. Distributed intelligence

Finally, viability is concerned with the meaning we create from infor-mation. Intelligence is the vital material needed to continuously nourish any living system so that it can self-organise and purposefully coevolve in relation to its environment. All viable systems are reliant upon intel-ligence for their very survival and adaptation. If intelligence is sub-verted, muddled or terminated the organism (or species) will die through an inability to adapt. Although the centre of intelligence in human beings was once thought to reside in the brain, that is now thought to be not entirely true. Intelligence is a function of the whole human body. The process of distributed intelligence is apparent from the way the brain distributes its operations into the furthest reaches of the body via the extensive system of nerves and synapses.

In terms of human enterprise, this nervous system is represented by the connections created between many autonomous members of an organisation or business ecosystem, where each member is able to react both individually and collectively to the state of their local envi-ronment according to an innate code of behaviour. These autonomous members are connected to each other, but not necessarily to any central controlling hub. They form a peer network. Since there is no central intelligence the management and heart of the system are said to be *decentrally distributed* within the system. In such a distributed system, isolated crashes or breakdowns are relatively unimportant, because of the nonlinear, or web-like, nature of the system. There is an obvious difference between distributed systems and situations where instructions from a central authority need to be obeyed, or where a group of individuals is required to react in 'lock-step' in order to deal with certain environmental conditions. In these situations, crashes and breakdowns can significantly affect the whole – occasionally causing total organisational trauma from which it may be impossible to recover.

Five literacies leaders recognise that, in certain environmental conditions, viable systems have enormous benefits over other, more conventionally structured, forms of organising.

Briefly, viable systems are more:

- Accommodating – adjusting to new, changing or changed circumstances is more easily accomplished.
- Evolvable – networks are able to shift their locus of adaptation over time from one part of the system to another in order to evolve.
- Resilient – small failures and individual mistakes do not count, or are infinitely less important, and big failures are held in check by becoming small failures at the next level in a hierarchy of nested systems.
- Boundless – by incrementally extending new structure beyond the bounds of its initial state a network can build its own scaffolding to initiate further structure.
- Novel – through the exponential combinations of many individuals as well as the tolerance of individual imperfection and variation, networks generate perpetual novelty.
- Optimal – built-in redundancy causes inefficiency, duplication of effort is rampant, resources are allocated higgledy-piggledy.
- Controllable – because there is no central authority, guidance or influence comes from applying appropriate leverage at crucial points and from subverting the natural tendency of the system to new ends.
- Predictable – complexity tends to bend the network in unforeseeable ways, and this factor may require a greater degree of control to be exercised in particular situations (for example, where such control is literally a matter of life or death).
- Fathomable – while linear causality is like clockwork, nonlinear, web-like networks are mysterious fields of intersecting logic and self-referential paradox. The credit for the true proportional mix of causes will spread horizontally through the network until the trigger of a particular event is essentially unknown and unknowable.
- Immediate – the greater the levels of complexity within a network the more time the system takes to respond.

Like natural ecosystems, each viable system is a dynamic web – always in flux, always in the process of reshaping itself. This is as true of human beings as it is of social ecologies and organisational cultures. They, too, must also be in a constant state of flux and reinvention in order to persist. Thus, life itself is a networked process – a distributed intelligence. It is one organism extended in space and time. Indeed, it is entirely possible there may be no such thing as individual life. Life is all about relationships, links, shared multiples, interconnections, alliances. Life is always plural! Translating these seven principles into business terms, Table 8.2 illustrates the major factors that allow *five literacies* leaders to distinguish and create a vibrant and innovative organisation compared with one that is unhealthy, in a state of atrophy and essentially non-viable.

Table 8.2 The signs of a non-viable, unhealthy organisation compared with a viable healthy one.

Non-viable	Viable
Internally driven strategic focus	Systemically aligned strategic focus
Disconnect between management's view of the world and the staff's view of the world	Aligned understandings, albeit from different and multiple perspectives
Unclear future and intent	Clarity of intent and future possibilities
Self-destructive culture	Self-sustaining and integrative culture
Disconnected communications	Collaborative, shared intelligence
Disengagement between external and internal views	The corporation's boundaries favour and allow connectedness within the niche
Counter-cultures abound	Aligned cultures abound
No acceptance of responsibility though attention given to accountability (apparent through blaming, scapegoating, and separation ('us' versus 'them'))	Responsible and responsive culture (apparent through individual expression and group ethos)
No energy for change which is always portrayed in negative terms	Energy for change and confidence for action
Inertia, difficult to change, average performance	Speed of response and change with focused energy
Learning not valued – therefore static	Learning is valued – therefore adaptive
Rationalising away data	Using information wisely
The past used as a justification for maintaining the status quo	The past, present and future used as a resource for innovation
Future as threat and high risk	Future as opportunity and high value
Present as default	Present as choice
Value-cost trade-off	High value but low cost

NOTES

1. Witness the growing number of spiteful, occasionally histrionic, wars of words between various historians who hold to one or more ideologies and whose version of history is subsequently coloured by that fact.
2. Any totalitarian state, as George Orwell so famously made clear in *Nineteen Eighty-four*, must monopolise the past to control the future.
3. The political rigidity of the Communist Party of China (CPC) has meant that China has never been forced to confront its own horrendous past or come clean about the enormous violations of human rights it has committed over the past 80 years. Beijing has never felt the need to apologise for occupying Tibet; attacking India, Burma and Vietnam; creating Pol Pot's Cambodia; bankrolling Enver Hoxha's Albania; and fuelling devastating insurgencies across southeast Asia and Africa. According to freelance journalist Jasper Becker, this is because China has clung to a version of history which allows the Chinese to see themselves only as victims. At the same time, Beijing stirs up outrage at Japan's alleged unwillingness to repent for its invasion of east Asia and for using textbooks that falsify history.
4. These filters commonly include any assumptions, beliefs and values we might hold that ultimately determine our attitudes, opinions and behaviours regarding any given issue.
5. The atemporal zone is where past, present and future collapse into a dream-like state. According to descriptions from high-performance athletes and performing artists, although events are passing rapidly in clock time they appear to be floating in suspended motion as far as the performer's actual experience is concerned.
6. Autonomic processes are the unconscious mechanisms of the mind–body relationship. Like the process of digestion or the beating of the heart, for example, autonomic processes happen automatically and without the need for conscious regulation.
7. The Shell Longevity study cited in Arie de Geus, *The Living Company: Growth, Learning and Longevity in Business*, Nicholas Brealey, London, 1997.
8. The learning metabolism of an organisation is the time it takes the organisation to collect, process and act upon intelligence.
9. The ecological literature contains many conflicting definitions of the term 'keystone' and some debate the extent of its relevance. In the context of global business ecosystems it is used to denote a single enterprise (or possibly an industry cluster of SMEs) that governs most important aspects of ecosystem health, often without being a significant portion of the ecosystem itself.
10. Strategy as ecology, *Harvard Business Review*, **82**(3), March 2004.
11. A derived demand is a need that can be satisfied immediately – like flicking the switch when light is required.

12. Typically this can range from simple relationship diagrams and causal loops to quite complicated computer modelling.

13. As old legal and political institutions fail to keep pace in a world changing so fast, new web-based citizen's organisations are springing up specifically designed to put more influential power in the hands of ordinary people. A good example of this is *GetUp* – a new political activist movement in Australia. *GetUp* brings together like-minded people who use the latest online tools to act on the most important issues facing the country. Another example is UK-based Open Democracy – an online vehicle for disseminating information that frequently challenges the official versions of news stories conveyed in the conventional press.

14. As a general rule I use the term fitness to mean 'fitness for purpose' within the context of the most relevant business ecosystem(s).

15. This insight gained from Stewart Brand.

CHAPTER 9

LITERACY II – FUTURING

Life can only be understood backwards, but it must be lived forwards.

– Soren Kierkegaard

Most people think the future is a destination or a goal – somewhere we are headed in time. It is not. It is something we help to create every time we make a decision about what we will do next and then act out that decision. In spite of that, we can never be too sure about the future. Our lives are teeming with such intricacies that novelty is sure to take us by surprise sooner or later – even in the most certain of situations or when we are convinced of arriving at a particular outcome. The shock of the new is constantly with us these days. The future is essentially unknowable. Indeed it is impossible to predict how even the most ordinary of events might play out, though we frequently behave as if this were not the case.

Such irrational contradictions are part of the rich tapestry of life. Furthermore they translate into every facet of our being, from the mundane to the spectacular. Take, for example, the grandiose posturing of the world's trade ministers held in Cancun, Mexico, supposedly to hammer out a better deal for disadvantaged nations. Despite the deadlines set in Doha several years ago, the poor still find it impossible to buy cheap medicines and the governments of rich countries still strain every sinew to protect their corporate paymasters from genuine trade competition.[1] While it is apparently unreasonable for third-world manufacturers to make cheap copies of the life-saving drugs developed by the world's wealthiest companies, it is fine for those corporations to take out patents on seeds that third-world farmers have used for generations. This is the very antithesis of the oft-stated intentions, claims of breakthroughs and promises of a new era regularly emanating from the WTO. Western governments have convinced themselves that they behave in this high-handed manner to protect jobs or environmental quality or traditional ways of life. In reality the main beneficiaries are almost always large corporations. So what? Ambiguities, inconsistencies and double standards, some argue, are the epitome of what it is to be human. The danger, however, is habituated hubris. All manner of hazards are likely to befall those egotistical corporations and governments who are uncaring of the consequences resulting from their actions. History makes evident how extravagant plans can take on an almost siren-like character, seducing us into narcissistic quiescence if we allow them too much latitude or begin to marvel at our own self-propaganda.

How then to reconcile the power of human intention and invention with our apparent inability as a society to achieve even the most fundamental of life's basics – such as the elimination of starvation, poverty and conflict, and the protection of the environment on which we depend for our very existence? Perhaps the trick is to let go of the illusion that we can manipulate events to suit our purpose and seek more viable means of creating better futures. Now there's a scary thought, if only for the fact that this would require a far more profound comprehension of ourselves (especially the connections between our inner reality and the behavioural consequences and events that flow unerringly from particular sets of beliefs and worldviews) than we are usually willing to take on.

Each and every one of us joins in actualising the world we see and touch, although we are mostly unconscious of it. Even when we become more aware of our own culpability we are only willing to own up to that part we find to our liking. Greater knowledge of that elusive inner world might help restore wisdom and enable a healthier societal pathology once more. Sadly, self-knowledge remains considerably more of a mystery than does outer space! Uncertainty prevails even here in the microcosmic recesses of our minds.

THINKING MATTERS

In truth, there are few things of which we can be truly certain. Many aspects of the past and even the present remain, at best, ambiguous. But as far as the future is concerned, the magnitude of uncertainty can be overwhelming. There are only really three assertions we can make with any degree of confidence. They are that the future will be determined by:

- The choices each of us made yesterday, and will make again today.
- How this total array of choices might play out as they collide in time and space.
- The manner in which they happen to influence (or do not influence) each other.

Most decisions we make are probably routine; deliberate yet ultimately *inconsequential*. They affect relatively few people and their impact is usually short-lived, or so we assume. Each one of us makes countless decisions like this every day and instantly forgets them. Other, less frequent but more consequential decisions are made by politicians enacting new laws, entrepreneurs investing in a business, or military commanders directing their forces on the field of battle. These decisions impact more people and generally involve greater levels of 'risk'. Although they are calculated choices, they also rely heavily on *instinct* as well as knowledge and expertise. These decisions are *semi-structural* in nature.

From time to time, though, the decisions we make resonate far more widely. If we are influential individuals, or members of a powerful network, we are more likely to be involved in momentous decision making more frequently than those who are not similarly connected. This is due not to individual genius or the wielding of power but the degree of interconnectivity we possess.

Complexity scientists refer to this as 'fitness', meaning the ability to rapidly connect with other influential people and networks. Located at the opposite end of the scale, these kinds of decisions tend towards being *structural*, if *subliminal*, in nature. They often emerge not from a single deliberate act but from innumerable decisions that are, in themselves, mostly unremarkable.[2]

Structural decisions have the potential to change fundamentally the patterns of human beliefs and activity. Yet the wake emanating from wholly *structural* decisions are rarely identifiable as such in the present (in spite of the claims of self-proclaimed 'pop' futurists) and only then in the most faltering of ways. Nor do we usually become truly conscious of them until they are well and truly history. One might argue that a Gandhi or a Mandela understood only too well the implications of the stand they were taking against colonial power. Except that, by their own admittance, they did not!

Unremarkably, the future is constructed as much from numerous *inconsequential* decisions as from a few significant *structural* ones. This is because today's trivial decisions may combine with trivial others, morphing by sheer numbers into what to all intents and purposes become *structural* decisions at some stage in the future. If we locate all three decision types on a continuum depicting *structural* (and subliminal) impacts at one extreme and *inconsequential* (and deliberate) impacts at the other, we can presume that most important decisions will fall into an elastic, *semi-structural space* where there is some degree of intent as well as some degree of instinct present. And yet, as already noted, *inconsequential* decisions can rapidly cohere with each other in surprising ways to form more *structural*, if unintended, consequences.

For example, we might normally expect economic decisions made at an international level to be potentially more *structural* than those made by a family choosing to spend their annual vacation in, say, Bali. The latter are more likely to be part of an (equally intricate) web of decisions that dissipate rapidly and affect fewer people. Such *inconsequential* decisions invariably cause localised 'ripples' but scarcely ever incise deep enough patterns to change the structure of society in any meaningful or lasting way. To do so would require: (a) deliberate intent on the part of the decision takers; (b) the presence of a 'strange attractor' pulling networks of *inconsequential* decisions into more meaningful alignment; or (c) a serendipitous conjunction with choices made by others elsewhere.

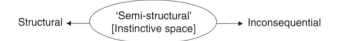

Figure 9.1 Depiction of the 'flatland' space within which most decisions of any consequences emanate, escalate and decay without any single controlling hand – a powerful argument for purposeful collaboration.

But imagine that our mythical family's decision to stay in Bali intersects in some way with Jemaah Islamiyah's bombing of a crowded nightclub in Kuta. Now the family's original decision becomes part of a more complex, yet far less deliberate, chain of events. Public outrage is tinged with a mixture of disbelief. Shock and grief deepens even further when a suicide bombing occurs in Jakarta months later. Righteous anger leads to an escalation of activities on the part of security agencies and emergency services. Arrests are made. Terrorists are tried and convicted. Meanwhile the terrorists achieve their ends. Dread. A fearful brake on normality. Tourism drops away from this already fragile economy.

Imagine now it is March 2010. The events of Bali and Jakarta, and more recently London, still linger in the public's consciousness. The threat of terrorism in our regional backyard still remains a distinct possibility. Halfway around the world, a team of scientists at the University of Texas decipher and publish the genome of Spanish flu – an air-borne, self-mutating virus that killed 40 million people in the early years of the twentieth century. The instant this blueprint is in the public domain, criminal development of the deadly bacteria becomes feasible. Realising the threat, public authorities move to immunise more people. Laboratory security is raised, antiviral drugs are stockpiled and filters and sensors are fitted to more and more buildings in the hope of protecting occupants. Public concern wanes. Some months later, Emirates flight EK410 leaves Singapore on schedule at 8.45 pm bound for Sydney. Somewhere over the Indian Ocean, unnoticed by crew or passengers, a 15-year-old Pakistani passenger armed with an inconspicuous breath freshener, sprays the weaponised virus into the air, setting off a global pandemic . . .

The weaving of such plausible events into a story allows us to play with the dynamics of how a particular future might unfold and what we might do about it if we wanted to change the course of such events. Such 'play' tests the resilience of our current thinking (and strategies) as well as shifting the 'unthinkable' into the realm of the possible. In our scenario, it is reasonable to suppose that the uncertainty arising from such a complex interplay of circumstances would at some stage generate entirely *structural* (if subliminal) decisions. For example, current policies might substantially shift as the community chooses to trade-off aspects of personal privacy for increased public safety.[3] In fact this kind of consequence happens all the time. Called *emergence*, it is a natural corollary of any complex system and can be deeply unsettling. In complex environments, *emergence* ensures that even short-term predictions cannot be made with any degree of accuracy – in a linear cause and effect sense at least.

DEEP STRUCTURAL PATTERNS

We now realise the emergence of *structural* outcomes from a mess of interconnected but mostly commonplace decisions is a universal characteristic of certain kinds of complex system. It also helps explain the 'flocking' behaviour apparent in society's long-term lock-in to certain technologies. Why does the US have so many gun killings when Britain has so few? Why is traditional medicine still practised in many parts of Asia when it is only a new-age novelty in most of the so-called developed world? Why does a mountain of debt make the first world, led by the US, the likely next candidate for a seismic crisis when the recent history of Argentina is an object lesson in how *not* to run the global economy? Why does Europe have more efficient urban public transit systems than the US? The evolution of these, and other emergent phenomena, is explained at least in part, by the above model.

Lock-in is especially significant in creating long-term conditions over which control is all but relinquished. Take the issue of how public transport systems have evolved over the past century, for example. In the US during the early years of the twentieth century, the right of every individual to own one of the new automobiles rolling off William Ford's production lines went unchallenged. In fact it was almost regarded as a human right in a society that virtually invented the free market ideology. Consequently, innumerable deliberate decisions were made on the part of citizens to buy motorcars. This initiated a 'flocking' effect that only became evident as the decisions, unremarkable in themselves, escalated accumulating into a collective 'choice' that was far from deliberate. As the population of the US grew and families began to purchase two or more vehicles, highways were needed to convey the growing numbers of automobiles around the cities. Then highway systems were required to link highways with other highways until eventually the entire country was covered in one vast network. This led to the (presumably unintended) consequences we see now in the traffic gridlocks of New York and chronic pollution in cities like Los Angeles. It is unlikely that the original 'decision' (to allow everyone who wanted an automobile to buy one) would have gone unchallenged had people anticipated the likely outcome a century later. Meanwhile, choices played out differently in Europe, where community-minded values prevailed over individualism and public funds were channelled into urban public transit systems.

These decisions, and others like them, continue to resonate today. They are the profound yet unconscious upshot of many inconsequential yet deliberate choices, the collective outcome of which can never be predicted. Structural 'decisions' at these profound levels are capable of etching deep patterns in the structure of society, giving rise to conditions that trap us into persistent ways of behaving, sometimes for decades at a time. The success of Microsoft's Windows, an operating system loaded in 86% of all PCs, Google's overwhelming dominance of Internet browsers, the use of English as the standard language for international air safety and tourism, even the system of ideas comprising scientific method, are all examples of this extraordinary phenomenon.

AND YET STILL DEEPER . . .

So far we have been contemplating some ways the future emerges. Equally important, however, especially if we desire to create better futures, are the various mechanisms we use to perceive reality. Many of these have to do with unconscious (or subliminal) conceptual frameworks used in society both to *sense* and *make sense* of things. These, too, may emanate from numerous decisions of an inconsequential nature that rapidly replicate, taking on *structural* characteristics at a societal level. We commonly refer to this framework of ideas as a *paradigm.* The dominant paradigm in society is our 'window on the world' – an implicit framework that shapes assumptions, values and beliefs and filters out anything that would appear illogical in the context of this self-referential system of ideas.[4] Moving under the surface of society's awareness, such subliminal knowledge (often referred to as commonsense or even conventional wisdom) becomes the natural order of things – the way it has always been and will always be. It is as real as the oxygen we breathe – unseen yet ever present. Snarled within its embrace we accept it as readily as the goldfish does water or the bird does air. After all, who are we to challenge what God has put in place?

Paradigms are not static. They shift imperceptibly over geographies and time. However, because the pace of paradigmatic change is slow, usually decades, the verity of 'what we know' at any time goes mostly unchallenged. The political freedoms and privacy accorded individuals in Western democracies, for example, appear strange and out of kilter with the more communitarian systems of Asia. The developed world's notion of industrial economic rationalism differs markedly from its agrarian predecessors. Islamic states hold very different truths to the alleged Christian ethos of some other contemporary secular nation-states. And yet all these, together with nomadic and tribal paradigms, coexist in today's world.[5]

In theory, no single paradigm is inherently superior to any other – even when we imagine ourselves more civilised or our 'truths' more advanced than some others. The real test is whether the prevailing paradigm continues to make sense and to be useful to the majority in a particular context. Nor do paradigms just fall on us from another galaxy. We all contribute inadvertently to their manifesting, for which we should accept collective responsibility. And we are all responsible for their continuance by the choices we make day by day. For the past 300 years or so the industrialised world has embraced a materialist paradigm characterised by the need to manage tangible things. Within this framework we have extolled economic progress and development, valued empirical research, and celebrated science, technology and innovation. Knowledge accrued within this paradigm has helped us to solve the most vexatious problems of our time. No longer can we claim that to be the case. There is now accumulating evidence to suggest that society's current paradigms are incapable of resolving today's most pressing concerns.

If this is so, new paradigms will emerge, even though it may take decades. Indeed the turbulence and chaos of our times may already be heralding such a transition. Certainly much past knowledge seems to be increasingly redundant as the world becomes more connected and the global economy goes real time and digital. It is far too early to predict the distinguishing features of the new paradigm. Except that it will probably be characterised by the need to cope better with complexity. And how it manifests will depend on the choices all of us make today! Because the personal decisions we routinely make seem inevitably to be driven by self-interest, the sets of assumptions that shape our identity, and consequently underpin our beliefs about what is important (or not), are extremely significant in this respect. They help forge a collective view of the world within which the choices we make can be explained and made to appear rational. Furthermore, they will be recognised as such by others.

In other words, our personal window on the world, our 'world-view', isn't simply a framework for the thinking we use in order to

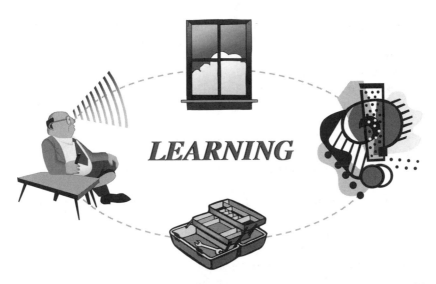

Figure 9.2   The power of dominant worldviews trap us into seeing the world a certain way. We instinctively then reach for our toolkit when we should first become more aware of our 'window' on the world(view) which defines everything we perceive to be real.

make the choices we make, but also serves to validate and affirm those choices as being *logical* – the 'right' decisions. In addition, because we constantly find ways of communicating, asserting and adjusting the logic of our particular worldview (for example through our interactions with society's institutions, entertainment and trade) to suit our immediate purpose, they become, to all intents and purposes, a shared, continually reified, *ideology*. This is constructive. It allows us to identify matters that need resolution and to come to some agreement fairly quickly. But there is also a downside to paradigms, for while they remain subliminal they blind us to alternatives. They cause us to accept the world as we have been told it should be, seeing it in starkly monochrome terms, and trapping us securely in the past.

VIEWS FROM THE FUTURE

Clearly, given these hypotheses, there are certain tensions inherent between our technocratic attempts to construct a linear future that suits us, compared with *emergence* – the system's way of keeping us on our toes, with richly serendipitous trends appearing to propel us forward towards some unknown end-game. There is something incalculably discomforting in this, just as there is in owning up to the power of paradigms compared to our avowed capability for creativity and originality. For much of the twentieth century it was fashionable to assume we could achieve our objectives merely by planning the right sequence of steps towards their realisation. Hey presto! Mission accomplished. It was as simple as that. We now know such beliefs to be at once naive and an oversimplification of our capabilities. For a start, the dynamic context within which human aspirations are played out is continuously shifting in ways we least expect and cannot divine.

Discrete individual goals are relatively easy to achieve. They only require clarity of purpose, sustained focused energy, dogged persistence and time. It is far more problematic to control the fickle array of factors implied in the harmonious alignment of other human beings to ensure the realisation of infinitely more ambitious goals – such as the eradication of poverty, for example, or the reversal of global warming. The new science of complex, scale-free, preferential networks demonstrates this paradox only too well. Together we possess unbelievable potency to shape better futures. At the same time we must resign ourselves to an intrinsic inability to do anything much to control how the future takes shape. A little fine-tuning at the edges is about the limit of our current capability.

To do anything more will require us to change our minds about human fragility, our relationship to each other and to the planet on which we rely for our very existence. It will necessitate the curbing of human ego in order to focus on protecting and creating wealth for all humankind. We will need to admit the paucity of human progress, acknowledge our mistakes at the same time as celebrating our resilience and willpower, so that our attention can turn to the things that really matter. It will entail an awareness of the toxic nature of current paradigms and an ability to design ones that are infinitely richer and more equitable. And it will require new tools and methods to bring clarity from complexity and meaning from chaos.

If only we could find ways of disrupting our current thinking sufficiently, and of visualising information in such a way as to put prejudices aside – to see the world afresh!

That's a big ask! Perhaps it would simply be better to watch how the future evolves and, quite literally, attempt to go with the flow.

Except that it is not in our nature to do so! Many futurists believe the answer is staring us in the face. They point to innumerable moments in history when challenge to the current order, by revolution or accommodation, has occurred through narrative and oratory. One has only to look at the scriptures to see the power of tales. Story telling is one of the most ancient forms of communication and learning. It also happens to be one of the most useful for us today.

Particularly enlightening is the relating of stories about how the future *might, could* or *should* be in the context of how things actually are. This is the art of strategic foresight – infuriatingly reduced, more often than not, to trite scenarios exhibiting little comprehension of today's actual dynamics let alone rigorous challenge to the established order. Scenario planning, as it is known and practised, is often deficient in at least the following respects: firstly, predicated on the assumption that by 'thinking the unthinkable' fresh insights about what is possible will occur, classic approaches often ignore the opportunity to step into a new epistemology – to recast the dominant paradigms of human knowledge in order to imagine entirely different classes of 'unthinkable'. Secondly, seduced particularly by scientific discoveries, socio-political manoeuvrings, cataclysmic events and gee-whiz technological toys, many pop futurists fall into the trap of scanning only external realities. After all, we can all 'see' events unfolding. Right? And we all know if something we 'see' is the truth. Correct?

Well, NO actually! Everyone 'sees' and interprets events individually – and differently. Even basic absolutes, for example, like the colour red, actually occur differently to all of us. Not only that, but different (often even conflicting) meanings are continuously constructed from what we see 'out there'. We even use psychological devices to help protect our spin on 'the truth' – like the myths we fabricate and project into situations to help validate feelings and reinforce assumptions. Indeed, human consciousness is not some absolute stream shared by all humanity. Rather, it is a continuously evolving and intensely personal rationalisation of our own creation. Disregarding or ignoring such psychological and cultural underpinnings is to overlook the internal realities shaping our 'window on the world'. Thirdly, by focusing purely on the forward view, relevant information drawn both from resonant memories and present experiences can all go missing.

Foolishly, people are often instructed to 'forget the past' so as to 'focus on the future'. Apart from the fact that a separation such as this is not possible in a healthy human mind (past, present and future memories being inextricably interwoven from one moment to the next) this exhortation pays no heed to the fact that the main reason for crafting scenarios is to better understand what decisions need to be made in the present! Obviously it is impossible to totally decouple past experience and memory from our current actuality. But we can become more conscious of their tendency to hold us back. Inhabiting the past only allows incremental change – at best! Also real transformation can only occur when we allow ourselves opportunities to explore the future, imagine our desired actuality and then reinvent and shape our capability to achieve this.

Although conventional scenario practice can be of enormous value, it too often falls foul of methodological stupor. The results are then little more than bizarre, tedious fictions. Bearing little relevance to particular circumstances, and disconnected from any strategic intent, scenarios crafted in this manner do not stretch thinking sufficiently to be anything other than nondescript curiosities. They certainly don't change the world. Nor do they, as far as I can tell, unleash significantly different behaviours. Why? Because human intent remains intact – unmoved by such banalities.

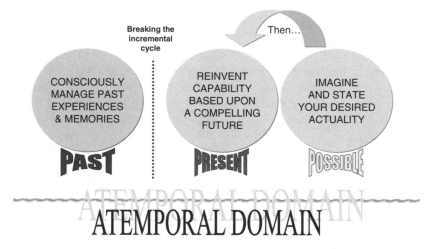

Figure 9.3 Past, present and possible are not discrete 'modes' of experience – they are not sequential, however, we may experience them as such, nor can we somehow delete the past. All three domains have knowledge that is integral to creating better futures while the atemporal domain of 'unconscious competence' allows us to achieve a state of high-performance using positive energy rather than heroic effort.

The same cannot be said for paradigmatic discourse and narrative. Poised at that fragile intersection between human and natural systems, between our inner and outer realities, and between the significant and the inconsequential, paradigmatic narratives are deliberately disruptive and profoundly disturbing at a worldview level. Rejecting the notion of artificially sustaining a single 'logic' these narratives embrace instead serendipity, complexity and the inconsequential, blurring the edges of 'the known' in ways that facilitate multiple pathways and novel eventualities, just as in real life. Narratives arising from paradigmatic discourse enable us to grasp how others perceive their world, with its distinctive axioms, customs and idiosyncracies and, as a consequence, comprehend how they habitually think and act. Unlike conventional scenario planning, they do this not by exploring linear storylines around *external* realities that happen to appeal to our egocentric sense of technological progress and therefore feel *coherent* from within the comfort

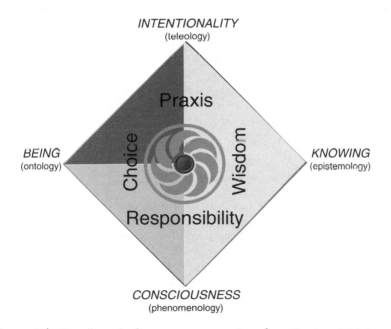

Figure 9.4 Paradigmatic discourse covers a 'transformative terrain' integrating the domains of ontology, epistemology, teleology and phenomenology. Strategic conversation conducted at this level raises the consciousness of an entire organisation, community or society.

and familiarity of our own worldview. Rather, they evoke the essence of complex emotional responses, myths, credos, enacted beliefs and other forms of *internal* reality that ultimately give rise to behavioural patterns or compel events to unfold in particular ways.[6]

Indeed, their discursive nature intensifies our natural predispositions, compelling deeper and more expansive reflection on even the most inconsequential of human interactions and behaviour. Eventually attention shifts from *outcome* to *intent*. Now opportunities to reassign society's mind open up. Wisdom is engaged. In these ways, rather than by pompous predictions and fantastic revelations, paradigmatic scenarios astonish and confront our most deeply ingrained beliefs about *what* is important and *why*.

Suddenly we find ourselves naked and exposed. Armed with new intelligence we find new truths. But in so doing we lay bare the fallacy of real alternatives. For ultimately choice may be merely another delusion, society's Prozac, aimed at comforting fragile egos, when what is actually going on is intention manifest in behaviour. Delusions like this prevent profound whole-system change because they have already trapped us in the comfort of current worldviews. Yet this awareness pries open a different consciousness, enabling better decisions and the opportunity, perhaps, to consider subsituting current intent for something healthier and wiser. Perhaps when we are able to speak about such things openly we will find ourselves capable of solving the world's great problems. And perhaps then starvation, poverty and terrorism will become things of the past.

NOTES

1. Since Doha, the US has raised its farm subsidies by 80%. Thus the poor nations of the world are oppressed by the rich nations in the interests of the rich. It is apparently necessary for poor countries to accept every detail of the neo liberal creed, cutting tariffs, ending subsidies and privatising services. But it is equally necessary, it seems, for rich countries to act to retain subsidies and keep tariffs high when there is a threat to a domestic industry, whether it is steel, textiles or agriculture. The situation is exacerbated by the proliferation of bilateral trade deals or 'preferential trading agreements' – otherwise known as PTAs. Far from strengthening multilateral trade, PTAs have made a mockery of the World Trade Organisation system, which was genuinely devoted to even-handed, or most-favoured nation, treatment of all trading partners.

2. It is but a small step to speculate that an organisation's 'vision' is not dependent upon any one individual (as is commonly supposed) but only becomes feasible through the emergence of appropriate systemic conditions – particularly the harmonious actions of the community of individuals comprising the whole organisation.

3. Every event, link and thread in the above scenario arises from empirical research. The story is only fictional in the sense that it hasn't yet happened. But there is no doubt that it could!

4. A term first used, to my knowledge, by Richard Bawden, a distinguished Australian scholar who has pioneered social ecology and generative learning.

5. In an article in *The Age* newspaper on Thursday 31 August 2006, Julia Suryakusuma, a Jakarta writer and the author of *Sex, Power and Nation* and Tim Lindsey, Professor of Asian Law at the University of Melbourne, point to the potential overthrow of the secular state in Indonesia. 'This nation of 230 million mostly Muslim people is in the middle of an explosive debate about whether conservative Islamic morality will become enforceable law. It is a debate that threatens to unravel the secular foundation of the republic itself. Amid street protests, the DPR, Indonesia's newly democratic legislature, is debating a reactionary Anti-Pornography Bill that is really an attempt to introduce hardline interpretations of sharia (Islamic law) by stealth. The bill would criminalise much sexuality, force women to cover up almost completely, largely exclude them from public space and tightly censor the arts and media. If passed, it would give Islam a new, dominant position in law and politics that generations of Indonesian leaders have tried to avoid. And it would inevitably create huge difficulties for the nation's relationships with some neighbouring nations like Australia, for example. How did Indonesia get to this frightening position? A wave of local elections through to late 2005 seeking to implement democratisation and decentralisation delivered dramatic political change in Indonesia, cementing a broader social process under way since 1998, when the dictatorial Soeharto lost power. Of a hundred local elections conducted to date, some 40 per cent or so resulted in the rise of new elites. Many of these are traditional male leaders pushed to one side under Soeharto's 'New Order' who draw their authority from traditional local sources and look for legitimacy for conservative and socially regressive values linked to local identity. In many regions these groups have replaced Jakarta-endorsed bureaucrats, who, for all their many failings, often had a strongly secular nationalist bent and some commitment to a modernising agenda. The old-for-new elites are influencing local policy right across the country'. The battle between pluralism and fundamentalism, leading to the de-secularisation of nations in this manner, may well result in even more complicated geopolitical scenarios in the future, especially in cases where secular US interests (energy or security) are threatened.

6. To do things differently we need to perceive things differently. The processes and systems surrounding us in our globalised world are complex and ambiguous. But that should not stop us from making them intelligible and knowable.

CHAPTER 10

LITERACY III – STRATEGIC NAVIGATION[1]

The great thing in this world is not so much where we stand, as in what direction we are moving.

– Oliver Wendell Holmes

While the kind of strategic foresight (integral reflection, dialogue and action) portrayed in *futuring* is unarguably a prerequisite for *five literacies* leaders, it is still considered to be something of a luxury or a rare gift – outside the comprehension of most of us or, within the context of organisational life, not deemed sufficiently important to be a core competence and embedded within good business practice. In fact the arguments both for and against including foresight in contemporary strategic management practice are still being keenly fought decades after it proved its worth in various other contexts, including nation-building (witness the empowering use of scenarios in the transition from apartheid in South Africa),[2] urban development (*Imagine Chicago, Australia Tomorrow,* and other civil engagement visions) and land stewardship (Land & Water Australia's pioneering Future Landscapes project), for example.

In situations where its insights are valued, foresight projects are most often outsourced to professional futurists. There are numerous examples of small yet influential firms that specialise in particular aspects of foresight, as is the case with Global Business Network in San Francisco and the Neville-Freeman Agency in Sydney with their generalised approach to alternative scenarios methods, John Elkington's SustainAbility in London, which focuses on the future of the environment and corporate social responsibility, and Thoughtpost in Australia with their 'art of uncommon strategy' theme.

Yet in cases where internal expertise is deployed, mostly through the personal interest of a certain individual, constructive results often ensue. However valuable futuring is in challenging mental models, it is actually the compression of past, present and future into an atemporal consciousness, together with the navigation within that zone (or *expanded now*) which is critical for leaders today.

This ability transcends conventional strategy or management planning expertise and practice. Navigation is very much a leadership art. Yet it is precisely this art that will ensure every member of an enterprise responds, responds appropriately and in real time, to emergent strategic issues. And it will assist in coevolving the business to higher levels of wisdom where people can collectively be conscious of their choices and the consequences flowing from those decisions. Marvin Oka and I call this capability Strategic Navigation. Strategic Navigation is a continuous conversational braiding of collective reflection and decision making informed by real-time intelligence. It is also the art of confidently and ethically finding viable paths into the future, nego-

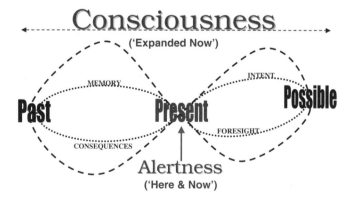

Figure 10.1 The continuous process of weaving the present 'here and now' from the past and the future in an 'expanded now' of higher awareness is the source archetype for strategic navigation.

tiating unknown terrain and unprecedented complexity while retaining integrity and relevance.[3]

PLANNING IN REAL TIME

When the world was less volatile, most markets were local, and life felt more certain, strategic planning was used to help determine how best to optimise a business in terms of the marketplace. Stemming from military planning and logistics operations developed during World War II and subsequently honed by academics like Igor Ansoff (strategic marketing) and Michael Porter (competition strategy), strategic planning was widely adopted as a must-have discipline in most large organisations during the later part of the twentieth century. Indeed, many corporations still practise strategic planning, unthinkingly trusting that this will enable them to compete effectively in the information economy. In a sense it can. It is always better to have chosen the direction in which one is headed and to be growing internal capability. But that is not sufficient.

Conventional strategic planning is dead! In a world where strategy is a commodity, navigation and imagination become the critical factors from which value is extracted. When almost anyone can think strategically about anything, the locus of value creation shifts from outmanoeuvring everyone to out-imagining them. The prime mover of value creation becomes putting the capability to adapt and innovate (goods, services, processes – even strategies and business models) at the heart of the enterprise. There is evidence of this revolution everywhere one turns and it is already generating enormous challenges for firms – challenges that can only be faced by stepping into new epistemologies, transforming worldviews and fostering creative and innovative cultures.

All of which implies a sea change in the ways we lead, manage, coordinate and monitor business and far more mature ways of thinking about value creation through innovation, not planning. Strategic Navigation adds a level of elegance to conventional planning that is altogether different and more sophisticated. It is a further distinction between the science practised by managers and the art of leaders.

> There is a difference between leadership and management. Leadership is of the spirit, compounded of personality and vision; its practice is an art. Management is of the mind, more a matter of accurate calculation,

of statistics, of methods, timetables and routines; its practice is a science. Managers are necessary; leaders are essential (Field Marshall Lord Slim).

Connectivity and the universal flow of ideas and information making up today's economy have shrunk our world as Marshall McLuhan predicted half a century ago. Connections, trusted relationships, uniqueness, attention and adaptiveness are the keys to survival in this world. Consequently, contemporary business, learning and government institutions need a far more dynamic approach to strategic development than has been the case in the past. Today, the most forward-looking of our leading edge enterprises aspire to remain viable, or self-sustaining over time, so as to be better able to survive and prosper within an increasingly complex, highly uncertain and forever-changing social and business environment.

Incorporating an awareness of social and political trends into an organisation's strategic consciousness strategy has become overwhelming. Issues such as privacy, gender and diversity, offshoring, the safety of pharmaceutical products and even public health problems like obesity can alter the ground rules within any business ecosystem. For example, in response to a growing public debate about the possible connection between soda and childhood obesity, several of the largest US beverage distributors agreed in April 2006 to stop selling carbonated beverages in most schools – a move that highlights the growing importance of social issues to business. The financial and reputational impact of mishandling these issues can be huge although they also create new market opportunities that nimble companies can exploit. Strategic Navigation teaches us to look for signs of emerging hot topics, be ready to respond to them rapidly, and place a series of small strategic bets that will create value should the sociopolitical landscape shift.

In a hyperconnected world such as ours, the external environment in all its surprising richness needs to be the primary target of our attention. The classic approach to growing internal capability, for example by focusing on skills development, process fitness, cost control and resource deployment, is no longer enough to guarantee business success. Capability building must now look outside of the enterprise at the business ecosystem. It must include collaborative co-design; distributed innovation; word-of-mouth marketing; and network presence through mastery – a deeper understanding of the dynamic interface between the business's internal capability to innovate and to change, and the constantly shifting realities of global business ecosystems. Likewise, strategic planning (a mechanism, remember, devised primarily for inventing, aligning and communicating high-level goals and subsequent operations) has been gazumped by the nimbleness of Strategic Navigation and similar methods. While strategic planning remains a mostly technocentric procedure, inviting input from a limited number of experts, Strategic Navigation has the potential to engage literally everyone across an enterprise – and beyond into the broader business ecosystem. As such it is legitimately an ecosystem-wide capability and not necessarily just an occasional high-level exercise undertaken by an elite within a single enterprise. In a world of industry clusters, peer-to-peer networks, dynamic business ecosystems, constant technological innovation, customer-designed products and shifting social values, Strategic Navigation has become one of the most effective means for everyone in an enterprise to collaborate, thus helping to assure the long-term viability of the whole system. In this instance, viability is both the objective and the solution.

To the best of current knowledge the unequalled exemplars of viability already exist within natural systems – ecologies and organisms, like you and me. Consequently, if we were about to design an enterprise from scratch, one that was assured of being healthy, responsive, adaptive and productive, we would most certainly look to nature (other than perhaps the more ancient wisdom practised to this day within some vernacular societies) for guidance. In spite of the growing use of biomimicry in all walks of life, such an approach would still be counter-intuitive, so inculcated are we with rational, economic-based models of growth and development in designing organisations.[4] That fact alone deters many people from pursuing methodologies like Strategic Navigation. It seems like too much freedom for some to handle!

Strategic Navigation uses our knowledge of living systems in the creation of an entirely upgraded *operating system* for managing complexity as practised by smart leaders. An operating system more in keeping with the specific socioeconomic needs of the global community. An operating system founded upon principles derived from chaos, complexity and network science – the knowledge that has changed forever our understanding of the world, our relationship to it, and to each other.

This *five literacies* approach to Strategic Navigation is in stark contrast to more orthodox Western management practices, where planning leads to the maximisation of profits for a relatively small number of parties with vested interests – mostly investors and shareholders. Strategic Navigation, by comparison, is an *eco*diagnosing and *eco*-designing model for assuring ongoing viability of the whole business ecosystem. In that sense it is a methodology utilised mainly by *keystone* companies. Here *ecological* metaphors (concerned primarily with learning and transformation) balance more familiar *economic* metaphors (concerned primarily with controlling and producing) to create a moral purpose. Whereas classic strategic management practices, informed solely by *economic* metaphors, have generated incredible material wealth for a few and inconceivable poverty for many, navigational processes focus on continuous, pragmatic, long-term navigation of uncertainty leading to optimisation of the whole system for the benefit of all stakeholders. This is known as *systemic viability* – a concept I introduced earlier.

Naturally, such a distinctly different model, for what in most circles is still regarded as *planning*, albeit at the very highest strategic level, requires a considerable shift in our perceptions. So considerable, in fact, that the paradigm shift from (managers) planning to (leaders) navigating can be likened to that experienced by computer users having to come to grips with Windows when all they had previously known was DOS. Practically everything has to be learned again – even including the *raison d'être* for systemic viability. It is tantamount to stepping into a new epistemology. Yet ultimately, this shift heralds greater user friendliness, better economic use of scarce resources, increased yields, improved design capability, an enhanced potential for innovation and creativity and, last but by no means least, greater benefits for greater numbers of people.

Essentially, the Windows operating system turned the world of computing on its head, just as DOS had done 20 years earlier. Strategic Navigation is doing the same to less sophisticated, more narrowly focused forms of strategic thinking and planning. Although it does not necessarily preclude the need for more traditional forms of planning where relevant, the underlying assumptions and principles of this new strategic leadership operating system are different – borrowed not from physics and economics but from the life sciences and ecology. They reflect the laws of the new global environment in which we interact and transact business today, stressing the need to embrace uncertainty rather than to maintain tight control; the need for adaptiveness over efficiency; the need to collaborate and to share ideas with each other rather than to keep secrets; and the need for new tools and maps to help visualise the terrain we are attempting to navigate.

These assumptions also require leaders to recognise that their organisations, however large or successful, can never be exempt from needing to ensure their own viability. Even being part of the public sector does not necessarily guarantee the future for a government agency. The larger ecosystem in which the department is located may change so utterly that the business niche can become redundant, or the current form of the organisation may need to be replaced by a more optimum form.

Of course this happens in business all the time. Self-renewal and regeneration are healthy and should not necessarily be threatening; although imposed changes of any kind frequently generate cynical and defensive responses, especially from those within organisations that exhibit high levels of management control and where obedience and compliance is valued more than passion and imagination. In fact the process of ensuring systemic viability through Strategic Navigation can be exciting in its potential. How this is experienced by people in the organisation, though, depends upon how well they are able to develop capabilities to effectively coevolve with the ecosystem in which their organisation exists. In other words, the business needs to continuously reinvent its niche.

Naturally one cannot just substitute alternative assumptions and underlying principles without also creating the need to rethink other taken-for-granted conventions. And so the key concepts of Strategic Navigation, based upon pathological diagnosis and systemic leverage, are different from established norms. The key methodologies, derived from systems dynamics, are different too. The tools, techniques and mechanisms for Strategic Navigation are different – requiring different ways of apprehending and comprehending, a different skills set, and an altogether more strategic breadth of perspective than is apparent with more conventional systems for managing planning. Finally, entirely new classes of proficiency are required by leaders. These include enhanced *intellectual* skills (involving systems thinking and managing paradox); finely tuned *emotional* skills (such as being comfortable with non-closure, uncertainty and ambiguity); and exceptional *relating* skills (such as collaborative learning, strategic conversation and group reflection).

IMITATING NATURE[5]

So Strategic Navigation implies an entirely new set of strategic management and leadership arrangements than much of the conventional wisdom we have come to take for granted. The most frequently used expression for talking about and making sense of how we think about working together is the commonly used term *organisation*. In conventional thinking *organisation* is most often conceived as the process of ordering, coordinating and developing labour (in addition to other resources, such as materials, tools, money and time) so as to achieve mutually agreeable ends such as, for example, the creation of wealth or the production of goods and services. Thus, this type of thinking would have us believe that there is such a thing as *the organisation* – a separate, concrete entity that has a life of its own, to which we are contracted and have membership. In other words, we join *it* and undertake certain prescribed tasks for *it*, which we then label *work.*

We do not often reflect upon what we actually mean by this term *organisation*. If we did we would realise that the implications of our willingness to concretise are quite profound, prescribing all manner of coordinative and administrative mechanisms, including what we believe we can achieve together, as well as the means used to achieve it. But that is not all. Through a process of socialisation and induction we are expected to feel at one with *the organisation*. We are expected to *fit* into it. Deviation from the norms and standards set by the organisation, made visible by myriad cultural artefacts, is not tolerated. Heresy is frowned upon. Change, even of an innovative nature, is often considered to be a threat. More often than not, a history and a moral purpose are ascribed to *the organisation*. Why, we have even done that here! The organisation is assumed to have a memory and a particular way of doing things. We project such human qualities on *the organisation* that it almost assumes a separate identity, a persona, so *real* does it become in our minds. Nowadays, we are even asked to believe that this entity has the capacity to learn!

The superordinate goal in this classic view of *the organisation* is equilibrium: equilibrium of strategic direction, of functionality (often termed *mission*) of procedures, behaviours and tasks. The fact that this so evidently conflicts with the continuously evolving helter-skelter of our private lives has resulted in our leading double lives. Lives where work is quite separate from our normal, private existence and where the myth of achieving work–life balance prevails. In living systems, equilibrium equates to death.[6] In corporate life, too, the schizophrenic existence led by many workers can cause enormous stress, especially where the organisation's endeavours and ethics appear to conflict with individual values and aspirations. Nevertheless, conventional management thinking would have us believe that we must place the organisation's values and goals above our own. That we should become subservient to *it*.

The praxis of Strategic Navigation posits an altogether different meaning for this term *organisation*. Instead of being a metaphor for a discrete, unified entity, *five literacies* leaders think of *organisation* as the process used to create and sustain a purposeful social ecology within any group of people brought together for a particular reason. If the full potential of a group is to be realised, relationships and interdependencies between its autonomous members become critical. Involving the invented array of explicit architectures and implicit protocols that enable the realisation of strategic intentions, *organisation* now becomes a mechanism for liberating a *community of praxis* (a unique way of thinking, doing and being) that can be observed, understood, codified and leveraged.

The implications of this biomimicry approach to *organising* are profound.[7] For one thing, potency is ascribed to individuals working collaboratively rather than to some discrete, cold, homogeneous entity. Moreover, as autonomous yet functioning members of the whole group, every individual is connected to every other member in a system of distributed intelligence. In this context the linking in of every single person within the enterprise (and beyond) invariably creates additional diversity and social richness. As new ideas are shared and become valued, and strategic *fitness* (to achieve a shared intent) is openly pursued by the community, the addition of each new member creates a further node in an ever-expanding, generative learning community, a living network, enhancing the potential for adaptiveness and ensuring both robustness and resilience of the business.

STRATEGIC ACTIVISM

The same concretisation that popularised our thinking about *the organisation* as an entity (complete with desirable and less endearing human traits) has also been widely used to define *strategy*. Formerly a military term defining predetermined offensive and defensive moves and countermoves deployed by an army in the heat of battle, this traditional approach to strategy arises out of the cause and effect hypothesis of games. The intention of strategy in this context was to capture territory or dominate the psyche of the enemy by inflicting casualties on a scale that would convince them to surrender. Incidentally, a basic idea here which, as it turns out, also appears to be a fundamental flaw, is that there must always be a winner and, *ipso facto*, a loser. In theory, of course, it is convenient to portray the outcome of a game in such orderly terms. In the hurly-burly reality of today's volatile and unpredictable world, however, where new and unholy alliances form and dissolve so rapidly, such a simplistic concept is bound to cause confusion as much as it creates impossible expectations. In spite of this, the militaristic notion of strategy has been enthusiastically (if mindlessly) adopted by the majority of our corporations and their leaders.

Originally, when applied to business, planning was not in the least bit strategic in nature. On the contrary, it was simply a response to the complexity of production – an attempt to coordinate people, equipment and resources to be more effective. Eventually, as methods became more reliable, planning became longer term. By and by, as managers realised they could sell more goods (thus optimising the capacity of their production plants) by predicting which of their products would sell and to whom, various forms of forecasting and budgeting were built in. Eventually, with computer planning technologies, the whole operational value chain could be bundled into a real-time, whole-of-enterprise, resource-planning package.

However, planning only really became strategic, in the truly militaristic sense of that term, following World War II when the global business environment began showing such signs of competitiveness that each corporation was required to outmanoeuvre the other if they wished to survive. Initially, relatively unsophisticated 'power plays' were implemented around branding and positioning. Eventually, however, new technologies coupled with highly developed strategic management systems allowed corporations to change the rules of competition at a moment's notice. The game had become so engaging that entire units devoted to strategic planning were set up.

Today, more often than not, strategy has become a linear process where secret plans, goals and targets are established by an elite group of senior managers who may or may not be in touch with the real world. Because the process of strategic planning has become such an infrequent event – often occurring only once a year and undertaken by the senior executives within the corporation irrespective of their ability to think strategically, any resulting plans tend to lock the corporation into a single future path, usually within an horizon of between two and five years.

We are all too familiar with the implications of this approach: the unavoidable result is that strategy devised in this manner is too often based on mediocre intelligence and is consequently unambitious, inappropriate, wide of the mark in terms of its relevance, and difficult to realise with available resources. For one thing, changes in environmental conditions always demand continuous corrections but senior managers rarely have the time to spend making changes to and refining their original ideas, seeing this as a waste of time when they could be busy *doing* something. For another, the bureaucratic systems and procedures that, with re-engineering, could enable optimal deployment of any new strategies often remain untouched due to a lack of understanding, resources or will. And then, even when the strategy is sufficiently robust to withstand the test of time, people may continue to do what they have always done. Ask them why, and they are likely to respond with a million good reasons. Yet inevitably the root of the problem can be seen in weak overt communication as well as the underestimated power of implicit, more informal, cultural interchange. Indeed, much of the research into social organisation carried out over the past 20 years points to the importance of implicit messages embedded within group culture. Up to 80% of actual performance may be directly reliant upon embedded communication of one kind or another – habits, gossip, assumptions, tacit knowledge and the like. This is the organisational *cafe* at work. Conversely, less than 20% is directly attributable to explicit plans, rules or goals mandated by the *cathedral*, however well communicated these may be. The lesson here is to do with the significance of what we glibly refer to as *culture* – uncontrollable and fickle – in determining what is done as well as how it is done.

Explicit communication of strategic plans and goals, therefore, often has very little effect on the performance of an enterprise. Perhaps people aren't convinced the new strategy can work and so continue to do what they have always done. Perhaps their personal values clash with what they are being asked to do. Or perhaps they simply do not fully comprehend how any new strategy affects them and the work they actually do. In some cases they may not even have heard about some significant strategy. This is particularly the case when cagey managers deem it necessary to keep things secret! But whatever the reason, the results betray the inevitability of a self-fulfilling prophecy. Managers spend indiscriminate proportions of their time attempting to influence and get buy-in from their staff, industrial relations problems abound, there is a preoccupation with implementation and *doingness*, and issues of accountability never quite seem to get resolved. Arguably of more consequence, the strategic responses intended by the organisation's leaders remain ever only partially realised while a critical mass of the workforce continue to do what they've always done – thus limiting potential change and development.

As with the term organisation, I prefer to confer a very different meaning by using the term *strategy*. From an ecological perspective, strategy doesn't actually exist – at least not as a visible, palpable thing. Like many words in the management lexicon, which we take for granted, strategy, even in its more conventional sense, is only a metaphor, a mental map that we use to help us make sense of our reality. From within the framework of Strategic Navigation, strategy is simply distributed consciousness – an alignment of epistemologies and intent where cognisance is both implicit and explicit *knowing*. Strategy is dynamic, transparent and constantly present; manifested in every moment.

In this context, then, strategy is not merely a set of programmed responses to changing environmental conditions, but a characteristic 'mode of thinking' from which a rich repertoire of different types of responses can be distilled and actioned. Strategy as a characteristic in this sense will normally be defined by explicit intentions (such as a salient driving force and worldview ambitions, for example) and characterised by distinct ethical or moral qualities. It also uses different time frames (past, present and future) to make sense of apparently unrelated patterns of events for creating intelligence and, over time, results in the distribution of context-aligned responses and initiatives throughout the enterprise. These responses and initiatives are most effective when they integrate business and social factors into a whole system – a Strategic Navigation system.

One hears a lot of talk about 'systems' in management circles today. Hard and soft systems methodologies, systems dynamics, complex adaptive systems, critical systems thinking, the socioeconomic system, systems of enquiry, information technology systems, management information systems – the list is as endless as it is confusing . . . Little wonder that the concept of systems, though by no means a new idea, is so misunderstood.

Conventional interpretations of a system range from definitions (for example, 'an organised method or process') to questions like '*What's a system?*' In Western society, our minds have become so programmed to accept numerical patterning as a means of making sense of the world (rather than genealogical patterning, for example, which appears to be hard-wired into the community of mind of many indigenous societies), that we are inclined to embrace *systematic* processes almost without challenging their basis for being. Indeed, such patterning has become so ingrained within our consciousness that we have actually come to believe it is in the nature of things to be systematic. Conversely, many people believe that it is unnatural to be anything other than *systemic*! Whereas a *systematic* process is engineered to have an ordered sequence of events that can be consistently repeated, *systemic patterning* has to do with a whole messy world of interconnecting processes and their dynamic relationships to each other. It is an entirely different way of viewing and understanding reality. Most managers talk about systems yet feel distinctly uncomfortable with their disordered and chaotic messiness. After all they are being paid to exercise control and to maintain order.

The world of difference between these two terms is tantamount to comprehending the difference between the rich ecology of an equatorial rainforest and the bureaucratic procedures we have to go through to get a visa to go see the rainforest. The rainforest is complex and forever changing. It is almost unfathomable – or *systemic*. The *systematic* thinking underpinning bureaucratic procedures, by comparison, is quite linear and simplistic. Because the primary mode of processing here is reductionist and analytical, the emphasis must always be on problem solving and the adoption of standardised solutions. Consequently, thinking systematically often results in an inability to deal effectively with complexity. Although undeniably useful in many situations, while we continue to predominantly perceive the world in a systematic manner we should always be prepared to be taken by surprise by life's spontaneity, unpredictability and sheer systemic richness.

Ecologists will tell you that, from an ecological perspective, every organism is a system; an abstract idea representing a complex, identifiable *whole* composed of other interacting *wholes* whose dynamics are consistent over some period of time. How this mutual interaction occurs can be better understood by identifying a specific model and *keystone* principles, which are universally applicable to each part of a system, as well as the system itself. It might be argued that such a model (or generalised theory of systems) not only provides us with a more complete understanding of the world but plays a role similar to that of Aristotelian logic in antiquity. For the latter, static *classification* was the means by which meaning was made. Today, dynamic *interaction* is the fundamental issue in all fields, and its general principles are formulated in Ludwig von Bertalanffy's general systems theory.

There are a number of implications arising out of this way of thinking about systems as the context for Strategic Navigation that need to be appreciated. Undoubtedly the most significant is the use of non-linear thinking in Strategic Navigation. Nonlinear thinking uses synthesis (rather than analysis) as the primary mode of cognitive processing. It is therefore integrative of differences rather than selective, seeks to transcend the perception of any evolving situation rather than just solve the problem as first perceived, and looks for systemic leverage to influence or shape the system in question, rather than to solve a discrete problem. Within this context, surprise (or novelty) is to be expected. Indeed it is often deliberately sought.

This perspective also requires that we re-examine the nature of individuality. Within our model, the myth of the rugged individual – standing alone, self-contained and able to survive as an entity – is an illusion. In our model each individual is a mobile community – a symbiont being living in close contact with others. All are elements in a global system of interlocking, mutual interactions within a self-sustaining ecosystem. Conversely, any social organisation, such as a family, a church, or a society, may be accorded the status and identity of an individual. That this type of individuality is no mere phantasm is clear when one realises that since 1886, the US Supreme Court has recognised the real existence of corporate personalities – that a business corporation is indeed a 'person' and thereby subject to the same Constitutional protections afforded other persons. And that's what scuppers the whole nature of conventional leadership.

EXIT THE WHITE KNIGHT

Leadership has to be the single most talked about (and our commonly held perceptions of what it is, the most irrelevant) phenomenon of our time. A vexed and vexing issue, leadership, at least as it has been consistently portrayed in history, is infused with overly-aggressive heroic characteristics such as might, assertiveness and supremacy – qualities closely resembling the mythical disposition of Greek gods and biblical patriarchs. In conventional terms a leader is someone possessing preeminent status, power or charisma. It is the leader who forges the vision and issues clear directives, accepting as part of their leadership role, responsibility for the overall performance of the enterprise. The most frequently used metaphors for this 'white knight' style of leadership range from the general leading his troops into battle to the orchestral conductor, the situational leader – even the servant–leader

concept of Robert Greenleaf, on which so much contemporary leadership theory is based.

The implications arising from positioning leadership as a heroic
function are quite profound. For a start, the dualistic nature of such
thinking gave rise to the need for the leader to have followers – passive
subordinates who needed to be told what to do, motivated to do it
and, quite often, instructed on how to do it. Inevitably, information
flowed in one direction (top-down) and genuine communication was
smothered. Instead of the enterprise being suffused with purposeful
intentions, all effort was reflected in the single-minded purpose of the
all-knowing and all-powerful leader. Where the leader occupied a
preeminent position, the likelihood was that everybody waited to be
told what to do and valuable resources were wasted trying to convince
people to follow and to change. With only a small elite group of people
supposedly thinking for the enterprise, the lack of differing perspectives, combined with insufficient intelligence, dramatically reduced the
capacity of the enterprise to deal with complexity and surprise. But at
least there was always somebody to blame!

Strategic Navigation necessitates a very different kind of leadership.
Five literacies leadership is not so much a role as it is a process
of shared learning – a catalyst for changing the status quo. Here
the act of leading is *a collaborative process of realising potential for
purposeful advancement of the human condition.* In one sense, of
course, this is even more 'heroic' than more conventional meanings
of that term. But the heroic act has become a collective one in
this context. Undertaken consciously by the community in order to
survive and develop its potential to the full, such collaborative individualism is intent on creating a better society for all. The true measure
of leadership now becomes *survival value* – in other words the contribution being made to enable the long-term survival of the society,
community or enterprise as a whole. It is immediately engaging and
can emanate from any member anywhere within the enterprise or
community, depending upon the circumstances. There is no need to
sell a vision as the community is continually intent on learning how
to co-create the future it wants for itself. But it is socially demanding,
requiring the members of the community constantly to engage in dialogue regarding their purpose as well as the development of a philosophy on the ethics that will guide their actions. In the conversational
communities initiated by *five literacies* leaders, reflective practice
replaces specification, inspiration replaces information, enquiry replaces
assertion.[8]

(RE)DEFINING MANAGEMENT

It is impossible to redefine *leadership* in this way without also having to (re)define what we mean by *management* – if only to distinguish between the two. Conventional thinking, together with vast numbers of management textbooks, suggests that management is about things like control, resource allocation, getting things done through people, planning, delegating, organising, coordinating, monitoring and evaluating. All of these may once have been relevant in the age of Henry Ford. Today, however, the world has changed, and with it our understanding of how things work. We know, for example, that corporations are not machines in which workers slave blindly like cogs, unknowing and numb to their surroundings. We know that forecasting will remain forever inaccurate and that the future will always contain surprises, however well founded our intentions and how refined our forecasting methods. We know, too, that people will always do what they want to do, rather than what anybody else (including managers) believes they actually instructed them to do. In effect, we have learned that the mechanistic Cartesian view of the world is no longer sufficiently adequate to explain our reality. For that we need to increasingly rely on quantum mechanics, chaos and complexity theory, even though these fields of new knowledge are still mysterious and a virtually unexplored terrain.

Of course you wouldn't know it, judging from the state of many contemporary corporations. For in spite of this new knowledge, most managers still perpetuate the myth that managing is pure science, continuing to act as if they were controlling and motivating unskilled workers in Henry Ford's factory. They believe that management is a position – their role one of trying to dampen down any perturbations in the system rather than maintaining the processes that eventually lead to self-regulation. Those who haven't yet made it into the ranks of management are merely doers, not necessarily thinkers. Thinking is the dominion of managers and they protect that jurisdiction with all their energy. For them, outputs are king. KPIs rule! Efficiency and effectiveness are all that matter. Their focus is primarily internal, as a result of which inappropriate measures are applied and micro-management and meddling is rife. Such traditional methods are no longer viable in today's environment. In fact they can create more damage than not to the organisation as a whole.

From our viewpoint, the *management* applied by *five literacies* leaders is a principle. This means the function of *managing* will change, depending upon one's perspective. It may also look very different in different situations. And although management must be seen as a function of everybody's work, as Stafford Beer suggests, ultimately it is the process of organising and coordinating resources to optimise the whole business as a viable enterprise that really counts.

This means executives need to redefine their role and practice on a continuing basis, as do others in the enterprise. It implies that the focus for ecologically minded managers must be on the viability of the system as a whole, on different levels of feedback (rather than on measurement per se), on the ability to deal with complexity and to utilise that knowledge effectively, and the generation of higher levels of consciousness throughout the business. All very different tasks from those usually considered to be within management's domain but all aimed at raising the 'consciousness' of the organisation to comprehend everything that is going on within and around it in order to be able to respond more intelligently.

(RAISE)ING CONSCIOUSNESS

Strategic Navigation makes use of five leverage points we call the RAISE factors. These are elements we would expect to see in any healthy, adaptive (or *viable*) system and that help the organism learn, grow, develop and change. Natural systems (dissipative structures such as living organisms, ecosystems, networks and social communities) have properties that are very different from other, less adaptive structures – especially those artificial, naive and fairly simplistic configurations that are traditionally used in corporations in a vain effort to maintain control of people and of their production. In this regard there are a number of essential properties that are particularly important for us to understand.

Firstly, natural systems remain healthy and viable by distributing intelligence outwards. Unlike most corporate structures, they do not organise themselves around any central authority nor, indeed, from any one part of the system. Instead, members of the system are interconnected. Systemic viability is dependent upon the participation of every single member feeding back information from every other part of the system. Through this process of self-reference and communication, natural systems are naturally self-renewing – or what the biologist Humberto Maturana defined as *autopoietic*. Like life itself, they experiment, play and create their world into being at every moment. To the observer, they appear to be totally unpredictable – *and* uncontrollable.

Can you imagine what a scary proposition that is for conventional managers!

In effect, the naturally adaptive system self-organises, evolving in relation to its niche, continually growing and mutating by sensing important changes in its environment, then changing appropriately to meet these changed circumstances. This property of self-renewal results from the ability of the system to learn from, and respond immediately to, significant stimuli in the environment. The property of self-renewal, therefore, is all to do with the principle of *responsiveness* – the first of the RAISE factors. It is perhaps worth noting that, in the context of natural living systems, management (at least in the form of the somewhat artificially imposed discipline with which we have become all too familiar through corporate life) does not exist, just as it didn't exist in pre-industrial society, nor, indeed, in vernacular communities. Healthy adaptive systems, in fact, thrive without the need for *management* as it has been traditionally operationalised in factories and in offices throughout the industrialised world. Management as it is practised today is purely a man-made fabrication that has not kept pace with external realities. Initially it appeared to work. But there are now serious doubts that traditional ways of managing could ever be sufficient to take us into the knowledge-creating age. We can only conclude that there are better ways to manage complex business ecosystems and social ecologies – which is why we define management as a *principle* within the context of Strategic Navigation.

The second property of living systems we need to appreciate is that their self-renewing, evolutionary growth occurs as a direct result of their deliberate search for eccentricity, richness, diversity and fluidity. This fluidity generates unlimited novelty, variety and restlessness, like a stream of foaming water tumbling over rocks. Paradoxically it also builds resilience, robustness and stability, even enabling the system to change *how* it changes and, therefore, the degree to which the organism is able to adapt and survive when the going gets tough. In essence, the more a natural living system embodies diversity, the greater is its ability to sustain itself – to accommodate to any situation at all. This encouragement of diversity and fluidity is all to do with flexibility. It enables the second of the RAISE factors – that of *adaptiveness*. Within the context of responsiveness, adaptiveness is required of any system when external pressures (in the form of a catastrophe point comprising new and unexpected classes of needs, new quantities of needs, or a sudden complexity of needs) triggers the need for self-transcendence or transformation.

The third important property of natural systems that we need to note is the tendency of their members to 'flock' – rather in the manner of a swarm of bees, or a shoal of fish. Without any apparent management control or visible guiding force the individual members of complex adaptive systems behave as if they are wired into a unifying identity, a *community of mind* moving effortlessly as if they were one super organism (or vivisystem).

In human social ecologies, this tendency for individuals to link with each other and to form relationships results from the need to *belong*. *Belonging* ensures that the individual can survive by drawing upon the resources and reserves of the entire community. Ultimately, this need to *belong* leads to processes and structures that enable the principle of *sustainability* – of surviving and prospering in the long term. This is the third of the RAISE factors.

These three principles – *responsiveness, adaptiveness* and *sustainability* – are obviously vital aspects around which any viable model for a strategic management system based upon living systems must be designed. By combining these three factors we can at least be assured of designing a system that will learn and evolve over time. But is that sufficient for our needs? Probably not if coevolution is our *raison d'être*. Nature, as we know, is harsh and indiscriminate. Natural systems tend not to manifest nostalgia for the past. Evolution doesn't care what happened yesterday. Neither is it particularly concerned with what might happen tomorrow. Every ounce of energy is focused on surviving now.

Human beings, however, have an innate need to exercise choice over the future. We possess free will and a desire to direct, or at least influence, our destiny. Thus, we are concerned to mutually coevolve within the larger systems of which we are a part. As a consequence, there is a fourth and vital factor which, though we don't usually encounter it in the natural world, needs to be taken into account when designing a social ecology.

Social ecologies appear to require civilising factors – critical features that enable people to connect, contribute and to feel that they belong. These include:

- An overriding moral purpose (or purposes) on which to focus attention.
- The potential and capability for each individual to contribute and make a difference.
- A shared identity (or moral centre) comprising a dominant worldview, together with coherent corresponding principles and ideals.

- Cultural and behavioural symbols of this identity; and
- The opportunity to continually create new meaning with each other.

Together, these create an essence or 'soul' that is rarely found in non-human systems. And this leads to the fourth of the RAISE factors, the principle of *intentionality*.

Finally the fifth of the RAISE factors, which sets both the context and moral compass for *intentionality*, is *ecority*. Ecority is a term coined for the Gaian belief that all life is sacred and one – that it is our collective responsibility to protect the rights of all living things to live peacefully together on the Earth. When coupled with the willingness not to cause damage to others and to avoid actions that might put undue stress on the natural environment within which life exists, ecority sets new standards for what it means to be human – standards to which all human activities, especially production and consumption, need to adhere.

Before the twenty-first century, ecority was considered inimical (or at best a distraction) to running a profitable business or successfully governing a nation. Religious dogma also upheld the view that human beings were put on the Earth to dominate and subdue nature. Within the corporate domain, early advocates of environmental sustainability and corporate social responsibility were mostly ridiculed because of this. Today that is certainly not the case. In fact the reverse is true. While not all business leaders have come to terms with the fact, the business case for strategic ecority is overwhelmingly persuasive and on so many different levels. It can no longer be ignored. Customers are acutely aware of this. Regulators and activists avidly monitor corporate behaviour as never before. Employees demand ecority as the trade-off for giving their ideas, time and labour to the enterprise. Besides, the planet will not accept anything less. Over the past few centuries, the world's developed nations have plundered the resources of the planet, creating a situation where there is quite literally no alternative. Most people recognise that every decision and action we take must now observe the principle of ecority for without it we are set on an inevitable voyage of global destruction.

NAVIGATING EMERGENCE

The principles of viability all exist in the source model for the practice of Strategic Navigation. Although this model might look complicated

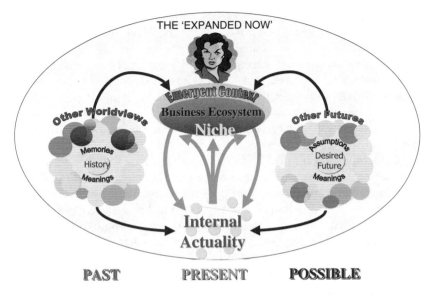

Figure 10.2   The Hames–Oka Strategic Navigation model depicts those conversational domains from which continuous strategic intelligence and extended periods of collaborative enquiry are required in order to navigate prevailing conditions successfully.

at first glance it is, in fact, fairly simple. Each of the five RAISE factors, in conjunction with other principles of natural living systems, such as emergence and the intelligence used to make decisions, are directly related to, or are implied in particular elements of this model. Domains of conversation are indicated, as are critical links and connections. The four most critical regions of the Strategic Navigation model are as follows. The model is brought to life through strategic conversation which is discussed in Literacy IV – Deep Design.

Region 1 – Stepping into a new epistemology

The bubbles on the far left of the model (*PAST*) represent the symbolism inherent in how we *see*, *recall*, and therefore *construct*, the world differently both as individuals and as societies. Although we may believe we are unbiased (or impartial) in the way we *know* things, our thinking is actually structured and patterned in ways that, while allowing us to see some things clearly, inhibit our seeing other things at all, or seeing them in a way that distorts their true meaning. Another way of looking at this is to imagine you, the reader (the human head at the top of the model) staring out at the external world of natural events and social activities. What you 'see' will depend entirely on the mental models and other frameworks you have acquired since birth. In fact, to be able to know precisely what you are seeing and feeling, one would have to have recourse to all your life events – down to every millisecond of experience.

Individual, institutional, communal and societal worldviews are all fabricated from a mass of implicit assumptions, which we blindly take to be universal truths. More often than not, however, they have formed over time as an expression of our direct and indirect experiences – our personal history. These unstated assumptions create the paradigms that frame *what* we see, *how* we make meaning of what we see, and *why* some things are more important for us than for others. So history varies according to who is narrating and who is listening. In this sense, our history is as uncertain as the future, so skewed is it by our preconceptions and mental models of reality.

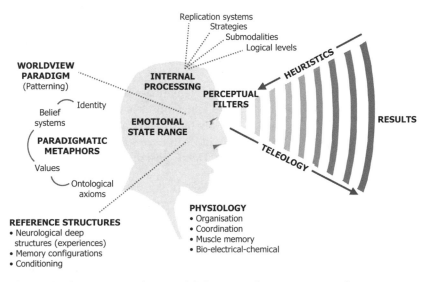

Figure 10.3 Marvin's Oka's model depicting the conscious and unconscious activity of the human mind 'being' in the world.

Occasionally personal and social worldviews will correlate in some form of approximate alignment (as, for example, in the common belief among most social groups, irrespective of geography or environment, that the theft of someone else's property is 'wrong'). At other times they diverge, sometimes significantly (as in the case of differing political ideologies or religious doctrines, for example) thereby allowing conflict, hostility and misunderstanding to take root. Shared understanding, together with the alignment of differing worldviews, will only occur when we consciously cooperate in experiencing our reality of the world with others who are doing the same. It requires the building of what is called a *community of praxis.*[9] The hypothesis behind the model of Strategic Navigation supposes that this is best done through strategic conversation during the process of design.[10]

Region 2 – Strategic alignment

The overlapping oval-shaped domains in the centre of the model (*PRESENT*) are to be read as a single vertical slice illustrating today's capability for *responsiveness.* These elements represent the *here and now* capability and performance gaps between the needs and expectations expressed by key external stakeholders (you might care to think of these as the critical needs that must be satisfied if the organisation is to achieve success within its chosen operational *niche*) with the current capability of the system to precisely meet those needs. If you prefer, it is a 'snapshot' of today's reality – a measure of the degree of *alignment* of the system with its niche. The niche, in this sense, represents the chosen transactional environment (market) over which a corporation presumably exercises some degree of influence and control. As greater alignment is achieved over time (through self-organisation as well as precisely targeted interventions to the organisation's structure, culture, systems, skills base and strategies), niche and internal capability merge, the system's intelligence increases, and the enterprise is better able to meet the needs of all its stakeholders. It achieves, and maintains over time, what we call 'strategic fit'.

Clearly, as greater numbers of critical factors change in the business ecosystem, additional shifts are required internally to maintain ongoing alignment. Nothing less than a constant flow of pertinent information (specifically facilitating ongoing comparisons of internal capability with external needs) will allow us to come to grips with the changing nature of today's reality from a total stakeholder perspective. Consequently, *responsiveness* can only be sustained where iterations of this process of strategic alignment occur on a regular basis. Continuous monitoring of the alignment of the enterprise as a system is needed to ensure that the enterprise is not veering off track or being seduced by conventional thinking or the latest flavour of the month.

As ever, there are additional benefits to be gained by talking to stakeholders on a daily basis and by inviting them to participate from time to time in co-design of products and services, expeditionary marketing and evaluation activities. Collecting current data, listening to what is said, watching what is done, learning and trying to make sense of this information as a whole, furnishes us with an enhanced appreciation of the critical strategic dilemmas impacting the business today and allows us to continually test our assumptions about stake-holders' needs and expectations and our capability of delivering those needs. Armed with this precious knowledge, we can then find more systemic ways of liberating the intelligence within the enterprise, and within the broader stakeholder community, to address both today's actual (and tomorrow's anticipated) needs.

Region 3 – Future perfect

By now, observant readers are sure to have noted that the niche, as illustrated, nestles within a larger bubble labelled *context*. Context here denotes the broader global external environment over which the enterprise has little or no direct influence. Unhappily, contextual intelligence is frequently neglected, misunderstood, or totally overlooked, by managers whose role it is to devise strategy for the enterprise. They posit that, because this environment is largely beyond the control of any individual corporation, there is little point paying much attention to it. *Five literacies* leaders understand this fallacy. History has proven again and again the foolishness of such a proposition. For it is here, in the complex, oft concealed and apparently irrelevant milieu of social, political, economic and technological complexity that the seeds of the future are revealed – that the structural drivers for change first manifest. It is a particular human failing that we tend to filter out of our consciousness anything we believe to be irrelevant to the accomplishment of our goals. Yet comprehending the structural nature of the global forces shaping change often provides the means whereby a corporation's survival is assured – even the largest and most successful multinationals.

IBM, for example, simply failed to comprehend a more informed society's need for the PC and lost its strategic impetus for a decade as a result. The Body Shop, on the other hand, intuitively felt the implications behind the community's increasing concern for social justice and environmental quality and built an entire empire almost overnight on this unlikely trend in public opinion. More recently, Apple Computers failed to keep pace with the demands of their customers for personal service. Initially propelled by a strategy of innovation and user friendliness, Apple now has to contend with the fact that today's PCs easily emulate the sophisticated graphic capabilities of the Mac – formerly the company's key strategic advantage. The jury is still out as to whether Apple is sufficiently future-focused to be able to truly understand this shift in customer expectations and reconfigure the company's strategy accordingly – although the success of the iPod and Apple's strategic realignment with the music industry seems to confirm the ability of Steve Jobs to remain at least one step ahead of the competition in this respect.

The kind of knowledge entailed in identifying and comprehending the driving forces for change is commonly called *foresight*. Foresight, therefore, is the third key element in Strategic Navigation. And the links between the *contextual* environment and the various *futures* bubbles depicted on the far right-hand side of our model (*POSSIBLE*) illustrate this capability. Here, any number of potential future possibilities interact and overlap, vying for supremacy from one moment to the next. The dynamic between the opportunistic creation of a *preferred* future (conventionally referred to as the *vision* or *ambition*) and the future as argued by experts (the *official* or *expected* future) is depicted as a tract that needs to be navigated. The extent of the gap between these two potential futures indicates the degree to which the *preferred* future will need to be invented by the organisation. Signifying considerable human effort, this element of the model illustrates the principle of *intentionality*. Meanwhile, a confusing muddle of other alternative futures (perhaps 'unthinkable' or 'too fanciful' to be considered likely) depict the need to prepare for entirely unexpected or unforeseen situations – the kind of unpredictable and unforeseen situations we referred to previously as *emergent* properties.

Researching and playing out a number of alternative (yet conceivable) futures not only enhances the quality of our strategic thinking, allowing us to appreciate worldviews other than our own, but also encourages far greater discrimination between what really matters (even when these are currently 'weak' signals) and what is merely distracting noise. It is through developing foresight that we are better able to con-sciously invent the future we desire, anticipating difficulties or opportu-nities with ease, avoiding potential traps, and rehearsing what we would do if the future we most want, or expect, does not eventuate.

The development of foresight, together with its associated tech-niques, can also help delay, or even prevent, the likelihood of events taking us by surprise. In today's volatile and unpredictable business environment, for example, virtually any proposal for capital expend-iture should be viewed as high risk if it doesn't stand up to scrutiny in at least three different possible future environments.

The principle of *intentionality* (together with implied ideals of *ecority*) is really the only uniquely 'human' factors in the entire Strategic Navigation model. The other principles are evident to some degree within all natural living systems. And so it is vital that we use that fact to help design and bring into being the future we want rather than be directionless, like a cork bobbing up and down on the waves of the ocean. In fact, one could argue that *intentionality* is the whole point behind the concept of Strategic Navigation. Uniquely among sensate beings, humankind can contemplate the future, developing foresight about what might happen, and rehearse appropriate responses should danger threaten or unanticipated opportunities present themselves. In that sense, navigating prevalent conditions allows us to act with some conviction in an ocean of uncertainty.

Region 4 – Learning our way forward

The fourth key element (not explicitly depicted) in the Hames–Oka Strategic Navigation model is the process of continuous strategic learn-ing. Integrating past, present and future it directs our focus and attention towards a *preferred* future. *Knowledge Designer* – a simple eight-step learning heuristic – depicts the energy for learning and confidence for taking action required from *five literacies* leaders in order for their business to remain viable. Experienced as a continuous braiding of thinking and acting, and navigating the waters between the past and the future, it is the propensity towards shared learning that creates the momentum for change without which any preferred future is sure to fade. This learning heuristic illustrates the principle of *adaptiveness.*

As can be seen from this illustration, *Knowledge Designer* is a simple tool comprising an eight-step sequence nesting within four

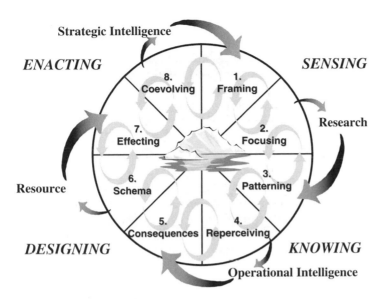

Figure 10.4 Although the Hames–Oka strategic learning heuristic or *Knowledge Designer* is here depicted as a simple eight-step cycle, it is actually a spiral that enables a shift of thinking into new epistemologies. The iceberg model of strategic questioning is embedded within the process at every level.

quadrants. Some readers may be familiar with these quadrants as they broadly follow the cycle of learning proposed by David Kolb – a cycle that involves four components, namely:

- *Sensing* or experiencing something concrete happening.
- *Knowing* conceptually (making sense) by integrating what has been discovered with what is already known in order to discover significant trends or patterns.
- *Designing* appropriate responses in the light of this new knowledge that will change or improve the situation at hand.
- *Enacting* the results of these strategies.

The Hames–Oka *Knowledge Designer* articulates a finer granularity of processes within the Kolb cycle. Each pairing in this sequence represents the continuous balance required from *breathing in* (providing space for reflection) and *breathing out* (providing energy for action) without which learning remains ineffective and essentially non-strategic. The basic learning cycle follows the following sequence. In step one we frame the circumstances of our experience by setting a context that anchors our current understanding of it. Next we focus in on all the elements that appear to be important, given our current information, so as to fully comprehend what is going on. In step three, alternative perspectives and new learning are integrated into our understanding of what is happening through some form of enquiry – this might be based on feelings, intuition, instinct or on hard facts. Following this, we attempt to reperceive our understanding by finding other ways to view the issues, or by filtering out elements that appear to be unhelpful in terms of leading us to a wiser, more comprehensive, or more elegant understanding of the situation. In step five we examine any issues, together with their implications and consequences that may have surfaced or mutated as a result of our new appreciation of the situation. We are then able to design pertinent responses to the situation in step six, testing the viability of our strategies against the criteria we have established during the learning process. These designed changes are then implemented in step seven. Finally, monitoring the situation on a continuous basis, we are able to reflect on the impact our changes are having on the original situation and how they might be having unintended consequences within the enterprise or the broader business ecosystem.

The cycle is repeated as often as needed in order to introduce new knowledge, monitor environmental conditions, review and assess what effects our actions are having on the original situation and whether those consequences are still valid, and revise our strategy or our intentions as appropriate. We will see, too, how our decisions may well change the context, which will require us to focus on different issues, and so on. . . . Using this simple eight-step sequence allows us to learn how to respond to situations with greater conviction. It also encourages us to integrate new knowledge into our capability for designing. This is the level of applied learning. And applied learning allows us to act and improve our actions. But, as suggested above, use of the strategic learning spiral can do a lot more than just that.

Employing the phase labelled *coevolution* as a reflective bridge into a higher level of learning enables us to use the eight-step sequence again. This time around, however, it can be used not only to learn new actions, but also to learn about how we are learning to think about and *do* new things. In this case, we can use the spiral to reflect on the very processes we've used to develop the responses we've come up with in order to address the situation at hand. This level of *meta-learning* is the level of systemic patterning.

Finally, additional insights can be found by using the same coevolutionary phase from the level of patterning as a reflective bridge into an even higher level of learning (that of learning about the nature and structure of *knowing* itself). Here, the eight-step learning sequence can be used to critically examine our fundamental worldviews. This level of learning is precisely the level we shall need to access in order to re-organise our core epistemologies, guiding principles, morals, ethics and aesthetics.

One should not think of these different levels of learning as 'good and bad', or 'better and worse'. Such distinctions are of little real value as human beings use all three levels most of the time in addition to a level we haven't even considered here, that of conditioning, or automatic response – the kind of learning that has taken place when we

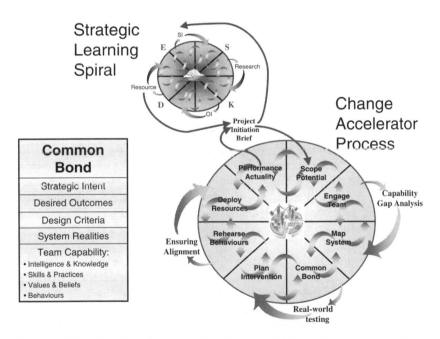

Figure 10.5 The Change Accelerator Process (CAP) replicates the structure and logic of *Knowledge Designer* at the operational level of project management. The CAP was created by the author in collaboration with Geoffrey Dale.

do things instinctively. That acknowledged, what is important, especially to *five literacies* leaders charged with the task of navigating their organisations through uncertain or uncharted waters, is the relatively sophisticated competence to appreciate what level of learning is required at any given moment, and for any given situation, sufficient to provide the context for beneficial reflection and dialogue. To become so mindful is to achieve *unconscious competence*, to use the expression coined by Carl Rogers. The real value of *Knowledge Designer*, therefore, resides in this intrinsic development of higher levels of consciousness. Because this strategic learning heuristic is an integral component of strategic conversation – the basic element of Deep Design – more detailed information concerning its use can be found in that section of this book. The *Knowledge Designer* process can also be replicated at an operational level to provide order and to accelerate the implementation of any projects emerging from the strategic learning process. We call this the *Change Accelerator* process.[11]

Region 5 – Strategic conversation

There is a further region implied by the philosophy underpinning Strategic Navigation. Once again this is not explicitly depicted on the source model. It is the strategic dialogue enabling Deep Design and development of the business ecosystem. This fifth key element of the navigational model arises from the diverse exchanges undertaken by members of the organisation as they attempt to help design and shape a socially dynamic, mutually engaging and ethical enterprise together. It can be envisaged as a sensory web, stretched like a skin over the enterprise, monitoring and analysing the signals arising from within and across the enterprise and out into the furthest reaches of the business ecosystem.

Understood by *five literacies* leaders as an enabler of Deep Design, strategic conversation is the primary means whereby each of the other four elements in the Strategic Navigation model are integrated into a unified, purposeful, collaborative dialogue – a *community of praxis*. Some die-hards might query the need for such a dynamic braiding of strategic thinking and doing arguing, instead, for a more rigorous formal strategic planning process. Sadly, the most common outcome of most strategic planning is an elegant plan; an (often secret) repository of incongruous dreams and well-intended, yet fanciful, unresourced or impractical objectives. Although we do not advocate that strategic conversation should necessarily displace other dynamic strategic planning methods (although it may in certain circumstances – such as in highly volatile situations where, quite literally, nothing is certain for long) the strategic management of a contemporary corporation, institution or government department cannot be considered comprehensive unless there are more relevant and engaging ways of addressing strategic learning, other than through formal processes of planning.

One incontrovertible problem for today's leaders is that very few things appear to be certain. And without certainty it becomes impossible to predict, and therefore control, events. In this context, long-term planning becomes inadvisable to say the least. In such circumstances, it seems wiser for managers to engage in continuous intelligence gathering that leaders can use to constantly feel their way forward – making corrections to strategy as circumstances demand, rather than sticking to some predetermined, centrally controlled game-plan that might rapidly become irrelevant.

Where insights for control and certainty, together with their antitheses, are vital for the viability of any business, it makes sense for leaders to find ways of creating alternative kinds of dialogue that transcend fixed thinking habits and the inflexible views they inevitably produce. This is where alternative scenarios come in handy; it is unusual for scenarios not to provide at least some fresh insights that can then lead to a set of new strategic options. Occasionally these options may even require us to review those things we had thought fixed or out of our control. The following cycle provides a useful trajectory for facilitating rudimentary strategic conversations.[12] Starting from what we understand to be enduring rules, we can use a process of collaborative enquiry to challenge some of these beliefs. Conversation can then be steered into the domain of uncertainties, from which alternative scenarios can be crafted. These scenarios can then be used to offer up original options that, coincidental with a greater degree of certainty, can be used to make strategic decisions.

There are other issues to keep in mind. One of these is the actual time and effort it takes to create and disseminate a strategic plan possessing any degree of sophistication. It goes without saying that *intentionality* should ideally be agreed, shared and clearly understood by every member of the organisation. But one really has to wonder whether, today, any enterprise can afford the luxury of committing precious resources producing a plan that might very well become out

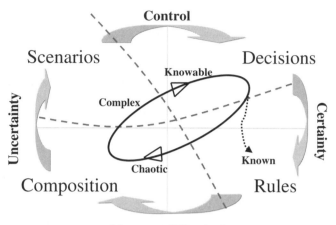

Figure 10.6 A basic trajectory for guiding simple strategic conversations. Snowden's decision flows model overlays a standard matrix thus forcing a dialogue between what is certain (or not) and what degree of control can be exercised over specific issues (or not). Different conversations may use different dilemma parameters.

of date almost before it has been printed and bound – let alone deployed throughout the enterprise.

Another has to do with the potential for wasted effort. We now know that possibly 75% or more of an organisation's performance is directly attributable to the more informal aspects of organisational life – things such as gossip, habits, spontaneous actions, unspoken rules and assumptions about work, and the like, which are extremely difficult to control, rather than the more formally planned visions, goals and objectives we habitually lock ourselves into.

These examples merely demonstrate the need for vigorous processes that are able to address strategic issues in real time. No conventional strategic planning process, however rigorous or flexible, can possibly deal with the degree of organisational informality and levels of complexity in today's global business environment. They are not *sticky* – nor are they *viral* enough. Even the most rigorous and successful strategic plan will only ever deliver around 25% of an organisation's performance. Hence, if an enterprise doesn't develop some kind of process for dealing with the more *informal* aspects of organising, that is of harnessing the natural energy and vitality for change in the *cafe*, it becomes totally reliant on dictates from the *cathedral* to manage its capability for being adaptive. As we have seen, this is simply insufficient and lacks the variety to be effective.

Strategic conversation, we believe, is an ideal vehicle for dealing with those dynamic, unforeseen factors, just as strategic planning was an ideal vehicle for addressing the more generic, foreseeable aspects of organising and managing in a more predictable world. The golden rule appears to be that a strategic plan can only ever be genuinely effective in circumstances where key events can be accurately forecast, or where the external environment is stable and relatively unchanging. Otherwise strategic conversation within and across organisational communities is far more viable. Ideally, a balance is required between the two.

Strategic conversation is not merely better quality talk. It clearly is a different, more integrative and more dynamic way of engaging people in sharing diverse opinions, values, assumptions and worldviews by high-jacking the conversational space within the enterprise. Nor can it work effectively without participation. It really is a means of involving people in creating that *characteristic mode of thinking*, which was the way we have previously described the term 'strategy'. If people are continuously engaged in critical reflection of the many things happening around them (and have both the tools and skills to make that meaning significant and enabling) then we have the potential to create an authentic strategic conversation.

In effect, strategic conversation makes sense of the various components in the Strategic Navigation model by enabling a dialogue which continually shifts the context between the various key elements. Thus, the distant future can be discussed within the context of what is required today, while the relevance and appropriateness of today's internal capability (and its subsequent degree of alignment) can be viewed within the context of what it is we are ultimately trying to achieve. Likewise, leadership can be thought of as the facilitation of a collaborative process for the optimisation of the organisation's potential, while that same potential, in the form of learning, can be seen as a continuing 'songline' drawing from a known past, through the eye of the present, into a future yet to be invented.

The 'community of praxis', brought into life by this fifth element of strategic conversation, reinforces the notion of *identity* and illustrates the principle of *sustainability*. When viewed as a whole, these principles, together with the property of emergence, effectively raise our consciousness of the system – both its pathology and its potential. It is for this reason we call *responsiveness; adaptiveness; intentionality;*

sustainability and *ecority* the RAISE factors; an easy acronym to help us remember the significance of these life-giving principles.

UPGRADING THINKING . . .

The idea that strategic management can, or should be, based around the existence of indeterminate, mutable, protean forces that can neither be predicted nor controlled with any degree of certainty is, in itself, a frightening and difficult psychological chasm for so many individuals in so many corporations and limits the extent to which Strategic Navigation can be used effectively in those organisations. In fact, once an organisation becomes convinced of the need to upgrade its operating system from a planning-based to a navigation-based system (perhaps through an empathy with ecological principles or, more likely, through the simple realisation that traditional forms of strategic planning have become too unreliable and unwieldy, too slow, too much of an economic gamble in today's volatile, hostile and notoriously fickle business environment) it is already faced with having to deal with the reality of 'lock-in'.

After a century and a half of management and organisation development – a programme of modernisation which has taken us on a magical mystery tour from Taylorism, through the sociotechnical methods of the Tavistock Institute, to teamwork, total quality management and organisational learning – we are psychologically, technologically and culturally 'locked-in' to the paradigm of management professionalism. Inevitably, we are also 'locked-in' to the accumulated wisdom, expectations, tools and techniques spawned by this ever-burgeoning industry – encumbrances and artefacts ranging from workforce planning and design, enterprise bargaining, human resources departments, spreadsheets and performance systems to statistical process control charts, cause and effect diagrams and a host of planning-based management tools. After a lifetime spent using these technologies, and of identifying personally with these systems, they have become like a second skin that we wear almost without noticing. Indeed, so natural do we find many of these developments that we have come to believe that it is in the nature of things to be just so. We tend to be sceptical, even downright suspicious, of any system based upon a different set of assumptions and propositions.

To some extent, the history of planning has paralleled the history of management. It certainly shares the same typology in terms of the increasing sophistication of a single paradigm. Starting in the mid-nineteenth century with simple production coordination and planning techniques, developing into more or less accurate short-term budgeting and forecasting methods, and ending with even more comprehensive systems for long-term strategic planning, this typology has been amply documented in the numerous management texts, educational programmes, fads and commercial products littering the landscape of organisational and business life this century.

Although each change was initiated by some methodical advance on the original idea for production coordination, the only truly quantum leap in thinking, in an otherwise linear progression of improvements, was triggered by global competition and the realisation, not commonly felt or agreed to by any means, that plans could be made far more resilient to changing market conditions if they took the firm's external environment, including customers' needs, into account. It was, without doubt, this development that gave rise to today's more refined methods for strategic management and real-time navigation.

However, what must be of concern to all of us, is that our emotional attachment to, and nostalgia for, the actual experience contained within such accumulated paraphernalia now traps us within a world-view that is vastly out of date. It means, quite simply that, even when there are highly rational social and economic reasons for changing to a new operating system, such as Strategic Navigation, we are inclined to resist – no more than any system instinctively resists trading its illusion of equilibrium and comfort for a world of commotion and uncertainty.

Quite obviously, unless there is, for some reason, an unacceptably high risk attached to the perpetuation of a planning-based system of strategic management, the resources of most organisations do not run to being able to implement a totally comprehensive Strategic Navigation system overnight – much less replicated throughout a distributed community such as exists in many a medium to large-scale corporation or government department. Besides, current management practices, such as the processes for governance and performance management, for example, along with any recently introduced or important new strategic initiatives, need to be critiqued, have their viability accepted within the newly defined strategic framework and, where appropriate, integrated into the Strategic Navigation system. This will take time and reflection, not to mention a shrewd migration strategy. It will also take targeted leverage to grow appropriate internal capabilities. In this regard Marvin Oka and myself have identified several leverage points that are critical to understand in order to get the best out of Strategic Navigation.

1. Leadership

Fairly obviously, the first of these is the enormous leverage obtained for systemic change through applying *five literacies* leadership – where 'leadership' becomes *a collaborative process for the purposeful advancement of the human condition*. In other words, leadership within the ecological framework and philosophy of Strategic Navigation is a catalytic energy, enabling such processes as organisational learning, strategic conversation, and the creation of a genuinely *appreciative* social ecology (all examples of social processes that cannot be imposed by diktat or by force of personality) to occur and burgeon.

While the term leadership is a much used, misused and abused term today, it does point to a phenomenon which when properly understood, can be a great point of systemic leverage for organisational change. The immediate difference between more traditional forms of 'servant as leader' and *five literacies* leadership (or what, perhaps, is increasingly better understood as *collaborative individualism*) will be seen to be that the ecological leadership experienced within Strategic Navigation cannot possibly emanate from a position or function. It is not the ultimate title accorded the CEO, nor is it the role of an elite group of people in the organisation. Just as followers, like observers, cannot actually exist within the context of viable systems, so leadership, in terms of ecology, is simply an emergent property of the system. It now becomes a process that can engage and be engaged in by anyone, at anytime, whenever there is a need for conscious change – change that ultimately betters the human experience of any situation or condition. There are several aspects to this new emergent form of leadership that need some explanation in order to fully comprehend its potential within the context of Strategic Navigation.

To focus on ecological leadership as leverage for systemic change means to bring a strategic consciousness to, or wisdom to bear on, the organisation. This entails positive energy – sufficient to overcome the natural inertia to be found in most traditionally managed organisations. Sufficient energy, too, to begin and maintain a focusing of people's attention on strategic imperatives – or what is commonly referred to as the 'big' picture. This 'big' picture should encompass intelligence about the external environment and how it is changing, the niche into which the organisation fits, the purpose of the organisation existing, the principles that are to be lived, and from which meaning of events, decisions and actions can be made. In other words, *five literacies* leadership is about the managing of meaning that is being made by everyone, moment by moment.

Additionally, a critical obligation of *five literacies* leadership must be to create the conditions necessary for a learning environment, within which transformative change can take place. In this regard, *five literacies* leadership catalyses energy for learning and instils a confidence for new actions to be taken. And ultimately, such leadership behaviourally symbolises and demonstrates how essential values can be embodied and lived in a practical day-to-day context and in responding to real-life conditions.

Without these aspects of *five literacies* leadership – without the means to bring new levels of consciousness into the organisation – the status quo of the current culture will always find ways to counteract the efforts for change initiated by a strategic management system, bolstering inertia and ineffective practices as surely as the ocean's drag on the boat's rudder. One cannot expect radically new methods for organisational management to succeed if these are introduced from within an old paradigm, or applied with the same level of consciousness that produced the current, less than ideal, conditions in the first place. It takes the energy and focus, attention and passion of *five literacies* leadership to break the inertia of any pre-existing paradigm through conscious intent.

2. Mastering complexity

The second leverage point is the ability of *five literacies* leaders to master the complexity surrounding them. In any business or government environment that is dynamic, ever changing and multifaceted, it is absurd to continue using management methods that are linear or reductionist in their approach and scope. Unfortunately, most conventional management methods are exactly that! So what do smart global leaders reach for instead? Well first, let's define what we really mean by the term 'mastering' complexity.[13] I believe it to be *the skill of understanding and capitalising on the dynamics of interrelating systems over time.* That probably sounds glib, but it actually takes quite a while to appreciate the full extent of just what that means. First, it is a skill and, like any skill, it can be learned, practised and mastered.

Furthermore, it is a skill of *understanding*. Many people might not accept that *understanding* can be a skill. However, just as the ability to understand technical matters requires a different set of intellectual skills, or strategies, to understanding human relationships and feelings, so there are particular kinds of strategies we can engage in, and tools we can use, to understand complexity and systemic emergence.

Mastering complexity, though, is not just the skill of understanding complexity; it is also the skill of capitalising on the dynamics of complexity. As systems interrelate and interact with each other, dynamics occur, sometimes quite chaotically. It is precisely the dynamics arising from systemic interactions that we can use as leverage for change. A simple example will illustrate what I mean. A famous story is told of an ancient Chinese feudal ruler who was constantly oppressed by a neighbouring feudal warlord. It was a relationship that could best be described as one of cordial hostility. While they were on speaking terms and engaged in mutual events between kingdoms, there were always undercurrents of covert power plays between them. It seems that the weaker of the two had a psychological barrier wherein he believed the other to be the stronger and more powerful, and would always win in any power struggle between them. He therefore ruled his kingdom accordingly, albeit unconsciously, and the morale of his people was low as they lived in abject fear of the neighbouring kingdom.

Apprehensive of a possible attack from the more powerful warlord, the weaker sovereign sought counsel from a well-known military strategist. The military strategist was quick to note that the sovereign already believed that any engagement in war would lead to his eventual demise, believing that he was weaker and could never win. Now it seems that every year, these two warlords would stage a horse race between the two kingdoms, each warlord racing their top three horses against each other. The weaker lord placed much significance on these races as being symbolic of his relationship with the more dominant lord. And each year, the weaker lord's horses would always lose every race.

Now the military strategist, being a keen observer of dynamics, realised that here was the potential for leverage to help raise the morale of the entire kingdom, as well as create a better foundation for building their military strength in case of attack! How? Well, he knew that if his lord could ever win the races, his confidence would be boosted and his self-esteem would be considerably raised. But how could he win the races?

The strategist saw that the other lord's horses were only slightly better than theirs, but there was a marked difference in quality between each of the three categories of horses, being the best horses, second best and third best. So the strategist suggested to his sovereign, 'Sir, I recommend that you race your third best horse against his first best horse. Then you race your first best horse against his second best, and your second best against his third best. In this way, you will win two out of the three races and be the overall winner.' And so the sovereign did as his strategist suggested and won the horse race. His confidence was boosted immediately. His self-image was so enhanced by the knowledge that he had actually beaten his more oppressive opponent that he subsequently ruled his kingdom with considerably more confidence than previously. So noticeable was this change in self-image that a significant change in the morale of his people was also apparent. And, after many years of feeling inadequate to the opposing forces, his army now had a feeling of hope and the thought of possible victory should they ever have to engage in battle with the oppressive warlord.

As quaint as this story is, it does illustrate how complex situations can be mastered and dealt with in ways that might at first seem counter-productive or irrelevant to the primary issues, yet in the end leverage a significant change to the system. *Five literacies* leaders understand this. They appreciate the power and utility of technology to effect change and help bring about transformation.

3. Harnessing new technologies

The third leverage point accessible to those practising Strategic Navigation is the harnessing of new technologies for strategic purpose. This can be defined broadly as *the repackaging of work, re-engineering of processes, and redefining of context given new technological capabilities.* The essence of this definition can be found in a quote from the world-renowned management guru Peter Drucker. In the early years when computers were just becoming more and more accessible, Drucker declared, 'Most organisations are asking the wrong question. They are asking, "How can we use computers in our business?" What they should be asking is, "Given that computers now exist, how should we structure our business?" ' Organisational performance today is constrained by the fact that we still tend to package the work that needs to be done into artificially bounded compartments we designate as 'jobs'. If, for example, creative thinking isn't written down as part of the job description, the average worker will believe they are meant to park their brains at the door each morning and just do as they are told by their (it is assumed more competent) supervisor. In order to really harness the potential of new technologies we will need to redesign all work into entirely new, far more flexible envelopes. And that also means we will need to reimagine the processes of how we do that work, and even redefine the work context – given what our technologies can do. And here I'm not just talking about computer and information technologies but entire knowledge fields, such as the very language we use to express how we are thinking; behavioural technologies that increase human capabilities; large group processes such as 'open space' that are facilitative and energising in nature; even biochemical technologies which, through the use of nutritional supplements and dietary planning, can produce remarkable results, not only in one's health but also in abilities such as memory enhancement, the combating of mental fatigue, increasing cognitive capacities and the enhancement of emotional well-being.

Embedded, too, within any Strategic Navigation system will need to be collaborative mechanisms for surfacing and understanding the relevance of emerging technologies. These mechanisms will have to include everything from identifying what the technologies are, to the conducting of impact analysis studies. Just because an individual or department embodies technical expertise today does not mean they will be the required technical expert for tomorrow, unless of course, they are able to learn to master entirely new technological formats on an ongoing basis.

4. Strategic innovation

Our fourth leverage point is strategic innovation. Innovation doesn't just mean adding more technology to our lives. It also means liberating people to do the kinds of things that technology cannot do. By referring to *strategic* innovation, we are immediately concerned with *the ability of an organisation to continuously find ways of exploring, discovering and developing new and additional levels, and even entire forms, of uniqueness.* In other words, it is the ability of the organisation to continually create and adapt to its niche as its environment incessantly changes. As Gary Hamel repeatedly says, this amounts to building an organisation that is 'as flexible and adaptive as change itself'.

Obviously, the opposite of this is to *not* strategically innovate – to continue with the current ways of thinking and doing. Consequently, in the context of strategic innovation, leaders will need to encourage the challenging of all forms of sacred cows and so-called 'methods that work'. Often, when executives say that they are taking a particular approach to an issue because it works, what they are really saying is that the approach they are using has worked in the past. Unfortunately, there is no guarantee that it is the ideal approach to be using as we head into the future. Strategic innovation requires a breaking of 'status quo' perspectives and attitudes. It not only deliberately encourages, but also finds ways of nurturing, differences of perspective. The person with a *different* way of 'doing things around here' is not shunned because he or she does not fit in but, instead, is respected for their different angle on things and their courage to challenge the norm. To really develop this leverage point is to actively seek strange, novel, even weird perspectives from people who have strange and unusual ways of looking at the world – and the organisation.

5. Speed of learning

And finally, the fifth leverage point for increasing the momentum of strategic change is the speed of learning – or the organisation's 'learning metabolism'. By this I mean *the time taken to optimally engage in the process of transforming information into purposeful change.* Reg Revans, who coined the term *action learning,* also proposed an equation which states that the rate of learning for an organisation must be equal to, or greater than, the rate of change in its environment. In other words, if the environment is changing at a faster rate than the organisation can learn to make changes to itself, it will become extinct. The speed of learning within any organisation is critical to its survival. In essence, it is the rate of metabolism of the organisation to ingest new information, digest it and turn it into nutrition to help the organisation remain healthy, strong and to grow. The speed of organisational learning also has to do with the cycle time involved in making changes. This applies not only to the organisation as a whole, but also to groups and even individuals within the enterprise.

Some of the keys to enhancing the speed of learning have to do with the speed of access to useable information; the speed of effective methods of information processing; the opportunities made available for the rapid integration, utilisation and practise of new learning; and a focus on short, quick feedback loops between actions and results. Executives with a natural bias for action, fairly common in Western organisations where managers are not known for their patience, should note that this emphasis on speed is not intended to short-circuit genuine learning. On the contrary, the use of 'timeouts' (or reflection sessions) which may appear to slow things down are actually about engaging in learning and critique. Without reflection between one action and the next, there is no learning, there is only activity – no wisdom, only mindless conditioning! We are sure that it is not necessary to remind our readers here of Mr Pavlov and his dogs. The paradox of it all is, that in order to increase the speed of learning, one needs to take the time to learn. And what determines how long that time needs to be has as much to do with the other leverage points we've already mentioned.

CHANGEBRAINS AND STRATEGIC DECISION THEATRES

Strategic Navigation can only work effectively where there are groups of people devoted to working *on* the system – rather than working *in* it. Their role is to use *Knowledge Designer* and similar processes to synthesise intelligence, create maps that cut through the complexity to visualise reality and communicate derived meaning, monitor the dynamics of the business ecosystem and use the leverage points outlined above to propose and initiate strategies for the development of the business, the business ecosystem and the organisation. We call this function the *ChangeBrain* and the environments within which *Change-Brain* staff work, strategic decision theatres.[14]

Directed by corporate navigators, the *ChangeBrain*'s role is firstly to *sense* and to *make sense* of changing systemic conditions. Strategic learning of this nature is accomplished through a constant monitoring and mapping of the system's dynamics.[15] Consequently, information from all stakeholders (and from every part of the system) is collected and synthesised into maps that explicitly depict critical factors, relationships, issues and events in the organisation's system. A variety of colourful maps adorn every available space in these decision theatres. These allow comparisons to be made and specific dynamics tracked over time, while acting as potent reminders of the novelty that exists within and between the organisation's internal and external environments.

In collaboration with others, *ChangeBrain* staff detect and communicate significant patterns and trends. Differing hypotheses are proffered to explain changes in the system's dynamics. Rapid response action-research projects may be undertaken to plug critical knowledge gaps, while generative scenarios are used to play out different possibilities as how best to sustain organisational viability given current resources and their deployment. Within hours of any significant discerned change in the system's dynamics, *ChangeBrain* staff have moved into their next principal role – that of *designing* and *actioning* appropriate strategies to initiate, intervene in or counteract specific dynamics. Mapped depictions of the current state of the system are now used to identify leverage points and appropriate interventions to maintain strategic alignment with the company's niche are *designed* and *deployed.* Short planning cycle times and feedback loops help to ensure that nothing undertaken by the company is quarantined from evaluation or permanently locked in.

Because resource deployment is continuous rather than fixed over the life of an arbitrary annual budget, new projects can be started and redundant ones terminated without sending the organisation into unnecessary trauma. *ChangeBrain* staff then continue to observe and evaluate results to ensure that the organisation's original intentions are being met. If they are not, swift corrective actions, sometimes in the form of quite subtle adjustments to strategy, are constantly being taken.

The learning environment itself is a critical, though often neglected, element of effective strategic conversation. Even the most enlightened management and leadership dialogue typically occurs in sterile spaces where participants are given little or no assistance in documenting narrative, visualising relationships, recalling crucial data – or even creating new knowledge. When information is available it is commonly expressed in a form (e.g. spreadsheets, lists and graphs) that is difficult to share or alter, operates as a convergent (rather than a divergent) factor, ignores tacit knowledge and hinders comprehension of systemic dynamics and leverage, evolutionary trajectories and unintended consequences. Moreover, such information will often be open to wild misinterpretation, depending upon personal perspective, memory, political games, face-saving devices and individual assumptions. Because of these constraints, even the most enlightened dialogue will only ever be effective at the level of simple business problems, not entire systems. Complex systems are far more difficult to grasp. Consequently they require more sophisticated means for visualising the information from which intelligence can be synthesised and acted upon.

The design of strategic decision theatres that attempt to overcome at least some of these inadequacies can be traced back to the work of Stafford Beer in pre-revolutionary Chile. Beer was a pioneer in creating environments that enabled deeper conversations (and consequently wiser decisions) through the identification, collection and synthesis of real-time systemic intelligence. Later, his work became the basis for the *ChangeBrain* decision theatre environments and associated processes.[16] Strategic decision theatres are increasingly used in companies, governments and research institutions around the world as intelligent enablers of new knowledge and fresh insights where the process of transformational narrative is facilitated by dialogue-literate *ChangeBrain* staff.

These conversation spaces are most effective where the issues under scrutiny are contextualised within a dynamically emergent environment and where there are no simple black and white solutions to this emergence. The inputs to transformational narrative are relatively straightforward: monitoring the dynamics of change, *ChangeBrain* facilitators track the emergent properties of their system (an organisation, project or strategy, for example) in real time. This constantly evolving information is displayed live on four walls as an interconnected, real-time, knowledge system:

- Wall 1 is a synthesis of PAST STATES. It comprises anecdotes, diagrams, photographs and learning histories to depict the evolution of the system up to and including the present day.
- Wall 2 is a synthesis of possible FUTURE STATES. It comprises descriptions of the official or desired future, possible alternative worlds within which the organisation may need to live, succession matrices, aspirational statements, etc.
- Wall 3 maps the system in its IDEAL PRESENT STATE. It comprises a high-level map of stocks and flows, supply webs and value chains as well as intended value points, feedback loops, transformations, etc. The information on this wall can also be used as inputs to simulations of one kind or another in which various assumptions can be tested.
- Wall 4 maps the ACTUAL PRESENT STATE. It comprises relationship diagrams, causal-loop diagrams, theories in use and any additional data that can be used to expose the underlying behavioural DNA of the system as it manifests in real time.

The process of strategic conversation (often using transformational narrative methods) is moderated within the decision theatre space in ways that allow the dialogue to flow within and between the various domains. The knowledge product at the conclusion of each conversation becomes the critical domain of attention (CDOA) – a shared expression of the threads of critically interrelated ideas, dynamics, models and consequences that are strategically relevant in decision making. Frequently the CDOA from one conversation becomes the input to the next conversation with another group of people. In this way ideas are shared and explored across various constituencies.

Strategic decision theatres are increasingly replacing the boardroom in companies that recognise the need for the space itself to act as an enabler for deeper systemic consciousness of strategic issues, dilemmas and paradoxes. Although decision theatres and the role of the *ChangeBrain* is critical to Strategic Navigation, the engagement of the whole organisation as a learning community epitomises *five literacies* leadership. And for this, all-encompassing processes of engaging the organisation in strategic conversation are needed. Ultimately though, it is how intelligence from the *ChangeBrain* feeds into strategic dialogue across the enterprise, and beyond, that enables Strategic Navigation to fulfil its promise. That is achieved through our fourth literacy, that of Deep Design.

NOTES

1. Because Strategic Navigation is such an extensive methodology, comprising philosophy, theory, methods, processes, tools and techniques, only a brief description is possible here. Further information on Strategic Navigation and its associated methods can be had via email from The Hames Group at http://www.hamesgroup.com.
2. Referred to as the Mont Fleur scenarios. Completed in 1992, these scenarios sought to answer the question 'What will South Africa look like in 2002?'. The Mont Fleur scenarios were one in a series of scenario exercises in South Africa at the turn of the 1990s.
3. Richard Hames and Marvin Oka pioneered Strategic Navigation in collaboration with the Australian Taxation Office from 1996. Assuming various guises, strategic navigation has since found its way into many government departments and multinational corporations.
4. 'Biomimicry is a revolutionary new science that analyses nature's best ideas and adapts them for human use', in J.M. Benyus, *Biomimicry*, Penguin Books, New York, 1997.

5. Biomimcry has many uses. For example, scientists in search of a super adhesive have examined the structure of the spider's foot that allows it to cling to a ceiling and measured that they can carry up to 170 times their own weight with the force of attachment. They are now looking to replicate this in a new generation of post-it notes. This is part of the process of biomimicry – looking at how nature does things better than we can and copying the structure or processes involved.

6. 'Equilibrium equals death. Companies . . . may enjoy a period of time when equilibrium really works. It may give them a dominant position, and it may result in outstanding economic rewards. But it makes them increasingly vulnerable to the moment when the game changes. Because when the game changes, their winning formula from the previous period becomes their own worst enemy,' Richard Pascale, co-author, *Surfing the Edge of Chaos*.

7. Biomimicry analyses nature's best ideas and adapts them for human use. This revolutionary new science is captured in a book by science writer Janine Benyus, *Perennial*, HarperCollins, New York, 1997.

8. Theodore Zeldin has set up an organisation called The Oxford Muse to help people and organisations converse to good effect. He uses simple tools, such as a 'Muse Conversation Menu', which typically lists around 24 topics through which people can discover different aspects of each other. These range from topics like aspirations and fears to curiosities, goals, friendships, beliefs, etc. One eminent participant during a dinner organised by Zeldin at the World Economic Forum in 2005 said he would never again give a dinner party without this menu because he hated superficial chat. Another maintained he had in just two hours made a friend who was closer than many he had known much longer. A third said he had never revealed so much about himself to anybody with the exception of his wife.

9. The notion of a community of practice (knowledge plus practical application) is here extended by taking into account how the individual will become different through the experience of using and applying knowledge – hence praxis.

10. Design is the first sign of human intention to act to change what 'is' to 'what might be'.

11. Designed by Geoff Dale and Richard Hames as an eco-design replacement to standard project management methods.

12. Taken from Clem Sunter and Chantell Ilbury's book, *The Mind of the Fox: Scenario Planning in Action*, Human & Rousseau Tafelberg, Cape Town, 2001.

13. Complexity comes from the root 'plexa' meaning a woven pattern is present. This is different from being complicated, which comes from the root 'plica' meaning fold upon fold upon fold. Human beings tend to make things more and more complicated by adding additional layers of stuff.

But mastering *complexity* means being able to find the simple patterns that are woven into the information. Thus complex and complicated are not at all the same thing.

14. I first came across this term being used by Arizona State University which has a highly sophisticated, computerised, decision theatre – a learning and decision space in which the latest understanding of complex social, economic and natural processes and their interactions are visualized. Previously, we had referred to these spaces as navigation centres.

15. These maps, which are used to discern significant patterns and trends within the noise of data impacting the organisation, range from stock-flow diagrams, relationship diagrams and causal loop diagrams to soft systems maps and rich pictures.

16. Transformational narrative, of the kind that resculpts entire paradigms, requires profound conversations that evolve the consciousness of participants. It also demands (physical and virtual) spaces that embody critical atemporal information. These conversations are an art, arising from integrating new intelligence (about ourselves and the business yesterday, today and into the future) into a flowing discourse. Thus strategic dialogue, facilitated by *ChangeBrain* staff and conducted in decision theatres where the technological infrastructure is robust, becomes an adventure in learning – a liberating process of intelligence gathering, collaborative enquiry and systemic mapping where exploring and responding to complex realities is made explicit and shared with others so as to arrive at wiser decisions.

CHAPTER 11

LITERACY IV – DEEP DESIGN

The days of the celebrity solo designer are over. Complex systems are shaped by all the people who use them.

– John Thakara, *In the Bubble*.

Design is the first sign of human intention to change from what is currently available to something better.[1] Until recently *design* was not a word one often heard mentioned in the context of business. Nor, in the past, has it necessarily been linked to creativity or the practice of innovation. Why is that? After all, design affects every aspect of our lives. We live in a totally designed world. Design is not merely an afterthought or an aesthetic add-on but integral to how products and processes connect, interact, behave and age. It is what humans do. Everything from where we live, to how we get to work, to what we eat and wear, is the result of an endless series of design decisions by countless individuals. Design captures the flow and interfaces of our lives.

In spite of this, design has been a seriously neglected discipline in the field of business, governance and organisation. Rarely is thought given to the design of whole processes or attention paid to how systems should work together. Effectiveness is often sacrificed for cost. Because much of the design in our world is undervalued it is also flawed, and with each new technological advance we find ourselves faced with yet another set of unintended consequences. I seriously doubt that future generations will tolerate the damaging consequences of short-term thinking in their design of the present, where end-to-end lifecycles are sacrificed for the sake of cost and long-term consequences are mostly ignored.

Taking note of the driving forces of change, adopting more integral approaches to design and challenging basic beliefs, for example that human industry must inevitably damage the natural world, will all help rectify this state of affairs. In this regard *Deep Design* is a way of thinking about the way we create, manage and sustain relationships of all kinds. It is the essence of our connection with those with whom we interact – from investors and staff to customers (and even non-customers), analysts, suppliers, regulators and citizens. It is also the emotional resonance created by our connection with the objects we choose to purchase and live with. So critical has it become to business success that a number of smart leaders are predicting design will be the next testing ground for competitive advantage.

The *five literacies* approach to design, therefore, is not an abstraction. On the contrary, it defines who we are, even extending to a direct visceral manifestation of one's entire philosophy, beliefs, emotions, values – and intentions. This is the essence of *Deep Design*. Deep Design stretches far beyond the material tangibility that convey signs of sentient life (such as individual goods, industries and architectures). Beyond, too, the more subtle processes, artefacts and interactions of a civil society (such as institutions, media and governance structures) to the basic patterns of human consumption and production and even knowledge itself. Far more integral and expansive than the discrete nature of most conventional design disciplines, Deep Design is a new conceptual framework: a framework in which economic activity creates goods and services that generate ecological, social and economic value; where waste is a thing of the past; and where human needs are balanced by nature's realities.

Systems, products and services designed according to Deep Design criteria are characterised by being:

- **Integral** – Consciousness and compassion must permeate every aspect of the lifecycle from innovation through production to delivery, usage and beyond. The deepest assumptions and beliefs under-lying design decisions must be made explicit so that the burden of choice becomes transparent at every stage of this cycle.

- **Benign** – For Deep Design to be acceptable no damage must be done or accrue to people or to the environment. Sustainable prac-tices must be used at all stages in the lifecycle.
- **Resonant** – Deep Designs are a part of our identity and must align with our most deeply felt values and ethos. The whole design of integrated intangibles is far greater than the sum of the parts for the purchaser.
- **Low impact** – Ecological linkages ensure the use of *soft* pathways where the costs are accounted for over the full lifetime of the product or system and meet key criteria for renewability, recyclabil-ity and non-toxicity.
- **Strategic** – Deep Design is sustainable in terms of being socially desirable, ethically defensible, culturally appropriate, ecologically responsible and economically feasible, now and into the future.

There are two important aspects to design of any kind: the first has to do with what we fabricate (let's call that the *content*) and then there is the means we use to inform the content (which I will call the *method*). Although an understanding of both content and method is critical for effective Deep Design, *five literacies* leaders often focus more on method than on content. That is because, while there are always a surplus of experts on hand to design content, expertise in ecologically intelligent systemic method is hard to come by. Also, content flows from method – not the other way round. Let us look for a moment at an example of content to illustrate my point before moving on to method.

BITS AND PIECES WE PAY FOR

We can reflect on the future of content by examining past intentions and beliefs. Take urban planning, for example, as an urgent issue deserving of more ecologically intelligent Deep Design.[2] It is quite easy to see what our intentions were in the past. Imagine that the city skyline represents the changing pageant of these intentions. Eight hundred or more years ago, the inspiring architecture of cathedrals and temples thrust towards the heavens, signifying our belief in mysterious forces beyond our comprehension. From the seventeenth century these sacred spaces were gradually eclipsed by monoliths to government, depicting the growing influence of the nation state and the importance of the political process on our lives. Today, corporate skyscrapers (together with the colossal cranes constructing them at such a feverish pace) dominate the skyline, towering over the slums, dwarfing government offices and casting their shadows over the temples and museums; ample evidence, if that were needed, of our intention to pursue material wealth irrespective of political persuasion or spiritual fulfilment. I often pause to wonder what the city skyline of the twenty-first century will tell future generations about our intentions and whether the principles of Deep Design will have enabled a new sensitivity to nature and to each other. Time will tell.

Sometimes it takes just one human being to tip the scales and change the course of history. In 2007, that human being will either move to or be born in a city, and demographers watching urban trends will allude to it as the moment when the world entered a new urban millennium, in which the majority of its people will live in cities. Coincidentally it will also see the number of slum dwellers cross the one billion mark, when one in every three city residents will live in inadequate housing, with few or no basic services that the rest of us take for granted. About 70 million people a year are migrating from the country to cities. That is about 130 people every minute. All of the world's projected two billion population growth between now and 2030 will occur in cities. China is urbanising at just under 2% annually. Translating that statistic into terms we can grasp, it means that over the next couple of decades we can expect around 400 million Chinese people to move into a dozen new cities in China. Such development is unprecedented. Traditional design and planning models cannot cope with these growth levels, putting as they do such enormous pressure on traditional systems and amenities.

Intentional or not, we have designed a world in which much of *what* we do and *how* we do it simply cannot continue. Whole-system change in the pattern of human activities is required. And fast. Current models are not sustainable and have reached the point where our species is now threatened with extinction. In terms of our urban planning example, we need to rethink how we think about designing and planning our cities: from conceiving the city as a machine to understanding the city as an ecology. In other words we need to shift our thinking from how things *look* in the landscape to how things can *work* better for society – balancing nature's needs with commercial realities, but on a human scale. That is the role of Deep Design.

A century or more ago cities in the US, Britain and parts of Europe enthusiastically embraced what was destined to become one of the twentieth-century's most ascendant new technologies: powered by the internal combustion engine, automobiles rapidly overtook horse power as the most favoured form of transport. Ever since, urban planning and spatial design have been dominated by our psychological 'lock-in' to this technology, to the extent that most citizens now believe it is their god-given entitlement to own one or more automobiles. The more powerful and larger the petrol guzzler the better we like it. These attitudes have given rise to an expanding web of urban highways that gridlock with ever-increasing numbers of vehicles and that pollute the air causing stress and illness to citizens. Logically that cannot continue. Yet, paradoxically, it is politically unacceptable to try to change the current system. Even when the inefficiencies, costs, toxicity and ill-health are self-evident, cities from Mexico City to Bangkok and Shang-hai still eagerly pursue the same goals. So nothing changes . . .

How might the principles of Deep Design be used to turn conventional wisdom on its head in situations like this? What would happen, say, if we decided to retrofit our cities to an alternative 'lock-in' – putting people and their real needs, together with the flows of information, water, sounds, images, capital, goods and services that are so critical to progress in the attention economy, at the centre of our thinking? By shifting our thinking almost imperceptibly we might possibly conceive of a new conceptual framework for flexible urban design where the design criteria emphasised an improved balance between the natural environment, human needs and enterprise. We might use biomimicry and the principles of natural living systems to transcend the ways we have traditionally conceived of urban development. And we might find it easier to embrace complexity and celebrate the sheer joy and creativity of the human spirit as well as the abundance of nature.[3]

There are four critical design elements in Deep Design that distinguish it from more time-honoured approaches. They are philosophy, viability, ecology and governance. Let us look briefly at each of these in turn.

1. Philosophy

While most approaches to design focus on the product being manufactured or service being offered, the philosophy of Deep Design focuses primarily on human agency: How will this product be used? What could be its impact? What unintended consequences might occur and how would any unwanted or harmful effects be avoided or allayed? Central to this philosophy is the notion that design should be exercised 'on a human scale' and with human needs in mind – improving the complex ecology of dynamic flows and interactions as people go about their daily lives. As in the natural world, there should be no waste created in Deep Designs. On the contrary, systems are synergetic and regenerative. Applying the principles of Deep Design to urban planning would ensure that our cities have clean air, fresh water, diversity and aesthetic appeal – as a minimum.

2. Viability

Viability has to do with the consequences of our design decisions, both intended and unintended. Not everything can or should be planned in today's complex environment. Our civilisation has generated resilient, flexible, learning ecologies, in which self-organisation and spontaneity occur all the time at a community level, creating diversity and richness that contains much of real value. In a sense it is this richness that feeds back to nurture civilisation. Without it, civil society would collapse. The principles of Deep Design enable social infrastructures and decision-making processes that ensure viability. In terms of our previous example, viability might translate into a series of connected neighbourhoods and community hubs where retail, recreational and learning facilities are close at hand so that the need for travel is minimised. When travel is required (or desired) in a viable urban system, clean, energy-efficient, public transport systems (as well as safe walking paths and bicycle tracks) take precedence over the automobile.

3. Ecology

Deep Design takes a balanced view between economic and ecological benefit. Products, services and processes are planned as 'holons' that have future consequences and where ecologically intelligent outcomes are just as desirable as profits.[4] This means new disciplines such as biomimicry and industrial ecology are used to ensure permanent assets are created – rather than perpetual liabilities that future generations will need to attend to. Flows of energy and materials are continuously tracked and materials are cycled and recycled through products designed for disassembly. In the context of our urban planning example this will result in architectures that are socially, economically and ecologically advanced; where buildings using smart materials purify air and water, and produce more energy than they require; and where communities are reintegrated and nested more skilfully into nature. In effect, the use of ecologically intelligent Deep Design principles in this context would dramatically reduce the ecological footprint of the urban environment while aiming to make our cities' water cleaner, their air fresher, and their people happier.[5]

4. Governance

Conventional design assumes that products are designed *for* rather than *with* others. This has its origins in the industrial revolution when products were mass manufactured for the first time, thus separating manufacturers and customers. In this context, manufacturers make what they believe they can sell in the marketplace while governments impose regulations to ensure fairness, quality, safety, waste minimisation, and a myriad other socially acceptable requirements aimed at maintaining an economically viable society. The unintended consequences of this system include: (i) an enormous, and largely superfluous, compliance burden on business that grows each year, with the cost of compliance often passed on to customers; (ii) hidden costs of production that serve to keep the true costs of manufacturing hidden; (iii) an endless choice of goods and services that creates almost unlimited demand for new products; and (iv) the demand on business to comprehend the counterintuitive trend of selling less of more.[6]

Through the use of open-source development, cooperative industry clusters, 'creative commons' approaches to the sharing of intellectual property,[7] and similar collaborative mechanisms, Deep Design puts people, flows and cooperation at the centre of its governance agenda, turning conventional practices on their head. In terms of our urban development example, it means moving from minimal consultation to openly engaging citizens as co-designers: while guiding principles are set centrally by government, citizens themselves take responsibility for local rules, applying these and determining how such principles are interpreted and enacted. Applying Deep Design to urban planning and development we can imagine a city of the future designed almost from the molecule up:

While meeting standard requirements for cost, function and performance, the future city is also ecologically intelligent, serious about social justice, safe, healthy, has clean air, soil and abundant power and an individual vibrancy and character one expects from cities. Walkable, transit-oriented mixed-use neighbourhoods are structured around a series of green spaces. Workplaces and residences are close to transportation hubs, primary schools and interlinked networks of different habitats. The city is laid out so that pedestrians can walk in parks without crossing traffic. The entire city is connected via hi-tech communication networks. The buildings work like biological beings, using daylight while photosynthesising, producing and reusing their own energy. Waste is energy: methane is used to cook food and a quarter of the city's cooking is done with gas from sewage. The energy systems are mostly solar. Soil covers rooftops and is green. In effect the city of the future grows, breathes, and is ecologically sound, just as trees, forests, and gardens are. It uses energy, expels waste, and reproduces in ways that nature intended without destroying everything else around it (William McDonough, architect).[8]

THE VITAL STUFF (OR METHOD)

The Iron Age did not end because humans ran out of iron. It ended because it was time for a rethink about *how* we live. We have reached another watershed in human history. It is time for a further rethink about *how* we live. And we need Deep Designs to help us achieve that intelligently and benevolently. In spite of good intentions, smart individuals and so-called best practices, many products, services, living spaces, organisations, urban environments and entire global systems are toxic and are becoming more so every day. The issue is to rethink the essence of design at a time when old models are clearly non-viable. It is time for ecologically intelligent design. Spatial, ergonomic and ecological design that is creative, abundant, prosperous and intelligent from the start. It is time we adopted the principles of Deep Design to create a whole new world for the future and that of our children. That is our challenge and why Deep Design is so critical to our future health and well-being.

This challenge comprises considerable implications for the way we think about and apply design in our world. Which is why method is so critical. In the domain of method, Deep Design explores an integral way of thinking that invariably starts with questions like: 'What should be our ultimate aim?' 'Given the context, what is now possible?' 'What can we achieve that has not been possible before?' 'How can we create retained value for more people in this process?' Designs that begin with such questions, whether in products, buildings, technologies, communities or nations, are sensitive to all living systems and can accomplish their purpose without the side-effects of contamination, corrosion, congestion and trauma.

In any situation, be it business, government or community organisation, one of the most effective ways of ensuring we remain sufficiently alert to changing conditions, and that we are asking the most relevant questions in the circumstances, is through the pervasive use of generative learning environments and decision theatres, as well as process models like *Knowledge Designer*.[9] As previously described, this is one of the principal process tools used for strategic conversation, collaborative learning and systemic development within the Strategic Navigation methodology. It is also fundamental to the realisation of Deep Design.

Knowledge Designer is a tool for liberating strategic conversation and collaborative enquiry. It comprises a phased method of exploration, discovery and enquiry leading to informed and insightful action – or Deep Design. It is most effective in situations where:

- A level of uncertainty prevails around a number of critical variables.
- There are no obvious solutions to a problem or problems.
- Patterns and trends, for whatever reasons, are difficult to establish.
- Previous experience and/or knowledge appears to be of little use.
- The degree of complexity appears overwhelming.
- Emergent issues are creating threatening environmental conditions.

Knowledge Designer is a versatile tool. While intended primarily as a collaborative path-finding technology to ensure the integration of *active thinking* and *mindful action* in groups engaged in systemic development – especially where such ends require extensive strategic conversation around complex, uncertain and unpredictable issues and dilemmas – this spiral can even be employed by individuals as a more immediate, personal 'aide memoir' for unfettered thinking.

The eight phases of *Knowledge Designer* are arranged in four linked pairs, each pair representing one type of learning domain (sensing, knowing, designing and enacting). Although each discrete phase has its own processes and associated tools and techniques, feedback arrows denote a fluidity wherein each phase can simultaneously point forwards (in development) and backwards in time (in reviewing and evaluating).

And in addressing both of these as a continuous thread through the spiral, another aspect of learning, which is learning to *become* different, is initiated. In this way, the *Knowledge Designer* process facilitates the fundamental pattern and criteria of any complex adaptive (learning) system; namely, that it:

- Acquires information about its total environment.
- Acquires information about its own interaction with that environment.
- Identifies regularities in that information.
- Condenses those regularities into a model.
- Acts in the real world on the basis of that model.
- Qualifies competing models based on real-world results.
- Upgrades its models based on real-world results.

The most subtle, and arguably significant, aspect of *Knowledge Designer* lies in its eighth phase, *coevolving*, which, in fact, is the precursor to moving through the next round of the heuristic at a higher order of awareness. This coevolving phase entails being responsive to the effects of one's actions. The information that comes from these transactions is analysed and then fed into the *contextualising* phase as intelligence, thereby moving us into an iteration of the learning process at different learning planes where we are able to focus on: (a) the process of learning and (b) the nature of knowledge itself. In spiralling onto different learning planes, we are able to: (a) change what we do; (b) improve our understanding of how we are doing it; (c) reflect systemically and strategically on higher level issues so as to continuously question the value and purpose of what we are doing while simultaneously improving our understanding of its complexity; and (d) critique the quality of our own thinking, and expand our own paradigms and worldview.

Each learning domain in *Knowledge Designer* has products (or outputs) that act much like a propulsion agent as they provide inputs into the next phase. These four sets of combined inputs and outputs are called *transition systems*. These transition systems either provoke the collection and integration of useful information from a variety of sources into the ongoing process of knowledge creation or, as in the case of *resourcing*, replenish our capacity for actioning change. The first of these transition systems, *strategic intelligence*, enables us to more accurately assess the scale, urgency and significance of the systemic dynamics with which we are dealing. It allows us to comprehend the scale of our predicament. The second, *researching*, encourages us to explore certain issues in greater depth, where required, or to find out what we do not already know. *Researching* also broadens our perspectives. It confirms or challenges our assumptions and direction-alises us, showing us where we ought to be looking and supplying us with more thorough information concerning the various dimensions of our business context. As we begin to develop our ideas, the third transition system, *operational intelligence*, ensures that we take adequate note of the more practical aspects of what is (or is not) possible, feeding us information about what we don't know that could make a significant difference to our ability to (re)focus. Finally, *resourcing* encourages us to ensure that adequate time, skills, money, facilities, people, tools and equipment, and particularly relevant information, are readily available to those people who will be responsible for implementing strategy.

USING *KNOWLEDGE DESIGNER*

Although *Knowledge Designer* is visually represented here as a simple eight-step process, in practice it is a heuristic, facilitating an exploratory process of learning up and down a knowledge spiral. The basic steps are straightforward enough.

1. **Framing** allows us to perceive and establish a preliminary broad understanding of the systemic environment (or context) in which strategy is to be developed, reviewed or reinvented. Using strategic intelligence feeds, we ask: What are our general strategic concerns? What do we feel is going on around us? How do these concerns relate to the environment in which we are operating? What are the key characteristics of this environment? What is changing?
2. **Focusing** allows us to arrive at a shared, though preliminary, under-standing of the critical issues requiring our attention, together with the strategic impact of these issues. Here we ask: What are the most strategically significant issues requiring our attention? What specific factors make these significant? What are the relationships between these and other specific issues? How should we resolve dilemmas between what is strategically important versus what is not important but more urgent? What should we be attending to (and when) in order to ensure greater resilience and ultimate viability?
3. **Patterning** allows us to test and enhance the quality of perceptions in play through challenge, exploration and expansion of our mental

286 THE FIVE LITERACIES

models. Using any research we may have undertaken to understand these issues better, we ask: What are the gaps in our current thinking and our current ways of knowing? Where can we get the information and from whom? What assumptions are being made that we should challenge? What other perspectives are needed or could be useful? Are there any other ways of perceiving the issues that could raise different questions, problems, solutions and opportunities?

4. **Reperceiving**. Given the information surfaced in the previous phase, we can now move to a more insightful level of understanding (or reaffirm our original understandings) of the systemic dynamics of the environment and a precise description of the 'critical domain of attention' within that environment. We ask: What new light has been shed on the situation that was previously hidden? How have our beliefs about what is important changed? What has been confirmed from our previous understanding? How can we best represent the complexity of our critical domain of attention to others?

5. **Consequences** allows us to refocus by using our new understanding to establish design criteria for shaping the business ecosystem in ways that effectively address the 'critical domain of attention'. Using intelligence from our operatives, we ask: What are the most strategically significant issues now requiring our attention? What operational perspectives should we take into account? What should our plans address in order to ensure our strategic viability? What would be the consequences of these plans?

6. **Schema** is the explicit Deep Design of our entire array of strategic activities, together with project plans for the systemic facilitation of change. We now ask: What strategies are possible? What will work best given our current resources? What stays the same? What do we stop doing? How might our culture or natural inclinations need to be developed in order for our strategy to be more effective? What are the consequences, risks and opportunity costs of choosing these strategies? Are we sure that our strategies will address key systemic leverage points?

7. **Enacting** allows us to put our Deep Design into action, shaping changes to the business ecosystem in order to generate higher levels of strategic appropriateness and systemic viability. This manifests in enhanced strategic performance, which leads to increasingly viable organisational ecology and, ultimately, a capability for healthy, adaptive coevolution of the whole business ecosystem. We ask: What actions will we need to take to ensure that our intended schema

and strategies are realised? What do we need to ensure our deployment capability? How will we know if we are being effective? Are our results demonstrably generating our strategic intentions?

8. **Coevolving** enables the continual adaptation of the organisation's praxis, in harmony with the systemic changes caused by that praxis. We can now ask: How are the dynamics of the business environment changing as a result of our strategies? What signals will indicate that a fundamental change is occurring in the context from which we are defining our strategy? What are the critical, unintended consequences of our actions? Will our strategic framework now need to change? Do we now see flaws or gaps in our previous thinking? Are there any weak signals we are recklessly ignoring? How will we upgrade our current thinking accordingly?

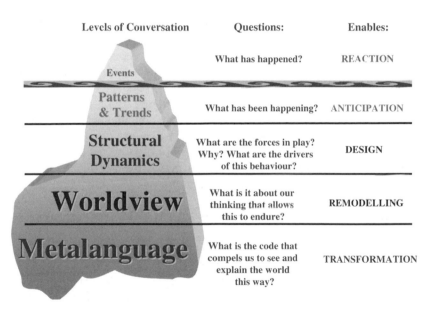

Figure 11.1 This 'iceberg' model represents how different levels of strategic thinking, triggered by different types of questions, allow for different responses to occur. Most conversations are reactive – occurring 'above the surface' of our perceptions. The challenge of deep design is to create dialogue that is more meaningful. This can only be done by exploring beneath the surface of discrete issues in order to find patterns, understand complex relationships and appreciate systemic dynamics.

These final questions in the *Knowledge Designer* enable far greater levels of consciousness, about ourselves as well as our relationship to the business ecosystem of which we are a part. To become so mindful is to achieve *unconscious competence*. The *Knowledge Designer* heuristic integrates multiple perspectives into our thinking; generates dialogue; and effectively maps the changing dynamics of our systems, allowing us to make more informed and insightful decisions for change. It is the continuous building of intelligence and learning from which planning and Strategic Navigation emerge. The real value of the *Knowledge Designer* heuristic, therefore, resides in this development of consciousness through processes of mapping and strategic conversation. To engage in strategic conversation is to engage in collaborative learning, which is the essence of Deep Design.

THE ART OF STRATEGIC CONVERSATION

Strategic conversation is an art – a particular class of dialogue and collaborative inquiry that integrates multiple perspectives from a diverse group of people for the purpose of enhancing the group's *strategic intelligence* in a process of transforming their activities. While there are undoubtedly many ways to define strategic intelligence, even within the context of strategic navigation, I prefer to regard this as *the information and capability required by an organisation if it is to learn to adapt to changes in its environment in ways that ensure its ongoing survival and well being*. Of course, this can apply equally to individuals.

An example from my colleague Marvin Oka will best serve to illustrate what I mean. Let's imagine your neighbour, Mr Pavlov, has a dog that likes to explore the vicinity, starting its adventures each morning by hurtling down the driveway and out into the big wide world. Now let's imagine that, on a particular day, Mr Pavlov fails to remove the rubbish bin from the drive after collection that morning. Picture the dog happily trotting down the driveway until confronted by the rubbish bin that now blocks its path. The dog, believing it can go no further because the bin is in its way, and confused by the changed circumstances, reacts by flopping down and howling until someone can come along and remove the bin from its path.

We would probably all agree that this particular dog is a very dumb dog. It is probably loved by Pavlov and his family, but it does not appear to be too intelligent. In other words, it doesn't really have much of an ability to adapt to changes in its environment. Nor does it process information well, other than through conditioned reflex perhaps. Your own pooch, however, might be a very different story. Let us suppose that it too likes to go for long walks, occasionally disappearing for hours on end while you frantically search the neighbourhood. For the dog's safety (and your own peace of mind) you decide you want to regulate when and where your dog is able to take exercise. So you build a fenced enclosure for the dog that becomes its 'home within a home' while you are at work. One day when you arrive home from work the dog is missing. Either it's been stolen, abducted by aliens, possessed by the ghost of Houdini, or has learned to jump over the fencing.

Being a practical type, and knowing your dog, you realise it is probably the latter, as a result of which, before you next place the dog in the enclosure, you ensure the fencing is made considerably higher. Over the next few weeks you realise just how gifted your pet is. It learns to dig its way under the fence, find a way to climb the fence, and even teams up with another dog that helps it to flip the handle on the gate to release the locking mechanism. Now, after all of this, you'd have to say that your dog was not a dumb creature. A nuisance, maybe, but pretty intelligent. In other words, your dog has a high ability to learn to adapt to changes in its environment.

Surprisingly, many organisations and leaders behave much like Mr Pavlov's dog. Their plans appear to work well enough as long as their goals are relatively easy to achieve, are simple to implement, or nothing major happens to stuff them up. And as long as no significant changes occur in their environment – like competition from an unexpected quarter, unanticipated technological breakthroughs, or legislative changes to government regulations, for example! If, or more likely when, such changes occur, bewilderment sets in. Reacting irrationally and with little foresight, the individual or organisation continues to do what it has always done – only with more enthusiasm and seemingly regardless of the (new) consequences. By contrast, an intelligent organisation (or a *five literacies* leader) thinks, plans and operates in ways that enable learning and adaptation to the numerous ongoing changes, foreseen and unforeseen, simple and intricate, occurring in the environment. Not once, but continuously. . . .

Here I need to qualify my coupling of the terms *intelligence* and *strategic*. As previously discussed, the concept of strategy can be thought of as a characteristic mode of thinking shared by the community of individuals comprising an enterprise. It guides all decisions, plans and behaviours that affect the very nature of the business and its future direction as an organisation, both consciously and unconsciously. A *strategically intelligent* enterprise or leader, therefore, is able to learn to adapt to changes in the environment in ways that ensure ongoing survival, health and well-being. In an organisation, this ability to adapt is qualified by its psycho-epistemology – or the way the enterprise defines the essence of its business and *what* it ultimately wants to become as an organisation.

Thus, the art of strategic conversation is a way of increasing our ability to learn to adapt to changes in the environment in ways that are ecological and congruent with the nature and direction of our intentions. At the same time it enables continuing alignment with the broader business ecosystem, often contributing to its overall health, especially in the case of *keystone* corporations.

SEEING THROUGH ANOTHER'S EYES

The second main idea in strategic conversation is the integration of multiple perspectives. Perhaps it would be easiest to begin this explanation with a quote from one of the great thinkers of our time, the late Gregory Bateson, who said *there is no wisdom in only one point of reference*. He had noticed that, in order to make a distinction, any distinction, at least two points of reference are needed. For instance, one cannot specify what is 'up' without specifying what is meant by 'down'. Neither is it possible to say something is 'good' without having a reference for what is 'bad', nor can one say something 'is' what it is without being able to differentiate what it 'is not'. It matters not whether you are a manager, a politician, a professor or a bureaucrat, whenever you are involved in dealing with complex issues, how do you know your decisions are wise and intelligent ones? Do your conclusions and plans incorporate different points of view, or are they based on only one, or at best one narrow set, of perspectives?

Certainly the tendency in many organisations has been to seek only a limited range of opinions, usually from those considered to be technical experts or the management elite. More often than not, this has resulted in inappropriate band-aids being applied because the complexity of the situation – in other words, its *systemic* nature – has not been fully comprehended. How frequently, for example, are marketing executives or customers called upon to assist manufacturing with a product design problem; or students requested to input to the university curriculum; or for that matter, a broad range of community thinking sought prior to important changes in government policies? And yet it is obvious that the timely integration of a broad range of perspectives can help eliminate blind-spots, building a far more comprehensive picture of the issue at hand than that seen by technical experts. Today, when there are so many variable factors to take into account and ambient conditions can change instantly and without warning, making momentous decisions is not something that can or should be undertaken by any individual or group coming from an expert viewpoint or singular ideological position. The systemic nature of complex issues, their interdependence and dynamic interaction with other such issues, demands an altogether different approach.

In any multifaceted or complex situation, capturing a variety of perspectives is vital: it helps sort the trivial from the significant, injects novelty and increased understanding, providing a solution that is ultimately more relevant, robust and sustainable in the long term. Moreover, this practice also has the benefit of assuring those who have been consulted of the importance of their input. Appreciation of the need to incorporate different viewpoints is a volitional characteristic of *five literacies* leaders – in fact of all healthy, adaptive human beings, just as the lack of such appreciation characterises maladaptive ones. It is worth recalling the sensible words of strategist Pierre Wack who warned *the majority of errors in strategy are not errors of analysis, they are errors of perspective.* When IBM nearly collapsed due to enormous losses, it wasn't because they didn't do their spreadsheets right, it was because their strategic perspective was so narrow it completely missed the impact of the PC against the mainframe. In recent landslide elections in Australia, it wasn't that the opposition party didn't do its campaign planning right, it's that the party was coming only from its own narrow outlook about what would work and that, at the time, was so very much not the perspective of the majority of Australians. Essentially the same thing happened in the UK in 1997 when, to the utter dismay and disbelief of many Tory supporters, Tony Blair's New Labour was swept to power after so many years in the political wilderness.

These, and numerous other instances of poor decision making, are examples of errors of perspective: errors based on expert opinion or on too narrow a viewpoint when making strategic decisions and plans, errors of not actively seeking (and integrating) as many viewpoints as possible in order to make wiser, more intelligent choices. The paradox is that in spite of the contemporary emphasis on individuals – their rights, roles and responsibilities – good decision making requires input from as wide a range of people as possible. From a *five literacies* leadership perspective, then, it is clear that humility must be a key personal character trait required in order to engage in strategic conversation. Simply, it is our willingness to recognise that we have only a singular perspective on any situation (a particular set of beliefs and assumptions through which we filter reality) and that this one perspective is insufficient for vibrant decision making. It's the acumen to recognise and accept that our single perspective may not always be appropriate or complete enough. It's the humility to recognise and appreciate that it is unwise and unhelpful to argue who is 'right' but, instead, be willing to learn from others by discovering how to share and understand their perspectives. Strategic conversation requires the kind of humility that leads to mutual respect and appreciation of very diverse points of view. To put it simply, true strategic conversation is both unifying and coevolutionary.

GROWING COHERENCE

This brings us to the notion of integration. As astute readers will have realised by now, the art of strategic conversation is not one of persuasion, but one of evolving coherence. Not one of influence, but one of synthesis. Not one of debate, but one of learning where information is replaced by deliberation. Because strategic conversation seeks integration (by synthesising many perspectives into a comprehensive *meta* perspective) we cannot hastily delete or discard any information as irrelevant. Instead, we must account for it. In a pluralist society such as ours, the lack of a pluralistic method for communicating meaning (the kind strategic conversation readily facilitates) guarantees poor or ill-informed decision making; the adoption of rigid conceptual positions that often prove to be irrelevant, socially inappropriate, or based only on partial understanding; and the perpetuation of argument and analysis based upon 'objective' evidence as the sole basis for *knowing*. Yet, it must be conceded, most of our social systems, legal institutions and scientific constructs (and consequently the routine conduct of our daily lives) are founded upon such dualistic concepts – still permeated by such thinking 'hand-me-downs' from Plato, Aristotle and Socrates.

Dualistic, or reductionist, thinking has many benefits, of course. For a start it simplifies complex phenomena, allowing us to analyse and *see* certain things and events with far greater clarity than would otherwise be the case. However, especially considering the hetero-geneous nature of many of today's most crucial issues, this dualistic framework can easily lead us into believing that literally everything can be reduced to simple, easily understood principles and processes. Indeed, it may even deceive us into believing that complexity itself is something inherently sinister or suspect, that anything resisting reduc-tion to a few simple elements is of no real value or has no useful purpose. This may account for the disturbing anti-intellectual attitude, prevalent in many contemporary Western societies and evidently sanc-tioned by their media, where serious, in-depth, debate of complicated issues is spurned in favour of superficial banalities, hype or commercial clichés; where it is commonly held that anything that cannot be said simply should not be said at all. In this respect, dualism's disadvantages should never be underestimated.

Using the reductionist approach of analysis and argument requires that a position be adopted. This position is usually fabricated from our most fundamental (and largely unchallenged) assumptions regarding what we believe to be *right* or *wrong*. Evidence is then acquired, albeit in a fairly biased and selective manner, to ensure we are able to defend our position should this become necessary. We then spend inordinate amounts of time attempting to influence and persuade others to our point of view, invariably seeking information that will validate our position, or refute any perspectives we would regard as being opposed to our own. After that, everything is perceived from one position or another – as if black or white, which is, after all, the whole point of reductionism. If we believe the data we collect does not validate the position we have adopted (that is, it does not make sense within our current frame of reference) we habitually discard it, label it as irrelevant or perversive, or even deny its very existence!

Occasionally, as is common in the political arena, we may even use it against our opponents as evidence that their position is inherently evil or seditious. Thus, it becomes extremely difficult, if not nigh impossible, to appreciate the systemic relevance of data to a situation where the reductionist paradigm of dualism is actively constructing how the various parties are thinking and behaving. Especially as everyone will be actively seeking only certain, limited types of information that will fit their own view of the world. By contrast, Deep Design requires *five literacies* leaders to expand their current perspectives to account for new, novel and often contradictory information, thereby broadening and intensify-ing how they think about any situation. From such an enriched perspec-tive, our decisions and plans increase in their levels of emergent wisdom. This entails integrating multiple perspectives into our thinking.

INTEGRATING MULTIPLE PERSPECTIVES

Through the assimilation of multiple perspectives, strategic conversation seeks, explores and critiques unconventional and innovative ways of thinking about an event or situation. It surfaces (and often constructively challenges) key assumptions we may have adopted in our thinking (albeit unconsciously) ultimately creating a shared, enriched understanding of the situation that could not possibly have been achieved by one person alone. In essence, Deep Design requires that we engage each other in strategic conversation, which is another way of engaging in collaborative learning. And, as I have already suggested, collaborative learning facilitates coevolution. Within the practice of Deep Design there is a need to integrate at least five key classes of multiple perspectives in order to achieve strategic conversation of the highest possible quality.

1. Perspectives of alignment

The first category of perspectives is that entailed through the process of alignment. Strategic alignment must include input from key external stakeholders, the organisation's members, competitors and any other individuals or bodies whose views may need to be taken into account. Strategic alignment also incorporates a unique perspective in Strategic Navigation, that of systemic facilitation, which pays particular attention to how the organisation interfaces with the external world – especially the global business ecosystem(s) that are of ongoing importance for the business. In order to achieve this 'helicopter' perspective, systems facilitators need to closely observe and map the hierarchy of relationship loops in play at any one time. This perspective is about connections, interfaces and the dynamics between the various elements of the system.

2. Perspectives of peripheral vision

The second category of perspectives we need to integrate into strategic conversation is that of peripheral vision, or what might be called 'going wide'. Developing a wider perspective involves seeking opinions that are novel and unique; input that, at first glance, might appear to be weird, strange or just plain off the mark! The development of peripheral vision is particularly important in corporations where it is quite common for members to become so single-mindedly focused on formal plans they often miss the significance of events that appear to have no relevance to them achieving their goals. Unfortunately, as history will attest, apparently 'insignificant' events can evolve into value-laden opportunities. Alternatively, they can turn nasty, creep up behind the largest and wealthiest of organisations when they are least expecting it, and knock them for six.

One of the ways such novel perspectives are sought is through the use of *remarkable* people. A term first used by Pierre Wack during his time as a strategist in Royal Dutch Shell, a remarkable person refers to anyone who is able to reperceive the context or issues facing an organisation – by virtue of their particular experience, originality, eminence, wisdom or heretical stance on issues. Remarkable people may be invited to contribute through interviews conducted by members of the organisation, as guest speakers in strategic forums, or even, at times, as part of the process of strategic conversation. Often, these remarkable people are from other industries, other environments, or are 'fringe dwellers' in our own society. The more 'outside of the box' they are, the more potential value they have for introducing novelty to our thinking, thus widening our appreciation of what is going on.

3. Perspectives of pattern and structure

The third category of perspectives required for high-quality strategic conversation is that of discerning patterns and structural dynamics – or what we refer to as 'going deep'. Here, we search for patterns under the surface of our normal perceptions and conversation, asking questions that we may not normally think to ask. A good way to understand what we mean by this is through a model that describes how strategic conversation may take place at varying levels of 'depth'.[10] The shallowest (surface) level is that where the primary content of the conversation centres on discrete issues and events. At this level, talk is largely superficial. It is concerned with what happened, who did what, why it occurred, what we are going to do about it, and the like. In other words, the conversation is content-driven, based on whatever the topic happens to be at the time of conversation. Such talk doesn't usually add much in terms of our understanding, especially if we have not personally witnessed the issue under discussion. A good example of this is the kind of conversation, often overheard at the hairdresser or around the water cooler, where people enthusiastically discuss the latest eviction from *Big Brother*, a blockbuster movie, celebrity antics or last weekend's sport.

Recurring issues and events, however (even football matches and television reality shows), will exhibit certain patterns and trends over time. The identification and recognition of these patterns is the second, deeper level of conversation in which it is possible to engage. At this level we are not as much concerned about going into the details of any one specific event or issue, but rather of seeking to understand and address entire patterns and trends of which the issues and events are merely signals. This level of conversation takes us to an understanding that comes from being aware of a much bigger picture of what is going on and how we should be responding. At this level, for example, our conversationalists will be more interested in the characteristics of *Big Brother* as a phenomenon of today's TV culture.

However, if issues and events are recurring often enough to produce discernible patterns or trends, deeper questions still might be asked. What are the underlying causes that continually produce such patterns and trends? What dynamics are in play, and what is the structure holding these dynamics constant? In other words, What is the underlying system responsible for producing these patterns and trends over time? This insightful, third level of conversational depth, can provide a profound understanding of the essential nature of the systemic conditions with which we are dealing. It can also reveal the location and identity of leverage points for changing the entire system. And yet, once again we can continue to ask deeper questions. For example, If that is the underlying system from which all the other things spring forth, what keeps this underlying system in play? Why has it come to be the way that it is and why doesn't it just change? This fourth level of conversation explores the mental models and worldviews that drive the preeminent underlying system. Finally, in the fifth and deepest level of conversation, we explore the critical aspects of the collective human psyche that actually cause the very conditions that humans must contend with. Here, we seek to understand ourselves as a 'community of mind' and how developed meta-language within society contributes to the manifested ecology of our own environment.

The art of strategic conversation traverses freely through all of these levels. It does not necessarily seek to occur only at the deepest levels for, obviously, we cannot even reach an understanding of mental models and worldviews without getting our clues from the issues and events they manifest. Strategic conversation is a continual weaving between the various levels, and it is through this seemingly roundabout conversation that great insight and wisdom can be gained.

4. Perspectives of time

Finally, the fourth key category of multiple perspectives needed to achieve high-quality strategic conversation is that of temporal or time-based perspectives. The classic example of the significance of this category is the all-too-familiar distinction between basing decisions and plans on short-term or long-term views: as we know, the difference in the viability of results can be quite dramatic. Organisations with a short-term perspective may well opt for immediate results by borrowing from, or gambling, their future, while those with a longer term view frequently sacrifice instant results for the promise of even greater gains in the long term. The ability to consciously 'go atemporal' (the rarefied and highly sought after domain of sustainable excellence in any human field of endeavour) guarantees that an enterprise will be able to deliver good short-term results while steadily growing its long-term capability – in any situation, however volatile or distract-ing those conditions might become. Such concentration is one of the visible signs of *five literacies* leadership. There are many other temporal perspectives one can take that are also quite significant in their impact on the viability of any strategic decision. One of these is the difference between whether we decide to plan our future based on *extrapolations* from the past and the present, or if we pin our hopes on an ideal future and *backcast* to the present in terms of identifying what will need to happen in order to achieve that ideal. The former may well impart benefits in the form of improvements to the current paradigm, while the latter can spark truly visionary and transformative change.

   Within Strategic Navigation we not only propose a need to take a temporal perspective based on the future and what it means to how we might act with wisdom in the present, but also include the notion of multiple futures. As explained above, an organisation's ability to navigate in the 'now' (based on its understanding of the various futures that could manifest at any time) is critical to its ongoing viability.

5. Facilitating dialogue

As a particular class of collaborative inquiry, strategic conversation integrates multiple perspectives for the purpose of enhancing strategic intelligence. Typically, strategic conversation also has distinctive flows, patterns and typologies. The following model, adapted from some of the work being undertaken by Dave Snowden and his colleagues at Cognitive Edge (formerly the Cynefin Centre for Organisational Complexity) illustrates the many classes and levels of thinking (and tools) that can be accessed to enhance genuinely strategic conversations.[11]

It is important here to understand the difference between dialogue and discussion. The distinction was first popularised by noted scientist David Bohm. He pointed out that the etymology of the word *discussion* had links to words like 'concussion', and 'percussion', which

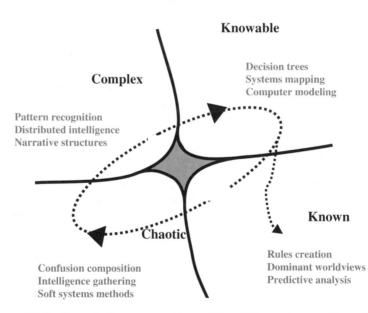

Figure 11.2 Snowden's representation of five different types of knowledge and decision flows, together with examples of tools and methods are appropriate within the flow of dialogue. The central domain represents disorder. Reproduced from Snowden, D., Complex Acts of Knowing: Paradox and Descriptive Self-Awareness, *Journal of Knowledge Management*, **6**(2), 100—11, 2002.

are words that have to do with hitting, striking, or being forcefully impacted. In fact, if we look up the word discussion in the dictionary, one of the definitions is 'to debate'. The concept of a dialogue, however, is based on the Greek root *logos* or logic, and *duos*, meaning two. The concept of dialogue is one where, through a particular way of conversing with another, we share, integrate and transcend each other's perspectives into an emergent perspective, which neither of us could have arrived at on our own, nor without the process of dialogue to get us there. Consequently, dialogue nearly always results in surprise. The essence of true dialogue is at the heart of strategic conversation. Combined with all of the other principles we have covered so far, strategic conversation is also able to bring forth a process of how any individual or an organisation can learn to continually redefine how much it delineates from, or merges itself with, the ecosystem of which it is a part.

As I have stated time and time again, the most viable of systems are natural systems, and one of the most natural ways humans share, transfer and build intelligence is through conversation. The notion of strategic conversation is a natural method for involvement in collaborative learning that is inherently heuristical and ecological. The art of strategic conversation plays a critical role in any system for strategic management. It is much more than just the kind of *business speak* we use when planning. Rather, it is a conscious building of intelligence from which Deep Design emerges and Strategic Navigation is made possible.

In any enterprise there are two main contexts in which strategic conversation should be fostered. The first is in the formal context of meetings and strategic workshops. The second is more informal: given new tools and techniques, people are able to engage in strategic conversation during coffee breaks, lunches or car pooling. Basically anytime and anywhere members of an enterprise meet to talk about organisational matters the conversational space can be highjacked by an intent to create a strategic emphasis. Such activity fulfils the principle of 'distributed intelligence' I talked about earlier in this book.

Five literacies leaders, however, recognise that the real power of strategic conversation derives not just from its capacity to amplify distributed intelligence, but also in the way it integrates and braids the two primary strategic streams of any viable organisation, namely the organisation's business strategy (focused on the external environment) and its social, or cultural, strategy (obviously focused on the internal arrangements of the enterprise). In other words, strategic conversation also builds and nurtures a strategic culture that resonates both externally and internally with maximum alignment and coherence. Not only that, it must achieve this integration at both individual and whole-of-system levels. The work of Ken Wilber has done much to focus our attention on the need for more integral conversations of this nature.

Additional to Wilber's work, four interdependent elements are needed for an enterprise to effectively engage in high-quality strategic conversation. Firstly, the organisation's members, and especially its leaders, need to understand and value strategic conversation, and to also appreciate the consequences of what happens when strategic conversation is not being utilised. Secondly, new skills need to be learned and developed. Strategic conversation requires new ways of thinking, linking, visualising and communicating. Thirdly, opportunities must be created in order for strategic conversation to be practised. Strategic conversation is the practise of collaborative reflection and requires an attention to creating the 'shared space' in

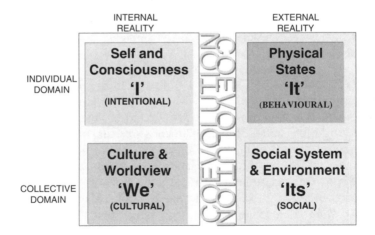

Figure 11.3 A diagrammatic summary of how Wilber's Integral 4Q model can be used to depict four knowledge systems required in order to develop greater self-consciousness in conversation with others. Adapted from Wilber, K., *A Brief History of Everything*, Shambhala, Boston, 1996, Figure 5.1, p. 71.

which to practise it. And finally strategic conversation requires a vehicle. It needs the relevant content to carry it. This can be in the form of scenarios, or the strategic framework for the organisation (such as its unique guiding principles, aspirations, and the like). Equally, it can be about specific strategic issues, the business model being used by the organisation, the corporation's planning cycle, in fact just about anything that is of strategic relevance to the Deep Design of the business ecosystem.

OPERATIONALISING DEEP DESIGN

Any operating system claiming to provide a comprehensive means for Deep Design and Strategic Navigation must enable every member of the organisation to use strategic conversation to fulfil three fundamental functions:

1. Asking the right questions

The first of these is to enable the organisation to surface the most pertinent strategic questions to be asking. Most organisations lack the means for asking the right questions. Unless they are fortunate enough to have a 'remarkable person' or a corporate philosopher in their executive line-up it is extremely unlikely that they will even know how to begin to ask strategically appropriate questions. Others, in spite of their well-intended efforts, may simply ask inappropriate or irrelevant questions. They will probably end up solving the wrong problems and unwittingly reinforce the fact in some people's minds that it may be better not to ask such questions in the first place! If, for example, management believes there is a problem with the quality of the services they provide when, in fact, they are providing the wrong services in the first place, they could end up investing time, money and effort in improving what is neither needed nor wanted at great cost to the business. There is a significant difference between the question, *How can we improve our services?* and, *Are we delivering the right services?*

One might reasonably ask how, in today's constantly morphing environment, anyone can possibly know which questions they need to be asking at any particular time? The answer is that they cannot. We know of no simple formula, no prescriptive made-to-measure consultant's package able automatically to pinpoint the right questions to be asking at all times. This is precisely why the prime function of a robust system for Deep Design must grow this capability – enabling the organisation to surface the right questions to be asking given the unique dynamics of any particular set of strategic issues. That is, it must create opportunities for the right questions to be exposed and examined. Surfacing the right questions is what provides the organisation with the means to then search for the most appropriate strategic framework it should be operating from, given the intelligence it has available to it at that time. The critical question demanding a satisfactory solution from our Strategic Navigation system, in fact any system purporting to effectively create and execute strategy, must be how does an organisation surface what questions it should be asking in order to even begin establishing its strategic framework or business idea? Furthermore, how does it know if earlier questions that were asked, maybe only a few months or weeks ago, are still the right questions to be pursuing? And, possibly most important of all, how can an organisation ensure that it is able to repeatedly provide itself with the opportunities and means that will continually surface the right questions it should be asking? This is precisely what processes of Deep Design must be able to facilitate.

2. Strategy finding

Deep Design must also enable the enterprise to engage in the process of constantly redefining an appropriate strategic framework that will guide all strategic decisions, intentions, values and behaviours. This key process is one of *strategy finding*. It is worthwhile noting here that the primary function of 'surfacing the right questions' to be asked does not, in itself, establish the strategic framework for the organisation. What it does do is to ensure that the most strategically appropriate questions are being found and investigated in order that an appropriate strategic framework can be detected and instituted. It is through this second function of strategy finding that contemporary strategy is conceived, put together, worked on, challenged, refined and tested. And it is through this process, too, that we are able to develop, specify, continually reinterpret and critique the *characteristic mode of thinking* that ultimately becomes the 'theatre' for all our strategic endeavours and decisions.

3. Transformation

Ultimately the purpose of Deep Design is to implement an array of beneficial strategies that improve the health of the business ecosystem for all stakeholders. This can be extended to include high-level aspirations such as the design of an appreciative society, for example. But in order for this to be a realistic proposition, new mental models must be created to enable the possibility of transformation. This requires processes that are able to challenge the status quo, transform current thinking and practices, and legitimise new paradigms. Although I have always found *Knowledge Designer* to be most useful in this regard, an alternative and vastly under-utilised model is Richard Slaughter's Transformative Cycle.[12]

Preceding both Ken Wilber's work and my own *Knowledge Designer* model by several years, the Transformative Cycle is also both integral and discursive. Its generic nature means that it is effective in the analysis of the change process at all levels: personal, organisational, societal and even global. Like the recent work around narrative undertaken by

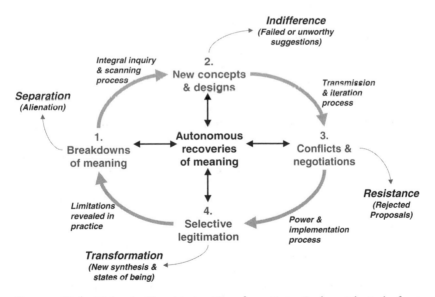

Figure 11.4 Richard Slaughter's Transformative Cycle. Adapted from Slaughter, R. et al., *The Transformative Cycle*, AFI Monograph 6, Swinburne University, Melbourne, 2004.

Dave Snowden and his colleagues at the Cynefin Centre for Organisational Complexity, Slaughter's cycle is particularly useful as a guide for unlocking deeper conversations that have the potential, with smart facilitation, to reveal the triggers and impetus for transformation, opening up entirely new possibilities and pointing to ways in which these might be legitimised. Slaughter's tool goes straight to the epistemological heart of change; in terms of the breakdowns of meaning that invariably occur when current ideas lose their legitimacy, before cycling through the development of new possibilities, negotiating conflict and building legitimacy for the new.

NOTES

1. A magical phrase used by John Thakara in his book, *In the Bubble: Designing in a Complex World*, MIT Press, Boston, 2006.
2. Urbanisation globally is now occurring at the rate of about 70 million people a year. That is approximately 130 people every minute.
3. Although urban planning is just one example, the principles of Deep Design can be used in almost any context from reimagining society beyond capitalism to liberating hope in the developing world, to dealing with some of the most troublesome geopolitical hotspots of our time, to conventional product development that takes full costs of development and production into account. In spite of efforts by *five literacies* leaders, most of the world still uses obsolete means in an effort to control, dominate and conquer that simply add to the difficulties and do nothing to resolve human conflict, poverty, inequality, environmental toxicity or any of the other issues with which we are having to deal today.
4. Holons are whole systems in their own right as well as subsystems within a larger dynamically complex system.
5. In industrial ecosystems the waste from one process is used as raw material for another, just as in nature waste from one organism is food for another.
6. Refer to *The Long Tail* by Chris Anderson, published by Hyperion, New York, 2006, for the reasons the future of business may be in selling less of more.
7. The 'creative commons' is a movement designed to deal more effectively with the inequalities arising from standard intellectual property law. The core of the creative commons is a license aimed at freely distributing certain 'common properties' so that everyone can benefit rather than just a few. The idea was invented by Professor Lawrence Lessig of Stanford University.
8. This scenario is not science fiction. It is happening as you read this book. This quotation, from Canadian designer and architect William McDonough,

is taken from his book *Cradle to Cradle*. If you need evidence of Deep Design today just look at the work being done in China and elsewhere by architects and designers like McDonough.

9. Refer here to Figure 10.2.
10. Refer here to Figure 10.4 – The iceberg model of levels of conversation.
11. Cognitive Edge Pty Ltd. http://www.cognitive-edge.com.
12. The original T-Cycle paper was published in *Educational Change and Development*, 1987, by the Department of Educational Research at the University of Lancaster, UK.

CHAPTER 12

LITERACY V – BRAND RESONANCE

Nothing great has been and nothing great can be accomplished without passion.

– G.W.F. Hegel

MARKETS ARE CONVERSATIONS

As global brands become ubiquitous commodities to be found on almost any main street in the world, we are all on the lookout for products and services that reinforce a sense of our uniqueness – that reflect our identity. The emotional and psychological attachment we bring to the products we buy creates a highly personalised 'resonance' that helps each one of us project a more desirable public image. Para-doxically, it enables us to stand out from the crowd while remaining part of the pack! This 'resonance' is applicable to individuals (the branding of self) as much as goods and services – and even commun-ities and nation-states. The idea of an individual or a fabricated object (like a watch, a car, a tee shirt, ultra-personalised banking cards and products,[1] or a house, for example) absorbing and projecting more than just its own materiality is known as *brand resonance. Brand resonance* enables us to create deep emotional attachments of *belonging* to objects, each other and entire communities. *Five literacies* leaders use *brand resonance* to assure, rather than to subvert, authenticity – aligning themselves and their ideas with the zeitgeist of the times but also being themselves, only intensely so.

In the field of marketing, *brand resonance* has recently become a trend that is taking us way beyond fashion as we currently understand it. But it also has important implications for corporations as they seek the attention of purchasers by trying to remain distinctive in an otherwise bland global marketplace where invisibility can mean death. Nor are governments immune from the need to recognise the value of *brand resonance*. The ability to project a compelling national 'brand' with unique characteristics when promoting the virtues of industries like scientific research or tourism for example, requires governments to think very carefully about *brand resonance. Five literacies* leaders understand this and use it to their advantage.

Brand resonance is not an entirely new phenomenon. For some time now, companies have had to address the migration from mass customisation to mass individualisation in their production processes to keep pace with new branding possibilities in an era of unprecedented consumer choice, ever-changing fads and capricious customer loyalty. However, through all this time, the demarcation between production and purchasing invariably remained clear. With the advent of more fluid interactive communications technologies, however, that boundary has become much more fuzzy. In many cases it has all but disappeared. These technologies – SMS and MMS texting, mashups, instant messaging, pod casts and vodcasts, VoIP, weblogs and broadcast email – are making the networks at the core of society today, buzz with new life.[2]

The information flowing through these networks has altered the rules of the game for many industries – partly because there is simply so much of it to comprehend. Swamped with data and information, much of it self-indulgent, ephemeral, prejudiced or just plain useless, consumers have become far more discriminating than was previously the case. One of the strategies used by corporations to counteract increasing customer demands and lower tolerance for less than excellent service is to offer customers the prospect of co-designing products and services. Some companies even go so far as to hand over the creative design process entirely to customers. Peer curating, too, a related phenomenon in which recommendations are shared, reducing the chaos of infinite options by allowing every consumer to create their own personal store, have become commonplace in transactions ranging from the purchase of books, videos and DVDs to eating in restaurants and booking hotel rooms. What is most interesting and worthwhile quickly becomes most visible – an example of the 'rich get richer' phenomenon of scale-free networks.

These trends are not altogether surprising when one realises that almost all contemporary economic activity is converging into a single market space; a collective global mind based on flows of ideas. Ideas, of course, procreate ideas. Indeed they need other ideas in order to come alive and be of any value. Most contemporary ideas can be captured digitally, which means that they can flow freely between consumers. Consequently it is the flows of innovative ideas and intellectual property that dominate today's markets. In this flow economy, visibility is essential. Invisibility is death! Which is why companies will do anything to attract your attention. But just attracting attention is not sufficient. Companies also have to earn your *trust*. *Brand resonance* is the most intelligent way of capturing both of these essential qualities. Increasingly that means engaging collaboratively with customers.

The incidence of corporations creating goods, services and experiences in cooperation with consumers, tapping into their intellectual capital and giving them a direct say in what actually gets produced, manufactured, developed, designed, serviced, or processed in exchange, is a trend that has been slowly building over the past few years. Through technologies like the Internet, webcasts, podcasts and instant messaging, which encourage the instant interchange of value-laden information and intelligence, we are now seeing the emergence of co-designed, customer-made and consumer-curated strategies as a business-as-usual routine.

As a direct consequence of *brand-resonant* approaches traditional value chains are being distorted (and even eliminated). Meanwhile the old-fashioned hard and fast delineation between designers, manufacturers and consumers is dissolving into a single, fluid market space. Counterintuitive strategies underpin much of the success of the *brand–resonant* tactic. Take, for example, the ultimate in curated consumption – elitism plus chic. Use no other means of marketing your product other than through a word-of-mouth community, thereby making client acquisition an organic process arising purely from favourable experiences, and you have Thoughtpost, one of Australia's foremost boutique business consulting firms. Or limit your customer's choice to one product a day, add a pinch of eBay-style excitement and bargain hunting and you end up with Woot – a hugely successful 'one day, one deal' business enterprise.

Woot founder Matt Rutledge came up with the concept back in 2004, as an Internet offshoot for his Dallas wholesale business. Since then, Woot's combination of great deals, highly novel approach and irreverent attitude has created a huge following. Thousands of regular buyers and visitors perch in front of their computers before midnight every day, hitting the refresh button to be the first to buy the new deal when it's announced at 12:00 am Central Time. On average, 27% of sales occur in the first hour, and items typically sell for about one-third of their retail value. The number of units on sale isn't announced until the item is sold out, and all items are in stock and shipped within a few days. Woot had 300,000 registered users as of February 2006, and the Woot community is an important part of its popularity. Hundreds of comments are posted about each item, and Woot feeds back data like 'first sucker' and 'speed to first woot' to help build community identity.[3]

Since Woot do not ship their goods outside of the US, a firm called iBood ('Internet's best online offer daily') saw a golden opportunity. Launched in October 2005, this Dutch company ships to most European countries. Although it lacks Woot's wacky personality, sales certainly aren't lagging. In its first two months of business iBood's turnover was 1.1 million euros. Expected turnover for 2006 is between 6.5 and 8 million euros. Plenty of *brand-resonant* opportunities exist for wholesalers partnering with smart online companies. Who will offer Turks or Thais a deal a day? Both Woot and iBood lean heavily towards electronics, so how about targeting a different audience? Daily deals for teens, teachers, parents or women, all at bargain basement prices perhaps? Nor do *brand-resonant* strategies necessarily have to remain the prerogative of private enterprise. What about local government, for example? Initiated in February 2005, LoveLewisham involves residents in keeping this London borough clean. It also helps engender civic pride in a community that was plagued by racial tensions only a few years ago. After installing special software on their cameraphones, observant citizens can snap a picture of offending graffiti or overflowing litter bins, enter location details and send it to the local council. The picture is then posted on the council's website, and cleaning crews are sent to resolve the issue. This is a similar concept to New York's 311 phone number, which also provides residents with quick, easy access to government services. Judging from the number of recent snapshots on Love Lewisham's picture pages, local people really have become involved. Apart from the user-friendliness of the system, this particular council also understands the need for feedback, probably the most important reason the experiment remains vibrant and popular with townspeople. People can track the progress of their submissions online, as well as having the option of receiving information directly from the council.

Connecting, growing, nurturing and liberating communities have become an increasingly important part of many *brand-resonant* strategies. Riding on the popularity of social networks like YouTube and MySpace (for teens) and Flickr (for anyone with a camera), major players are forming partnerships to create interactive communities. These interactive networks aren't necessarily intended to be permanent either, as evident from the many instant 'pop-up' communities that are created around specific events or opportunities. The Swatch Instant Store, which sells limited edition watches, has popped up in cities like London, Paris, Barcelona, Amsterdam and Berlin. The target audience is 15 to 25 year olds and the duration is flexible: as soon as the masses find the store, it will close its doors. The company's rationale for such apparent quirkiness is actually quite simple:

> The pace of life is forever increasing. The public is becoming more and more unpredictable. Trends come and go at an ever faster pace and often spread across the globe instantly. In large cities one finds generally the same chains of stores along the most famous shopping thoroughfares, at most in a different order. With its Instant Stores, Swatch has decided to remedy this state of affairs.

In the run-up to the 2006 World Cup, Nike and Google partnered to create Joga, the first invitation-only social networking website for soccer fans. Joga is short for Nike's slogan *Joga Bonito* – Portuguese for 'play beautifully'. Up and running in 14 languages, Joga is meant to be a global community for the world's most popular sport. Members can create subcommunities for their favourite player, city or field while Google takes care of the technical side, including plenty of moving images from Google Video. *Wired* magazine has also bought into the action of pop-up stores. Their New York pop-up in 2005 was designed as a destination that would move e-commerce into a bricks and mortar space and let shoppers test drive the latest consumer gadgets and gear. The store allowed customers to sample more than 65 products ranging from a new Motorola cell phone to the Ultimate Gaming chair to a once-in-a-lifetime suborbital space adventure. Purchases could be made on digital checkout, allowing shoppers to leave the bags and hassles behind. Partners in this venture included American Express, VW, 3M, Adidas, Biomorph, Braun, Cingular, Epson, Flavorpill, Grey Goose, Klipsch, Logitech, Motorola, Napster, Nikon, Nokia, Oakley, Oregon Scientific, Rockstar, Samsonite, Sanyo, Sonos, Sony, Symantec and Tassimo.

Pop-up spaces are beginning to morph into another form of successful *brand-resonant* idea; that of *being spaces* – a trend first identified by Springwise.[4] With face-to-face communication being rapidly replaced by email and chat, goods and services being purchased online, and big city apartments shrinking year by year, urban dwellers are trading their lonely, cramped living rooms for the real-life buzz of *being spaces*: commercial living-room-like settings in a public space where catering and entertainment aren't just the main attraction but are there to facilitate out-of-office or out-of-home activities like watching a movie, checking email, reading a book, or meeting friends and colleagues. *Being spaces* charge customers for eating, drinking, playing, listening, surfing, working, or meeting, just as we would at home or in the office, while successfully reintegrating us into city life. Starbucks, Borders Bookstores and Kinko's are terrific examples on a global scale, while many companies in Japan, China and South Korea offer deluxe gaming and manga-reading facilities, as well as semi-private DVD booths.

The need for *being spaces* is nothing new. Sociologist Ray Oldenburg coined the phrase 'the third place' in his 1990 book *The Great Good Place*, describing it as a celebration of places where people can regularly go to take it easy and commune with friends, neighbours and whoever else shows up. In Oldenburg's view, this complements the Freudian concept of well-being (having someone to love and work to do) by providing a dependable place of refuge where one can escape the demands of family and work and thus temporarily forget about one's sorrows and shortcomings. What has changed since 1990 is a slew of new uber-commercial players (with Starbucks leading the way) who have actively launched thousands of *being spaces*, twenty-first century style, complete with WiFi and easy chairs, and are now cramming even more of them into supermarkets, hospitals, hotel lobbies, cinemas, universities, libraries, bookshops and airports. The next generation of *being spaces* will really begin to deliver on the 'markets are conversations' mantra by creating less grandiose, more interactive offers to consumers who are not only looking for entertainment, but also for uniqueness, discovery, trying out, hanging out, empathy and even transformation.

BRAND NEW WORLD

In all these *brand-resonant* examples, technology has shifted the balance of power away from corporations to consumers – and from governments to (yes, you guessed it) citizens. Oh yes! *Brand-resonant* policies are alive and well in state governments. Take for example Brazil's most successful democratic innovation to date – the Participative Budget process that has been introduced by the Brazilian Workers' Party in over 100 of the major cities that they govern. In 2002 the success of the Participative Budget process in transforming the lives of millions of Brazil's poorest citizens was one of the key factors in the Brazilian Workers' Party winning the presidential and federal elections.[5] More recently, the power invested in a vocal minority of determined citizens in Bangkok was sufficient to bring about the (temporary) downfall of Prime Minister Thaksin, the allegedly corrupt if richest and most powerful individual in Thailand, during that country's 2006 election – an election that was eventually deemed invalid and will lead to new elections before October 2007. In Nepal, the monarchy was overthrown. People power has come of age with these new technologies.

It probably helps that many of these people (both consumers and citizens) are part of a younger, creative generation, that increasingly have access to professional hardware, software and online distribution channels to show and dictate to companies using text, sound, picture and video in ever more powerful ways, what it is they expect from them. This is a headache for many corporations – and all governments! But for those leaders who dwell on possibilities rather than on problems and are willing to take advantage of their customers playing an entrepreneurial and creative role in the processes of design and production, (or policy setting in the public context) it is a blessing. It can lead to breakthroughs in design, less wasted effort, more efficient operations and increased customer intimacy.

Speeding these trends in a purely innovative and commercial sense is the NBR (nano/bio/robotics) convergence revolution. Using smart materials and a precision of scale that was barely imaginable even a few years ago,[6] we are beginning to conjure up new possibilities in everything from the electrochromic polymers in 'chameleon' clothes that can change colour to mimic the wearer's surroundings or even flash signs like a neon billboard, to genetically modified goats that can produce human medicines in their milk, thought-controlled bionic limbs, super repellent plastics where even honey rolls off the surface, polythene bags that lengthen the shelf-life of supermarket fruit and vegetables, ultra thin films that are only five nanometres wide but as hard as a normal diamond, and airplane wings that deform during flight. These same technologies are also allowing for softer, more benign design pathways. This is resulting in whole industrial ecologies where the smooth flow of information and resources work hand in hand to eliminate all waste and pollution.

It is evident that the new technologies are also facilitating a shift from a focus on 'value-add' to 'value-retained' impacts – offering long-term benefits (such as recyclable materials and the use of renewable energies, for example) that are increasingly being demanded by consumers with scruples. As value players gain share, at varying speeds, within business ecosystems and across the broader economy, they are creating attention-grabbing amounts of shareholder value. As they gain share, they transform consumer attitudes about the need for trade-offs between price and quality, thus the nature of competition is changed.

Five literacies leaders acknowledge the prime importance of creating uncontested market space through collaboration, of innovation, of strategies that help render competition less relevant. At the same time they also understand how mainstream competition is getting tougher and more intense. When they are forced to compete with value-based rivals, it is essential that the perennial routes to business success are reviewed: finding sources of differentiation and managing costs and prices effectively, for example. New product and service categories, formats and the like can also help. But flawless execution is crucial for competing with value players. For this reason *five literacies* leaders focus their efforts on the development of superior customer insights, strategic innovation, effective pricing and promotions, and frontline efficiencies. In the future, the real challenge will be diagnosing accurately where the company's capabilities fall short and then finding the talent needed to plug these gaps faster than their competitors.

Changes like these continue to revise the rules of business in quite fundamental ways. Sure, some companies are now beginning to engage creative customers in new ways. Brands like Coors Light and Mercedes Benz, for example, recently invited customers to co-create advertising campaigns, with Mercedes encouraging proud owners of a Benz to submit snapshots of themselves next to their automotive objects of desire. Mazda and Condé Nast have just partnered to create a similar contest whereby contestants can submit photos representative of their interpretation of Mazda's popular 'Zoom-Zoom' slogan. These companies are clearly aware that tapping into the collective intellectual capital of their customers yields enormous creative content. However, not all of these conversations will be about communications and branding. On the contrary, such cooperative ventures are set to extend to virtually everything a corporation does simply by making the customer an integral part of every creative process.

And it doesn't even stop there. Markets are conversations now – at least for the 1.5 billion people living in the developed world where materialist frenzy continues to run rampant. These webs of global conversations involving millions of consumers are not just taking place between corporations and consumers; they are also *about* corporations. Moreover, these conversations manifest through new rather than traditional technologies. Here, it is blogging and other forms of online viral communication that are potent, while more conventional forms of informing the masses such as via television and newspapers are in decline. Blogging disseminates information in ways that are utterly different from how the news has traditionally been written and broken. Newspapers can't go to print saying 'we've heard something but we're not too sure'. With blogs, on the other hand, this is not only possible but also desirable. A blogger says: 'I've noticed something, what do you think?' Others add to the story and the blogger updates it. It is almost like continually updated, globally distributed gossip, interspersed sporadically with opinions and observations.

For example, Toshiba recently developed a system with their barcode reader phone that links purchasers to blogger reviews of the product they are thinking of buying. By taking a photo of the bar code on the packaging potential purchasers can get immediate reviews and feedback on the product. 'OK', I hear you say. 'But surely very few people actually read and write blogs?' Not at all. Boing Boing, a six-year-old 'directory of wonderful things' attracts more than 1.7 million readers a day.[7] That is the kind of following that can give a website serious clout. It was Boing Boing that first observed that 'black people loot, white people find' groceries in the now-infamous captions of news photographs taken after Hurricane Katrina. In January 2006 the site campaigned against a Canadian MP, Sarmite Bulte, who accepted (legal) donations from the entertainment industry while she was drafting copyright laws. She lost her seat and blamed the blog. In February 2006 readers alerted the site to spyware in the latest version of Apple's iTunes, and the resulting fuss persuaded Apple to change their software.

According to the search engine Technorati, there are now more than 35 million blogs worldwide. While most bloggers only write for small audiences, they can sometimes achieve much wider fame and are increasingly becoming the focus for consumer campaigns. Companies such as McDonald's, the lock manufacturer Kryptonite and computer firm Dell as well as the US government's foreign policy and treatment of civilians in Iraq, have all fallen foul of bloggers' buzz in recent years. Because search engines like Google can allow grassroots campaigns to become highly visible, decisions can be shaped by just a small number of activists. Consequently, while 'active' web users make up only a small proportion of the online population, they are exerting a disproportionately large influence on society by dominating public conversations and creating business trends.

On numerous websites like Planetfeedback, Complaint Station, AlterNet and Epinions, and on hundreds of thousands of blogs, community sites, forums, viral emails and bulletin boards, consumers are uncompromisingly exchanging views, complaints and commentary about products, services, brands – and companies! Why? Because they finally can. As Ross Dawson so eloquently puts it:[8]

> For decades, consumers have been saving up their insights and rants about the stuff they consume, simply because there were no adequate means to interact with companies, or with other consumers. No longer. These fickle, wired, empowered, informed, opinionated and experienced holders of a MC (Master in Consumerism) are getting used to 'having it their way', in *any* way imaginable, which includes wanting to have a direct influence on what companies develop and produce for them'.

All of this – the pervasiveness and transparency of living networks, the phenomenal speed of transactions and interactions, the increasingly insatiable desire of individuals everywhere to find new ways of expressing their identity – are contributing to a commercial, communications and sociopolitical upheaval. The promiscuously fluid territory of electronic peer-to-peer networks is challenging global business and government ecosystems alike. It is also fundamentally transforming the value of information and, therefore, knowledge.

Could this be the beginning of expanded freedoms where citizens are better able to shape the forms and meanings of social communication? Or does it offer an invitation to entrench state surveillance and closure? Nobody knows for sure. Certainly there can be no doubt that the use by non-state networks of new communication technologies like the Internet is challenging long-established ideas about citizenship, democracy, security and the nation-state. So-called 'nefarious' networks are constantly being identified by governments as posing a threat. As

the National Security Strategy of the United States of America, published in September 2002, asserts:

> Defending our Nation against its enemies is the first and fundamental
> commitment of the Federal Government. Today, that task has changed
> dramatically. Enemies in the past needed great armies and great industrial
> capabilities to endanger America. Now, shadowy networks of individuals
> can bring great chaos and suffering to our shores for less than it costs
> to purchase a single tank. Terrorists are organized to penetrate open
> societies and to turn the power of modern technologies against us.

The rise of distributed information systems certainly complicates,
even undermines, the sense of stability within a nation-state. The
nation-state is an information system in itself. Among the various roles
it has taken upon itself, regulating flows of information is perceived
to be critical. This is apparent even in the most 'democratic' of nations.
The problem with networks is that they are invisible, dispersed, distributed, encrypted and ubiquitous. That is especially scary for those
charged with governing. In response, the impulse to restrict or suppress
is shared by states as ideologically different as Australia and the
People's Republic of China. One has only to consider the reaction of
the Australian government to a fairly harmless but amusing spoof site
fabricated by well-known Australian satirist Richard Neville in March
2006 to recognise the sensitivity of non-sanctioned information (of any
kind) within government circles these days.[9] The site was closed down
peremptorily by Australia's Security Intelligence Organisation (ASIO)
without Neville even being approached! From this single act one can
venture to redefine a nation-state as a particular method of information
management.

An important characteristic that distinguishes dictatorships from
democratic republics, apart from their resort to physical repression and
denial of basic rights, is how they restrict the flow of certain kinds
and pieces of information and the technologies that carry them. An
authoritarian state, as Hannah Arendt argued, is the constant reminder
that the state is the source of 'official' information, and that all other
information is suspect. If the closure of an innocuous site in Australia
causes so much consternation from government officials, how can the
most oppressive of world states, such as in Myanmar (where the
shunned military regime appears to be in a state of social, economic
and political meltdown), Saudi Arabia and the People's Republic of
China, not be expected to install restrictions on the communicative
technologies at their citizens' disposal? Australia, of course, is not an

isolated exception. Most relatively liberal nation-states like the United States, Japan, Singapore and the United Kingdom routinely attempt to block or monitor legitimate flows of information, ignoring concerns for due process or free speech. And because many of these initiatives are emerging through multinational organisations and corporations, citizens have no forum for debate or appeal.

For reasons such as these it is no accident that unintended consequences are multiplying like a rash all over the public sector. The traditional mechanistic approach to policy has been savagely undermined by increasing complexity and interconnectedness. In a more connected world, devising robust policy really does become more difficult, to the extent that without a change of method, failure will be increasingly commonplace. Meanwhile, eaten by their toxic incentives, public-service organisations run by targets on command-and-control lines will, as an absolute certainty, become more dysfunctional and more neurotic until they either seize up or implode. That is the kind of *brand resonance* nobody wants! But while governments continue to ponder and fret about such issues, for business these trends boil down to just one thing. Adapt or perish!

WILD ABOUT WORK

If markets are conversations, so too are organisations. If contemporary global markets are dominated by flows of innovative ideas and intellectual property, so too are organisations. However, these facts are usually ignored when organising business. There are so many reasons not to go about designing organisations the way we have traditionally done, none more so than the fact that the axioms underpinning the global business environment have changed, and are continuing to transform at warp speed, that it no longer makes any sense whatsoever to rely on past orthodoxies to guarantee success. This is why *five literacies* leaders throw out conventional thinking and practices, instead embedding a capacity for continuous reinvention and collaborative development and stripping away anything that impedes the growth of deep, trusting relationships with customers, business partners and with the business ecosystem's community.

In place of habits learned in the factories and classrooms of the nineteenth century, such as discipline, diligence and obedience, and attempting to counter the blind faith many of us have acquired in numbers as well as the curious (but effective) mix of assurances and fear proffered by many old-style, charismatic leaders, *five literacies* leaders understand the need to think more systemically while liberating creativity, entrepreneurial passion and tolerance for the new. *Five literacies* leaders persistently work to free the mind, thus avoiding structure-function traps and unshackling imagination. They seek to free the spirit from oppressive practices, trite visions and superfluous regulations. They seek to free the soul from the drudgery and indignity of futile work that adds no value to anything or anyone. And they seek to ignite integrity, loyalty and the sheer joy of living – both within themselves and within others. These are the impulses *five literacies* leaders bring to knowing and developing themselves. They are also the motivations for designing better business models and organising more effective enterprise the *five literacies* way. I must stress here this is not because these are *good* things to do, rather they make good sense. In this day and age they are the *intelligent* things to do and they are reflected in the *five literacies* business model.

Amplified by *brand resonance*, *five literacies* business models create value for more than just a single stakeholder in the business ecosystem. Driven by collaboration, creativity and a sense of community, the generic *five literacies* business model makes it possible for a company (or government) to leverage its unique knowledge, talent and energy to meet an identified societal need while creating value for itself and its clients. In this way, *five literacies* leaders deliberately try to improve the overall health and well-being of society. No finer examples exist than Lord John Browne's objective for his company, BP, to help change the entire nature of how we use energy on this planet (to go 'beyond petroleum' towards renewable sources of energy);[10] Bill Gates' ambition to realise the potential of the global knowledge economy for the benefit of all; or Premier Wen Jiabao's determination to reverse the effects of environmental degradation and pollution in China (through what he calls *mature* sustainable development). The new ethos is well summarised by ANZ Chief John McFarlane after 10 inspirational years creating 'a very different bank':

> As I reflect on what makes a great organisation, two themes emerge. Firstly, that those companies that find their unique place in the world and develop and execute the factors that determine its uniqueness win over others who are not unique. In other words those that have a sustainable reason for being in business beat those who don't. They are very clear why a customer should deal with them and not with another, why their people should invest their working lives in their adventure, why the community should trust them, and why shareholders should invest in

them. They focus on making a long and lasting contribution to the world. The second is that it is people, and how they work together that makes a company great. We often forget that our responsibility as leaders is to create an exciting but safe adventure for our people, that is worthy of their devoting their lives to it. People are seeking real meaning in their lives, particularly at work. Unfortunately it is rare that they find it.

Of course it is not just the leaders of financial services firms or global energy companies that are striving to change the world for the better. All sorts of organisations are now applying *five literacies* business models; The Body Shop was one of the first but now they range from NGOs like Médecins Sans Frontières and OneWorld Health and social entrepreneurs like the Grameen Foundation, Kickstart and Heifer International, to for-profit companies like Bendigo Bank, Airbus, Guild Insurance & Financial Services, Whole Foods Market, LEGO, Toyota and even Google![11]

To be sure, goals like John Browne's and John McFarlane's are heady and noble aspirations from mostly large organisations. But there are many examples of *five literacies* leaders who are doing much the same, with resounding success, in their own backyards. They are not household names – yet. Often they are unheralded and do not enjoy much public exposure. They are not on massive salaries, nor do they have thousands of people reporting to them. In fact they often struggle to achieve their goals. But they are part of a global *five literacies* business model revolution that is set on changing the world. The motivation for their business could be the absence of medical diagnostic labs in the developing world, which is driving the PATH organisation to create a portable, disposable lab that fits onto a plastic card. PATH's simple, life-saving solutions, such as clean birthing kits and disposable vaccination syringes that prevent reuse, belie the diligence and expertise required to produce these sorts of solutions routinely. In Zambia, where malaria causes 40% of deaths among children under age five, PATH is part of a $35 million partnership to broaden use of simple malaria-prevention techniques such as insecticide-treated bed nets. Their aim is to reduce deaths from malaria by as much as 75% in the next three to five years. For Room to Read's founder John Wood the stimulus was a trek through Nepal. While there, he visited several local schools and was amazed by the warmth and enthusiasm of the students and teachers, but also saddened by the shocking lack of resources. Driven to help, John quit his senior position with Microsoft and built a global team to work with rural villages to create a sustainable solution to their educational challenges. Today, Room to Read has become an educational juggernaut, building nearly as many new libraries each week as Starbucks opens latte-slinging storefronts.[12]

The tiny village of Baan Nong Pai (population 500) in rural northern Thailand is literally situated in the middle of nowhere. But this village has become the test bed for an ultra broadband solution to bridging the 'digital divide'. There are no fixed-line telephones here and mobile phones do not work unless people stand outside or on a roof. But these villagers now have a 'Classroom for Life' that gives them access to email, e-commerce, video conferencing and a video-on-demand library – all thanks to the work of a certain Canadian-Australian by the name of John Hawker who was inspired by Meechai Viravadhya's concepts of bringing the market to the village. The silk woven by the villagers, which used to be sold to local agents for 150 baht a metre, is now sold directly to purchasers in the US for many times that amount. And all without contributing to the huge social strain on family ties and overcrowded cities like Bangkok.

A few further examples from my own country, Australia, demonstrate the breadth of social entrepreneurship in the world today.[13] Take 32-year-old Tracy Bialek, who has created a range of water-saving devices for the home while protecting and marketing what will become a valuable brand in sustainability. Her company, Ripple Products, isn't driven solely by profit as evidenced by the following mission statement:

> What we do, what we say and how we act can cause a ripple in our community. Help yourself, teach a friend or educate your children. It will all make a difference. It will create a ripple.

In Canberra, a different approach to sustainability has created one of Australia's first five-star rated 'green' buildings at Brindabella Business Park.[14] Driven by the personal vision of Terry Snow, the project began with energy efficiency but has evolved with each building in a much more comprehensive view of sustainability, including use of non-toxic materials, waterless urinals, recycled concrete, fresher air and more. The project has pushed revision of building regulations (in concrete recycling, for example) and has had other spin-offs as contractors applied what they learned in other areas.

Land-based entrepreneurs are combining a love of nature, concern for the planet and the need to make a living. One exhausted grazing property near Byron Bay has been restored to life by Danielle Leonard, using whole-systems farming practices. No pesticides or chemicals are used, and the farm turns over about $A5000 a week through the sale of vegetables to local restaurants. Food scraps are collected and brought back for compost, forming a closed loop. Melbourne agriculturalist and aid worker Tony Rinaudo promotes the desert survival skills of Australian Aborigines in helping the people of Niger, where drought and locust plagues have combined to create famine that threatens 4 million Nigerians, a third of the population. Using advice from CSIRO, Tony arranged trial plots of Australian desert trees and ran tests to ensure that nuts from the hardy acacia were safe to eat. They proved to be very nutritious. The trees also provide fuel and the leaves make good fertiliser.

Of course, any robust business model has strong implications for what is done and how a company or government institution will organise itself to do what is done – its very self-concept or identity as an organisation if you like. Again, this should be apparent from the previous examples. Conventional business models are mostly driven by an overriding need to create value for the owners of the business. *Five literacies* business models are also driven by ethical ecority; the desire to build better futures for all stakeholders permeates everything and is highly visible in the way activities are designed, communicated and marketed. As with any business model, the *five literacies* genre must achieve alignment with the organisation's overall strategic framework and congruence with its broader social role in the business ecosystem.

Although an appropriate business model will help realise brand-resonant strategies this can never be sufficient by itself. *Brand resonance* is intangible. It cannot be seen or held and is not as easily pursued as sales targets, for example. Rather, it is like credibility and reputation, acquired little by little from others, especially customers, as a result of deep and trusting relationships coupled with consistency of performance, integrity of purpose and a unique, even wacky, value proposition. That said, much can be done to bring *brand-resonant* strategies to the attention of the market, especially through viral forms of communication.

Word-of-mouth marketing (what is said) and word-of-mouth ethics (what is done) create ripples of attention in the market. Consequently they are now the most important forms of communication within *five literacies* companies for supporting the expansion of *brand resonance* into the broader business ecosystem – and for reflecting this image back on itself into the enterprise. Word-of-mouth methods have always been around, but have become all the buzz lately. This is partly a result of the new technologies we have already discussed but also the fact that relationships are a greater priority than awareness (of a particular product) today. Take someone suffering from allergic rhinitis, for example. She may have seen a number of advertisements for Claritin in the local pharmacy and on television, but may not buy the product until a friend innocently inquires, 'Have you ever tried Claritin?' In other words, advertising may have achieved front-of-mind prominence for the product, but that only goes so far. When consumers are given opportunities for that awareness to become real – especially during conversations between friends – word-of-mouth marketing comes into its own. Experience has shown that it also helps where the product is associated with some kind of novelty, surprise or a suspension of belief. One has only to recall the hugely successful marketing campaigns surrounding Optus Communications in Australia and The Blair Witch film project in the US, for example, to see how effective this can be. A recent buzz campaign by Freestyle Interactive and Ammo Marketing scattered oranges in the streets of major cities for the launch of *The Godfather: The Game*. Curiosity and the surprise element of walking to work and seeing oranges everywhere compelled people to investigate.

A word of caution to the overzealous. The use of word of mouth for increasing *brand resonance* must never descend into spin. Increasingly, corporations and governments alike are resorting to spin to cast a more positive light on issues that may otherwise be a concern to the community. This is a false hope and also fairly amusing coming just at a time when consumers are not so easily duped and are able to sniff phoney behaviour, false claims and sham bona fides. Such bluster can be deadly and is not recommended. *Five literacies* leaders know better. We are all naked in the attention economy. Trust is absolutely essential now. There is no substitute and a vital competitive factor is the capability to grow trust fast. Consequently developing trusting relationships in every aspect of the business must be accelerated and amplified in every way possible. That cannot be accomplished by using spin. In fact spin is detrimental in the long run as it invariably conceals some aspect of the truth. It can be achieved, however, through highly personalised connectivity and the deep integration of processes and systems, such as are increasingly evident with customer-curated and customer-made activities.

Of course, to be really beneficial, *brand resonance* must reverberate internally within an enterprise as well as reaching far beyond its boundaries. In this regard, *five literacies* leaders also advance, with all the passion they can muster, a moral purpose that taps deeply into the their own soul and into the beliefs and values of their enterprise. In this way authenticity is built organically into the business, lighting an entrepreneurial fuse that links creative ideas, capital and talent in generating some of the most universally revered and trusted brands in the world.

NOTES

1. Garanti Bank's Flexi Cards, for example, allow customers to personalise the look of their bankcards. But Garanti takes the concept a bit further: customers can develop their own banking products. Flexi Cards are Visa cards that let the cardholder make a few key decisions, allowing them to set over 10 parameters. When applying for a card, customers can manipulate variables like reward rates and types, interest rate and card fee. The rewards system is especially flexible, not only letting customers determine reward ratio and type (cash or points), but also enabling them to choose which payments will earn them extra rewards: whether it's broad categories like restaurants, or specific stores like Zara. Interest rate, bonus rate and card fees are selected by sliding bars that render various combinations of rates and fees. Card fees, for example, can be pushed back to zero by committing to a monthly spending minimum. A lower interest rate leads to a lower bonus rate, etc. Lastly, after making serious decisions about financial terms, customers can design their own card, choosing from different colours and a gallery of images, or uploading their own image. There's even the option of picking a vertical card, which is a world's first for Visa. Mutual benefits are apparent. While customers appreciate being in control and creating a tailor-made card, inside and out, the bank is able to test various value propositions, gaining valuable insights into which customer segments choose which options. In other words, self-segmentation through ultra-personalisation.

2. In the equal-opportunity world of the blogosphere all manner of interest groups are creating attention that would otherwise be denied to them by the corporate world. Take political feminism for example: in the US, Ana Marie Cox broke into the scene a few years ago with the political blog Wonkette (wonkette.com). Across the Atlantic, left-leaning Lynne Featherstone (lynnefeatherstone.org), a member of the British Parliament and Antonia Bance (antoniabance.org) a Labour councillor on the Oxford City Council, both keep blogs that mix professional and personal anecdotes with heated opinions. The F-Word blog (thefword.org.uk/blog) started by British feminist Catherine Redfern, is now a significant forum for feminist and women's political issues. For those leaning towards the right, *Daily Mail* columnist Melanie Phillips (melaniephillips.com) sounds off on hot-

button issues, most recently the UK's immigration problems. For more proof of this new women's revolution, check out the Girls Blog UK Web ring (bloguk.com) which links to a canon of female-penned online commentary.

3. These extensive insights on 'customer-made' and consumer-curated products from Springwise.com.
4. www.springwise.com.
5. Roy Madron, Democracy from the South, Unpublished paper, July 2003.
6. Nanotechnology refers to design at the molecular level.
7. Boing Boing is co-edited by Cory Doctorow. A Canadian-born, London-based journalist, author and activist, Doctorow is well known for his work on digital copyright issues. He appeared before the United Nations to argue against regional restrictions on DVDs, campaigning against the one-use limitations programmed into digital television technology and championing creative commons. This is a new kind of copyright contract that allows writers, musicians and other artists to encourage copying, reproduction and sometimes alteration of their works.
8. Dawson, R. *Living Networks*, FT Prentice-Hall, 2003.
9. This site, openly constructed and managed by Neville, contained a speech supposedly given by John Howard, the current prime minister, in which he declared himself, Blair and Bush culpable for the poor judgement and subsequent execution used by the 'coalition of the willing' in invading Iraq.
10. 'The misconception that there is serious disagreement among scientists about global warming is actually an illusion deliberately fostered by a relatively small but extremely well-funded cadre of special interests including Exxon Mobil and a few other oil, coal and utilities companies'. Browne was the first oil man to acknowledge global warming as fact rather than theory (Source: Gore, A. *An Inconvenient Truth*, Rodale, PA. 2006).
11. I am referring particularly here to google.org – the unlikely 'for profit' philanthropic arm of Google Corporation.
12. These examples are from the Fast Company/Monitor Group Social Capitalist Awards for 2006.
13. These examples are all provided by Jan Lee Martin of the Futures Foundation. They appeared in the March 2006 edition of *Future News*, Vol. 11, No. 1.
14. The City of Melbourne in Australia recently opened its new offices building which is one of the first in the world to carry a six-star energy rating for sustainability.

PART FOUR

ESCAPE VELOCITY

The energy required for a space vehicle to escape the Earth's gravity is colossal. It is called the vehicle's 'escape velocity'. The Five Literacies Code Book (specifically designed to be used by five literacies leaders in their organisations) performs the same function, gathering and focusing the energy needed in order for the organisation to break free from the gravitational pull of past habits and unchallenged practices. Without this energy any enterprise will remain earthbound and captive to its past.

CHAPTER 13

CRACKING THE CODE

The system of industrial economism we in the West invented in the middle of the eighteenth century, and which we now frequently equate with progress (and indeed democracy), has spawned consequences that are only now revealing themselves. Consequences we had surely never intended. Ranging from the ethics of technologies that disrupt the patterns of human production and consumption to climate change, and from the obscenity of abject poverty in the third world to the inadequacy of once-venerable institutions such as the law and the political process to cope, these issues are not simple but complex and overwhelming. Furthermore they reveal deeply flawed designs not to mention dubious intentions.

It matters little where you live on the planet for no one is immune now. We have exported our problems to every corner of the globe. People from Brazil to Zaire and from Thailand to New Zealand are concerned about these very same things. They have spread like an unstoppable pandemic across the planet. Nor does it matter how you cut or prioritise them. Ultimately, though, these problems remain only the tip of an iceberg – visible signs of a deeper malaise that is far more disturbing; a paradox of Gaian proportions at the heart of which is embedded the competitive and rapacious nature of humankind itself and the discriminatory system of global debt we've created to ensure that rich nations get richer (by controlling resources needed to create wealth) and the poor continue to suffer.

Take just one example of the extravagance and wasteful disposition of developed nations compared with the ingrained poverty found in every country of the world but particularly in weaker nations where education has been suppressed and their economies deliberately undermined. Walk into the heart of any city. Look up at the towering skyscrapers. Ignore the beggar on the street corner. Walk in and look at the names on the office doors. Now pay attention to the work that is being done behind these doors. Do you get it? This is how we distribute wealth – through excess and pointless and demeaning work. Those monolithic buildings are the bricks and mortar of monopolies that intercept wealth rather than creating it. Through this system of plundered and stolen wealth, distributed through diplomatic warfare, fictitious free trade, conflicts, illegitimate regimes and cartels, arguably half the labour, capital and resources available to us are squandered needlessly. Furthermore, it is through this theft of the wealth from the impoverished world by the powerful that we are able to enjoy such a high quality of life compared with some others.

The political and corporate power brokers know this very well of course. We have all read the statistics on wealth distribution; the top 1% owns more wealth than the bottom 90%. Eliminate the wasted labour, capital and resources through which this wealth is distributed and we stand exposed as nothing less than a duplication of the aristocratic system that supposedly disappeared centuries ago. Then eliminate the military and government spending protecting these monopolies, together with the garbage of those monopolies themselves, and there are enough resources on this earth for all. Indeed, if we were able to reconceptualise capitalism to create a more cooperative and equitable system, poverty could be eliminated in a decade and a quality life for all attained within 50 years. Under such a system of 'cooperative capitalism' the average standard of living would rise rapidly even as the GNP and the hours worked per person dropped by possibly half.[1] In spite of this of course we continue to examine and treat all such issues either as just too hard, or as if they were simple, discrete concerns requiring simple, discrete policies.

Nothing could be further from the truth. Philosophers, scientists and poets alike have warned that issues can never be resolved by using the same levels of thinking that caused their genesis in the first place. Perversely, we mostly choose to ignore such warnings. Like ostriches with our heads in the sand, we choose to analyse the same old data, arriving at conclusions which conveniently affirm our own vested interests, then prescribing the same old medicine via the same old processes and institutions, all the time expecting different results. But all we get is more of the same, wrapped up in a semblance of progress. Why? Could it be that we actually do not want to change? Could it be that we are so greedy we have washed our hands of those who are less fortunate than us? Is it fear of those who worship other gods? Or is it that we are sufficiently arrogant to believe our inventive prowess will eventually find a way out of all our problems? I hope not for the mirror of history does little to support such a scenario.

Sixteen hundred years ago, all around the Mediterranean, societies were well developed with extensive educated populations and with large libraries and cultural centres. In other words they were intellectually and culturally advanced much as we are today.

Under the alliance between the Roman Empire and the Christian church in 324 AD, all other religions and the empire's educated came under assault. Over a period of 350 years all the libraries within the Roman Empire were systematically burned, education was taboo, Hellenic cultural centres were destroyed and their priests and educated were assassinated or forced underground. Those 350 years of assassination and suppression of the educated classes propelled Western society into the Dark Ages. They no longer had sufficient numbers of educated people necessary to run their economy.

I wonder if we are not doing the same thing today. And if we are, what is the reason we do not see it? Perhaps it is the insidious nature of the Matrix at work. Living at the heart of this empire, we are cradled within its tyranny of created beliefs in enemies. Fear of one's enemies. That is how the masses of every society have been controlled throughout history. Perhaps that fear is why we cannot see the reality. But let it be recognised that the consequences of this predicament are dire. For a start, it means that what we may perceive to be sound policy, driven by high morals and informed by the very best of intentions, serves only to maintain a status quo that, at least in terms of progress and improvement, is but an illusion.

There appear to be only two antidotes to our apparent inability to seriously challenge current assumptions and subsequent behaviour: in the past we have used revolution – sometimes successfully, sometimes not! Today's most viable alternative is the design of an entirely new systemic framework for perceiving reality, talking about it and taking action to change and improve it. During the course of human history we have traversed such rites of passage many times. Scientists refer to them as paradigm shifts. The great ideas revolutions of the past (from Copernicus to Einstein) have allowed us to reflect differently and to appreciate our reality with far greater awareness of how things actually work. But they have yet to unwrap the mysteries of human consciousness. And there can be no doubting that our emotional makeup and behaviours have not kept pace with technological progress. In that sense at least, progress itself is a deception . . .

There is yet another problem we need to face. Time is running out much faster than many of us would care to believe. Humanity is poised on a knife-edge and history's page may yet turn in ways that wipe our species from the face of this Earth. Few educated people now doubt there is time to lose. We must once again take a giant leap forward to shift human behaviour from the toxic practices of industrial economism of the past 300 years to the more benign systemicity of global ecority. In our hearts we understand that this is the case. We feel passionately the need to create better futures for those who will follow us. In fact not to do so is unthinkable – we would be negligent in shirking our responsibility to future generations.

But we must also be courageous enough to face up to the fact that our generation has created, and is perpetuating, a future that the young people of today do not value. Nor, by all accounts, do many others if the increasing numbers of terrorist acts by extreme fundamentalists are to be believed. To allow things to continue as they are is not an option. There is a clear and present danger to which we must respond. This danger exists along many fronts. That at least is apparent. Ultimately, though, it is only through purposeful action that things can change for the better. For centuries we have called this 'leadership' and the people that undertake such activities in the full spotlight of our lives we ordain as 'leaders'. We look to leaders in our society to inspire purposeful action for change. Sometimes they let us down, causing us greater pain than would have been the case if they had done nothing at all (tyrants such as Pol Pot and Saddam Hussein and the military juntas in Myanmar and North Korea, for example, spring immediately to mind). Yet even the most sincere and capable of leaders can do great damage by denying, ignoring or misconstruing the consequences of their tendency to act unilaterally. At other times of course they make matters worse simply by insisting that they are in the right or (worse still) have 'god' on their side.

Part of the difficulty lies in our stories of leadership. Invariably these narratives ensnare us either in some obligatory technical prowess or in past heroics. For example, we are taught from an early age that leaders are a rare species – particular kinds of people with a certain kind of mind – like lawyers who can dazzle juries, engineers who can build entire cities, or accountants who can manipulate numbers with such aplomb. We are also told that leaders possess the kinds of incomparable courage, wealth, power and status of which mere mortals can only dream. These people are members of an exclusive club – born-to-rule high-flyers whose celebrity, charisma, initiative, fortitude and conviction are prerequisites for membership. It also helps to be male, Caucasian, with a university degree in accounting or law and, in many parts of the world, a military career coupled with an ability to tell half-truths without flinching. Romantic nostalgia from a 'Boy's Own' world of playground contests, these stories speak almost exclusively of daring deeds and the superhuman prowess of a select few. Like celebrity athletes at the peak of their powers, this elite band is impossible to ignore. They are there to be noticed. They scream their credentials at us constantly. You won't find many women's tales in this stereotypical male domain. Nor do deeper more spiritual aspects of our humanity get much of a look in. This is a world where actions always speak louder than words, where using one's intellect is derided, and where expressing deeply held feelings is too sissy by far.

In an age characterised by immediacy of communications, rampant materialism and the desire for instant gratification, this extreme sport of leadership fits like a glove with our expectations. Like other forms of extreme sport, it is addictive, appealing to the ego to such an extent that those who practise it frequently do so to excess. Nor are they ever likely willingly to give it up or change the conditions whereby they are able to receive such instant adulation for their efforts. It is exciting to watch! We glorify it. And we yearn for more. If this isn't leadership, what is?

Today the exercise of leadership as an extreme sport casts a dark and cruel shadow over what leadership can be and should be. This leadership archetype generates an expectation that we are all merely players in a story being directed by the rich and powerful. What arid nonsense! But here's the rub. Those men and women inhabiting the corridors of power who practise this obsolete form of leadership are bluffing. They cannot resolve the most critical issues of our time. If they could they would have done so by now. Deep down they know it. Cracks appear daily in their demeanour. And we are beginning to notice too. As a consequence, 'Where have all the leaders gone?' is a cry increasingly heard in the media, in our corporations and on the streets.

But what if we've been looking in the wrong place? What if we're seeking the wrong qualities in the wrong people? What if the leadership we need in order to change the human condition is something quite different from that we are used to? Without a shadow of doubt the nature of leadership has changed and is continuing to change beyond recognition. The keys to the kingdom are changing hands. The extreme sport of leadership we have come to expect, respect, and for which many of us still secretly yearn, is no longer relevant or sufficient for our needs. Great leadership has become something less heralded, but more pervasive, and it taps deeply into the zeitgeist of our times. It doesn't mean that leadership has disappeared. Rather, it has adopted a new guise. After all, the world is always changing; old certainties and established truths are continually being adjusted or swept away.

Through the ages it was claimed that death and taxes were the only certainties. Today even this must be in doubt. Astonishing break-

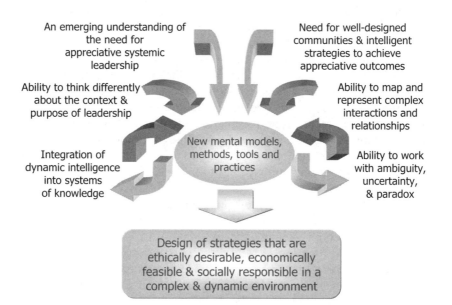

An emerging understanding of the need for appreciative systemic leadership

Need for well-designed communities & intelligent strategies to achieve appreciative outcomes

Ability to think differently about the context & purpose of leadership

Ability to map and represent complex interactions and relationships

Integration of dynamic intelligence into systems of knowledge

New mental models, methods, tools and practices

Ability to work with ambiguity, uncertainty, & paradox

Design of strategies that are ethically desirable, economically feasible & socially responsible in a complex & dynamic environment

Figure 13.1 The context for leadership has changed, and with it the capability to lead.

throughs in knowledge are undermining almost everything we once held true. New technologies are disrupting long-established patterns of human activity, banishing the familiar and eroding certainty in every corner of our minds. Traditional value systems, centred on the family, the Church and the corporation, are rapidly mutating. Incredibly, even our most venerable institutions are threatened as – through the rapid fusion of ideas, technologies, markets, cultures and entire belief systems collide and ricochet – indifferent to established boundaries.

At the same time, communications gadgets plug us in to the diverse clamour of the global village. What it means to be human (its ideals and its anguish, its joys and its horrors) confronts us constantly. It is hurled in our faces, 24 hours a day and 7 days a week. The intrusion of the mass media into our daily lives ensures there can be no escape. Trapped in prisons of our own invention, but able to interact instantly with people in different environments and from utterly dissimilar cultures, we happily impose our opinions on anyone who will listen, wherever they happen to be. The need to be heard and to be appreciated matters more than anything else, or so it seems.

Certainly the pressures on leaders appear overwhelming. Technology has changed *what* we do, *how* we do it and even *how long* we can go on doing it before we need to stop and do something else. Now governments react nervously to changing conditions. Clinging to the coat-tails of American militancy, Chinese pragmatism or religious zealots, their own authority has evaporated with a steady decline in national sovereignty. Companies and countries alike resort to obsolete business models (probably because that is all they know) apparently unconcerned with the risks they face by remaining the same. Spin-doctors talk up growth and profitability, glossing over the look-alike plans they know will stifle innovation and strip value out of the enterprise. The landscape has become littered with mindless, short-term, survival tactics. And, just to add a further frisson of uncertainty, a rising tide of corporate scandals is shaking world markets as terrorists fly planes into buildings, the Catholic Church staggers from one crisis to another, politicians look even more like clowns, anarchists use the Internet to plot the destruction of capitalism and global warming threatens our very existence! No wonder the business world is in such a state of bewilderment and disarray.

As these dynamics have acquired a seemingly unstoppable intensity they have given rise to an increasingly unstable environment in which the rules (and much of the knowledge) of the past 600 years are simply irrelevant. How can we possibly know what matters any more? Suppose for one moment that we can get new information and communications technologies to work for the poor. This would mean that remote villages in the world's most disadvantaged nations, with no experience of electric power, telephone cables or money, would get low-cost computers and broadband wireless Internet, plus Internet telephony (VoIP). This, in turn, would enable sustainable economic growth, education, good health care, access to government and jobs.

Suppose that all of this works everywhere, and that it eventually breaks the cycle of dependence on government aid, replacing it with self-reliance. If the likely backlash of protectionism from the United States and the European Union as they fight against increased agricultural and manufacturing exports from rapidly developing countries could be avoided, we will begin to hear the voice of the poor for the first time in history. When poor people can speak, the world will change. But what will they say? And to whom? What will they talk about and with what results? As the voices of the world's five billion poor rise in chorus, what will they utter. What will they tell us about their poverty and about our common future? What will they say about our lifestyle and how we choose to spend our money? What will they say about our corporations and about our notions of leaders and of leadership? Will they see leadership as it is commonly practised in the West of any relevance to them? Will they demand a new kind of leadership instead? I should think so. But even if we could nurture new leaders, what should they do in times such as these? So ambiguous is today's environment it seems almost impossible to achieve anything much. Chaos and anxiety have usurped certainty. And yet, paradoxically, almost anything is now possible.

Learning from the past we see that real progress is not about having a vision, instituting controls for its realisation and persuading others of its virtue. That is precisely how we got ourselves into this predicament in the first place. On the contrary, transformation of our world requires that we transform ourselves first. This is the real challenge of contemporary leadership: letting go of our old self-serving scripts and creating new stories that allow our authentic selves to emerge whole once again. That is the essence of *five literacies* leadership.

History tells us that Christopher Columbus set sail for India in 1492. He went West and never found India. But the natives he saw he named Indians. And upon his return to Spain he reported to King Ferdinand and Queen Isabella that the world was round. We believed him. The new religion of science, after all, verified as much. Columbus was both right and wrong. Planet Earth is indeed round. The global village we inhabit, however, is not. But how could he possibly have predicted today's bewildering reality. As US journalist Thomas Friedman recently noted in his book, *The World is Flat*, we live in a world that is highly interconnected. The economy in this world of *zero geography* is a stream of global flows, ever-changing relationships and mercurial inter-actions and transactions. Volatile and dynamic, it is punctuated by momentous events while information and communications technol-ogies continue to shrink the world daily, allowing work to be done by anybody almost anywhere.

Today when networks of peasant families in Wenzhou capture 90% of the world market in lighters and when students in Bangalore operate call centres more efficiently than we can in Australia or the US or Germany, any competitive advantage the West once had has disappeared. We are now exposed in this world. There is nowhere left to hide. And the extreme sport of leadership doesn't fit well in these circumstances.

Zero geography demands an alternative belief system and practice both for leading and for leaders. We need to transcend the practise of leadership as an extreme sport. The future belongs to a very different kind of leader with a very different kind of mind and very different values: those who can create and connect; those with compassion; story tellers and meaning makers. These people are the leaders of the future.

Today's dynamic is one of living global networks in which flows of ideas and information ricochet and collide in continuous streams of opportunity. In this context, network sports are in. Living systems leadership is in. We must think systemically, working together to learn how different conditions can be shaped to effect more sustainable and beneficial change for all of humankind. And the world's truly smart leaders in all walks of life are discovering that fact. This new reality demands insightful thinking, purposeful dialogue and collaborative action. This leadership praxis is the well-spring of the *five literacies*. *Five literacies* leadership allows us, if we have the willpower to over-come the seduction of nostalgia and the gravitational pull of the past, to bring higher levels of consciousness, wisdom and knowledge to bear on improving the human condition. Anywhere we encounter that need – be it in global institutions, state governments, corporations, non-government organisations or local communities.

Integrating intelligence, foresight, innovation, design and personal resonance, the *five literacies* enable a form of stewardship in which individual egos are set aside in favour of collective wisdom. This is a new form of leadership and it is well understood by the smart leaders of our time. They know that their own dreams may galvanise and impel action. But that alone is not sufficient. It is how we collectively *feel* and *think* and *act* that matter now. The *five literacies* compel us to aspire to higher, more virtuous goals. They also enable other possibilities to emerge in terms of structures and institutions. But mostly they allow us to re-engage as a society with the urgent issues of our time.

Ultimately, the aim of the *five literacies*, to accelerate change in the nature of leadership itself, must resonate in you, the reader. It cannot just reside in the dry words of a book. Success will only come through each of us recognising our role as a leader, learner and activist and joining together in concerted action. Are we are a smart mob? That remains to be seen. For the challenge now is to liberate the collective knowledge and wisdom we have acquired over generations and across continents. In spite of the many millions of dollars spent each year, the strategies we have mostly used to develop leadership have totally failed to deliver the kind of leaders we need. They have, instead, reinforced in our minds the model of leadership as an extreme sport. That path is now bankrupt. The story that has dominated Western society for well over two centuries has been one of servitude, conformity, and efficiency. It has fuelled an *age of progress* in which materialism has flourished and self-interest limited to the notion of material gain. This story is no longer sufficient to generate a sense of meaning and well-being. It has led to an impoverished view of self, and an ethos of dependency within society. Furthermore, because it has failed to remind us of our dependence on the environment in which we live (so often seen merely as a means of production) we have damaged the Earth's resources, and lost our sense of relationship to the planet that sustains us. This script is past resurrection. It is has lost all legitimacy. The new story, emerging, barely sensed and certainly not yet understood with any degree of clarity, is about integration, collaboration and sustainability. It is about an entirely new and as yet uncommon form of leadership. This is leadership with an entirely new moral purpose. *Five literacies* leadership.

Of course, the integral body of knowledge embodied within the *five literacies* is not news for those extraordinary leaders among us. It is understood and appreciated by them. They have processed this knowledge and apply it in the course of their daily lives; in all their encounters; in everything they do. This book will only affirm what they already know in their minds and have discovered in their hearts. But this praxis also happens to be the wisdom the rest of us are scrambling to discover. At some point in our lives, we have to put aside our masks to accept and express who we really are. It is not possible to lead fulfilling lives and be content with being what others want or expect us to be. We have to weave our own story. In this story we must each learn anew to accept responsibility for our own lives as well as the world in which we live. As long as we can tap into and liberate our passions and our convictions with unflinching courage, engage authentically with the world, create greater integration between our lives and our work and discover a more sustaining and meaningful story, we are capable of transforming ourselves. And when we change ourselves, we change the world.

The challenge of leadership today is no longer just a personal one – although it is still a challenge facing us all. The courage of the solitary hero and his epic journey is not what leadership can be about any more. The power of great leadership now resides in the invisible – in integrity, in identity and in intentionality. As a consequence, the

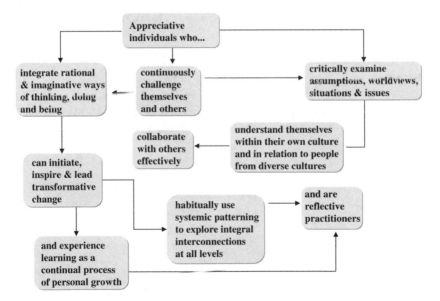

Figure 13.2 A high level (yet clearly observable) view of the behavioural profile of *five literacies* leaders.

mind of today's leader is focused on Deep Design, meaningful narrative, dynamics, aesthetic, composition, conviviality and play.

But having understood that, a vital question still remains: what will you do to change the way things are? How will you engage others in collaboration? Will you wait for those who practise leadership as an extreme sport to observe and to comment on your behalf before shrugging their shoulders in pessimistic resignation that it is all too difficult for them? Or will you step into a *five literacies* epistemology, accepting the challenge of collaborative individualism?

Will you use the *five literacies* as a new beginning – a springboard from which to engage others in appreciative dialogue and committed action that really changes the course of the future for the better? Will you overturn the ridiculous orthodoxies that hamper and hinder our advancement at every turn – perhaps even those you yourself helped to install? Will you start to pose more strategic questions? Will you find in your own experience perhaps an affirmation of the wisdom of *appreciative* practice?

I hope so. For that will mean that you have chosen *five literacies* leadership as the way forward. You will have joined the ranks of those very few smart leaders who actually 'get it'. But remember the Matrix. Once you have taken the red pill of knowing there can be no turning back. That will take courage, an uncommon humility, and persistence. Good luck! We need you.

NOTE

1. This insight provided by Dr J.W. Smith in a keynote address given at Radford University, 26 May 2004.

FURTHER READING

Albert, M., *Realizing Hope: Life Beyond Capitalism*, Zed Books, London, 2006.

Atkins, R. and Mintcheva, S. (eds), *Censoring Culture: Contemporary Threats to Free Expression*, The New Press, New York, 2006.

Baggini, J., *What's It All About? Philosophy and the Meaning of Life*, Granta Books, London, 2004.

Ball, P., *Critical Mass: How One Thing Leads to Another*, Farrar, Straus and Giroux, New York, 2004.

Barabasi, A-L., *Linked: How Everything is Connected to Everything Else and What it Means for Business, Science and Everyday Life*, Penguin, London, 2003.

Bard, A. and Soderqvist, J., *Netocracy: The New Power Elite and Life After Capitalism*, Pearson Education, London, 2002.

Baudrillard, J., *The Spirit of Terrorism*, Verso, London, 2002.

Beck, D. and Cowan, C., *Spiral Dynamics: Mastering Values, Leadership and Change*, Blackwell, Oxford, 1996.

Benyus, J.M., *Biomimicry: Innovation Inspired by Nature*, HarperCollins, London, 1997.

Bruner, J., *Making Stories: Law, Literature and Life*, Farrar, Straus and Giroux, New York, 2002.

Buchanan, M., *Small World: Uncovering Nature's Hidden Networks*, Weidenfeld and Nicolson, London, 2002.

Callinicos, A., *Against the Third Way*, Polity Press, Cambridge, 2001.

Chomsky, N., *Government in the Future*, Open Media, New York, 1970.

Clippinger, J.H., *The Biology of Business: Decoding the Natural Laws of Enterprise*, Jossey-Bass, 1999.

Cohen, D., *The Wealth of the World and the Poverty of Nations*, MIT Press, 1998.

Cooper, R., *The Breaking of Nations: Order and Chaos in the 21st Century*, Atlantic, London, 2003.

Cowan, C.C., Lee, W.R. and Todorovic, N. (eds), *Graves: Levels of Human Existence*, ECLET Publishing, Santa Barbara, 2003.

Cowan, C.C. and Todorovic, N. (eds), *The Never Ending Quest: Clare W. Graves Explores Human Nature*, ECLET Publishing, Santa Barbara, 2005.

Dawson, R., *Living Networks: Leading Your Company, Customers and Partners in the Hyper-connected Economy*, FT Prentice Hall, New Jersey, 2003.

Dennett, D., *Kinds of Minds: Toward an Understanding of Consciousness*, Basic Books, New York, 1996.

Diamond, J., *Collapse: How Societies Choose to Fail or Survive*, Allen Lane, 2005.

Edelman, G.M. and Tononi, G., *Consciousness: How Matter Becomes Imagination*, Penguin, London, 2000.

Enriquez, J., *As the Future Catches You: How Genomics and Other Forces are Changing Your Life, Work, Health and Wealth*, Crown Business, New York, 2002.

Flannery, T., *The Weather Makers: The History and Future Impact of Climate Change*, The Text Publishing Company, Melbourne, 2005.

Ford, C.V., *Lies! Lies! Lies! The Psychology of Deceit*, American Psychiatric Press, 1996.

Freire, P., *Pedagogy of the Oppressed*, Penguin, London, 1970.

Frenay, R., *Pulse: The Coming Age of Machines Inspired by Living Things*, Farrar, Straus and Giroux, New York, 2006.

Furedi, F., *Where Have All the Intellectuals Gone? Confronting 21st Century Philistinism*, Continuum, London, 2004.

Gaita, R., *A Common Humanity: Thinking about Love, Truth and Justice*, Text Publishing, Melbourne, 1999.

Gazzaniga, M.S., *The Mind's Past*, University of California Press, 1998.

Genoff, R. and Sheather, G., *Innovation and the Knowledge Economy: Industrial Regeneration in Northern Adelaide*, City of Playford, SA, 2003.

Gore, A., *An Inconvenient Truth: The Planetary Emergency of Global Warming and What We Can Do About It*, Rodale, New York, 2006.

Gray, J., *Straw Dogs: Thoughts on Humans and Other Animals*, Granta Books, London, 2002.

Greenfield, S., *The Human Brain: A Guided Tour*, Weidenfeld and Nicolson, London, 1997.

Griffin, D., *The Emergence of Leadership: Linking Self-Organisation and Ethics*, Routledge, London, 2002.

Gunderson, L.H. and Holling, C.S. (eds), *Panarchy: Understanding Transformations in Human and Natural Systems*, Island Press, 2002.

Hames, R.D., Strategic Navigation: Learning Viability in a World Wired for Speed in S. Herman (ed.), *Rewiring Organisations for the Networked Economy*, Jossey-Bass/Pfeiffer, 2002.

Harford, T., *The Undercover Economist*, Little, Brown, London, 2006.

Hargroves, K.C. and Smith, M. (eds), *The Natural Advantage of Nations: Business Opportunities, Innovation and Governance in the 21st Century*, Earthscan, London, 2005.

Harman, W., *Global Mind Change: The Promise of the 21st Century*, Berrett-Koehler, San Francisco, 1998.

Himanen P., *The Hacker Ethic and the Spirit of the Information Age*, Secker and Warburg, London, 2001.

Hobshawm, E. and Polito, A., *The New Century*, Little, Brown, 1999.

Hutton, W. and Giddens, A. (eds), *On the Edge: Living with Global Capitalism*, Jonathan Cape, London, 2000.

Inayatullah, S. and Boxwell, G. (eds), *Islam, Postmodernism and Other Futures: A Ziauddin Sardar Reader*, Pluto Press, London, 2003.

Irwin, W. (ed.), *The Matrix and Philosophy*, Open Court, Chicago, 2003.

Johnson, S., *Emergence: The Connected Lives of Ants, Brains, Cities and Software*, Scribner, New York, 2001.

Kelly, E. and Leyden, P., *What's Next? Exploring the New Terrain for Business*. Perseus Books, Cambridge, MA, 2002.

Khoza, R.J., *Let Africa Lead: African Transformational Leadership for 21st Century Business*, Vezubuntu Publishing, Johannesburg, 2005.

Kuhn, T.S., *The Structure of Scientific Revolutions*, University of Chicago Press, 1962.

Landry, C., *Rethinking Adelaide*, Government of South Australia, 2004.

Leadbetter, C., *Living on Thin Air*, Penguin, London, 1999.

Lessig, L., *The Future of Ideas: The Fate of the Commons in a Connected World*, Random House, London, 2001.

Lomborg, B., *The Skeptical Environmentalist: Measuring the Real State of the World*, Cambridge University Press, 2001.

Low, N., Gleeson, B., Green, R. and Radovic, D., *The Green City: Sustainable Homes, Sustainable Suburbs*, UNSW Press, Sydney, 2005.

Lowe, I., *A Big Fix: Radical Solutions for Australia's Environmental Crisis*, Black Inc., Melbourne, 2005.

McDonough, W. and Braungart, M., *Cradle to Cradle: Remaking the Way We Make Things*, North Point Press, New York, 2002.

Madron, R. and Jopling, J., *Gaian Democracies: Redefining Globalisation and People Power*, Green Books, Totnes, 2003.

Mau, B., Maclear, K. and Testa, B. (eds), *Life Style*, Phaidon, New York, 2002.

Mills, R. (ed.), *Barons to Bloggers: Confronting Media Power*, The Alfred Deakin Debate, Miegunyah Press, Melbourne, 2005.

Monbiot, G., *The Captive State: The Corporate Takeover of Britain*, Pan, London, 2001.

Nisbett, R.E., *The Geography of Thought: How Asians and Westerners Think Differently and Why*, Nicholas Brealey, 2005.

Norris, D., Mason, J. and Lefrere, P., *Transforming e-Knowledge*, SCUP, Ann Arbor, Michigan, 2003.

Ogilvy, J.A., *Creating Better Futures: Scenario Planning as a Tool for a Better Tomorrow*, Oxford University Press, 2002.

Penny, L., *Your Call is Important to Us: The Truth about Bullshit*, Scribe Publications, Melbourne, 2005.

Piattelli-Palmarini, M., *Inevitable Illusions: How Mistakes of Reason Rule our Minds*, John Wiley & Sons, Ltd, 1994.

Pilger, J., *The New Rulers of the World*, Verso, London, 2002.

Pink, D.H., *A Whole New Mind: Moving from the Information Age to the Conceptual Age*, Allen and Unwin, Sydney, 2005.

Porter, D. (ed.), *Internet Culture*, Routledge, London, 1996.

Ralston, B. and Wilson, I., *The Scenario Planning Handbook: Developing Strategies in Uncertain Times*, Thompson South-Western, Ohio, 2006.

Ralston Saul, J., *The Unconscious Civilization*, Penguin, Canada, 1997.

Rapaille, C., *The Culture Code*, Broadway Books, New York, 2006.

Rifkin, J., *The Age of Access: How the Shift from Ownership to Access is Transforming Capitalism*, Penguin, 2000.

Rose, S., *The Future of the Brain: The Promise and Perils of Tomorrow's Neuroscience*, Oxford University Press, New York, 2005.

Rosenberg, J., *The Follies of Globalisation Theory*, Verso, London, 2000.

Sardar, Z. and Davies, M.W., *Why do People Hate America?* Icon Books, London, 2002.

Schwartz-Satant, N., *The Mystery of Human Relationship: Alchemy and the Transformation of the Self*, Routledge, New York, 1998.

Scoble, R. and Israel, S., *Naked Conversations: How Blogs are Changing the Way Businesses Talk with Customers*, John Wiley & Sons, Inc., New York, 2006.

Seddon, J., *Freedom from Command and Control: A Better Way to Make the Work Work*, Vanguard Education, Buckingham, 2003.

Senge, P., Scharmer, C.O., Jaworski, J. and Flowers, B.S., *Presence: Human Purpose and the Field of the Future*, SOL, Cambridge, MA, 2004.

Shaw, P., *Changing Conversations in Organisations: A Complexity Approach to Change*, Routledge, London, 2002.

Slaughter, R.A., *Futures Beyond Dystopia: Creating Social Foresight*, Routledge, London, 2004.

Slaughter, R.A. (ed.), *Gone Today, Here Tomorrow*, Prospect Media, Sydney, 2000.

Slaughter, R.A., Naismith, L. and Houghton, N., *The Transformative Cycle*, AFI Swinburne, Melbourne, 2004.

Slaughter, R.A., *Pathways and Impediments to Social Foresight*, AFI Swinburne, Melbourne, 2006.

Singer, P., *One World: The Ethics of Globalisation*, Text Publishing, Melbourne, 2002.

Strogatz, S., *SYNC: The Emerging Science of Spontaneous Order*, Hyperion, New York, 2003.

Suter, K., *In Defence of Globalisation*, UNSW Press, Sydney, 2000.

Taleb, N.N., *Fooled by Randomness: The Hidden Role of Chance in Life and in the Markets*, Random House, London, 2004.

Thakara, J., *In the Bubble: Designing in a Complex World*, MIT Press, Boston, 2005.

Theobald, R., *Reworking Success: New Communities at the Millennium*, New Society Publishers, Canada, 1997.

Viriolio, P. and Lotringer, S., *Crepuscular Dawn*, Semiotext(e), Los Angeles, 2002.

Virilio, P., *Ground Zero*, Verso, London, 2001.

Watts, D.J., *Six Degrees: The Science of a Connected Age*, William Heinemann, London, 2003.

Whyte, D., *Crossing the Unknown Sea: Work and the Shaping of Identity*, Penguin, London, 2001.

Wilber, K., *The Marriage of Sense and Soul, Integrating Science and Religion*, Hill of Content, Melbourne, 1998.

Wilber, K., *Eye to Eye: The Quest for the New Paradigm*, Shambhala, Boston, 1993.

Zizek, S., *Welcome to the Desert of the Real*, Verso Books, London, 2002.

INDEX

3M 312
360 Degree Feedback 93

abundance 29
accounting practices 135–6
action learning 267
active thinking 283
adaptation 203
adaptiveness 244, 245, 252, 259
Adidas 312
advancement, survival vs. 156
AirAsia 148
Airbus 320
Albert, Michael 5, 6
algedonic signals 100
Alibaba.com 148
alignment
  perspectives of 294
  system–niche 249
Allende, Salvador 98, 101
Alternet 102
AlterNet 316
altruism 88
Amazon 29, 148
ambition 251
American Express 312
Ammo Marketing 323

Andersen Consulting 70
Anderson, Ray 22
Ansoff, Igor 43, 229
antisocial values 163
AOL 131
Apple Computers 29, 251
  iTunes 315
applications 94–5
appreciative age 135, 142
appreciative conditions 204–5
appreciative ecologies 137–8
appreciative ideals 172
appreciative practice 340
appreciative social ecology 262
appreciative society 169, 170–1,
  174–8
appreciative worldview 159–61,
  168
architecture of participation 86–90
Arendt, Hannah 317
Aristotle 292
Asia-Pacific Partnership on Clean
  Development and Climate
  157, 158
atemporal zone 208
Atkins, Robert 127
attention economy 122

attractors 4, 12, 84–5, 91, 101
Australia Tomorrow 227
Australia's Security Intelligence Organisation (ASIO) 317
autonomic processes 208
autopoiesis 139, 204–5, 243
Avaki Corporation 194, 195
Aventis 195

backcast 297
Balanced Scorecard 93
Bance, Antonia 324
barriers to responsiveness 147
Bateson, Gregory 290
Bawden, Richard 225
Beer, Stafford 15, 43, 76, 77, 78, 98, 101, 243, 270
being spaces 312
belonging 245
Bendigo Bank 320
Bergson, Henri 3
Berlin Wall, collapse of 23–4, 141
Berners-Lee, Tim 32
Bertalanffy, Ludwig von 239
best practices 37, 282
beta tests 195
Bhopal disaster 171
Bialek, Tracy 321
Bill of Rights 49
bin Laden, Osama 98
bioeconomics 199
biomimicry 235, 271, 272, 279
Biomorph 312
biospheric worldview 158
Blair, Tony 49, 291, 325
Blair Witch film project 323
blogging 315
Body Shop, The 148, 194, 251, 320
Boeing 195
Bohm, David 298
Boing Boing 315, 325

Bono 18
Borders Bookstores 312
BP 22, 319
brand resonance 148, 307–24
Braun 312
British Telecom 131
Brown, John 320, 325
Brown, Lester 97
Browne, Lord John 319
Bulte, Sarmite 315
Bumrungrad International Hospital 148, 154
bureaucratic service model 65–7, 76–7
Bush, George W. 47, 48, 49, 93, 98, 141, 325
Bush, George, Snr 158
business ecosystem 71, 100, 139
business process reengineering 132

cafe, organisational 71–3, 74, 75, 82, 83, 91, 92, 95–6, 237, 258
capability building 230–1
capacity 99
capitalism 6, 7, 8, 13, 28, 69, 124–5, 176
Capra, Fritjof 35
Cartesian approaches 53, 55, 242
Cassels, Alan 120
cathedral, organisational 70–2, 73, 74, 75, 82, 83, 92, 95–6, 237, 258
censorship 128
chain of command configuration 62
Challenger space shuttle disaster 110–11
Chanel, Coco 128
Change Accelerator Process (CAP) 255, 256
change activities 65
ChangeBrain 268–71, 273
chaos theory 140
Chernobyl disaster 171
Chiat-Day 131

China 4, 12, 18, 54, 86, 126, 208, 278, 317, 319
Cingular 312
Cirque du Soleil 148
Citibank 140
citizenship 9
Clark, David D. 129
classification 239
climate change 157
clock time 101
clustering 97
CNN 148
Coach 195
coadaptions 203
code 85
coevolution 203, 254–5
coevolving phase 284, 287
cognitive dysfunctionality 165–6
Cognitive Edge 298
cognitive science 99
coherence 223
collaboration 29
collaborative individualism 262
collective memory 108, 116
  urban 173
colonisation 56
Columbus, Christopher 336–7
command and control 92
commonsense 111–12, 217
communecology 72
communication 17
community 90
community of mind 245
community of practice 272
community of praxis 235, 249, 256, 259
competitive behaviour 39–40
Complaint Station 316
complex adaptive systems 145, 154
complexity catastrophe 174
complexity, mastering 263–5, 272
Condé Nast 314
connectedness 83

connectivity 230
consciousness 65
consequences 286
consilience 18
context 143–4, 250
contextual environment 251
contextualizing phase 284
conventional wisdom 217
convivial society 6, 9, 13
cooperative capitalism 330
core group 70, 75
counterfeiting 20
Cox, Ana Marie 324
Creative Commons 21, 31, 281, 304
critical domain of attention (CDOA) 271, 286
CSIRO 322
culture 237
culture of permanence 41
Customer Relationship Management 93
cybernetic governance 80
Cybersin 98

Darwin, Charles 45, 203
data overload 174
Dawkins, Richard 100, 179
Dawson, Ross 316
decision flows model 258
decision-making 213–16
decision theatres 138
Deep Design 80, 81, 254, 256, 271, 275–304, 340
Dell 142, 148, 154, 316
democracy 5, 9
derived demands 60, 99, 147, 154, 193, 194, 208
Descartes 45
design solutions 63
dialogue, facilitating 298–301
distributed intelligence 205–7, 299
Doctorow, Cory 325
DOS 232

Dow 195
downsizing 103
Drucker, Peter 265
dualistic (reductionist) framework
     292–3
DuPont 41, 195

eBay 29, 142, 148, 195–6
Eckersley, Richard 162–3
ecodesigning model 232
ecodiagnosis 232
ecological fit 202
ecological leadership 262–3
ecological metaphors 232
ecological paradigm 40
ecology 201–2, 280–1
economic growth 112
economic metaphors 232
ecority 246, 252, 260
Einstein, Albert 42, 46, 98, 117
Eli Lilly 195
Elkington, John 228
emergence 55–6, 105, 203–4,
     215–16, 220
emergent properties 251
emotional skills 233
empowerment 87, 88
enacting 286–7
endism 131, 132
Enron 22, 70
entitlement 156
environmental sustainability 113–14
Epinions 316
Epson 312
equality, ideal of 172
ethical unity 177–8
ethnicity 24–5
e-topias 129, 141
European Union (EU) 12, 164,
     336
evolutionary hype cycle 140
expanded now 228
expected future 251
expeditionary marketing 29, 195
experience economy 140

extended enterprise 139, 154
extrapolations 297
Exxon Mobil 325

false assumptions in systems 111
Featherstone, Lynne 324
filters 186, 208
fitness 235
Flavorpill 312
Flickr 88, 311
Flight Centre 148
focusing 285
Ford, Henry 242
foresight 251, 252
foresight projects 227–8
framing 285
Freestyle Interactive 323
Friedman, Milton 176
Friedman, Thomas 337
future 183–9, 251
     as myth 114
Future Landscapes project 227
futuring 211–24, 227
F-Word blog 324

Gaddafi, Colonel 16
Gadsden, Henry 120
Garanti Bank's Flexi Cards 324
Gartner 140
Gates, Bill 319
GE 21
Geldof, Bob 18
General Motors 41, 69
genetically modified (GM) foods
     119–20
Getup! 102, 209
Geus, Arie de 42
ghost statements 74
Gingrich, Newt 98
Girls Blog UK 325
Gladwell, Malcolm 95
Global Business Network 228
global warming 157–8
globalisation 17, 28, 56–7,
     124–5

globalism 28, 56–7, 125, 126
glocalisation 38, 97
Going Deep 295
Google 29, 148, 217, 311, 316, 320, 325
Gorbachev, Mikhail 31
Gore, Al 141
Gould, Steven J. 179
governance 281–2
Grameen Foundation 320
Gramsci, Antonio 116
Granovetter, Mark 84
Graves, Claire 159, 160
gravitational pull of the past 64
Green Cross International 18, 31
Greenleaf, Robert 241
Grey Goose 312
Gross Domestic Product 12, 13
Guanxi 86, 101
Guare, John 90
Guild Insurance & Financial Services 320

Hamel, Gary 266
Hames, Richard 154, 271
Handy, Charles 100
harnessing new technologies 265–6
Hawker, John 321
Hegel, G.W.F. 307
Heifer International 320
Henderson, Hazel 53, 99
history 62–3
Hitler, Adolf 98
Hobbes, Thomas 45
Holmes, Oliver Wendell 227
Holocaust 127–8
holons 280, 304
Hopi tribe 170
hot-desking 131–2
Howard, John 158, 325
hub enterprises 192
Hubbert, Dr M. King 142
human fit 202

Human Genome Project 155
human rights 93
Hussein, Saddam 332

Iansiti, Marco 193, 197
IBM 21, 22, 131, 194, 195, 251, 291
iBood 88, 102, 310
iceberg model 287
identity 259
ideological superiority, myth of 112
ideology 219
Imagine Chicago 227
IMF 113
immigration/migration 130
impulsive behaviour 111
inconsequential decisions 214
India 12, 18, 54
Indonesia 225
industrial ecology model 32
industrial economism 7, 9, 10, 13, 30–1, 53–5, 109, 112, 121, 122, 134, 137, 141, 169
Industrial Revolution 17, 18, 52, 56, 78, 139
industrialism 123
infolust 192–8
Information Technology (IT) 189
    see also Internet
infotainment 25, 174
InnoCentives 195
instant messaging 92
instinct 213
institutionalised learning 112
intangible goods 135
Integral 4Q model 300
integration 292
intellectual property 19–20, 281
intellectual skills 233
intelligence 154
intentionality 204, 246, 251, 252, 257, 259
Interface 22

Internet 26, 27, 29, 30, 66, 73, 88, 125, 336
  activism 102
  security 129–30
  usage 129
ISO 9000 series 93

Japan 85–6
Jiabao, Wen 319
Jobs, Steve 251
Joga 311
Johnson & Johnson 195

Kahle, Brewster 21–2
Karinthy, Frigyes 90
Kauffman, Stuart 174
Kendrick, John 135
Keynes, John Maynard 69
keystone enterprises 192–4, 195, 196, 197, 208, 239
Kickstart 320
Kierkegaard, Soren 211
Kim, W. Chan 148
Kinko 312
Klein, Naomi 120
Klipsch 312
knowing 292
Knowledge Designer 252–6, 268, 283–8, 303
knowledge economy 140
knowledge system 46
Kolb, David 253
Kotter, John 43
Kremer, Michael 21
Kryptonite 316
Kyoto Principles on Climate Change 157, 158

Lackoff, George 47, 168
Laszlo, Irwin 39, 97
Lean Manufacturing 93
learning metabolism 57, 58, 59, 208, 267
learning, speed of 267–8
LEGO 195, 320

Lennon, John 6, 23
Leonard, Danielle 321
Lessig, Lawrence 20, 31, 304
Leviathan 45
libraries 21–2
Lincoln, Abraham 5, 6
linear thinking 110–11
linking 193
Linux 194
liquid identity 174
literate communities 52
living systems 149–51
lock-in 216, 260, 279
Logitech 312
LoveLewisham 88, 102, 310–11
loyalty 74

management 8, 58, 242–4
management factory 59, 60
Mandela, Nelson 18
manufacturing industries 125
material geography 19
materialism 50–1, 163
Maturana, Humberto 177, 243
Mauborgne, Renee 148
Mazda 314
McDonald's 316
McDonough, William 282, 304
McFarlane, John 319, 320
McLuhan, Marshall 230
Médecins Sans Frontières 320
media, dead 174–5
medical tourism 154
memory 116
mental models 114
Mercedes 314
Merck 120
metalearning 255
metatechnologies 87
Metropolitan Museum of Art 128
Mexican wave phenomenon 138
Microsoft 22, 196, 320
  Windows 29, 194, 217, 232
migration 24–5, 278

Milgram, Stanley 90
mind traps 152, 184, 186
mindful action 283
mission 234
Mitsui 41
modernism 175
Monsanto 69, 120
Mont Fleur scenarios 271
Montebello, Phillipe de 128
Motorola 312
Moynihan, Ray 120
Murdoch, Rupert 128
Muse Conversation Menu 272
MySpace 311

Napster 312
NASA 89, 110–11
nation-states 23–4, 130, 317
natural selection 45–6
natural systems 243–5
navigation centres 273
NBR convergence revolution 313
net social consumption 177
network mastery 83–6
networked intelligence 197, 199, 201–2
Neville, Richard 317, 325
Neville-Freeman Agency 228
new economy 122
newness, shock of 163
Newton, Sir Isaac 45
Newtonian science 53, 55
NGOs 28, 198, 320
niche, business 148, 154, 202, 203, 249
Nike 311
Nikon 312
Nixon, Richard 47
Nokia 148
nonlinear thinking 240
nostalgia 166–7

Oakley 312
official future 251
Oka, Marvin 154, 228, 261, 271, 288

Oldenburg, Ray 312
OneWorld Health 148, 320
Open Content Alliance 22
Open Democracy 102, 209
open source 88–90
operating system 94–5, 231
operational intelligence 285
Optus Communications 323
orderliness 83
Oregon Scientific 312
organisation 234, 235
organisational cafe 71–3, 74, 75, 82, 83, 91, 92, 95–6, 237, 258
organisational capability 73, 100
organisational cathedral 70–2, 73, 74, 75, 82, 83, 92, 95–6, 237, 258
organisational learning 43, 260
Orwell, George 208
ownership 39
Oxford English Dictionary 89
Oxford Muse, The 272

paradigm 217–18
paradigmatic discourse 223
paradigmatic narrative 223
Parecon 5, 179
participative architecture 86–90
Participative Party process 313
Pascal, Blaise 96
past, making sense of 184–5
Patent Commons Project 22
PATH organisation 320
pattern and structure, perspectives of 295–7
patterning 285–6
Pavlov 288
peer curating 308–9
performance excellence 145–6
performance management 78
peripheral vision, perspectives of 294–5
personal ecosystems 139
personal mastery 83–4

Pfizer 195
pharmaceutical industry 120
phase transitions 81–2, 101, 103
Phillips, Melanie 324
philosophy 279–80
Pinochet, General Augusto 98
piracy 20
Planetfeedback 316
Plato 292
Pol Pot 332
population 278
pop-up communities 311, 312
Porter, Michael 97, 229
poverty gap 31, 33
power, collapse of 108–9
PowerSeller label 196
preferential trading agreements (PTAs) 224
preferred future 252
pre-literate communities 52
Procter & Gamble 195
profits 176–7
progress, concept of 156–7, 170, 176, 177
prototyping 195
Ptolemy 89

quantum entanglement 46

RAISE factors 243–6, 260
ratchet effect 60–1, 66–7, 68
real time approaches 41, 98
Rebeiro, Jose Felipe 113
recognition, systems of 116
Redfern, Catherine 324
reductionism 90, 99
reductionist objectivism 169
relating skills 233
relativity 46
reperceiving 286
representative government 8
researching 284–5
resocialisation 175
resonance 307

resource nationalism 38
resourcing 284, 285
responsiveness, principle of 244, 245, 249, 250, 259
Revans, Reg 267
rich-get-richer phenomenon 91
Rinaudo, Tony 322
Ripple Products 321
Rockstar 312
Rogers, Carl 256
role models 163
Room to Read 320–1
Royal Dutch Shell 70, 295
Rutledge, Matt 310
Ryanair 148

Samsonite 312
Santayana, Georges 114
Sanyo 312
Saramago, Jose 6
scenario planning 221–2
schema 286
Schrödinger, Erwin 46
self-sufficiency 40
Semantic Web 32
semi-structural decisions 213
semi-structural space 214
Senge, Peter 83
September 11, 220–1 47, 48, 49, 185
servant–leader concept 240–1
service agreement model 66
service industries 125
shamrock organisations 100
Shapiro, Robert 119
Shell 41, 42–3, 97, 188, 200
short-termism 153
situational leader 240
six degrees theory 90–1
Six Sigma 93
Slaughter, Richard 303
Slim, Field Marshall Lord 230
Smith, Adam 194
Snow, Terry 321
Snowden, Dave 258, 298, 304
social ecology 245–6

society 90
sociological worldview 158
Socrates 292
Sonos 312
Sony 312
Soviet Union 54, 141
spam, email 130
speed of learning 267–8
Springwise 195, 312
Starbucks 312
statistical process control 132
Stora 41–2
story telling 221
strategic activism 235–40
strategic conversation 80–1, 259,
    288–90, 295–7
strategic decision theatres 268–71
strategic fit 202, 249
strategic innovation 32, 266–7
strategic intelligence 147–8, 284,
    288, 290
Strategic Navigation 81, 101, 138,
    152–3, 187, 197, 227–71,
    288
strategic planning 229, 231
strategy 238
strategy finding 302
structural capital 142
structural decisions 213–14, 215
structural outcomes 216–17
structure–function traps of
    convention 184
subliminal knowledge 217, 219
suicide rates 165
surprises in systems 110
survival value 241
SustainAbility 228
sustainability 245, 259, 260
swarm intelligence applications 196
Swatch 148, 311
Symantec 312
symbiotic design 61–9
synchronicity 102
systematic patterning 239
systematic processes 238–9

systemic alignment 202
systemic relationships 201
systemic viability 232
systems theory 161

tacit knowledge 43
tangible goods 135
Tassimo 312
Tavistock Institute 260
Taylor, Frederick 53, 99
Taylorism 260
teamwork 260
technological determinism 112,
    116
technological paradigm 157, 158,
    164–5
Technorati 315
telecommuting 131
terrorism 57–9, 215
Thakara, John 143, 275
Thaksin, Prime Minister 313
Thoughtpost Pty Ltd 153, 228,
    309
Time Warner 131
time, perspectives of 297
Tomorrow's Company 32
topology 85
Toshiba 315
total quality management (TQM) 260
Toyota 194, 195, 320
transformation 303–4
transformational competence 115
Transformational Narrative 81, 101,
    273
Transformative Cycle 303
transhuman forms 162
transition systems 284
trust
    in political process 163
    in technologies 163
tunnel thinking 133

unconscious competence 222, 256,
    288
understanding as skill 264

urbanisation 173, 278, 304
US National Security Strategy 317

value creation 229
variety 103
viability 78–80, 101, 148–9, 152, 199–207, 280
Viable Systems Model (VSM) 77, 78, 98, 101
viral communications 73
Viravadhya, Meechai 321
Virtual Society 129
virtuous investment 193
vision 251
VoIP 140, 336
volatility 188–9
VW 312

Wack, Pierre 295
Wal-Mart 194, 196, 198
war on terror 47, 54
ways of knowing 51
Weinberg, David 155
well-being 312
white knight style of leadership 240–1

Whole Foods Market 320
Wikipedia 89
Wilber, Ken 300, 303
Winfrey, Oprah 18
Wired magazine 311
wisdom 172
Wonkette 324
Wood, John 320
Woot 102, 310
World Bank 21, 113
World Economic Forum 116
World Trade Organisation (WTO) 113, 124, 212, 224
WorldCom 22, 70, 197
worldview 45, 46–7, 49–50, 51–2, 218–19
Wright, Robert 87
www.YouTube.com 31

Yahoo! 22, 29
YouTube 311

Zeldin, Theodore 272
zero geography 19, 146, 186, 189–92, 337

Index compiled by Annette Musker